What We Eat

....
ARTS AND TRADITIONS OF THE TABLE:
PERSPECTIVES ON CULINARY HISTORY

ARTS AND TRADITIONS OF THE TABLE: PERSPECTIVES ON CULINARY HISTORY

Albert Sonnenfeld, Series Editor

Spoiled: The Myth of Milk as Superfood, Anne Mendelson

The Fulton Fish Market: A History, Jonathan H. Rees

The Botany of Beer: An Illustrated Guide to More Than 500 Plants Used in Brewing, Giuseppe Caruso

Anxious Eaters: Why We Fall for Fad Diets, Janet Chrzan and Kima Cargill

Gastronativism: Food, Identity, Politics, Fabio Parasecoli

Epistenology: Wine as Experience, Nicola Perullo

The Terroir of Whiskey: A Distiller's Journey Into the Flavor of Place, Rob Arnold

Meals Matter: A Radical Economics Through Gastronomy, Michael Symons

The Chile Pepper in China: A Cultural Biography, Brian R. Dott

Cook, Taste, Learn: How the Evolution of Science Transformed the Art of Cooking, Guy Crosby

Garden Variety: The American Tomato from Corporate to Heirloom, John Hoenig

Mouthfeel: How Texture Makes Taste, Ole G. Mouritsen and Klavs Styrbæk, translated by Mariela Johansen

Chow Chop Suey: Food and the Chinese American Journey, Anne Mendelson

Kosher USA: How Coke Became Kosher and Other Tales of Modern Food, Roger Horowitz

Taste as Experience: The Philosophy and Aesthetics of Food, Nicola Perullo

For a complete list of books in the series, please see the Columbia University Press website.

WHAT WE EAT

A GLOBAL HISTORY OF FOOD

EDITED BY **PIERRE SINGARAVÉLOU**
AND **SYLVAIN VENAYRE**
TRANSLATED BY STEPHEN W. SAWYER

Columbia University Press

New York

Columbia University Press
Publishers Since 1893
New York   Chichester, West Sussex

"L'épicerie du monde," sous la direction de Pierre Singaravélou et Sylvain Venayre
© Librairie Arthème Fayard, 2022

Translation copyright © 2025 Columbia University Press
All rights reserved

Library of Congress Cataloging-in-Publication Data

Names: Singaravélou, Pierre, editor. | Venayre, Sylvain, editor. | Sawyer, Stephen W., 1974– translator.
Title: What we eat : a global history of food / edited by Pierre Singaravélou, Sylvain Venayre ; translated by Stephen W. Sawyer.
Other titles: L'épicerie du monde. English
Description: New York : Columbia University Press, [2024] | Series: Arts and traditions of the table : perspectives on culinary history | Originally published in French as L'épicerie du monde : la mondialisation par les produits alimentaires du XVIIIe siècle à nos jours. | Includes bibliographical references and index.
Identifiers: LCCN 2024024689 | ISBN 9780231213684 (hardback) | ISBN 9780231221474 (trade paperback) | ISBN 9780231559973 (ebook)
Subjects: LCSH: Food—History. | Food habits—History.
Classification: LCC TX353 .E6513 2025 | DDC 641.3009--dc23/eng/20241029

COVER ART : Ô Majuscule !
COVER DESIGN : Philippine Dejardins

GPSR Authorized Representative: Easy Access System Europe, Mustamäe tee 50, 10621 Tallinn, Estonia, gpsr.requests@easproject.com

Columbia University Press gratefully acknowledges
the generous contribution to this book provided by
the Florence Gould Foundation Endowment
Fund for French Translation.

Contents

Introduction 1

Acheke 8

Bagels 11

Baguette 14

Banh Mi 18

Barbecue 21

Beer 25

Beet Sugar 29

Cassoulet 33

Caviar 37

Ceviche 41

Champagne 45

Charcuterie 49

Chicory 53

Chili con Carne 57

Chili Pepper 61

Chorba 65

Christmas Pudding 69

Coca-Cola 73

Coffee 77

Condensed Milk (Sweetened) 81

Cornflakes 85

Couscous 89

Curry 93

Dafina 97

Dim Sum 101

Dogmeat 105

Döner Kebab 109

Feijoada 112

Fish and Chips 116

Fish Sauce (Nuoc Mam) 120

Food Coloring and Preservatives 124

Freeze-Dried Foods 128

CONTENTS ix

French Fries 132

Gin 136

Guacamole 140

Hamburger 144

Harissa 148

Hedgehog Stew 151

Hot Dogs 155

Hummus 159

Ice Cubes 163

Indomie 167

Injera 170

Ketchup 174

Lato 178

Maki 182

Margarine 185

Mate 189

Matzah 193

Mayonnaise 196

Naan 200

Noodles and Macaroni 203

CONTENTS

Olive Oil   206

Orangina   210

Oyster   213

Palm Oil   217

Parmesan Cheese   221

Pepper   225

Pet Food and Treats   228

Pho   232

Pizza   236

Poke   240

Port Wine   243

Raki   247

Ramen   251

Rooibos   255

Roquefort   259

Rum   263

Sake   267

Salt   271

Sandwich   275

Sardines (Canned)   279

CONTENTS xi

Singapore Noodles 283

Soy Sauce 286

Spam 289

Sparkling Water 293

Sushi 297

Tapioca 301

Tea and Chai 304

Tikka 308

Tofu 311

Turkish Delight 315

Vanilla and Vanillin 318

Vodka 321

Whiskey 324

Wine 328

Yak Butter 332

Yogurt 335

......

Index 339

What We Eat

Introduction

Global history is written from a particular place. The histories offered here were written from France, a country known throughout the world for its gastronomy and commitment to the culinary arts. Essential to gastronomy is the pleasure of nourishing oneself and the words used to describe such *jouissance*. As a result, discourses on food are central to its past. Yet discussions of food vary throughout the world, not only because gastronomic cultures differ from place to place but also because the dishes themselves are shaped by local circumstances and history. Talking about cassoulet in France has a whole range of connotations that are entirely different in the United States, where on the evening of Barack Obama's first electoral victory as president on November 4, 2008, a banner bearing an image of a "cassoulet" unfurled by French journalists in Times Square, was picked up by the world's media just weeks before the first competition for the world's best cassoulet was held in New York. Conversely, for the French, the hamburger still seems a rather recent appropriation, while for an American it would seem to be part of an ancient and storied past.

The tension between the familiar and the exotic can be fertile. Historians do not enjoy the privilege of extraterritoriality. They too must strive to think from the point of view of others. Such is the purpose of this book: to recognize that we continue to be caught up in the turbulence of our situatedness, just as we try to see beyond it. As a result, readers from different parts of the world may be struck by some of the perspectives and even absences in this book. But such is the process of any culinary discovery, the addition or removal of an ingredient may shock even as it marks a first step toward further understanding.

Much less ambiguous are the essential vectors that revolutionized the global history of the culinary experience from the second half of the eighteenth century onward, which form the throughlines of this book: the growing expression of food identities, the industrialization of the agri-food sector, and the acceleration of global circulations.

Historical research has shown how, since the eighteenth century, a multitude of institutions have contributed to the creation of cultural markers and social practices, designed to bind communities together. Certain symbols of this process have now become self-evident (flags or anthems, for example), or those shared memories promoted in the public arena under the name of "traditions" or even "history."

Cuisine has been an essential part of this process. Common dishes and foods have become expressions of local or national identities. Legends have developed, such as that of Margherita pizza, named in honor of Queen Margaret of Savoy, whose three colors—red (tomatoes), white (mozzarella), and green (basil)—evoke the Italian flag. On another scale, Christmas pudding became the emblem of the British Empire, to the point where in the 1920s certain colonies complained to London that their produce was not included in the recipe. Governments unavoidably entered the fray. In Japan it was decided in 1913 that only national sake should be served at official celebrations to the detriment of foreign champagne. The phenomenon gained momentum in the second half of the twentieth century: feta cheese was recognized as typically Greek in 2002, while ceviche was declared the cultural heritage of the Peruvian nation in 2004.

These identifications were the culmination of a long process. As early as the nineteenth century, universal exhibitions or world's fairs were the preferred venues for the expression of these identities. Roquefort cheese and farmed oysters were presented in Paris in 1867, Turkish delight in Vienna in 1873, and cornflakes in San Francisco in 1915. These great festive gatherings were a means of showcasing the culinary "genius" of nations the world over.

Even though certain foods have been known since antiquity, they came to be defined as the result of subtle refinements perfected over centuries by small, talented communities. Wine is undoubtedly the best-known example of such a process, seen both as proof of civilization, in the broadest sense of the term, and as the product of the originality of a particular people, summed up in its terroirs and the way its winemakers were able to make the most of them. But the same could be said of yogurt, whose recent Bulgarian identity conceals a very long, much more shared history. As the origins of most dishes have been lost in the mists of time, they have in turn been appropriated by the great names of national histories, such as the French baguette, whose existence can be traced back to Napoleon's military campaigns, or Indian tikka, whose invention is sometimes attributed to the founder of the Mughal empire, King Babur. Whether it is question of mayonnaise or the bagel, there is no shortage of origin myths. (The legend that the word ceviche comes from the expression of an astonished English sailor—"son of a bitch!"—is undoubtedly one of the most humorous.) In Yokohama, where ramen is said to have been invented, two museums are dedicated to it.

Such identity claims obviously give rise to conflicts, which are equally serious for their symbolic power: For example, the "hummus war" that Israel and Lebanon have been waging for the past fifteen years, or the spirited reaction of Tunisia, Morocco, and Mauritania to Algeria's claim to be the homeland of couscous. We could also mention vodka, the invention of which is claimed by both Poland and Russia. In England, the French gradually became frog-eaters and the Germans sauerkraut-eaters, while on the Continent the English were assimilated to the "*rosbifs*" they supposedly consumed daily. Such humorous stigmatization can also go too far, as in the contempt in which Europeans have sometimes held hedgehog-hunting "gypsies" or dog-eating Chinese. And what about the despicable legend that the blood of Christian children is needed to make matzah?

That global culinary history is rife with politics should come as no surprise. It is not merely a question of taxation and duties on foodstuffs, as with the Boston Tea Party in 1773 or the organization of the Salt March by Gandhi and the Indian Congress in 1930. In the twentieth century, chili peppers played a major role in shaping revolutionary culture and Chinese regional identities, as popular songs celebrated the virtues of Hunan cuisine and its spicy flavors were said to cultivate the virility of the province's great leaders, such as Mao Zedong.

The products themselves are not the only elements to consider, however. Around them, cultural practices are expressed through rituals and table manners. Drinking tea in England, maté in Argentina, or raki in Turkey is done according to certain rules that have not only varied over time but have also punctuated daily life. In Brazil the consumption of feijoada has been so closely associated with special moments of celebration that in Portuguese the very word has come to designate a festive gathering. As for "fast food," it too has been accompanied by new forms of sociability, centered around french fry bars, pizza trucks, and, of course, fast-food outlets where people eat sandwiches, hot dogs, and hamburgers on the go. All these developments have a social dimension as well. In Great Britain, fish and chips was a working-class delicacy before becoming a national dish, while on the West Coast of the United States, the development of vegetarian specialties and a taste for raw fish were initially part of the urban California lifestyle.

This social history is also a history of how roles are distributed according to gender. It is not enough to say that cooking has long been, overwhelmingly, a

4   INTRODUCTION

woman's business. Indeed, this basic fact has evolved very differently in different
places and at different times. In the lagoon societies of Côte d'Ivoire, for example, if the making of acheke (*attiéké*) has been the prerogative of women, it is
because of their importance in the matrilineal order, a status far removed from
that of the chili queens who sold chili con carne in Texas. In Western societies,
the arrival of industrialization reinforced the prejudice associating women with
cooking: on the assembly lines of the new agroindustrial plants, the vast majority of workers were women.

The development of the agri-food industry was the second phenomenon to revolutionize the global history of the culinary arts. In France around 1830, such
development led to preserving sardines in oil or making macaroni. Emerging in
the United States at the end of the nineteenth century—in the Heinz factory in
Pittsburgh, for example, or among the meat-packers of Chicago—automation
of production lines soon became the norm. Industrialization of food was
accompanied by a packaging revolution. In the grocery stores of the early twentieth century, sugar loaves disappeared in favor of boxes of sugar cubes or granulated sugar. Since it was no longer possible to see or taste the product before
buying it, there was only one way for customers to be guided in their choice:
trust in the brand. Only the brand guaranteed what was to be found in the
carton, the bottle, the can and then, as technical developments progressed, in
concentrated, dehydrated, frozen, and freeze-dried products.

Hence the rise of advertising and packaging. As early as 1916 the Coca-Cola
Company distinguished itself from other beverages by a singular bottle shape,
recognizable in all contexts thanks to its logo carved into the glass. Subsequently,
the entertainment society has been at the service of food products manufactured or sold by the biggest companies everywhere, from the French soccer team
of the Stade de Reims promoting champagne in the 1950s to Hollywood stars
extolling the virtues of whiskey and maki. Television commercials have become
the main vehicles for discovering new products. In the United States, Kikkoman Japanese soy sauce first appeared on TV screens in 1956, a few minutes
before the announcement of the future president. In Nigeria advertising played
a decisive role in the recent success of the Indonesian instant noodle brand
Indomie. The culmination of this process was the transformation of certain
brands into common names, like Spam, the canned pork that seemed so univer-
sally widespread that its name came to designate the countless unwelcome
emails in our inboxes.

Industrialization has given rise to new concerns about the impact of food on health. Whiskey and port wine were reputed to aid digestion in eighteenth-century England, while tapioca, invented in the nineteenth century, was prescribed by French doctors to children and the elderly for its analeptic properties. Soon, however, new food products were damaging the health of hundreds of millions of people, fostering a climate of mistrust toward new products. For half a century people have been concerned about the quality of the minced meat in hamburgers or the health risks to children of sweetened condensed milk. The food served by fast-food chains is blamed for the current obesity epidemic in many countries around the world. The palm oil boom has led to alarm about the deleterious effects of saturated fatty acids, as well as the environmental damage caused by large-scale plantations. Industrial cured meats, in particular, have generated concern: due to the presence of harmful nitrite salts within them, in 2015 the World Health Organization made them the only food products currently classified as "definite carcinogens." There is certainly an amusing irony in the fact that cornflakes, now often too sweet, were created for dietary purposes and that Coca-Cola and Pepsi-Cola were invented at the end of the nineteenth century by pharmacists extolling their health benefits.

These health threats prompted an effort to standardize production and a growing demand for regulation from consumers and public authorities alike. As early as 1858 the city of Amsterdam set up a municipal food and drink control department, and two years later, the British Parliament enacted the first framework law against the adulteration of any food product. Most other European states adopted comparable legislation at the end of the nineteenth century. Subsequently, the function of indications of origin was not only to publicize and valorize local cultures and homelands but also to enforce certain standards. Though originating in countries of the Western Hemisphere, the movement has recently become globalized: in 2013 nuoc mam (fish sauce) made on the island of Phu Quoc was the first of Southeast Asian products to receive a protected designation of origin (PDO) from the European Union, while white pepper from Penja, Cameroon, became one of the first three protected designations in West and Central Africa.

In recent decades, increasing numbers of the affluent classes of Western hyperproductivist societies, concerned about their health as well as animal welfare, have reacted by criticizing what they consider the overconsumption of meat. Since the 1970s, Asian tofu has been making inroads in North America and Europe. Many youths in this part of the world are now adopting vegetarian diets that have long been widespread in other parts of the world, such as India, where a third of the population does not eat meat for religious reasons. As a result of this new demand, traditional dishes have been reinvented such as cassoulets, which can now be found garnished with soy sausages.

Finally, no global history would be complete without considering the acceleration of circulations of ideas, practices, and tastes, for cuisine is not only determined by its provenance, its products, indigenous knowledges, as well as the flavors and recipes that are so often presented as "traditional," readily embodied in familial figures such as the grandparent who bequeathed an inimitable recipe. In reality, food has never stopped traveling.

Our vocabulary bears witness to this long-standing phenomenon. "Sugar" and "pepper" are derived from Sanskrit. "Maize" comes from the Haitian Arawak language, Taino. "Tomato," "cocoa," "chocolate," and "avocado" come from the Nahuatl of the Aztecs. We owe "coffee" to the Arabic *qahwa*, which comes from Kaffa, the region in southwest Ethiopia where the coffee tree flourishes. Some etymologies are more complex, occasionally revealing the different phases of globalization. While most European languages adopted tea (*thé, tee, té,* and so on) from the phoneme *te* belonging to the Minnan language used by traders in southern China, the beverage has been known by Russians, Arabs, Turks, and other Asian societies for much longer, under another name derived from the Mandarin of northern China, *chai.*

In the beginning, then, was the exchange of products along the great trade routes. Consumed in Central America for almost ten thousand years, chilis were imported by Iberian colonists, who brought them to Europe as well as to their Asian trading posts, where they soon replaced pepper, which was too expensive. There is no end to the number of dishes whose basic ingredients come from the other side of the world. Manioc originated in South America and is now mainly grown and consumed in Africa, where it is used in many dishes, such as acheke. Of American origin, beans form the basis of not only Brazilian feijoada but also Moroccan loubia, Indian rajma, Turkish kuru fasulye, French cassoulet, British baked beans, and Beninese doyiwé.

Since the eighteenth century, two phenomena have dramatically accelerated these circulations. The first is the mass migration that began to take place worldwide in the 1830s. This led the Irish, Scots, and English to promote whiskey throughout the world; the Italians brought pizza and olive oil; the Japanese shared maki and sushi; the Turks döner kebab; the Indians curry and tikka; the Chinese dim sum; the Vietnamese, pho soup. In California, Japanese immigrants reinvented maki in the form of the California roll, replacing raw tuna

INTRODUCTION 7

with avocado and crabmeat. In Mexico, Lebanese Maronites, inspired by the Levantine shawarma and Turkish döner, came up with stuffing corn-based tacos with pork, which became *"al pastor."* In some Indian restaurants in France, cheese was added to bread preparations of naan, a recipe that had already traveled extensively.

The second factor that intensified trade was war. During the Napoleonic era, Britain's blockade led Europeans to replace cane sugar and coffee with beet sugar and chicory (cane sugar continued to be used mainly in rum, while Westerners became accustomed to sweetening their coffee with the beet-based product). During the Crimean War, British companies decided to sell stocks of Indian tea destined for Russia to the Maghreb. There it was mixed with a traditional sweetened mint infusion, which became the norm for consuming tea in the Arab-Muslim world. During World War II, supply difficulties led British troops to replace tea with rooibos, while the government of Nazi Germany promoted Fanta (*Fantastik*) to replace Coca-Cola. In the aftermath of the war the United States encouraged the production of ramen in occupied Japan to sell their wheat on a massive scale in the archipelago. The Korean War was a key vector in the spread of Spam, whose combination with kimchi, tofu, and noodles gave rise to *budae jjigae* (literally "army stew"), now one of South Korea's national dishes.

Despite the spread of sandwiches, sodas, french fries, and hamburgers, this protean globalization of food cannot be summed up as a Westernization of culinary habits and practices. Before it spread around the world and across social classes, rum was invented in the seventeenth century by African slaves seeking to escape the horrors of servitude on the plantations of the West Indies. Though considerably less spicy than the original, Indian curry is now the most popular dish in Japan. In 2001 Robin Cook, the British foreign secretary, solemnly declared chicken tikka the true national dish, replacing traditional fish and chips. As for the French, they have been massively adopting couscous for some time now, thanks both to immigration from the Maghreb and to its adaptation by the pied-noir culture (to which the French owe the introduction of merguez).

Roland Barthes has said that food gives rise to three pleasures: conviviality, by sharing the same dish; reminiscence, by bringing us back to the tastes of our childhood; and novelty, by attracting us to that we do not yet know. Without ignoring the suffering caused by malnutrition that still afflicts two billion people around the world today, the story of globalization through food products also means recounting these mixed emotions, to better experience the proximity across the world.

Acheke

In 1938 the French inspector general for agriculture in the colonies, Edmond François, published an article entitled "Le manioc, sa production et son utilisation" (Cassava, Its Production and Uses). The publication came at a pivotal moment in the root's history, when the colonies were transitioning from rural to protoindustrial and industrial farming. This industrial agricultural revolution later paved the way for the creation of a new dish in the postcolonial Côte d'Ivoire: acheke (*attiéké*) in the form of cassava semolina.

The story of cassava took a turn when Europeans discovered its consumption in Latin America, particularly in Brazil under Portuguese colonial rule. Cassava grows as two types of tubers: bitter cassava, which is poisonous, and sweet cassava, which is edible. In the sixteenth century the first globalization of the Atlantic took place mainly south of the equator, with the slave trade bound for Brazil. It was through this southern hemispheric trade that Portuguese sailors imported cassava into Central Africa (from the island of São Tomé to the Kongo kingdom and the Luanda trading post). Over the centuries, the tuber became an important crop in Central Africa, gradually making its way inland, following trade networks and agricultural markets. Cassava trade and consumption further globalized in the eighteenth and nineteenth centuries. On the continent, it spread from Central Africa to the coastal societies of West Africa (from the Igbo to the Akan), where millet, sorghum, and yam had previously been grown. While there are many similarities between yam and cassava, there are two main differences. First, cassava is easier to grow. Second, yam is associated with community ceremonies, such as the *elulie* or yam festival in Sanvi, the lagoon kingdom of the Akan, while cassava remains a more commonplace food that was consumed by both slaves and warriors. Within the context of empire, commercial links developed in the eighteenth and nineteenth centuries between Latin America, Africa, and the Indian Ocean, supported by technical innovations in agriculture. Production improved during the industrial age in the open-air laboratories of colonial plantations. In 1886 the Colonial and Indian Exhibition in London showcased cassava starch from Malakoff & Alma. The French colonial administration promoted the cultivation of cassava throughout its tropical territories. Cassava's nutritional and caloric value, combined with its low production costs, offered numerous advantages for ensuring food security in colonized societies.

In the nineteenth and twentieth centuries, cassava became a staple food in the Gulf of Guinea, so much so that many African consumers have forgotten the tuber's Latin American origins. This shift in collective memory may be explained by the way African culinary arts have reappropriated cassava (which has become less widely consumed in South America) and invented new recipes over the centuries. While sweet cassava was initially eaten raw, the first changes came through cooking (boiled or cooked cassava). A variation was introduced by cooking not only the tuber but also its leaves, as in the very popular Congolese recipe for *saka-saka*, which combines it with spinach, peanut paste, and fish. There was further culinary innovation in the processing of the tuber. Using bitter cassava to make tapioca, opened the tuber to several other experiments, including its transformation into semolina, which became the basis for the invention of acheke. For this preparation, the cassava is first peeled, ground, and mixed with a small quantity of already fermented cassava, or *magnan* in Ebrié. It is then fermented in water, dried in the sun, ground, dried, and winnowed, before being steamed. These acheke beads can vary in size.

Grasping the evolution of acheke requires an appreciation of its social history over the long term. Cooking and the culinary arts were traditionally the women's prerogative, practiced collectively in the villages of lagoon societies. But the ostensibly trivial relationship to cooking shifted across the twentieth century as community and village practices gradually gave way to the rise of agri-food industries in the second half of the century.

Several variations of acheke exist in Côte d'Ivoire: *abgodjama* (historically reserved for ritual ceremonies such as funerals or inheritances), *attiéké petit grain* (the most popular, for commercial use) and the famous *attiéké de garba* (fried acheke-thon). In the last quarter of the twentieth century, acheke exploded onto the scene and became a central foodstuff in Côte d'Ivoire. This was due first and foremost to the transition from a rural acheke economy to an industrial one, as part of the buildup of the Ivorian agro-industrial chain developed by

President Félix Houphouët-Boigny. The Société Ivoirienne de Technologie Tropicale, headed by Diarra Oumar and founded in 1979, played a key role in this industrialization, which led to an increase in production. A second element, closely linked to this agroindustrial strategy, was the tuna fishing policy stimulated by the minister of animal production appointed in 1970, Dicoh Garba, a veterinarian who had previously been deputy director of maritime and lagoon fisheries. The acheke-fried tuna dish soon took his name. It became a huge popular success since it was initially available for just 100 CFA francs. The urban population explosion in Abidjan also considerably increased popular consumption of the dish. The success of Garbadromes (a neologism referring to large collective restaurants) from the 1990s onward, with zouglou music playing in the background, is the best indicator of this. But the trajectory of Ivorian acheke did not stop there. It has become an export product (in dehydrated form), mainly to Africa and Europe. In the twenty-first century, globalization has made acheke an emblem of Ivorian cuisine, and since April 2021 it has been the object of an application for recognition from the African Intellectual Property Organization under the name "acheke from the lagoons" (*attiéké des lagunes*), which will mark a new stage in its globalized patrimonialization.

Jean-Pierre Bat

FURTHER READING

Judith A. Carney and Richard Nicholas Rosomoff. *In the Shadow of Slavery: Africa's Botanical Legacy in the Atlantic World*. Berkeley: University of California Press, 2011.

Jean-Pierre Chrétien. "La dimension historique des pratiques alimentaires en Afrique." *Diogène* 144, no. 9 (1988): 92–114.

Henriette Dagri Diabaté. *Le Sanvi: Un royaume Akan (1701–1901)*. 2 vols. Abidjan/Paris: CERAP-IRD/Khartala, 2013.

Dominique Juhé-Beaulaton. "De l'igname au manioc dans le golfe de Guinée: Traite des esclaves et alimentation au royaume du Danhomè (xviie–xixe siècle)." *Afriques* 5 (2014). https://journals.openedition.org/afriques/1669.

FURTHER TRAVELING

Palm Oil, Tapioca

Bagels

In 1963, Murray Lender, heir to a family-run bakery based in New Haven, Connecticut, called Lender's Bagels, revolutionized bagel production by adopting a bagel-making machine patented on the West Coast three years earlier. Mechanization enabled much faster and more voluminous production. Lender's could now make up to ten thousand bagels a day! The company broke with tradition by giving a new look to the bread ring that had remained the same for over three hundred years.

Long associated with Jewish diasporic life, this bread ring was distinguished by a specific baking method—balls of sourdough with holes were boiled before being put in the oven—and born of a singular history of transfers and reinterpretations.

This round roll, so characteristic of Ashkenazi Jewish life in the shtetls before their destruction by pogroms and the Holocaust, may be attributed to any number of places along the shores of the Mediterranean. One might go back as far as *bucellatum*, the circular biscuit used in rations distributed to soldiers in the Roman Empire and baked twice to ensure that no moisture remained in the dough; or *kaak*, the crown-shaped biscuit so common from Lebanon to Morocco. Or perhaps the bagel's ancestor is to be found in a bread produced by the Uyghurs in northwestern China? Among all these legendary origins, there is one more direct lineage: *tarallo*, made by Pugliese bakers in the fourteenth century. Known as *taralli*, it was brought to Poland by a young aristocrat who went on to rule the city of Krakow. It then borrowed a few features from *obwarzanek*, a round, whitened bread commonly served by Catholics. The bread born of this encounter is said to be bagel or *beygl*, from the Germanic root *beigen*, to bend.

The Ashkenazi fate of the round bun with a hole was sealed in 1610, when, according to the statutes of the Krakow Jewish community, the city council decreed that bagels could be offered at circumcision celebrations and given to mothers and their relatives at births. They were also offered at funerals: the roundness of the buns being seen as a symbol of protection. The bagel therefore played a central role in the Polish Jewish world, both in rituals and in everyday life. When made with almonds, they could be offered on the feast of Purim, which celebrates Esther's intervention to save the Jewish people from annihilation at the hands of Haman, a minister of King Ahasuerus. They could also be eaten on the eve of Tisha B'av, the fast day commemorating the destruction of the Temple.

Small in its original version, the bagel has the advantage of being transportable. As the saying goes, you must eat three to satisfy your hunger. Its production is demanding for bakers, who spend long hours preparing it alongside boiling kettles and scorching ovens. In Warsaw in the nineteenth and early twentieth centuries, these bakers endured harsh working conditions, while at the other end of the chain, the street vendors who sold them lived in extreme poverty and were some of the first to suffer from anti-Semitism.

The bagel crossed the Atlantic in the 1890s, accompanying Jewish migrants to the United States fleeing poverty and the violence of pogroms. This young country, which welcomed exiles from Southern and Eastern Europe with open doors, became the home of the bagel for the next hundred years. In the squalid New York neighborhoods of the Lower East Side, where most of these migrants settled, the dough rings were produced in damp, dark, vermin-infested basements. The coal-fired ovens required constant supervision and generated extremely almost unbearably high temperatures. The bakers worked between fourteen and twenty hours a day, finding a few hours' rest on a bench near the ovens. However, the bakers were able to organize themselves to defend their rights. The Bagel Manufacturers' Union was founded in 1907. Renamed Local 338, it ensured that the bagel recipe remained in the hands of its members alone. Through strikes and battles to prevent production in nonunionized bakeries, it won improvements in working conditions and pay. Fearing the loss of jobs, Local 338 also resisted the mechanization of production, which remained manual and traditional until the 1950s.

In the postwar period, the toasted bagel with smoked salmon and cream cheese, eaten as a family breakfast on weekends, became a ritual for Jews in New York, Florida, and California, reconnecting them with the origins of a forgotten past and allowing them to maintain their roots even if they were unable to practice all the rituals associated with Judaism. A 1951 Broadway comedy, *Bagels and*

Yok, made it popular with a wide audience, and publication of the recipe in *Family Circle* magazine established it as a national delicacy. Its production outside New York by nonunion bakeries brought the golden ring to middle-class bread baskets. In New Haven, Lender's Bagels, quickly bought out by Kellogg's, slightly modified the dough to make it softer and tastier for all palates; they used freezer technology to sell them presliced and packaged in plastic bags gradually distributed to supermarkets nationwide, offering bagels flavored with onion, cinnamon raisin, and poppy seed.

The bagel's move into the supermarket sector pushed it into every refrigerator and onto every table in the country. Its spread was supported by the multicultural shift of the 1970s, which also encouraged greater acceptance of culinary diversity. To keep up with black rye pumpernickel and white sandwich bread, bagels had to undergo a makeover. They became bigger (they too had to be supersized) and whiter, with a greater variety of flavors. The bagel boomed. By the early 2000s annual bagel sales in the United States had reached $1 billion. The ring-shaped dough was ready to conquer the global market. Bagel shops sprang up in the world's major capitals, often drawing on the roll's Jewish origins, but proudly displaying its New York history.

Pauline Peretz

FURTHER READING

Maria Balinska. *The Bagel: The Surprising History of a Modest Bread*. New Haven, CT: Yale University Press, 2008.

Matthew Goodman. "The Rise and Fall of the Bagel." *Harvard Review* 28 (2005): 91–99.

Solomon H. Katz and William Woys Weaver, eds. *Encyclopedia of Food and Culture*. New York: Scribner, 2003.

Irving Pfefferblit. "The Bagel." *Commentary*, May 7, 1951, 475–79.

FURTHER TRAVELING

Baguette, Banh Mi, Hamburger, Hot Dog, Sandwich

Baguette

The first official mention of "baguette" did not appear until 1902, in a patent listed by the French Office National de la Propriété Industrielle (National Office of Industrial Property). A long loaf of bread, now standardized at 250 grams (8.8 oz.), the baguette is crisp when fresh out of the oven but must be eaten quickly before becoming too hard or too soft. It is no doubt the food considered to be the most distinctively French. Paired with camembert and red wine on a checkered tablecloth, or cut into half-slices, buttered, and dipped in a bowl of café au lait, the baguette seems as French as it does immemorial. Its manufacture made it a candidate for world cultural heritage. On March 26, 2021, the French minister of culture, Roselyne Bachelot, announced that she would support the baguette's candidacy for UNESCO's "intangible cultural heritage," which UNESCO accepted in 2022. Despite the contemporary diversification of eating habits, the baguette remains one of the most common everyday food items in France after drinking water.

Yet buying one's daily bread from a baker only dates back to the massive urbanization of the late nineteenth century. It is not surprising, then, that far from the French capital, the term "Parisian baguette" has entered common usage. The transition from round bread baked at home or bought to be eaten over several days to smaller, longer loaves, produced daily, took place amid the development of small local shops and daily shopping, a break with rural practices prior to the exodus to the city. However, concern raised about individual baker's ovens continued and in urban areas, large ovens remained the norm. The proliferation of bakeries resulting from urban growth was also a consequence of the evolution of urban cooking. The eighteenth century witnessed the spread of small ovens heated by embers brought in from an outdoor fire to well-to-do homes. They were used to keep food warm, particularly soups (hence its name, *potager, potage* meaning soup in French), but also to fricassee, flambé, and set sauces as well as prepare beverages such as tea, coffee, and hot chocolate. The rise of the iron and steel industry in the nineteenth century led to the transition from the masonry potager to a cast-iron version, followed by stoves and the democratization of related culinary practices. Ovens, as well as other heating methods like cast iron stoves, would not have been possible without an invisible revolution in building architecture: individualized chimney flues thanks to standardized ceramic conduits. New fire regulations thus shaped eating habits. Roasting over an open fire and baking bread in an oven that had been cleared of embers became impossible for urban dwellers and was reserved for professionals. Moreover, raising and kneading bread dough with nineteenth-century flours and yeasts required time, space, skill, and physical strength.

While state control of bread prices eased in the liberal context of the Second Empire in France (1852–70), civil protection regulations increased. In October 1862 Frédéric Le Play pleaded with the highest administrative court in France, the Conseil d'État, to deregulate bread prices, while the prefect of Paris, Baron Haussmann, opposed the idea. The subject was politically sensitive, since any uncontrolled increase in bread prices could provoke revolt and barricades across the streets of the French capital. In the end price freedom prevailed, albeit with additional restrictions, including a 4:00 a.m. limit on the start of operations in bakeries to limit noise and the risk of fire in the middle of the night. This constraint accelerated the trend toward the production of quick-baking breads, that is, thin and elongated, but with a short shelf life. The Parisian regulations were gradually adopted in all major French cities. The baguette did not originate directly from official regulations imposing standardized characteristics. It was not until 1920, in the inflationary context of the aftermath of World War I, that a prefectoral decree in the Seine Department defined the size (maximum length 40 cm/15.75 in., compared with 80 cm/31.5 in. today), minimum weight (80 g/2.8 oz.), and maximum price (35 centimes, but soon to be raised). At the same time, the abolition of night work in bakeries was reaffirmed (March 28, 1919), this time in response to workers' demands.

All of this amounts to a rather prosaic and recent story for a food that has become a national totem. So it is hardly surprising that several legends have sprung up around its origins. The left-wing press still occasionally celebrates the birth of democratic bread on November 15. In 1793 the National Convention during the French Revolution decreed that from that date forward all citizens should eat the same bread. They declared there would be no more distinctions in which flour was reserved for the rich and bran for the poor. There would be one bakery product for all: "bread equality!" The republican imagination later drew a connection between this revolutionary bread and the baguette, even though the baguette was born a full century later. Another legend attributes it to Napoleon I, because its elongated shape made it easy to carry in soldiers' *basques* or trousers. A final version plays on the imagery of the "dangerous classes" of the early days of the French Third Republic in the late nineteenth century. The Prefecture of Police is said to have favored elongated loaves, which were easy to break and divide with one's hands. As a result, workers would not need to carry knives that could easily be used for something other than cutting their bread. A variant of the latter legend even attributes this decision to Fulgence Bienvenüe, the builder of the first Paris metro, who was keen to avoid fights between migrants from two distant regions of provincial France, in particular between Bretons and Auvergnats during the construction of the metro tunnels. Even in these imagined stories, the genesis of the baguette remains indissolubly associated with Paris.

Today, the baguette is regulated by the decree of September 13, 1993, signed by then Prime Minister Balladur. Only wheat flour, water, salt, yeast, or sourdough may be used. Three adjuvants are authorized in minute proportions: bean flour, soy flour, and wheat malt flour. These precise guidelines respond to the concerns of artisan bakers faced with the explosion in supermarket sales of breads that have all the appearance of baguettes, at least at the time of sale, but with increasingly imaginative compositions. The increase in the quantity of water and the reduction in baking times make it possible to advertise prices that are much lower than those of small shops. In January 2022 the Leclerc baguette cost about thirty-five cents. The Balladur decree has thus played a major role in maintaining bakeries and pastry shops in France, which sell the lion's share of the six billion baguettes produced in the country every year.

Beyond this newfound dynamism, the baguette has also become a globalized product, offering easy access to French gastronomy without high expense. Two waves of baguette world distribution have overlapped. The earliest was linked to the legacy of colonization. In practically all the former French colonies, even working-class urban dwellers ate bread made from leavened wheat and shaped longways. In the Middle East the practice of round, flat bread is still widespread, while in the Maghreb the baguette is widely consumed. Daily consumption, even beyond coastal towns, is more surprising in intertropical Africa, which does not produce wheat. And yet, at even the smallest taxi station, there are always baguette sellers who also offer instant coffee. While this French bread has hardly been changed in Africa, its spread to Indochina, where rice flour is more familiar, has given rise to a crossbreeding of foods in the form of banh mi.

A second process of diffusion took place with the accelerated food globalization of the late twentieth century. In the Anglo-American world, then in East Asia, the use of French bread for sandwiches, rather than as an accompaniment to a meal, has become widespread. Several upmarket French bakeries, pioneered by Lionel Poilâne, opened stores in the United States, Australia, Japan, and China. The Paul company opened its first franchise in Nagoya in 1990. By 2020, 355 Paul bakeries in forty-four countries from Morocco to Singapore and from the United Arab Emirates to Japan offered baguettes, among other products. Baguettes thus represent France's contribution to world food, alongside the other internationalized products from other countries such as sushi, hamburgers, and pizza.

Christian Grataloup

FURTHER READING

Alain Bonjean and Benoît Vermander. *L'homme et le grain: Une histoire céréalière des civilisations*. Paris: Les Belles Lettres, 2021.
Raymond Calvel. *La boulangerie moderne*. 1952. Paris: Eyrolles, 1979.
Steven L. Kaplan and Jean-Philippe de Tonnac. *La France et son pain: Histoire d'une passion*. Paris: Albin Michel, 2010.
——. *Pour le pain*. Paris: Fayard, 2020.
Claude Thouvenot. *Le pain d'autrefois: Chroniques alimentaires d'un monde qui s'en va*. Nancy: Presses Universitaires de Nancy, 1987.

FURTHER TRAVELING

Banh Mi, Coffee, Hamburger, Pizza, Salt, Sandwich, Sushi, Tea and Chai, Wine

Banh Mi

In 1954, the end of French colonization in Indochina coincided with the democratization of bread consumption in the former colony and the spread of banh mi, a sandwich whose recipe blends French influence with local tastes. Introduced to Indochina by the French in the nineteenth century, the bread was initially called *banh tay* (Western bread) by the local population. The term reflects the stark divide that existed at the time between French colonial society, which was mainly urban-based, and colonized Vietnamese society, which was largely rural. Bread was part of a repertoire of foods consumed by the French, like butter (*bo*), cheese (*pho ma, pho mai, pho mach*), and steak. In colonized Indochina, its consumption was an element of distinction for French settlers, and only the wealthiest Vietnamese could afford to buy it, topped with imported butter, pâté, ham, or gherkins. Until the 1940s–50s, exoticism and luxury were thus associated with French bread in Indochina.

After the departure of the French in 1954, bread lost its foreign character and became part of Vietnamese cuisine under the name *banh mi*, "*banh*" designating flour-based foods (cake, bread, galette) and "*mi*" referring to wheat. In Saigon (now Ho Chi Minh City), where such cuisine was more sought after than in the north of the country, vendors began offering *banh mi thit nguoi* (bread with cold meats) as early as the 1940s, *banh mi* referred to both the Vietnamese baguette and the sandwich emblematic of the Saigon region.

The term is also a phonetic reference to "sandwich bread," and in the 1950s, one could find two types of banh mi: one based on sandwich bread, the other on baguette. A luxury version, sold in boutiques, offered banh mi in small oval loaves, topped with mayonnaise, roast chicken or French ham (*giam bong, jam bong*), lettuce, tomato slices, and white onion. A second version combined charcuterie—sausage or pâté—with the same vegetables. The addition of mayonnaise, which is less liquid than the French recipe and contains no vinegar or other acidic ingredients, has helped make the dish popular by moistening the bread, a quality much appreciated by the Vietnamese.

At the same time, street stalls started selling a more affordable version of banh mi, in a variety of recipes. One consists of a piece of Vietnamese baguette, spread with mayonnaise, butter, or pâté. The garnish includes slices of Vietnamese mortadella (*gio lua* or *cha lua*) or roast pork, coriander leaves, slices of cucumber, and chopped red pepper, as well as carrot or daikon (white radish) pickles, replacing expensive pickles. A few drops of bottled Maggi flavoring, known simply as *Maggi* to the Vietnamese, or soy sauce are used to spice up the taste, as is often the case with dishes and ingredients borrowed from the French and considered too bland. Banh mi is then toasted on the small charcoal grills of street vendors. The variety and type of topping are determined by how much the customer wants to spend on their sandwich, the custom being for vendors to ask: "How much for your banh mi?" Other types of filling are also proposed, such as dumplings in tomato sauce or sardines in tomato sauce, two recipes that are popular with the South Vietnamese.

The Vietnamese baguette, which is split in two before being garnished, has become common over time. Adapted from the French baguette, it features a mixture of wheat and rice flour, making the bread lighter and the crust thinner and crispier. The introduction of rice flour, which is less expensive than wheat, also helped to popularize banh mi consumption by lowering its cost. The shape of the Vietnamese baguette, shorter than the French version, makes it particularly suitable for use in sandwiches. Vietnamese bakers have taken to baking two batches a day, as the baguette quickly becomes hard in the country's climate.

The successive transformations of banh mi are closely linked to the colonization of Indochina, but also to major population shifts across different historical moments. Thus, while different preparations of banh mi developed in Hanoi to the north and Saigon to the south, the emigration of several hundred thousand North Vietnamese to the south after the partition of Vietnam in 1954 contributed to the evolution of Saigon cuisine. Vendors were already offering a banh mi filling based on Vache Qui Rit, a processed cheese paste commercialized since 1921 by the French Jura-based cheesemaker Bel, which exported it to the colonies in a metal box. However, this garnish was less successful than the others, which has been attributed to the fact that the taste of the processed cheese did not go well with the pickles and other condiments.

From 1954 onward another version of banh mi with cheese (*pho mai*) was created, taking advantage of the cheddar deliveries arriving in the country via American food aid for North Vietnamese refugees, which also included powdered milk and canned meat. The cheddar, either orange or red in color, was delivered in forty-centimeter (15.75 in.) blocks. For many North Vietnamese living in remote villages, their shape and size were reminiscent of the soap sold in bars in the market. Huge quantities of cheddar, rejected by the refugees, were sold or used by street stalls, which incorporated them into their toppings to offer a low-priced banh mi. Associated with food aid and the ubiquity of cheddar, banh mi pho mai was even less popular than banh mi à la Vache Qui Rit. In fact, these two toppings have never managed to compete with recipes based on charcuterie or cooked meat.

Banh mi, which has become emblematic of Vietnamese street food, is still regarded as a snack, unable to match the hot rice-based meals served for lunch or dinner in the eyes of the Vietnamese. So, in the 1960s and 1970s, as many offices reduced the length of their employees' lunch breaks—which could last up to two and a half hours during the French colonial period—employees turned to new hot meals (*com van phong*) offered by street vendors, many of whom went on to open specialized restaurants in the office districts.

After the Communist takeover of Saigon in 1975 and the reunification of the country, many Vietnamese refugees went into exile in North America, France, and Australia. Most of them settled in the United States, where in the 2000s there were more than a million people of Vietnamese origin. From the late 1970s onward this migration led to the opening of restaurants serving local cuisine, particularly in California, such as Little Saigon (in Orange County, near Los Angeles), home to the country's largest Vietnamese community. The opening of specialized banh mi shops, initially by refugees from the Saigon region, has since spread throughout the world. Today there are many variations of banh mi, which are now offered on the menus of fast-food chains around the globe.

Emmanuelle Cronier

FURTHER READING

Nelly Krowolski and Nguyen Tung. "Note sur les pratiques alimentaires vietnamiennes et les influences étrangères." *Pratiques alimentaires et identités culturelles: Études vietnamiennes* 55–56, nos. 125–26 (1997): 361–400.

Vu Hong Lien. *Rice and Baguette: A History of Food in Vietnam*. London: Reaktion Books, 2016.

Andrea Nguyen. *The Banh Mi Handbook*. Berkeley, CA: Ten Speed Press, 2014.

FURTHER TRAVELING

Bagel, Baguette, Charcuterie, Chili Pepper, Mayonnaise, Sandwich, Soy Sauce

Barbecue

Recounting his shipwreck on the Mosquito Coast, the English slave trader Nathaniel Uring noted the ingenuity of his seamen as hunters and cooks. Failing to kill a large iguana, they slew black monkeys, singed off their hair, and cooked them whole on a wood frame he called a barbecue. They looked "so like young children broiled." Uring's recollections of Honduras hark back to the early, often fantastical European accounts of the New World depicting smoked or dried meat as human flesh.

The preparation of meat by grilling and smoking, following methods of the New World, became known in Europe either as *barbacoa*, in Spanish accounts, or as *boucan*, in French and English texts. *Boucan* is a word from the language of the Tupinamba, the tribe that helped Huguenot colonists during their expedition in 1557 to *la France antarctique* (modern Brazil). The chronicler of that voyage, Jean de Léry (1536–1613), describes a vertical frame of wood, topped by thick branches, on which the Tupi cooked fish and animal flesh over a slow fire "sometimes more than twenty-four hours." As for *barbacoa*, it originally had nothing to do with meat. According to Gonzalo Fernandez de Oviedo y Valdes (1478–1557), who reached the Americas a few years after Columbus, *barbacoa* was a term for wood scaffolding topped by a roof of reeds, which the Taino (of modern-day Haiti) built in cornfields. From atop the *barbacoa*, children surveyed the harvest and scared parakeets off the crops.

The arrival of European colonists to the New World radically altered the meaning of barbecue. With the extinction of the Taino people, the island of Hispaniola became a vast reserve of formerly domesticated Spanish quadrupeds (pigs and cows). In the seventeenth century, French buccaneers made a livelihood of hunting wild bovines and selling the skins to commercial ships. Early travel accounts compared these cow-hunting buccaneers to Spanish matadors. The meat of wild cattle was, however, too sinewy to eat. According to the French adventurer Alexandre-Olivier Exquemelin, "They usually just eat the nipples of cows." Buccaneers preferred swine, which recovered their fur and tusks in the wild. They cured their meat through a method unlike that of Amerindians in Brazil or on the isthmus of Panama. The *boucan* in Hispaniola was a sealed "hut covered with *taches* (skins)." Inside the hut, they placed long strips of the meat on a wood rack and "burn[ed] all the skins and bones of their boars to make a thicker smoke." The buccaneers sold smoked pork in bundles wrapped in animal skin to passing ships; they sold the lard, called *matengue*, to locals.

From its beginnings as an indigenous practice in North America, barbecue became part of the fabric of New World slave societies. Washington's letters and social calendar are full of such events, which marked everything from boat races and whist parties to army musters and elections. Alas we know little about the preparation of meat on those occasions. Several conflicting definitions of barbecue circulated in the eighteenth-century Anglophone world. Daniel Lescallier's *Vocabulaire des termes de marine anglais-françois et françois-anglais* (1777), which dates from the American War of Independence, mentions *barbique* as an English word for a spit used to roast or dry meat. In England, by contrast, *barbecue* had nothing to do with smoking. According to Johnson's *Dictionary*, to barbecue was "a term for dressing a hog whole" (1774).

As the birthplace of modern barbecue, North America was distinct from Caribbean slave societies. In eighteenth-century North America, indigenous people coexisted with settlers and slaves who learned from native practices. Though enmeshed in the history of slavery shared with other Southern food traditions, barbecue is also distinct from them. Staples of modern-day soul food (yams, black beans, okra, watermelons, and certain chilis) were domesticated in Africa and then transported to the North American continent. By contrast, West and Central Africans rarely ate meat at the time of the transatlantic slave trade. The massive consumption of animal flesh is a peculiarity of the New World, dating back to the arrival of Europeans on American soil. Further, while peoples throughout the globe developed methods for curing meat, those techniques outside the Americas—in China, the Maghreb, Turkey, Central Asia, sub-Saharan Africa—generally required salt.

Enslaved people comprised the production team of every barbecue party in the antebellum South, whether partygoers were white or black. The preparation of meat for these carnivalesque gatherings bore no resemblance to the *boucan* or barbecue among the Tupi, Cherokee, or buccaneers. Thomas Main Reid's novel *Bruin* (1860), set in antebellum America, offers a detailed barbecue scene involving dozens of slaves. They dig a pit, set the timber, kill an ox, gather paw-paw saplings to perfume the meat, manipulate the fire, then baste and apply their secret seasoning. "Proudly presiding over the operation was the major domo of the planter's household assisted by several celebrated cooks of the neighborhood," who applied a celebrated mixture of "salt, pepper, and herbs in a composition for which he has a great reputation." As the fear of slave revolt swept the South in the 1820s, white elites came to see slave barbecues as danger-ous events. Barbecues were seen as occasions where slaves hatched criminal plots. To wit, the Nat Turner revolt in 1831 began with a barbecue.

In the twentieth century, the automobile redefined American barbecue as a food preparation and a social experience. After 1945 the massive construction of new highways helped to suburbanize the country, especially in the North and West. A 1951 cartoon in the *Evening Star* (Washington, DC) depicted the new suburban barbecue culture. "I'm having a barbecue this afternoon for the boss and a few men from the office," explains a male homeowner in a chef's hat to his assistant, a bellboy in livery. (Just below the bellboy, in bold letters, appears the slogan "Do you inhale?" of the Philip Morris tobacco company.) During the Cold War era barbecue became a symbol of male middle-class sociability in much of the country, apart from the South.

The car and the highway shaped Southern barbecue by popularizing and reinforcing regional foodways. Barbecue stands, differentiated by local styles, became fixtures on new roads and at gas stations. The postwar highway culture (which created the now-iconic BBQ sign) helped Southern barbecue to thrive as a regionalized road food until its eclipse by the hamburger. Capitalist moder-nity, as a capricious force that wrecks some traditions, preserves others, and sanctifies the past, has further reinvented barbecue by creating a cult of nostal-gia. Through the marketing genius of local business leaders, Memphis, Tennes-see has been home to the World Barbecue Championship since 1978, where the only authentic meat is pork. Elsewhere, one finds other authentic meats: brisket in Texas, mutton in Kentucky. Whatever the regional tradition, barbecue is now America's quintessential slow food, which incarnates a lost world to revive and consume.

Miranda Spieler

FURTHER READING

Jean de Léry, Frank Lestringant, and Claude Lévi-Strauss. *Histoire d'un voyage fait en la terre du Brésil: 1578.* 2nd ed., 1580. Paris: Le Livre de Poche, 2016.

Daniel Dupre. "Barbecues and Pledges: Electioneering and the Rise of Democratic Politics in Antebellum Alabama." *Journal of Southern History* 60, no. 3 (1994): 479–512.

Alexandre-Olivier Exquemelin. *Histoire des aventuriers, flibustiers et boucaniers qui sont signalés dans les Indes, contenant ce qu'ils y ont fait de remarquable, avec la vie, les mœurs, et les coutumes des boucaniers et des habitants de Saint Domingue et de la Tortue, une description exacte de ces lieux.* 2 vols. 1686. Paris: Presses Universitaires de Paris Sorbonne, 2005.

Lucia Rojas de Perdomo. *Cocina prehispanica: Comentarios a la cocina de las altas culturas prehispanicas: Azteca, Inca y Muisca.* Santafé de Bogota: Editorial Voluntad, 1994.

James R. Veteto and Edward M. Maclin. *The Slaw and the Slow Cooked: Culture and Barbecue in the Mid-South.* Nashville, TN: Vanderbilt University Press, 2012.

FURTHER TRAVELING

Hamburger, Pepper, Salt

Beer

On December 31, 1904, Europeans and North Americans living in China, and particularly in the Shandong region, enjoyed an initial sip of "Tsingtao" beer. This so-called German-style beer was billed as the first produced on the Chinese mainland, originating from a brewery founded by German settlers and later taken over by the Anglo-German Brewery Co. Ltd, a Hong Kong–based company. Tsingtau, or Qingdao, was intended for Westerners, since it was assumed that the Chinese market was not yet sufficiently accustomed to such a foreign taste. Advertisements deliberately emphasized Tsingtao's proximity to Pilsner light beers and Munich dark beers. On that day, drinkers celebrated the arrival of a taste that seemed to them—and perhaps not without some nostalgia—to be all-European and very "modern," rooted in nineteenth-century industrial and national traditions. Few could have imagined that this drink was in fact just one piece in a long and rich history of globalization.

This history reflects a shared heritage across humanity. Historians and archaeologists associate the discovery of beer with a new phase in the development of human societies, at the beginning of the Neolithic period (9000–7000 BCE). The beverage, produced by fermenting barley, wheat, oats, or sorghum, marked a turn in human settlement toward sedentary communities. Its presence is attested in the famous Fertile Crescent, between the Tigris and Euphrates rivers, at Uruk, in 6000 BCE. In line with the hypothesis of a polygenesis of human inventions and activities, it is also found in China as early as 7000 BCE. The ancient Egyptians used to drink this beverage prepared in brasseries, which were also often brothels. This beer, whose quality changed according to social hierarchies, was used to compensate for the lack of drinking water, to eat, and even to pay workers on the building sites of pyramids. The drink was also present in Socrates's Athens. In Latin America, recent archaeological discoveries attest to its use in the Wari state (present-day Peru) in the seventh through tenth centuries in the form of hallucinogenic beer. In other words, by the time of the nineteenth century, the drink already had a long world history behind it. The European monasteries of the Carolingian era had already inaugurated commercial brewing and long-distance export. Reminiscent of the eternal challenge of deciding when to harvest the hops, one is pushed to ask what moment might be chosen to signify beer's entry into the modern age?

Hops, a climbing plant so essential to beer production, is the ideal place to start. Although hops had been known since the fourteenth century, its use in beer increased from the end of the eighteenth century onward. While hops added bitterness to the product, they also allowed for greater preservation, enabling it to adapt to the industrial changes underway. Alongside industrialization, the emergence of the modern state also contributed to its transformation. As was often the case, the starting point for this innovation was Great Britain. To finance the wars that would ensure its power in the seventeenth and eighteenth centuries, the British crown heavily taxed French wines during this period. The measure in turn necessitated the creation of an alternative beverage for the growing ranks of workers in big cities, especially port workers. This became the era of "Porter" beer, a particularly hoppy brown ale. Less tasty, less expensive, and produced in large volumes, it ensured the fortune and political power of the London brewers, who had become major industrialists.

Scientific and technical discoveries also played a role in the acceleration of beer production in the nineteenth century. In the 1840s brewers in Pilsen, Bohemia, in what is now the Czech Republic, adopted a Bavarian production technique known as bottom fermentation, in which fermentation is pursued at lower temperatures. The result is a clear, golden-colored beer of consistent quality. It became known as "Pilsner" and enjoyed great commercial success in Prague. This type of beer, known as "Lager" (from the German for "preserve"), benefited from other innovations at the end of the century, such as self-cooling tanks in the 1870s, the industrialization of bottle production, and advances in bottling. This enabled the company to conquer markets not only in rapidly expanding cities, but also on new continents such as the United States.

In the middle of the century, German emigrants set up the first lager breweries in North America. In particular, they produced Budweiser, named after Budweis, a Bohemian rival town to Pilsen. Its diffusion in this new land was hardly linear. Beer had been produced on the American continent since the seventeenth century. Then, stimulated by the California gold rush, European immigration, and post–Civil War industrialization, the number of breweries nevertheless rose from around a hundred in 1800 to twenty-five hundred by 1870. Taken as a whole, the change was impressive: on the eve of World War I, Germany, the United Kingdom, and the United States each consumed between five billion and seven billion liters (1.3–1.8 billion gal.) a year. Mexico also had an important place in this picture. What might be referred to as "old" beer, had been produced since Spanish colonization in the sixteenth century. It was consumed by the Spanish residents of Mexico City, while the local population preferred *pulque*, a slightly alcoholic beverage made from the partial fermentation of agave. Consumption of imported lager beer from the United States and Germany took off in the 1840s. New breweries were soon set up in Mexico, initially by European immigrants, as the country became part of the economic development of the Atlantic increasingly shaped by industrialization. The conversion was remarkable: in the 1880s, domestic demand for beer grew by 500 percent, while the share of foreign exports fell to less than 5 percent. By the dawn of the twentieth century Mexico had become a great beer nation and was preparing to export its *cervezas mexicanas*.

Of course, such a global rollout was not without its conflicts, rejections, and resistance. In Africa the first industrial breweries were set up at the end of the century, such as the famous South African Brewery (SAB), founded in 1895. However, many populations continued to prefer local beers with strong social and symbolic significance, such as the Bantu-speaking Hayas peoples of Tanzania, who drank "banana beer" made from banana and sorghum. In China, beer production also had a long history, even if it was not until 1903 that a brewery was set up in the German concession of Qingdao. At the same time, Russians were investing in Harbin, Japanese in Shenyang, and British and French in Shanghai. The first "modern" Chinese-owned brewery, known as the "Double Prosperity" brewery, opened in 1915.

Despite the diversity of its development across the century, a phenomenon of taste convergence also emerged, particularly around lager beers. Reproducing a well-known trend that can be found in other areas of development, beer types and taste underwent a process of increased differentiation as flavors varied according to the cereal, hop, water, or manufacturing techniques. This growing diversity took place within a realm of taste that was increasingly shared and distinct from previous experiences: beer increasingly became bitter, standardized, and light. Indian pale ale, which became a brand and style of beer in 1840, was another good example. Its drier, less sweet taste reflected the cooking methods and geographical features of the English region around Burton, in Wiltshire, as well as the expectations of British settlers in India. But its rise began with the return of these settlers to Great Britain, who ensured the beer's imperial reputation, and then with the opening of the Scottish and American markets at the end of the century.

So beer did indeed play a role in transformations across the nineteenth century. Just as during the period between 1900 and 1920, the effects of economic competition (which led to a smaller number of large breweries), the rise of other "global" beverages such as tea, coffee, and soft drinks, as well as the rupture provoked by World War I and the temperance and prohibition policies (particularly in the United States in the 1920s) that followed, led to a vast reorganization of production and consumption. The global history of beer has, of course, continued ever since. Today, against the backdrop of an explosion in consumption since 1980 and the inclusion of new markets such as Brazil, Russia, and China, three multinationals produce more than half the world's beers in the form of light lager beers. In response, over the last few decades, microbreweries have set out to recover old flavors or invent new ones, with an ever-increasing range of tastes, scents, and colors (lagers, browns, amber, whites, and so on). In short, far from the linear diffusion of beer from Germany to China imagined by marketers in 1905, it was a world historical development with deep roots in the nineteenth century that the Europeans in Qingdao enjoyed that evening when they toasted in the new year with a sip of beer.

Quentin Deluermoz

FURTHER READING

Robert Carlson. "Banana Beer, Reciprocity, and Ancestor Propitiation Among the Haya of Bukoba, Tanzania." *Ethnology* 29, no. 4 (1990): 297–311.

John V. C. Nye. *War, Wine and Taxes: The Political Economy of Anglo-French Trade, 1689–1900*. Princeton, NJ: Princeton University Press, 2007.

Mark Patterson and Nancy Hoalst-Pullen, eds. *The Geography of Beer: Regions, Environment, and Societies*. Berlin: Springer Science & Business Media, 2014.

Johan Swinnen and Devin Briski. *Bieronomics: Histoire du monde à travers la bière*. Paris: DeBoeck Supérieur, 2019.

Thomas M. Wilson. *Drinking Culture. Alcohol and Identity*. London: Bloomsbury, 2005.

Zhiguo Yang. "'This Beer Tastes Really Good': Nationalism, Consumer Culture and Development of the Beer Industry in Qingdao, 1903–1993." *Chinese Historical Review* 14, no. 1 (2007): 29–58.

FURTHER TRAVELING

Chicory, Coffee, Gin, Port Wine, Rum, Sake, Tea and Chai, Whiskey

Beet Sugar

In 1875 Eugène François, a Parisian grocer, patented a machine for cutting sugar into cubes. Though familiar to French consumers, the white square block of beet sugar hardly conquered the world. Written in the singular, sugar refers to sucrose extracted from two plants: sugarcane (*Saccharum spp.*) and sugar beet (*Beta vulgaris*). Until the early nineteenth century, the sugar market was based exclusively on sugarcane. Nineteenth-century Europe innovated by extracting sugar from beets to the point of competing with and then outstripping cane sugar. In 1890, beet sugar accounted for three-fifths of world consumption, rising to two-thirds by the early twentieth century. Today, the most widely consumed sugar comes from sugarcane, with beet sugar accounting for just a quarter of global production.

White or brown? In the West, social distinction has long been based on the whiteness of refined sugar on the table, while brown sugar was relegated to the kitchen. A veritable social hierarchy emerged along the spectrum from the purity of "royal sugar" through brown sugar to more common molasses, a brownish-black syrup. In the eighteenth century, molasses was widely consumed in North America because it was less expensive. As demand for sugar grew, consumers showed a preference for white sugar, a marker of modernity. In India, for example, while rural dwellers remain attached to unrefined or unrefined artisanal sugar, *gur* and *khansari*, city dwellers turned to industrial white sugar.

In the eighteenth century, sugar was sold in conical loaves. The characteristic shape of the sugar loaf comes from the truncated cone-shaped molds into which the crystallizing liquid sugar was poured to be drained and dried. Weighing from one to several kilograms, sugar loaves disappeared from the stores of the Western world in the 1950s but can still be found elsewhere. In North Africa and Mauritania, for example, they can sometimes be seen in their traditional blue-violet paper wrapping. To cut it, the grocer would use specific tools: a wooden block and a chopper, or a mechanical lever-operated sugar breaker, to break up the sugar loaf, followed by sugar-breaking tongs or sugar-breaking scissors to cut the pieces. Granulated sugar was made using a wooden mallet, sugar mill, or sugar grater. Stored in bulk in large containers, it was sold on demand by grocers. This sugar offered crystals of irregular size, sifted at the consumer's table with a perforated spoon. Introduced in the eighteenth century, such powdered sugar became obsolete in the 1930s in the face of fine industrial powdered sugar, which the Belgians refer to by the evocative name of semolina sugar, produced by grinding or sieving the crystallized product and delivered ready-to-use to grocery stores.

In the nineteenth century, Europe saw several artisanal attempts to calibrate sugar lumps, but it was not until the turn of the twentieth century that Théophile Adant industrialized the production of sugar lumps in Belgium: traditional sugar loaves were replaced by slabs of sugar sawed into bars and then into regular lumps. In 1949, the French company Chambon successfully developed a new industrial method: sugar was directly molded into lumps in rotary presses.

From the 1930s onward, lump sugar, sold in one-kilo (2.2 lb.) tins in European grocery stores, established itself as a simple, practical, hygienic, and modern product. At the same time, on the other side of the Atlantic, identical arguments were put forward in advertisements aimed at convincing retailers to sell Jack Frost sugar, one of the brands of the National Sugar Refining Company. Unlike bulk sales, packaged sugar enabled the product to be identified with a brand and guaranteed quality for consumers. Its success was thus linked to the rise of marketing. More generally, sugar packaging was part of a consumer revolution. Customers no longer saw the product, nor could they taste it. They now trusted a brand. As for the grocer, he no longer had to break up the sugar, weigh it, and package it, which represented an undeniable time-saver and reduced the loss of sugar crystals. Moreover, standardized packs were easier to store on shelves. Packaging enabled the transition from counter sales in the eighteenth and nineteenth centuries to open displays in the 1930s, and then to self-service sales after the war. In granulated or lump form, white or brown, packaged sugar introduced brands and their imaginary world to grocery store shelves and the everyday world of households: Domino Sugar in North America, Beghin-Say in France, Tate & Lyle in Great Britain, Cosuma in Morocco, and Mitr Phol in Thailand, among so many others.

From a semiluxury item in the eighteenth century to a basic necessity in the nineteenth century, sugar emerged as a staple foodstuff, entering the category of food reserves alongside oil and flour. It was used to sweeten hot drinks; tea, coffee, and chocolate all had it in common. It was also an unavoidable ingredient in many desserts and jams, as well as dishes in kitchens with a penchant for sweet and sour. In the form of confectionery, the purchase of sugar remained associated with festivities linked to the cycle of life and religious calendars: baptism, circumcision, weddings, breaking the Ramadan fast, Hanukkah, Easter, Halloween, the Mexican Day of the Dead, the celebration of Milād an-Nabī in Egypt, the feast day of Saint Nicholas, Valentine's Day, and birthdays.

As the twentieth century was increasingly shaped by the rise of agribusiness, the hidden consumption of sugar increased considerably, to the detriment of consumer health. It could be found in many breads, especially sandwich bread; in canned goods, including soups; in condiments and ready-to-use sauces, from pickles to ketchup; in frozen processed dishes; in ice cream; in cold meats and mixed salads. Industrialists came to use it as a preservative and as a means of improving the texture, color, and taste of a given dish. Sugar was also present in two of the flagship products of American soft power: soft drinks and breakfast cereals. In a bid to win the loyalty of children and teenagers, sugar was added to cereal boxes throughout the twentieth century. In 1949 Post Cereal successfully launched Sugar Crisp, puffed wheat coated with crunchy sugar. Kellogg's Honey Smacks contain 55.6 percent sugar, Post Cereal's Super Orange Crisp 70 percent. As for soft drinks, from the 1960s to the 1990s sucrose was gradually replaced by corn-derived high glucose-fructose syrup (HFCS), which has the same taste and sweetening power but is less expensive.

In Robert Stevenson's 1964 film, Mary Poppins sings, "A spoonful of sugar helps the medicine go down." Sweetness is an innate taste and a universal source of pleasure, but it is not the same sugar that is spooned out from one grocery store to another. Lump sugar is popular in France and Belgium and is also found in North and West Africa, but on a global scale it remains in the minority compared to granulated sugar. Consumers in northern France and Belgium appreciate the mellow consistency of blond or brown sugar. North Americans coat their pancakes with maple syrup. The British buy *moscovado*, raw cane sugar from Mauritius, and molasses sugar for puddings. Artisanal sugar production has continued in South America and Asia. The worldwide success of sugar is a fine example of local adaptations to food globalization.

Florent Quellier

FURTHER READING

Joseph Garnotel. *La saga du sucre entre douceur et amertume*. Versailles: Quae, 2020.
Sidney W. Mintz. *Sweetness and Power: The Place of Sugar in Modern History*. New York: Penguin Books, 1986.
Annie Perrier-Robert and Marie-Paule Bernardin. *Le grand livre du sucre*. Paris: Solar, 1999.
Philippe Reiser. *Avec ou sans sucre? 90 clés pour comprendre le sucre*. Versailles: Quae, 2015.
Andrew F. Smith. *Sugar: A Global History*. London: Reaktion Books, 2015.

FURTHER TRAVELING

Charcuterie, Coffee, Food Coloring and Preservatives, Ketchup, Tea and Chai

Cassoulet

On the evening of Barack Obama's election, November 4, 2008, the image of a "Cassoulet" banner unfurled by French journalists in Times Square was spotted by world media. A few weeks later, the world's first cassoulet competition was held in New York. This stew made from white beans and meat is associated with the history of regional cuisines and has become an emblem of French cooking. Suddenly it was in the spotlight in a city where food cultures from all over the world intersected. It was an example of how local cuisine could be combined with the diverse food culture of the world's major capitals. This widely publicized competition, covered in the *New York Times*, reflects the global history of cassoulet, with its rootedness, circulation, and syncretism. A staple of French gastronomy since the late nineteenth century, cassoulet is now celebrated in America, where some of its ingredients (beans and tomatoes) originate.

Cassoulet takes its name from the *cassole*, a wide, flat-bottomed earthenware vessel used to prepare it. As early as antiquity, this type of pottery was circulating in the Mediterranean to make a variety of stews. The origins of the dish we know today, however, are more directly linked to the arrival of beans (*Phaseolus vulgaris*) from Central America in Europe from the sixteenth century onward, followed by the slow spread of the tomato in the nineteenth century. Its roots go even further back in time, with common preparations in the Middle Ages of mutton stews (known as *haricots de mouton*) accompanied by fava beans (introduced to Europe by the Arabs in the seventh century). The use of cowpeas, a legume native to Africa also known as black-eyed peas, similarly reveals how much circulation there was in the Mediterranean region. However, the larger, more productive American bean supplanted these older species in the French region of Languedoc during the seventeenth and eighteenth centuries. Until the nineteenth century, cassoulet, like other popular dishes based on the use of a variety of ingredients, left little trace of its sources. Only the presence of *cassoles*, examples of which from the late eighteenth century were discovered by archaeologists in a Quebec pottery workshop, suggests that stews of this kind may have been prepared.

In the second half of the nineteenth century, in the wake of the regionalist movement, cassoulet became an emblem of Languedoc cuisine, with its many variations from Castelnaudary to Toulouse, via Carcassonne. In 1891, the French newspaper *La mode illustrée*, distributed not only in France but also in England, included a recipe for Carcassonne cassoulet (with mutton shoulder, garlic sausage, and tomato) in its readers' letters, a sign of the craze for this preparation that brought together Paris and the provinces.

But the national and international recognition of this slow-cooked dish is also closely linked to the history of the canning industry. With the development of the railroad and advances in the canning industry, cassoulet set out to conquer the French market. It was part of the boom in the food industry. Developed by Nicolas Appert, canning was initially used to consume seasonal produce such as fruit and vegetables throughout the year. Ready-made dishes, cassoulet among them, gradually began to feature in canners' catalogs, particularly in the French town of Castelnaudary. These preparations, packaged in metal cans, were seen as a way of saving time. From then on, cassoulet began to travel, as journalist Ardouin-Dumazet pointed out in 1904. According to Ardouin-Dumazet, it could be found in Paris, "where many restaurants offer cassoulet as one of their daily specials once a week. . . . Enthusiasts can also get cassoulet from Castelnaudary itself, where cooks make tinned cassoulet." Cassoulet thus appeared in the catalog of the Delhaize chain store in Brussels from 1914 onward.

However, it wasn't until World War I that cassoulet conquered the world, thanks to distribution in metal cans. During the war many soldiers discovered this canned dish (in the summer 1918 Au Bon Marché catalog, it was listed under the heading "For our soldiers"), which they found comforting in the trenches thanks to the parcels they received and shared. As with other foodstuffs, the army and wars accelerated transformations in eating habits. In the twentieth century canned cassoulet accompanied the French armies. At Dunkirk in 1940 it was used to feed French servicemen before their embarkation. Today it can be found in the most innovative forms of canned food, since the recipe is still used in rations for military missions abroad.

Promoted by the regionalist movement on the eve of World War I and by leading politicians such as President Armand Fallières, cassoulet spread throughout the world. Advertisements sought to include cassoulet in the history of France, with its great personalities and eternal countryside. Like all canned foods (sardines, truffles, pâtés, or game), it represented a form of social distinction, offering access to products from afar. At the same time, the renown of French cuisine, embodied since 1880–90 by Auguste Escoffier, ensured that cassoulet would be found on the tables of the finest restaurants and palaces. His *Guide culinaire*, a reference work for professionals the world over, included a recipe with mutton and garlic sausage. A local dish, cassoulet made its mark on globalization thanks to the expatriation of French chefs. On April 23, 1898, a cassoulet from Castelnaudary was served to first-class passengers aboard *La Gascogne*, a popular ocean liner. In November 1912 a mutton stew "in cassoulet" appeared on the menu of the Waldorf Astoria restaurant; in 1944 duck cassoulet from Toulouse was offered at the Cassonis Grill Room in Montevideo, Uruguay; and in 1987 The Greenhouse, the restaurant at the World Trade Center, made it one of the highlights of a menu celebrating French cuisine. At the same time, the spread of canned food on a large scale, embodied by industrial brands such as Olida and William Saurin, gave it a place of choice in popular diets of the second half of the twentieth century, alongside sauerkraut and lentils. Cassoulet has also been part of France's colonial history, from the colonizers who asserted their status through this dish to the soldiers who took part in the various conflicts in Indochina and Algeria.

In the twenty-first century, the Académie Universelle du Cassoulet has promoted the dish around the world, with ambassador restaurants in Belgium, Canada, and Japan. Chef André Pachon offers online sales of cassoulet in Tokyo. In the United States, thanks to French chefs who have settled there, cassoulet has even become a favorite among hipsters in the 2010s, with revisited versions (vegan versions with soy sausages and fish cassoulet, among others). There are also luxury versions such as the one served in Alain Ducasse's restaurants in New York. Some have even noted the incongruity of finding this rustic dish at high prices, consumed by urban elites. The worldwide habit of eating beans or broad beans as a stew (*feijoada* in Brazil, *doyiwé* in Benin, or *fèves au lard* in Quebec) has encouraged its international success. Though sometimes exaggerated, cassoulet that is either canned or prepared in restaurants has become the symbol of both gastronomic and everyday French cuisine with peasant roots.

Philippe Meyzie

FURTHER READING

Martin Bruegel. "Du temps annuel au temps quotidien: La conserve appertisée à la conquête du marché, 1810–1920." *Revue d'histoire moderne et contemporaine* 44, no. 1 (1997): 40–67.

Martin Bruegel, ed. *A Cultural History of Food in the Age of Empire*, vol. 5. London: Berg, 2012.

Hélène d'Almeida-Topor. *Le goût de l'étranger: Les saveurs venues d'ailleurs depuis la fin du xviii* siècle. Paris: Armand Colin, 2006.

Philippe Marchenay, Jacques Barrau, and Laurence Bérard. "Polenta, cassoulet et piperade, l'introduction des plantes du Nouveau Monde dans les cuisines régionales." *Journal d'agriculture traditionnelle et de botanique appliquée* 42 (2000): 65–80.

Fabio Parasecoli and Mateusz Halawa, eds. *Global Brooklyn: Designing Food Experiences in World Cities*. New York: Bloomsbury, 2021.

FURTHER TRAVELING

Feijoada, Sardines (Canned)

Caviar

In April 1998 CITES, the Convention on International Trade in Endangered Species of Wild Fauna and Flora, decided to place sturgeon on the list of protected species, banning all imports and exports of wild caviar from the Caspian and Black Seas eight years later. The situation was indeed worrying. Since December 1991 the implosion of the Soviet Union and the ensuing end of the Soviet monopoly on caviar rapidly aroused the appetites of the newly independent countries bordering the Caspian Sea (Kazakhstan, Turkmenistan, and Azerbaijan, joining Russia and Iran). Soon overfishing, illegal fishing, and the black market rapidly took their toll. Added to this was the increasing pollution of the Caspian Sea and the proliferation of dams on the Volga, which soon prevented the sturgeon from migrating upstream to their breeding grounds. In just a few years, these factors led to the rapid decline of one of the world's oldest fish species.

Around 350 BCE, Aristotle explained that for over a century the Greeks had been great fans of sturgeon, the primitive fish that survived from the era of the last dinosaurs. They most often enjoyed them grilled, but they also ate the eggs, which they likened to a divine, energizing, and invigorating food. But while the dish was known to gourmets in ancient Greece, it was the ancient Persians who first took an interest in *khagviar*, that is, "little black eggs." Fishing for sturgeon, and in particular for the abundant beluga which followed the Volga into the Caspian Sea, they ate the eggs after putting them in salt to make them easier to preserve and transport. Later, in 1432–33, Bertrandon de la Broquière, who was visiting Bursa in northwestern Anatolia, reported that *cavyaire* was eaten with olive oil, making it a relatively affordable product. The Burgundian traveler was hardly convinced by the taste experience, stating that *cavyaire* is consumed "when one has nothing else to eat" and that it "is only good for the Greeks."

In the Persian Empire, as in Greece, fish "pearls," dried or salted and then eaten (either as they are, drizzled with oil, or boiled), were therefore appreciated without being an exceptional delicacy. This all changed in the mid-sixteenth century, with Russian expansionism toward the Caspian Sea.

It was under the reign of Ivan the Terrible that, four years after taking Kazan, the Tsar's armies captured the Turco-Mongolian khanate of Astrakhan in 1556. The area bordered the Caspian Sea to the southeast and allowed Russians to become familiar with caviar. Little by little, the "black gold" appeared on the tables of Russian sovereigns, where it was eaten with vodka. It became so popular that in March 1675 Tsar Alexis Mikhailovich, son of the first Romanovs, imposed a state monopoly on caviar. The decision turned this rare and expensive delicacy—it can take seven years for a female sturgeon to lay her first eggs, and the eggs do not survive the extraction process—into a major source of revenue for the empire and a symbol of absolute luxury " *à la russe.*" For several centuries, caviar was available only to the elite and diplomats at the court of Saint Petersburg. Then, in the wake of the October Revolution, its consumption began to spread to wider circles. So while Russian sovereigns and elites have been fond of caviar since the seventeenth century to the point where caviar and Russia are often linked in the collective imagination, in reality the Russians played no role in the product's actual development, since its origins go back much further.

Be that as it may, until 1917 the Tsarist empire was the world's largest consumer of caviar, even if it did not have a monopoly on production. In France, under the influence of Colbert (minister to Louis XIV), a modest production appeared in the Gironde region, thanks to sturgeon migrating up the Garonne estuary. In the mid-nineteenth century, the United States became the world's leading producer of caviar from white sturgeon migrating up the Hudson, supplying trendy New York bars as well as European markets. Nevertheless, caviar from the belugas of the Volga and Caspian Seas remained of incomparable quality and a fixture in Russia's official celebrations. Until the middle of the nineteenth century caviar was eaten fresh only in winter (since it spoils very quickly in the heat), while the rest of the year it was consumed salted, dried, or pressed. Dehydrated and compacted, the grains were transformed into a very dense, highly flavored paste that was easy to store and transport. Whether fresh, salted, or pressed, caviar is often eaten *au naturel*, or with lemon wedges, chives, or chopped onions.

The October Revolution had a major impact on caviar production. In Soviet Russia the monopoly inherited from the Tsarist period remained unchallenged.

However, the growing enthusiasm for this delicacy among postwar European elites—and French elites in particular—led the Soviet government in 1927 to set up a Soviet-Iranian fishing company, in reality a cartel, to organize the exploitation of black pearls from the Caspian Sea. The agreement remained in force until 1953, when the Iranian state nationalized the company. Henceforth, Iranian and Russian caviars found themselves in competition, to the greater benefit of the former: less salty than Russian caviar, Iranian caviar, which is best enjoyed with champagne, was seen as the symbol of supreme refinement, reserved for the wealthiest consumers, including industrial magnates and Hollywood stars.

At the same time, the development of railroads and technical advances in refrigeration soon facilitated the transport of fresh caviar to European capitals such as Vienna and Paris, where the elite of the Roaring Twenties began to fall in love with the fine black or grey pearls. It was at this time that two brothers of Armenian origin, Melkoum and Mouchegh Petrossian, who had grown up in Baku and taken refuge in Paris in 1915, set up a boutique grocery store in 1919, selling Russian specialties to white Russians nostalgic for their imperial homeland. From 1920 onward they began to sell exclusively imported Soviet caviar in small blue tins. Although it immediately won over the Russian public, the product did not immediately win over Parisians, who considered it too salty. But soon the Petrossians, who were increasingly familiar with production techniques, succeeded in adapting it more to French tastes, thus winning over the capital's most chic restaurants, including the Ritz. At the same time, French caviar production developed under the influence of Émile Prunier who, in 1921, opened a production center in the Dordogne region of France using harvested sturgeon, echoing the first attempts during the reign of Louis XIV.

Until the beginning of the twentieth century, farmed caviar remained modest in scale. However, in view of the conservation measures adopted in 1998 and again in 2006, and the ever-increasing worldwide demand for caviar, farmed caviar became the norm. Farmed caviar is particularly popular in France (in Aquitaine, using sturgeon from Lake Baikal) and Italy (in Lombardy, using Siberian sturgeon). From 2013–14 onward, with an annual production of 26 to 30 tons out of a global total of 150 tons, Italy rapidly became the world's leading caviar producer, ahead of France. However, in 2019 Italy was in turn supplanted by China, which produced 43 tons that year. New Chinese elites were in turn converted to both the taste of "black gold" and the image of luxury it conveys. The little black pearls no doubt have a bright future ahead.

Marie-Pierre Rey

FURTHER READING

Charles de Saint-Vincent. *Caviar: Manuel décomplexé à l'usage de l'amateur*. Paris: Chronique, 2014.
Nichola Fletcher. *Caviar: A Global History*. London: Reaktion Books, 2010.
Horst Gödecken. *Le caviar*. Marseille: Jeanne Laffitte, 1986.
Natalie Rebeiz-Nielsen and Susie Boeckmann. *Caviar*. Paris: Hachette, 2002.

FURTHER TRAVELING

Champagne, Olive Oil, Salt, Vodka

Ceviche

Declared a cultural heritage of Peru in 2004, ceviche has in the past two decades become an almost metonymic reference to the country. The dish, which chef Javier Wong describes as "the perfection of simplicity" uses a limited number of ingredients and a simple, though not easy, method of preparation. The basic recipe is then adapted according to regional and national variations. A fish, often white and of medium quality such as corvina, is finely diced and cooked in a lemon-based marinade. It is then mixed with onion and chopped red pepper (*ají limo*), sprinkled with coriander, and accompanied by sweet potato and cooked (*choclo*) or grilled (*cancha*) corn. Ceviche must be eaten with a spoon to enjoy the full combination of flavors.

The dish is also available in the markets of the Andes and Amazonia, where exotic fruits are substituted for lemons, manioc for sweet potatoes, and freshwater fish for seafood. Central American cuisine tends to add tomato and mayonnaise. On Easter Island it is prepared with tuna rather than white fish, and in Ecuador with potato chips and popcorn. Nevertheless, Peru claims a special connection to the dish, which has become both a national symbol and an intangible export destined for global metropolises around the world.

The Peruvian banner thus flies high over this culinary preparation, which many blogs have called upon Peruvians to master as if they were composing the dish to the tune of their national anthem or, as it were, a Zambo Cavero song. In a recent short story, Claudia Ulloa portrays a mother about to welcome a future son-in-law from Norway to her home in Lima. After several days of intensive housework, she sees some images of Scandinavia that send her into a fit of anxiety, based on a feeling of national inferiority. This is gradually counterbalanced, however, by the discovery of Peru's treasures, compiled and marketed by the

National Tourist Promotion Agency: "My mother realized that we were living in a country where the buses were filthy and polluting, the waste useless and pestilential, the society macho and corrupt, the sky leaden; in a city that smelled of fish and mildew. . . . I suggested to her that we should go to Peru, where we'd be able to enjoy the beauty of the country. . . . I suggested that she take a look at the PromPerú web pages, so she'd have something to tell Lars about our country. She swooned over the cruises on Lake Titicaca. . . . Her state of mind changed. She was now filled with national pride, secreting endorphins . . . whenever she talked about our incomparable ceviche." A national beacon with the ability to "unite all Peruvians," according to the daily *El Comercio*, ceviche is thus entrusted with the overwhelming task of working toward national reconciliation, after a century marked by chronic inequality, democratic decline, and brutal domestic conflicts (1980–2000). At a time when the quest for a renewed social and political contract is still a mirage, it is doubtful that ceviche alone will be able to ward off the many biases that have made chronic violence possible. Thus, the Mistura gastronomic festival (2008–16), which aimed to celebrate the culinary fusion of differences as a national treasure, has been interpreted by anthropologists as part of a colonial takeover on the part of Lima and its hold over a "hinterland" that has been exploited and disregarded.

Castilians and Peruvians spell the dish differently: sometimes starting with an *s* or *c*, and sometimes *v* or *b* in the middle of the word: *seviche/ceviche, sebiche/cebiche.* The variations betray its hybrid etymology, which include stories of Arabo-Andalusian escabeche and more dubious anecdotes with little historical plausibility. For example, the first Englishman to taste the dish on the Pacific coast is said to have exclaimed in delight: "son of a bitch," and supposedly given the dish its name. The pickled fish technique may also have been carried from Polynesia to the Americas by Portuguese navigators. The question of "origins" is by definition unresolvable and highlights the obvious transnational dimension of culinary practices that recall the founding character of migration in Peruvian history. A culture dating back more than ten thousand years, marked by the juxtaposition of numerous microclimates, Peruvian cuisine and its evolution have been punctuated by the successive arrivals of foreign populations. After the long and eventful Spanish legacy, followed by a brief period of French culinary influence, which had no lasting effect since it was confined to the elite, the nineteenth century saw the arrival of populations from China, Italy, and Japan, bringing with them age-old popular traditions. Emigrants from Japan seem to have developed a particular attachment to fish-cutting techniques and a marked reduction in marinating time—two imperatives that have become dominant and endorsed by Lima elites.

The adjectives fresh and finely cut are not devoid of social markers. They suggest the advent of new ways of consuming protein in the age of healthier diets and the selective valuing of cultural diversity, as in the case of Hawaiian poke, which fast-food chains now offer in many variations. The ceviche "boom" that has been underway since the mid-2000s suggests the globalized dimension of the phenomenon, which began in the late 1990s with the expatriation of several up-and-coming chefs. Since 2006, when Lima was named "South America's gastronomic capital" at the Madrid Fusión festival, a flurry of accolades has followed. In 2012, star chef Ferrán Adriá directed a documentary entitled *Le Pérou a du goût: La cuisine comme arme sociale*, in which he is filmed traveling the country in search of its culinary resources, with some faint reminders of previous extractive practices. The Culinary Institute of America declared 2014 the year of Peruvian cuisine, while the World's 50 Best restaurants launched a Latin American section headed by Gastón Acurio's Astrid-y-Gastón. An entrepreneurial storyteller and ardent promoter of the "Peru brand," Acurio headed an eponymous group with some forty "international" restaurants. Ceviche has been transformed by this newly found legitimacy on a global scale. In Paris, for example, what used to be a slightly exotic traditional dish, served by Lourdes Pluvinage at Picaflor as early as 1994, is now found on the menus across the city. Pluvinage and Acurio have become ceviche pioneers. Sometimes labeled "Latino," cevicherias are revisiting the composition of ceviche, in particular *leche de tigre*. In the face of such reinvented traditions, purists may cry foul when coconut milk, for example, is added.

In his books (including several devoted exclusively to ceviche), Acurio is not afraid to look back on his childhood, when his appetite for a culinary career drew smiles from a father who was a senator and then minister. Times have changed, however, with the professional opportunities of Lima's elite now accommodating cultural variations, as long as revenues follow. Ceviche is now exported in huge quantities. The culinary fashion resembles the logic of an extractive boom, conferring symbolic and monetary value outside the territory where the product is harvested. And even if Peruvian economic history, with previous paradigmatic examples such as rubber, suggests that the boom may come to an end, palates are currently being won over by this surprising dish, which cuts against the grain of geographical associations to include rich sauces and potatoes.

Promoted for its concentrated flavors, ceviche also brings together several of Peru's contemporary ambiguities. Its circulation illustrates the paradoxical ways in which the Peruvian national culture is manufactured in Peru, often from a distance (as in the case of the tourist totem that Machu Picchu has become). It embodies the hope of sending back out into the world a festive and tasteful image after a twentieth century rife with violence and impunity. Last and perhaps most important, any cultural risk that may be associated with its exportation is reduced since its flavors are drawn more from the coast and its capital than the Andean-Amazonian hinterland.

Irène Favier

FURTHER READING

Claudia Ulloa Donoso. "De la glace pour les martiens." In *Nouvelles du Pérou*, trans. Marie Jammot, 9–28. Paris: Magellan & Cie, 2018.

María Elena García. *Gastropolitics and the Specter of Race*. Berkeley: University of California Press, 2021.

Elmo León. *14,000 años de alimentación en el Perú*. Lima: USMP, 2013.

Raúl Matta. "La construction sociale de la cuisine péruvienne: Une histoire de migrations et d'échanges culinaires." *Hommes et migrations: Revue française sur les dynamiques migratoires* 1283 (2010): 96–107.

Lourdes Pluvinage. *La cuisine du Pérou à Paris*. Lima: USMP, 2017.

FURTHER TRAVELING

Chili Pepper, Mayonnaise, Poke

Champagne

In the summer of 2021, the Comité Interprofessionnel du Vin de Champagne (CIVC), the powerful organization representing all the stakeholders in the champagne industry, was outraged: Russia wanted to delete the Cyrillic word "champagne" from the labels of French bottles sold in the country and replace it with "sparkling wine." From this point on, the term "champagne" was to be reserved exclusively for Russian sparkling wine producers, arousing the ire of the French and the mobilization of political, diplomatic, and economic authorities. Although Russia was only the sector's fifteenth-largest export market (1.7 million bottles in 2019 out of a total of 156 million), the episode testified to the importance of the international network. It also revealed the extranational dimension of champagne's historical development.

Even before the appearance of effervescent wines, still wines of Champagne, which had mainly been red wines produced in the region around abbeys since the sixth century, enjoyed a strong reputation in Europe. They were consumed in nearby Flanders and the German-speaking world as well as England. Contrary to legend, it was in England that a rudimentary method of champagnization was perfected. During the seventeenth century, wines from Champagne became popular with the English court. They were appreciated for their taste, resulting from a specific vinification process in which red grapes were harvested but then vinified as a white wine known as *"vins gris"* or "gray wines," and above all for their light effervescence. To enhance effervescence and raise the alcohol content of low-alcohol wines, the English came up with the idea of adding sugar in the spring, the best time to increase *"prise de mousse,"* the second fermentation that gives the wine its bubbles.

In Champagne, trade with the British Isles intensified, while production and packaging methods improved. Around 1670 the Benedictine monk Dom Pérignon, long hailed as the "inventor of champagne," perfected blending techniques with a relatively simple but revolutionary idea: select the best wines for blending. At the same time, to better meet the demands of a fragile product (bottle breakage was a real concern at the time), champagne producers drew inspiration from abroad by importing and copying the solid, dark-glass bottles of the English. They then began using corks from Spain and Portugal to facilitate transport and storage. A timid commercial network was then set up around local winegrowers and merchants, like the cloth merchant turned producer-trader Nicolas Ruinart and wine merchant Claude Moët.

The network grew stronger from the end of the eighteenth century onward, particularly with the arrival in the region of many young men from German families. Often joining existing firms as employees, they quickly became partners and then set up their own businesses. This was the case, for example, for Joseph Bollinger. Others, such as Florens-Louis Heidsieck or the Mumm brothers, were attracted by the region's prosperity and set up shop there to participate in the merchant trend. Through their origins, their networks, and their dedication they helped champagne spread throughout the world. Louis Bohne, the German traveler from the Cliquot Maison, was initially assigned to work in the English market but quickly turned his attention to the East, traveling thousands of kilometers to Vienna, Budapest, Stockholm, and Saint Petersburg in the 1800s. At the same time, Sultan Mahmud II regularly ordered champagne, his favorite wine, for delivery in Turkey.

This exportation, which took off in the nineteenth century as production, storage, and transport techniques were refined and perfected, was part of the very essence of champagne. A quality wine, requiring numerous complex and delicate manipulations, it was from the outset expensive, which had appeal for a relatively affluent clientele. Logically, this clientele could be found abroad, among the elites who set trends and fashions. The fashion for effervescence and foam explains its development in the seventeenth century, just as the refinement of food tastes in the eighteenth accounted for its expansion and ultimate success. Champagne merchants were quick to understand market mechanisms and the need to adapt to international demand. Depending on the area of export, the wines were sweetened to a greater or lesser degree, resulting in a standardized classification of market typicity (extra-brut, brut, dry, semi-dry, sweet), adapting to demand (dry to Anglo-Saxon countries, sweet to the Russian Empire). Above all, great importance was attached to external appearance, with carefully designed labels from the nineteenth century onward, enabling companies to stand out in an ultracompetitive international wine market.

The consumption of champagne and the entire imaginary that accompanies it has been supported by intense and inventive advertising. It also quickly transformed champagne into a mark of distinction, propagated by its influencers. An aristocratic beverage by birth and by association with European and then global elites, from the mid-nineteenth century onward it became part of bourgeois sociability. It then spread to Western or Westernized working classes in the twentieth century, for whom champagne became the wine of exceptional events, celebrating a birthday, a wedding, or a promotion. In modern times, local newspapers around the world carry classified ads from champagne importers. In December 1868, the Philadelphia *Daily Evening Telegraph* referred to the "youngest and liveliest of wines" in an article celebrating champagne, in a country where thirty years later some four million bottles were consumed. In 1913 the prime minister of Japan banned its consumption at official celebrations as too lowbrow, replacing it with the national drink, sake.

Unsurprisingly, champagne has been involved in all the major world events of our time. During World War I, for example, Allied and German soldiers consumed the wine abundantly, since it was readily available. In the twentieth century, world's fairs promoted champagne houses, while their products were shipped across the globe through the French and British empires, including the necessity of finding other markets in the 1920s when the American market closed under the effects of Prohibition. It also found a home in the world of sports. When the Reims soccer team was victorious in European competitions in the 1950s, newspaper articles across the continent regularly drew parallels with the excellence of the champagne beverage, popularizing the expression "champagne football," a lively, offensive style of play. The great motor racing competitions of the second half of the twentieth century also saw their champions drenched in champagne during the demonstrations of joy after victory. Geopolitical encounters have also been punctuated with meals where champagne toasts are the norm.

This explains why champagne is imitated the world over. Although sparkling wines exist independently of champagne, many are still inspired by it such as German *sekt*, Spanish *cava*, and Italian *prosecco*. Major frauds were noted as early as the nineteenth century. In Munich in 1883 and Odessa in 1896, for example, wines illicitly sold under the name of champagne were found. These frauds prompted local players to form professional organizations (the Syndicat des Négociants in 1882 and the CIVC in 1941), and to call for better protection, leading to the enactment of laws on contents and production (1911 and 1927 in particular). With this framework, producers and merchants defended the exclusivity of production in France and internationally, giving rise to fierce negotiations within the context of international conventions (the Treaty of Versailles in 1919, which institutionalized the notion of *appellation* at a world level) or global organizations (GATT, then WTO; EEC, then EU).

All this also explains why in 2021, when Russia represented only a small portion of a world market dominated by its historical partners, the United Kingdom, the United States and Germany, the industry's players were worried about changing the standards and commercial balances they had been striving to shape for over two centuries.

Stéphane Le Bras

FURTHER READING

Claire Desbois-Thibault, Werner Paravicini, and Jean-Pierre Poussou, eds. *Le champagne: Une histoire franco-allemande*. Paris: Presses Universitaires Paris-Sorbonne, 2011.

Bernard Destremau. *Le rôle des étrangers dans le succès international du vin de Bordeaux, du champagne et de l'eau-de-vie de Cognac*. Lille: ANRT, 1993.

André Garcia. *Les vins de Champagne*. 1986. Paris: Presses Universitaires de France, 1997.

Kolleen M. Guy. *When Champagne Became French: Wine and the Making of a National Identity*. Baltimore: Johns Hopkins University Press, 2003.

Benoît Musset. *Vignobles de Champagne et vins mousseux (1650–1830): Histoire d'un mariage de raison*. Paris: Fayard, 2008.

FURTHER TRAVELING

Beer, Gin, Port Wine, Rum, Sake, Whiskey, Wine

Charcuterie

A funeral dinner turned even more tragic in Ellezelles, Belgium, in December 1895. The cured ham served after the funeral had such a horrible taste that the guests covered it in mustard. Within a few hours some of the diners were seeing double, a dozen fell ill, and three died.

In charge of the medical expertise, biologist Émile van Ermengem quickly found the ham guilty. The pig had been killed in the middle of August, without refrigeration, and had been faultily bled. After slaughter, the meat was soiled and prepared with defective brine. It then spent months in a barrel, immersed in a liquid with insufficient salt concentration to ensure its preservation.

Spectacular as it was, such a case was hardly unusual. The catastrophe could have been avoided by respecting basic rules of hygiene, using more concentrated brines, or cooking the meat. As we know, for sausages and boudins extended cooking times are necessary to avoid any risk (this is the job of the charcutier, whose name means "meat or flesh cooker"). For "raw" charcuterie, that is cured meats, salt content matters most. And of course, hygiene is paramount. Doctors have been documenting these basic facts for over a century. As early as 1820 Dr. Justinus Kerner was already alarmed that sausages in Württemberg seemed to "be responsible for almost as many deaths as snakes in the tropics" (this was especially true of Saumagen, the huge "blood sausages" whose size made them difficult to cook thoroughly). Émile van Ermengem went further than his predecessors, using the new bacterial culture techniques he had learned from Robert Koch. He succeeded in identifying the bacillus responsible for the *botulinum* toxin, which attached itself to nerve receptors, causing muscle paralysis, blurred vision, and even death.

It may be discouraging to open a brief history of charcuterie with such a tragic tale. One might have started by recalling that charcuterie was already a delicacy in antiquity (Gallic salted pork, says Strabo, was highly prized in Rome) and contributed to the establishment of precise rules and standards. We might also have begun by drawing up a list of names that demonstrate the global dimension of charcuterie based on pork or other meats that have made mouths water around the world, including hams, sausages, pâtés, bacon, *soudjouks*, *soubressade*, and pastrami. Each of these names has been used in a variety of specialties and places, each producer prouder than the next of their recipe's originality.

However, the end of the nineteenth century marked a major upheaval in this long global history, accompanied by the discovery of Émile van Ermengem. The beginnings of this upheaval could be felt a few decades earlier, in the ham factories of County Cork in Ireland, in the large smokehouses of Hamburg in northern Germany, and in Massachusetts, where small abattoirs packed salted meat in barrels and crates for oceangoing shipping companies. But it was mainly around Cincinnati (nicknamed "Porkopolis"), and then Milwaukee and Chicago, that the true revolution took place. It was here that the "meat-packers" came into their own. These industrialists were at once butchers, packers, and shippers. Boosted by military orders during the American Civil War, the business triumphed in the northern United States from the 1880s onward. Travelers were amazed by the moving chains that grabbed the hog by the hind foot, hoisted it up, and then bled it dry before scalding, scraping, draining, decapitating, and splitting it in two. A process completed by flattening the bacon, mincing the meat, cleaning the casings, and filling them. By 1900, the Armour factory in Chicago was the largest meat factory in the world. More than fifty million pigs were processed each year in slaughterhouses in the United States, which accounted for 40 percent of the world's pigs.

At the same time, charcuterie was no longer reserved for the colder seasons. The cold had been mastered. This began with blocks of ice insulated with straw or sawdust. Then around 1880 came new ammonia refrigeration techniques. Vast charcuterie factories could now be set up just about anywhere, regardless of climate, and operate year-round.

Above all, this evolution necessitated the massive use of nitrate additives. The process was not new. A whole range of products were being used. Mexican cochineal powder was employed, for example, to give a red color to cooked meats, which would otherwise have a less appetizing gray or brownish color. The most widely used additive was potassium nitrate, known as saltpeter. The market was attractive enough that the first specialized sellers of meat dyes appeared at the end of the eighteenth century. From the 1820s onward, following the discovery of immense deposits at the foot of the Andes, sodium nitrate also known as Chilean saltpeter, began to be used.

At the end of the nineteenth century, these nitrates made a decisive contribution to the industrialization of charcuterie products. Not only did they give cooked meats an attractive pink color, but they also enabled raw meats to be colored more evenly and, above all, more quickly. Where ham massaged with salt used to take months to change color, as the iron in the meat was gradually replaced by zinc, it now took only a few weeks. As Benjamin Franklin had already noted, time is money.

Indeed. By enabling the same results to be obtained with meat from young animals that had hardly used their muscles, these additives allowed for the use of younger animals. This marked a real gain for manufacturers. For the animals, and pigs in particular, it was the beginning of a long confinement in soilless farms, which removed them from human sight at the very moment consumption of their meat greatly increased. For nature as a whole it was a catastrophe. These huge farms had deplorable consequences such as those that can be seen today in Brittany, France, where there is a proliferation of "green algae" on the coasts of pig farming regions.

Throughout the twentieth century, additive manufacturers celebrated their results in advertisements for cured meats. They did so further when a third, more effective additive was identified: sodium nitrite. Sodium nitrite was approved in the United States in 1925 and in France in 1964. Its use became even more necessary as new plastic packaging techniques were used to show the beautiful pink colors of pork products. These additives accompanied a phenomenal growth in consumption. In France alone, production doubled between 1980 and 2015.

It is well known that these additives are harmful. But when scientists began to express alarm in the 1960s, manufacturers responded that they were warding off the specter of botulism. It has been known for centuries that to produce tasty, cured meats that are harmless to humans, you need only two ingredients (in addition to meat): salt and time. But time had become too expensive.

It is all very well to enjoy cured meats (which is the case for the author of this entry). But the history of charcuterie since the end of the nineteenth century has involved so many additives that, in 2015, the World Health Organization classified it as "definitely carcinogenic." No other dish in this book has been characterized as such. But to borrow from the spirit of the French satirical newspaper *Le canard enchaîné*, which posted a headline when the WHO report was published, we'll "stop porcine the issue!"

Sylvain Venayre

FURTHER READING

Guillaume Coudray. *Cochonneries: Comment la charcuterie est devenue un poison*. Paris: La Découverte, 2017.

Roger Horowitz. *Putting Meat on the American Table: Taste, Technology, Transformation*. Baltimore: Johns Hopkins University Press, 2006.

Michel Pastoureau. *Le cochon: Histoire d'un cousin mal aimé*. Paris: Gallimard, 2009.

Alessandro Stanziani. *Histoire de la qualité alimentaire, xixe–xxe siècle*. Paris: Seuil, 2005.

C. Anne Wilson, ed. *Waste Not, Want Not: Food Preservation from Early Times to the Present Day*. Edinburgh: Edinburgh University Press, 1991.

FURTHER TRAVELING

Food Coloring and Preservatives, Salt

Chicory

Legend would have the development of chicory taking place in two phases: first the Deluge, and then Napoleon's continental blockade of November 1806. Pharaonic Egypt knew of, used, and appreciated the plant, while Napoleon I encouraged the development of the roasted root. But before going any further, a distinction must be made between legend and myth. Obviously this dual lineage served a specific purpose: a valorization of the product by making it part of the longest and most noble of histories. It provides a useful political history. But even if these two moments are not entirely a product of fantasy, they must be contextualized, and hence their importance must be relativized.

This is precisely what is uncovered by the history of chicory. Described and classified by Linnaeus in 1753, bitter chicory (*Cichorium intybus*) is a perennial herbaceous plant. It was identified as early as the first Egyptian medicinal text (the Ebers papyrus, dating from the middle of the second millennium BCE) for its digestive and other virtues, which are so numerous that, according to Pliny the Elder, it was "all-powerful" (*pancration*). According to Horace, chicory was a mainstay of his diet. However, the chicory under discussion here was transformed by human industry, first as a cultivated plant, then as a roasted root, which took its place among the stimulants that were so widely used in modern times. The values of the modern world have become entirely different: that of a society that values vitality and globalizes its processes.

In the case of chicory, the cultural has nourished the cultivated. The West of the "Great Discoveries" and the new colonial empires extended its diet to include a trio of plant-based stimulant beverages, generally served hot, which were consumed by the elite in the seventeenth century and that, right up to the present day, were characterized by the extra-European location of their cultivation. If on the one hand climatic constraint structured and justified colonization, it also led to the acclimatization of certain plants in Europe of Asian or, above all, American origin. In this respect, the eighteenth century—which, it should be noted, also witnessed the political development of the national state—was the century of the acclimatization of the potato and the tomato. The development of the roasting of bitter chicory root must be placed in this context.

The publication in Bremen in 1773 of Gottlieb Förster's pioneering work *The History of the Invention and Introduction of Chicory Coffee* provides insight into both the chronology and the geography of its development. As the title indicates, it is a question of substitution—in the twentieth century, the French language would incorporate the German word *ersatz* into its lexicon to refer to these stand-in products, mainly for food. A generation before the blockade of British trade from the European continent, decreed in Berlin by Napoleon I on November 26, 1806, it was already a question, in line with the Enlightenment, of ensuring that European technological progress served a dual response, from a new form of hegemony (national independence) to a selective market that left the working classes on the sidelines (presented as social utility). From the eighteenth century onward technical imagination multiplied the number of coffee substitutes, from beets—which the Frenchman Parmentier sought to promote before the Paris Agricultural Society—to holly, nutsedge, barley, and acorns. But chicory quickly took the lead.

The regions where root roasting (washed, cut, and dried) was tested and perfected were mostly around the North Sea (Sweden, North Germany, the Netherlands). It is significant that the establishment of industrial chicory cultivation in French territories took place not during the Empire but during the French Revolution. In anticipation of French domination of this market, the French Republic expanded the national borders by annexing what was later to become Belgium to the north. In 1798 Charles Giraud's experiments at Onnaing in the Valenciennois region, improved the drying of chicory into small pieces, known as *cossettes*. This marked the beginning of the French adventure in roasted chicory, whose *tourailles* (drying ovens) were installed on surrounding farms. In the next generation, Nicolas Alglave, a farmer from the neighboring village of Quarouble, mechanized the sowing process.

Although this approach already participated in a form of industrial patriotism in wartime, the economic and democratic argument that poor people's coffee was much cheaper than rich people's coffee enabled this fledgling industry to survive the fall of Napoleon. It was not, or no longer, the blockade—a situation that, incidentally, the producing countries were to face again during the two world wars of the twentieth century—that established the original albeit modest presence of "chicory coffee" in the Nord department of France, but rather the rise of popular consumption, in some cases by peasants, in others by workers who, along with economic accessibility, were able to fix a geographical or social identity.

In 1879 there were almost fifty roasted chicory factories in the Valenciennes district alone. The curve steepened quickly thereafter, though initially less because of the competitive development of more easily accessible coffee than the active policy pursued by the Leroux company. Based in Orchies, a town in the greater Lille area close to the Belgian border, Leroux moved toward a monopoly of technological innovation and advertising imagination in the sector from 1858 onward. While advertising relied on the reassuring image of the rural mother (the effigy of a young woman in a costume from the Audierne region, adopted in 1899, is reminiscent of the fashion for Breton culture at the end of the century), several means were used to diversify the product. For example, in the 1950s processes of extraction provided for soluble chicory and liquid concentrate. This centralization around Leroux did not contradict a geographical expansion that, after World War I, added the Auduicq region (Vieille-Église, Oye-Plage), in the Pas-de-Calais region near the city of Lille in France, where chicory dryers remain characteristic features of the landscape to this day. This commercial dynamism explains why, in the twenty-first century, France is still the world's leading producer of industrial chicory.

So the main driving force behind this story is economic and social, rather than political. Only time will tell whether the cultural motor, which was predominant before the invention of roasted chicory in discourses on the medicinal virtues of herbaceous plants, can halt the decline in consumption of the beverage or even reverse the trend. Such a reversal is not out of the question, given the advantages promoted by the advocates of this caffeine-free beverage, which is rich in inulin, a soluble dietary fiber with very few calories and is eminently prebiotic. But it is perhaps as a "fair trade" or "local" product—as opposed to the imported trio of coffee/chocolate/tea—that chicory might regain its rightful place as an ethical beverage in the twenty-first century. What more could we ask for?

Pascal Ory

FURTHER READING

Daniel Bordet, Anne-Lise Quesnel, and Michel Taeckens. *Les cent plus belles images de la chicorée*. Paris: Dabecom, 2006.

Philippe Cadet and Christian Defebvre. *Des racines et des hommes: La chicorée et l'espace agricole de la communauté de communes de la région d'Audruicq de 1885 à nos jours*. La Gorgue: Citoyenneté en Actes, 2010.

Yves Maerten, Nathalie Duronsoy, and Valérie Leroy. *La chicorée dans le Nord-Pas-de-Calais*. Béthune: Musée Régional d'Ethnologie, 1994.

Dominique Neirynck. *La saga Leroux: La chicorée dans le Nord, des hommes, une entreprise, une région*. La Tour-d'Aigues: Éditions de l'Aube, 1999.

FURTHER TRAVELING

Coffee, Tea and Chai

Chili con Carne

In 1893, during the Chicago exposition celebrating the four hundredth anniversary of Christopher Columbus's arrival in America, Texas sent the chili queens of San Antonio dressed in full-colored regalia to represent its gastronomy, offering visitors a stew made with meat and chili peppers. The association between chili con carne and Texas was further cemented a century later in 1977 when the Texas legislature proclaimed it an official dish of the state.

Chili con carne is without a doubt the Tex-Mex recipe par excellence. This dish, which has been designated as typically Texan, has an obvious kinship with other preparations eaten in Mexico that have not experienced such a revival. Spanish religious sources attest shortly after the conquest to Aztecs frying chili peppers with meat.

Unlike the richer Mexican sauces known as *moles*, chili belongs to the family of popular preparations made from the few ingredients available locally and whose recipes vary considerably. The military and civilian movements associated with Spanish colonization contributed to its spread and evolution as far as today's southwestern United States, where it incorporates cumin, perhaps imported by Canary Islands colonists settled in the 1730s by the Spanish crown. It takes its name from the chili pepper (*chile* in Spanish) used in its preparation, a fruit picked, cultivated, and transported dried by most native, mestizo, or Creole inhabitants, and which can be seen in strings on the flanks of pack animals.

It was only after the U.S. annexation of Texas in 1845 that the dish took on the name chili and became associated with the city of San Antonio. At the time, San Antonio was at the crossroads of Pacific and Atlantic trade routes as well as between Mexico and the United States, transporting, especially in winter, market garden produce not available further north, as well as the hygienic and health tourism that was developing in the South, renowned for its climate and sunlight. Travelers who stopped there discovered stalls set up in the central square for their meals. As elsewhere in Mexico, women, even couples and families, supplemented their income by selling dishes prepared in advance that they kept warm in fireplaces. Initially set up during festivals, these stalls became permanent in the 1870s as rail traffic increased. Together with their landladies, they soon became a distinctive feature of the city, described in travelogues and picked up by local newspapers as a picturesque, exotic, and even slightly adventurous attraction.

It was at this point that one of the ingredients, the chili pepper, ended up giving a unique name to a variety of dishes and especially to those who served them. The chili queens were a particular hit with visitors (although men also managed these stalls). Beef was the standard meat in the recipe, a legacy of the cattle farming that had developed with Spanish colonization and then Mexican control of the surrounding plains, and which industrialization, urbanization and population growth further stimulated. In the same years, several entrepreneurs sought to transform this Texan experience into a standardized and safe product, marketing a little adventure in a powder or a bottle. A grocer and then restaurateur, both Texans but not of Mexican origin, successively developed a dry blend of chili spices in the 1890s under a Hispanic-sounding name. Seeking to find a market for their products beyond their home state, one or the other may have played a role in sending the chili queens to Chicago in 1893. Because Chicago was the industrial capital of the meat industry at the time, the beef magnates were quick to offer their own canned chili, especially since grinding the meat could serve to mask the addition of meat waste products from the slaughterhouses.

At the same time, chili con carne also made its appearance in American cookbooks, such as *Favorite Dishes*, based on recipes collected at the Colombian Exposition by the event's "women's bureau" for charitable purposes. Chili spread throughout the Midwest, where dedicated chili parlors were opened. They encouraged job diversification and hybridization with other stews imported by European immigrants, such as Macedonians who introduced a cinnamon-flavored Cincinnati chili served with pasta. From then on there were national debates about the authenticity of this or that version, one of the most persistent of which concerned the addition of beans to the sauce, to make it more nourishing.

While the dish became part of U.S. culinary heritage, San Antonio's municipal elites developed and beautified the city according to the new standards of the time, transforming squares into green spaces destined to elevate the urban and popular classes. This meant the expulsion, not without difficulty, of the chili sellers, who were ordered to move into neighborhoods where the Spanish-speaking population had already been forced out of the city center by the arrival of the English-speaking population. This did not happen without resistance and marked a paroxysmal moment of nostalgic narratives featuring these famous "queens" whose descriptions betray the exoticizing and eroticizing fantasies of their authors. The early twentieth century also saw an influx of refugees fleeing the violence of the Mexican Revolution. Some, especially those of the capital's upper classes, sought to distance themselves as far as possible from this popular dish, which they considered "repugnant, with a usurped Mexican name." Indeed, even among the working classes chili remained an inexpensive dish. The accessibility and supposedly Mexican and historical character of chili also ensured its place among popular festivals. In 1936, for example, chili stands were included in celebrations marking the centenary of Texas independence, on condition that the cooks attended hygiene classes, which were offered in Spanish. In the 1940s, however, the war and the demand for female workers enabled them to escape this paternalism as they were hired elsewhere. As for canned chili, it was served to soldiers on the front. Each war that the United States joined helped spread its reputation around the world.

The cultural appropriation of chili was in full swing after the war, when the Chili Appreciation Society, founded in 1947, organized a fan club. Dallas journalist Frank Tolbert, author of a column on the peculiarities of Texan life and a book on chili con carne, launched a cook-off in 1967 to promote his book. The "chili cook-off" began as a competition between men in rural Texas, linking the dish to the traditions of ranching, in a version that was whiter and more English-speaking than Mexican, more cowboy than *vaquero*. Not only has the concept endured, since it is still held today, but it is also being emulated, testifying to the craze both for the dish and for what it conveys of the imaginary frontier.

But business and competition have not necessarily meant standardization: despite a few general rules, variations have been welcome. What makes a good Texas chili is its recognition by aficionados as well as the varieties of canned consumption. President Johnson took chili from his Texas home to Washington to ensure his survival between visits back to his ranch. Meanwhile, the idea of "Tex-Mex" took hold, at first with a pejorative connotation, to distinguish pale copies of "real Mexican cuisine," then finally as a means of asserting a positive regional identity. Chili was finally declared an official state dish in 1977 and gave birth to the successful eponymous restaurant chain.

In 1983, the first Tex-Mex restaurant outside the United States opened in Paris, under the leadership of Claude Benayoun, who had discovered this cuisine during a study visit. According to Benayoun, the success of Jean-Jacques Beineix's film *37°2 le matin* (1986), in which chili con carne is consumed in some of the film's most memorable scenes, gave the whole of Paris a frenzied desire to try the dish. It was only later that chili con carne was democratized with the arrival of Tex-Mex restaurant chains in shopping malls in the 1990s, first in the Paris region and later elsewhere in France. To appeal to an unfamiliar public, the chains played up the décor and the fun of the experience, imitating the theme parks that were developing at the same time, such as Disneyland Paris.

Emmanuelle Perez Tisserant

FURTHER READING

Sharon Hudgins. "Chili." In *The Oxford Companion to American Food and Drink*, ed. Andrew F. Smith, 231–33. Oxford: Oxford University Press, 2009.
Jeffrey Pilcher. *Planet Taco: A Global History of Mexican Food*. Oxford: Oxford University Press, 2017.
——. "Who Chased Out the 'Chili Queens?' Gender, Race, and Urban Reform in San Antonio, Texas (1880–1943)." *Food and Foodways* 16, no. 3 (2008): 173–200.
Maria Margarita Calleja Pinedo. "La interdependencia económica y cultural de Texas y Mexico: El caso del chili con carne." *Caravelle* 96 (2011): 217–34.
Francis X. Tolbert. *A Bowl of Red*. Dallas, TX: Taylor, 1988.

FURTHER TRAVELING

Chile Pepper, Noodles and Macaroni

Chili Pepper

Eliza Acton's cookbook *Modern Cookery, in All Its Branches* was published in 1845. A bestseller in England, it was one of the first to introduce the English public to Indian recipes, or rather recipes using Indian ingredients adapted to English tastes. The book met with great popularity in the first half of the nineteenth century and was reprinted throughout the rest of the century. Chilis and chili vinegar were the star ingredients of many dishes—for example, the famous mulligatawny soup, made with three to six onions, 100 grams of fresh coconut, 175 ml of stock, two tablespoons of curry powder, calf's head meat and sweetbreads, a cup of heavy cream, a teaspoon of flour, and a teaspoon of chili vinegar. The English palate gradually developed a taste for this pepper, imagined as a product of the great Indian empire.

In fact, chilis originated in America, where they were known as *ají* in the Caribbean and *chilli* in the Aztec Empire. Consumed since 7000 BCE and cultivated since 3500 BCE, they were an essential part of the diet of the peoples of Central America. At the end of the fifteenth century, Christopher Columbus reported the existence of this plant, which he named *pimiento*, drawing an analogy with the spice he was looking for at the time, that is, pepper, or *pimienta* in Spanish. Chilis were quickly adopted by Spanish and then Portuguese settlers, who spread them across the American continent and incorporated them into Iberian cuisine, for example, in the preparation of chorizo and in many traditional sauces. It was one of the main condiments in Spanish cookery books printed in Mexico and Peru in the eighteenth century. Doña Josepha de Escurrechea's *Libro de cocina*, printed in Potosí in 1776, features a recipe for chicken stewed in olive oil, which was common in Spain, with two New World ingredients added, tomatoes and chilis.

As soon as it was adopted, the chili peppers were taken on board transatlantic voyages by Iberian colonists. From the beginning of the sixteenth century, the Portuguese introduced it in their trading posts and the areas they colonized in Africa and Asia, where it met with immense success. In India it quickly replaced pepper, then widely used in cooking and medicine. Similar to pepper but cheaper because easier to grow and preserve, it was massively adopted by less affluent populations, to the point of being dubbed the "Savior of the Poor" by a South Indian poet. Even the scholars of Ayurvedic medicine, reluctant to introduce novelties into their treatments, replaced pepper with chili in numerous remedies. In the nineteenth century, chili soups were prescribed instead of peppered water to combat cholera. Similar developments took place later in China, where chilis were celebrated for their medicinal as well as gustatory properties, replacing more expensive spices—ginger in Taiwan, pepper in the interior of China, salt in the southwest of the country—to the point of becoming emblematic of the country's culture. In twentieth-century China, the chili pepper even took on a central symbolic role in the development of regional identities and revolutionary culture. Numerous songs and poems from Hunan Province established a direct link between the region's spicy cuisine, a guarantor of virility, and the revolutionary actions of the Chinese military and political leaders born there, such as Mao Zedong. Chilis remain at the heart of food cultures in India, China, and Indonesia, among other Southeast Asian nations. In 2021 these three countries were among the world's leading producers of the spice.

In Europe, the success of chilis was slower and less undisputed than in Asia. Initially used as an ornamental plant, it attracted the attention of botanists. It was then adopted as a mild condiment on the Iberian Peninsula and, above all, in Central and Eastern Europe. Introduced by the Turks to Hungary in the form of paprika, probably via trade with India and the Persian Gulf, it became emblematic of Hungarian cuisine. However, it failed to win over Northern European palates. In 1787 the English politician and author William Beckford complained that Portuguese cuisine was "so peppery and spicy that a spoonful of peas . . . is enough to set the mouth on fire." While it was finally popularized in England in the nineteenth century with the craze for recipes and ingredients from India, it was received much more cautiously in France, where it long remained a gustatory curiosity reserved for the elite. An anecdote told by American historian Hubert Bancroft states that on the battlefields during the Mexican Expedition (1861–67) the corpses of the French (who abstained from eating chili pepper) were eaten by wolves, while those of the Mexicans remained unharmed because they were saturated with the chili pepper they had eaten.

CHILI PEPPER

The anecdote highlights the use of chilis as a repellent or weapon—a technique already used by the Aztecs, which continues to this day. In the United States, gardening magazines of the 1980s were full of recipes using mixed chili peppers to keep cats away from flower beds and squirrels away from spring flower bulbs. At the same time, farmers were coating their sheep's necks with extracts of capsaicin, the main component of chili pepper, to ward off wolves and coyotes attacking their flocks. This substance is also the main component of pepper spray, used to suppress demonstrations in the United States. In many countries, such as Hong Kong, Iran, Iceland, and Belgium, it is used as a police weapon, even though it is banned as a weapon of war.

Extensive research has been carried out on capsaicin. Some believe that the burning sensation provoked by this substance is what makes chilis so popular: through negative stimulation the brain is tricked into releasing endorphins, the pleasure hormone. Whether the reasons are chemical or gastronomic, chilis are now at the heart of a globalized taste. The spread of this taste accelerated several times in the twentieth and twenty-first centuries. The first, from World War II onward, came with the spread of American culture, which had a fondness for the condiment, particularly in the form of hot sauce. Americans brought their culinary habits to countries where they had military bases—Germany and Japan in particular—and then to areas where they worked on oilfields, especially around the Persian Gulf . Later, in the 2000s, studies showed that chili had become the second most popular flavor in the United States after chocolate. This popularity has been growing over the last two decades, if the American and European craze for Chinese cuisine, from street food to gourmet restaurants, is anything to go by. More recently, the taste for chili has been renewed through chili competitions and their dissemination on social networks. Organized for several years in the United States, Australia, Canada, and the United Kingdom, these contests, which aim to ingest the strongest chilis on the standard measure of their strength, the "Scoville scale," went viral on TikTok, YouTube, Facebook, and Instagram in 2020, during the health crisis linked to the Covid-19 epidemic.

Julie Marquet and Margo Stemmelin

FURTHER READING

Eliza Acton. *Modern Cookery, in All Its Branches: Reduced to a System of Easy Practice, for the Use of Private Families* . . . London: Longman, Brown, Green & Longman, 1845.

Jean Andrews. *Peppers: The Domesticated Capsicums*. Austin: University of Texas Press, 1984.

Lizzie Collingham. *Curry: A Tale of Cooks and Conquerors.* Oxford: Oxford University Press, 2006.

Brian R. Dott. *The Chile Pepper in China: A Cultural Biography.* New York: Columbia University Press, 2020.

Stefan Halikowski Smith. "In the Shadow of a Pepper-Centric Historiography: Understanding the Global Diffusion of Capsicums in the Sixteenth and Seventeenth Centuries." *Journal of Ethnopharmacology* 167 (2015): 64–77.

FURTHER TRAVELING

Curry, Olive Oil, Salt

Chorba

It is five o'clock in the morning in the summer of 2015, and Istanbul is still asleep after a restless night. Upon leaving the 333, the nightly milonga on Taksim Square, there is nothing more natural following a night of dancing, with aching feet and endorphins flowing, than gathering around a good chorba (pronounced "tchorba") in one of the countless all-night restaurants on Istiklal Street. More reasonable clients as well as vegans or vegetarians choose the *mercimek çorbasi* made from coral lentils with a squeeze of lemon, while the more reckless—or those who may have had a little too much to drink—prefer the *işkembe çorbasi*, made from mutton offal and tripe, which is said to be "ideal for hangovers." And since "everything in mutton is good," the head and feet are used to prepare *kelle paça* in Turkish or *kalleh pocheh* in Persian, which, in Iran in particular, is recommended to be eaten before sunrise between 3:00 and 5:00 a.m. in restaurants exclusively for those in the know, because "it's very energetic," especially for men whose sexual energy is at half-mast.

Common to most of the Muslim world, from the celestial mountains of the Tian Shan to the white sands of the Sahara Desert, chorba refers to any form of water-based soup. The word has its origins in Persian, rather than in Arabic as is generally claimed: *shor* or *shur* for "savory" (sour or in brine) and *ba* for "broth" (stewed or simmered), a probable inversion of the Persian word *âb* (water). The term is thus declined into *shorpo*, *shorpa*, *sorpa*, *shurbo*, or *shulpa* if you are in Central Asia, the Uyghur region, or Tatar country; *shorwa* in Afghanistan and Pakistan (Pashto language); *chorba* in India, North Africa, and Bulgaria; *ciorba* in Romania; or even *shurpa* in Russia.

Despite its very similar sound, the word *shorba* should not be confused, in its various pronunciations, with *sharbat*, its sweet equivalent. This cold, nonalcoholic drink is made from fruit and sugar boiled in water. Cherries, plums, and apricots are the main ingredients. The term has also traveled far and wide: *sherbet* in English, *sorbetto* in Italian, and *sorbet* as well as *sirop* in French. The Soviets also appreciated this beverage, which was very popular in the canteens and cheap restaurants of the Communist era, but called it *kompot*, a word still used today in post-Soviet areas. *Sharbat* is said to come from the medieval Arabic *sharâb*, meaning a nonalcoholic beverage. It is a term also found in Persian to refer to "wine."

Why does the word *chorba* cover almost half the Eurasian continent and most of North Africa? According to a mythical story, nomadic Turkic peoples originating from Central Asia known as Oghuz migrated and were at the origin of the first Ottoman dynasties. This group developed the tradition of the kettle and the daily soup that united and welded the group into an elite military corps that forged Ottoman domination and diffusion through war and conquest. Such was the recipe for the transcontinental success of chorba. At the heart of this coincidence between territories under Ottoman control, from the fourteenth century to the fall of the empire in the throes of the Great War, and the circulation of the word *chorba* are the janissaries (*yeniçeri*—literally "new troop") and their military organization, whose ranks are directly related to soup and cooking pots.

The formal creation of this corps is not entirely known, but 1362 has been chosen as the date for these infantry units, made up of young teenagers who were selected from the conquered populations, particularly Christians. Recruitment took place in Macedonia, Greece, Albania, Serbia, and Bosnia and among Armenians, enabling the sultan to ensure strict discipline and unreserved loyalty, which lasted for over five centuries. The imperial guard was much admired by foreign ambassadors, who were impressed by the splendid, colorful uniforms. In fact, there were two janissary corps: the Constantinople corps for the Ottoman Empire, and the Algiers corps for North Africa, which recruited soldiers of Turkish origin.

To understand how military ranks and culinary denominations intertwined, it is necessary to return to the distant Ottoman origins, when nomadic traditions organized life around a daily meal and the hearth, *ocak* (pronounced "odjak") in Turkish. This is precisely the term used to designate the military "corps" of the Janissaries, made up of units (*orta*)—equivalent to a regiment—each of which possessed a cooking pot (*kazan*), which served as a rallying point for the troops and a place where warriors could be counseled. Each unit was commanded by the *çorbaci başı* (pronounced "tchorbadji bashi"), literally "chief of the soup-makers," a rank equivalent to colonel. He commanded, among others, the chief of barracks (*oda başı*), the guard of provisions and agent of expenses (*vekil-i harc*), and the chief cook (*aşçı başı*). The last also worked as a prison guard and wore a large kitchen knife as a sign of his rank. In the scale of punishments, being locked up in the kitchen was the lightest penalty. He then had under his control the head of the kitchen helpers (*baskara kullucu*) and the head of the water carriers (*sakka başı*).

Over time, the janissary corps became institutionalized as the guards of the sultan—the "foster father"—who paid them their wages after assembling them in the courtyard of the Topkapı Palace and having them distribute soup. Amid a paradise of wooden spoons and cooking pots, these men are remembered as unfailing warriors filled with military glories who specialized in sieges and were formidable in final attacks. They were also known for their bloody revolts. Overturning the pot or breaking it was a signal of revolt, and every janissary had to join the gathering place, armed or unarmed. The pot was also an object of superstition: losing it in battle was a bad omen, leading to officers being disgraced. In the seventeenth and eighteenth centuries, revolts became increasingly regular, culminating in the first two regicides of Sultan Osman II in 1622 and Sultan Ibrahim I in 1648. A ritual of revolt gradually became codified: a pamphlet of sedition, refusal to eat the soup offered by the sultan, then pots taken out of the barracks and brought to the central square or "meat square" (*et meydani*), today the Hippodrome in Istanbul. These revolts, which became all too frequent, earned the janissaries the nickname of "the gentlemen of the meat square" from the locals, who attended the spectacle at first, a performance that soon turned violent. This was followed by looting and attacks on the palaces of high-ranking dignitaries or fires on the outskirts of the city, which caused extensive damage because the houses were made of wood. Sultan Selim III's military reform of 1793 sounded the death knell for the janissary corps, while a new military order (*nizâm-ı cedid*) was put in place, creating the modern army. From then on, the cauldron was no longer a symbol of war councils or rebellion, and chorba's fame spread beyond the military order to become synonymous with a convivial moment around a table and a good hot, invigorating soup, after a hard day's work (or a long night of dancing).

Cloé Drieu

FURTHER READING

Alan Davidson, Tom Jain, and Soun Vannithone. *The Oxford Companion to Food*. New York: Oxford University Press, 2019.

Gilles Veinstein. "On the Ottoman Janissaries (14th–19th Centuries)." In *Fighting for a Living: A Comparative Study of Military Labour 1500–2000*, ed. Erik-Jan Zürcher, 115–34. Amsterdam: Amsterdam University Press, 2014.

Nahoum Weissman. *Les janissaires: Étude de l'organisation militaire des Ottomans*. Paris: Orient, 1964.

Ali Yaycioglu. "Janissaires, ingénieurs et prédicateurs." *Revue d'histoire du xixe siècle* 53 (2016): 19–37.

FURTHER TRAVELING

Couscous, Döner Kebab, Pho, Ramen, Turkish Delight, Wine

Christmas Pudding

On December 2, 1927, a curious ceremony took place just a stone's throw from London Bridge: representatives from all the territories of the British Empire attended the making of a giant Christmas pudding. One after the other, the pudding ingredients were solemnly announced as they were brought in by turbaned Indian servants. The participants, dressed in the traditional costume of the country they represented, then took turns mixing the pot's contents. The result, some twenty-kilograms (44 lb.) of cake, was then taken with great fanfare to the kitchens of the lord mayor of London's residence, where it was baked for twenty-six hours. The ceremony was filmed and shown in cinemas across the United Kingdom to celebrate what was billed as the most British of desserts.

The promotion of pudding to the status of national dish was by no means a foregone conclusion. Apart from the flour, beef kidney fat, milk, and eggs, the main ingredients all come from faraway lands (rum from Jamaica, raisins from Australia, sugar from the West Indies, cinnamon from Ceylon, cloves from Zanzibar, spices from India, brandy from Cyprus), and the recipe is the work of a Frenchman, chef Henri Cédard, who ran the kitchens of the English royal family from 1885 to 1935. Nonetheless, Cédard is not credited with having invented the dessert. The term *pudding* has been used in the English culinary repertoire since the Middle Ages. At the time, the name was generic, referring to a set of savory or sweet preparations made from animal fat, flour, or breadcrumbs and milk and wrapped in a cloth before being boiled. From the end of the Tudor reign, the elite sometimes added spices, raisins, and sugar brought back by British sailors from their expeditions around the world. Plum pudding may be ancient, but it was not until the nineteenth century that it became known as

"Christmas pudding," the inescapable dessert of the Christmas meal. It then took the form of a dome, sometimes topped with a holly leaf, which was flambéed with brandy in front of the guests. The invention of this tradition was largely the work of Charles Dickens. In 1843, the writer published a short story entitled "A Christmas Carol," about a dry-hearted old miser, Ebenezer Scrooge, and his clerk, Bob Cratchit, whose wife manages to make a magnificent Christmas pudding despite their meagre resources. The dessert quickly spawned a series of family traditions, such as "Stir-up Sunday," when, a month before Christmas, all members of the household gather and take turns mixing the pudding clockwise to ensure prosperity for the coming year. A festive dessert, pudding's ingredients come from the four corners of the empire, embodying British colonial and commercial power. Quickly promoted to the rank of national dessert, it was consumed by the elite as well as by more modest subjects. The latter sometimes joined "Christmas Clubs" that provided them with a turkey and pudding ingredients in exchange for an annual membership fee.

In the days of empire, making Christmas pudding became an identity issue for nineteenth-century British colonists as they tried to recreate Christmas festivities far from the mother country. They made a point of serving it on December 25, sometimes with a few adjustments. The cake was baked in boiling mud springs in New Guinea, made with rice and ostrich eggs in the South African veldt and with brandy-soaked cookies in the Australian bush. Attachment to this culinary tradition sometimes bordered on sacrifice. Indeed, it took a certain determination to consume, in the midst of the stifling heat of the Australian summer, a dessert that, in the words of gold prospector Francis Augustus Hare, takes "24 hours to cook and a week to digest." The symbolic importance of Christmas pudding is also reflected in the efforts made by British settlers in India to faithfully reproduce the traditional recipe, published without major alteration in Anglo-Indian cookbooks until the 1950s. Outside the British Empire, on the other hand, the pudding underwent substantial adaptations. In 1942 an American cookbook published an iconoclastic recipe for "White Christmas Pudding," made from gelatin, canned pineapple juice, coconut, frozen strawberries, and whipped cream.

The British patriotic and emotional attachment to Christmas pudding was rekindled during World War I, when collections were organized so that every soldier, whether stationed at the front, a prisoner of the enemy, or cared for in field hospitals, could enjoy the cake on Christmas Day. An object of nostalgia, the pudding was also a political dessert. Its characteristic shape makes it one of the symbols of Great Britain. One of the most popular postcards of the period depicts a Christmas pudding with the flags of Great Britain and its allies planted in it. However, it was the postwar period that witnessed the pudding's consecration. The return to normality gave Christmas celebrations, which were supposed to revive "Merry Old England," a special significance. In the 1920s, as memories of shortages and rationing began to fade, the festivities became the subject of an increasingly intense debate between protectionists and free traders. The former, anxious to encourage internal trade flows within the empire, convinced the British government to actively promote products from the colonies to the metropolitan market, through the Empire Marketing Board (EMB). It was during one of the campaigns organized by the EMB in 1926 that King George V and Queen Mary enjoyed a Christmas dinner made entirely of products from the British Empire (on the menu: soup, sole fillets, braised ham with spinach, turkey stuffed with chestnuts, lettuce, and cauliflower soufflé) and finished with an "Imperial Christmas Pudding," all the ingredients of which came from the British colonies and dominions. The recipe, which mentioned the origin of each ingredient, was published in national newspapers and was a huge success, prompting the EMB to repeat the feat the following year. While the pudding was celebrated as the national and imperial dessert par excellence, and presented as the fatty, sweet manifestation of British commercial power, its composition quickly became the focus of internal rivalries within the empire. Cyprus complained that its brandy was not included in the list of ingredients published by the EMB in 1926, and the following year Henri Cédard was forced to add Indian "pudding spices" to avoid a diplomatic incident. There was also fierce competition between South Africa and Australia, both of which produced dried fruit, and then it was question of whether New Zealand, Austria, Canada, or Great Britain would succeed in adding their apples to the recipe (Canada won that bout in 1927). The empire's internal lobbying was compounded by increasingly fierce foreign commercial competition. From the 1920s onward Australia, the empire's leading producer of raisins, faced competition from California, whose Sun Maid brand advertised aggressively even on English soil. Although it was increasingly abandoned in the twentieth century in favor of lighter, more easily digestible preparations, Christmas pudding remains to this day the emblematic dessert of British Christmas. Its recipe, published on social networks by Queen Elizabeth II's chef in November 2020, differs only slightly from that of Henri Cédard.

Stéphanie Soubrier

FURTHER READING

Natacha Chevalier. "Iconic Dishes, Culture and Identity: The Christmas Pudding and its Hundred Years' Journey in the USA, Australia, New Zealand and India." *Food, Culture and Society* 21, no. 3 (2018): 367–83.

Lizzie Collingham. *The Taste of Empire: How Britain's Quest for Food Shaped the Modern World.* New York: Basic Books, 2017.

Kenneth S. Inglis. *Australian Colonists: An Exploration of Social History, 1788–1870.* Melbourne: Melbourne University Press, 1993.

Kaori O'Connor. "The King's Christmas Pudding: Globalization, Recipes, and the Commodities of Empire." *Journal of Global History* 4, no. 1 (2009): 127–55.

Jeri Quinzio. *Pudding. A Global History.* London: Reaktion Books, 2012.

FURTHER TRAVELING

Rooibos, Rum, Tea and Chai, Turkish Delight, Vanilla

Coca-Cola

In the *Atlanta Journal* of May 29, 1886, a new product was introduced: "Coca-Cola! Delicious! Refreshing! Stimulating! Invigorating! The new and popular soda fountain contains the qualities of the wonderful Coca plant and the famous Cola nut . . . available at Dr. Pemberton's Jacobs Pharmacy." Advertising with a slogan of health and wellness ensured the product's popularity. Pharmacist Pemberton was already selling French wine, the famous coca wine made by Corsican chemist Mariani. The arrival of the prohibitionist wave in the state of Georgia prompted him to replace Bordeaux wine with carbonated, sugary water, and the product was promoted as an antialcoholic beverage. His accountant Robinson, a skilled communicator, came up with the name and the cursive lettering of the word in the now trademarked Spencer font.

Unfortunately, John Pemberton was ill and addicted to cocaine. As a result, he ran out of money and sold his invention to businessmen, including "Georgian Yankee" Asa Candler. By 1889 his company had taken the name of its flagship product: the Coca-Cola Company. Candler spent his life asserting his exclusivity and fighting the many counterfeiters (Africa Kola, Coq à Cola, Klu Ko Kola or Ola Cola). There were 153 imitations in 1916 alone! Candler set out to develop sales throughout the American market. He invented billboard advertising along roads and streets, which flourished with the automobile and urban revolution, and promoted the "5-cent Coca-Cola" or the "invigorating and refreshing Coca-Cola." Candler also invented "merchandising": transport vehicles, coolers, and even red salesmen's uniforms all imposed the brand's Spencer-typeface logo in public spaces. In addition to pharmacies, the product could soon be found in grocery stores, saloons, brand-new drugstores and bowling alleys in cities, and

74 COCA-COLA

gas stations. First offered in glasses, Candler soon approached bottlers all over the country to have special glass bottles made. His triumph came in 1916 when he succeeded in obtaining a fluted bottle imitating the shape of the sheath dresses of the elegant ladies of the time, the "contour bottle," "which even a blind man, as they say, will recognize."

Nothing could slow the drink's success. Neither the increasingly fierce competition (North Carolina pharmacist Bradham's Pepsi Cola dates from 1898), nor the push against drug addiction, which led to the de-cocainization of the coca leaf in 1903. Coca-Cola made so many Americas: a white, Anglo-Saxon, Protestant America sitting at the soda fountain; black Harlemites who drank it to reconnect with the Deep South; Russian immigrants who added vodka; or Italians who added chianti.

The drink was globalized at the height of U.S. imperialism. As early as 1898, Coca-Cola landed in Cuba to recover the sugar while Theodore Roosevelt's Rough Riders conquered the Spanish island. In the 1900s it expanded into Canada. In 1917, when the United States entered World War I, two million doughboys brought their national drink to Europe in American army vans. In 1919 a soda bar was set up in the land of wine on the Eiffel Tower. From 1923 onward the new president of 3C (the Coca-Cola Company), Robert Woodruff, even created a division and then a subsidiary dedicated to exports. In 1933 the Café de l'Europe in Montparnasse was selling Coca-Cola, and it was available from the Côte d'Azur all the way to Marseille. This comforted American political, moral, and cultural leadership. No doubt the ban on alcoholic beverages in the United States, but also in many parts of Europe, contributed to the spectacular spread of soda. In 1939, however, 3C was mainly present in Canada, Cuba, and Germany.

When the Second World War broke out, Coca-Cola Deutschland had to contend with a blockade of imported raw materials (cola nuts, coca leaves, lemons, and other exotic ingredients) and shortages of sugar in Nazi Germany. After the American declaration of war, the company invented an ersatz soda called Fanta (from the German *fantastik*), using substitute raw materials.

In the United States, Coca-Cola became a war product, mobilized for the national effort. Postcards, records, and radio broadcasts touted the product. The d'Arcy advertising agency that marketed for 3C put it bluntly when it argued that "Men work better with a refreshing drink. Current events guide the present as never before. A nation at war must intensify its productive efforts. So, in times like these, it becomes a necessity for workers."

The 3C chairman's good relations with U.S. President Franklin Roosevelt led to Coca-Cola's being included among the food products mobilized for the army.

The first bottling plant was built in Iceland, on Churchill's route between North America and the British Isles, just six months after Pearl Harbor (December 1941). Supreme Allied commander (and future president) Eisenhower then created a special unit, the T.O., Technical Observers, to set up Coca-Cola factories in Allied or reconquered territories and transport the precious product to the front line. A telegram dated June 29, 1943, explicitly ordered: "Convoy three million bottles of Coca-Cola, together with bottling, washing and encapsulating equipment, twice a month." Sometimes called "Coca-Cola colonels," these 3C employees also wore the uniform of the U.S. Army, with T.O. sewn on the sleeve. They were popular with the soldiers and their officers (Patton, Eisenhower, and Bradley were Coca-Cola drinkers). Some were even turned into heroes. Fred Cook, for example, completed a 1,300-mile raid "over the hump" of the Himalayas to bring supplies from a factory all the way to China. In Europe the first bottle of military Coke rolled off the line at the Oran plant during Christmas 1943, a year after the liberation of French North Africa. Coca-Cola embodied "a part of and a symbol of the way of life for which this war is being fought," said Woodruff's deputy.

After the war, bottling plants remained all over the world, climbing up to 64 in 44 countries. Coca-Cola spread the American way of life in liberated or occupied countries (Germany, Japan). Even in France the little bottle was a hit, despite the determined opposition of the French Communist Party, allied for the occasion with the wine lobby. Coca-Cola became the symbol of the free world. As the Soviets built their red world and built the Iron Curtain, as Churchill referred to it, Atlanticism triumphed in a movement of "coca-colonization," as it was known by Communists. Even in France, the Coca-Cola wave gained momentum from the 1950s onward. American advertising methods (large posters and TV spots) were adopted everywhere; packaging was renewed after 1960 with metal cans, which became "cannettes," as they were known by adoring fans.

The Coca-Cola expansion was global. Advertising was everywhere—even at the Olympic Games. Since 1928, and especially after the 1948 Melbourne Games, 3C has targeted sports, accompanying American athletes and entire sporting movements. Atlanta even became the "City of the Coca-Cola Olympics" in 1996. Of course, 3C's imperialism also encountered a few snags: competition with Pepsi turned into a catastrophe in 1985; in India, sales were hampered by the peasants' war on water: seven liters (1.85 gal.) of water are needed to make one liter (1.05 qt.) of soda; and the company struggled to communicate on the issue of sugar and aspartame, considered cancer-causing in high doses. But in the end the product bounced back. Production was cleverly diversified into Diet

Coke and Coke Zero, and the company joined forces with the McDonald's restaurant chain to communicate connotations of happiness, youth, and progress.

The little bottle has now become a giant. The product, which is both a brand and an industrial company, is now an everyday word found in the dictionary.

Didier Nourrisson

FURTHER READING

Jean-Luc Chalumeau. *Coca-Cola dans l'art*. Paris: Éditions du Chêne, 2008.
Aymon de Lestrange. *Angelo Mariani (1838–1914): Le vin de coca et la naissance de la publicité moderne*. Paris: Éditions Intervalles, 2016.
Bénédicte Jourgeaud. *Coca-Cola: Une passion française, 90 ans en bonne compagnie*. Paris: Le Cherche Midi, 2009.
Didier Nourisson. *La saga Coca-Cola*. Paris: Larousse, 2008.
William Reymond. *Coca-Cola: L'enquête interdite*. Paris: Flammarion, 2006.

FURTHER TRAVELING

Orangina, Sparkling Water, Vodka, Whiskey, Wine

Coffee

Is coffee *the* exemplary commodity of the modern era? It may indeed be if we consider its history. For the story of coffee must include the abuse and amputations suffered by hundreds of thousands of slaves in Saint-Domingue, who freed themselves from coffee plantations and set in motion a genuine Revolution in 1791. It was the famous French historian Jules Michelet who wrote,

> The three ages of coffee were also the three eras of modern thought. Each phase marked a solemn moment in the brilliant century known as the Enlightenment. The first was prepared by Arab coffee, even before 1700. Those beautiful ladies you see in the style of Bonnard with their noses above their little cups taking in the aromas of the finest Arabic coffee ... compared the boredom of Versailles to an Oriental paradise. Soon after ... the reign of Indian coffee began. It was abundant, popular, and relatively inexpensive. We transplanted coffee to our native island of Bourbon and generated an unprecedented success. Consumption of this coffee from volcanic soil exploded in the Regency thanks to the new spirit of the age.... As a result, neither Bourbon lava nor Arabian sand were sufficient. The Regent thus had coffee transplanted to the vast lands of the West Indies.... This strong, full-bodied coffee from Saint-Domingue ... nourished the mature thoughts of the century, the age of the *Encyclopédie*. Consumed by Buffon, Diderot, and Rousseau, this coffee provided the warmth of warm souls. It cast its light on the prophets assembled in the lair of the *Procope*, who read the coffee grounds in the bottom of their cups and anticipated the French Revolution.

To summarize Michelet's poetic account: Yemenite mocha in the seventeenth century, coffee from the East Indies under the Regency (1715–23), coffee from plantations in the West Indies until the French Revolution in 1789. Arabia, La Réunion, and Santo Domingo. Finesse, strength, and exaltation.

If this account provides a portrait of the modern age, it is less because it accurately denotes the layers of modern thought and more for what it says of the overseas expansion of concessionary companies, colonial empire, and then slave plantations. Even so, the view from the bottom of a coffee cup must be further explored.

In fact, if there are three ages in the history of coffee, they belong to a much more dilated stratigraphy, which may only be properly understood if we start from the present and look backward. We are in the age of zinc bar countertops and franchises; of espressos, americanos, lattés, and Turkish-style coffees; of cardboard cups and mugs; of cafeterias and vending machines; of brands and terroir, fair-trade or otherwise. There is little doubt that coffee is part of both a global economy and national cultures of consumption and taste. Let us then leave the Procope café, where the figures of the Enlightenment in Paris gathered, behind.

You find yourself in a hotel lobby or a modest *tin bunna bet* ("coffee house" in Amharic) on the roadside in Ethiopia. You've been invited to participate in a coffee ceremony. A young woman has laid out rushes on the floor, set up a cast-iron or terracotta pot, and brought in embers on which she places incense crystals. On an iron plate she roasts the green grains, inviting you to smell the fumes before crushing them in a mortar. The ground coffee is poured into a *jäbäna*, a narrow-necked coffee pot with a globular body, which she fills with water, along with some condiments (cardamom, chili, butter, salt, or sugar). The coffee boils for a few minutes, then thickens and settles before being poured into cups lined up on a wooden shelf. The first cup is served to guests in order of seniority or respectability, followed by a second, then third and so on until the last. The cup without a handle is called a *sëni*, or a "Chinese," because it is made of porcelain.

The folkloric dimension of this panoply of utensils and gestures is undeniable. But the coffee ceremony is also emblematic. It represents, and even captures or reinforces, national identity throughout the country as well as in restaurants abroad, and within the diaspora, in Israel, Great Britain, the United States, and elsewhere. It has been shown that this tradition is recent; its construction and pan-Ethiopian span have accompanied the history of Ethiopia since the end of the nineteenth century and the establishment of coffee cash crops in the southern territories incorporated into the empire. But like all traditions, the coffee ceremony exists to make people forget the history from which it springs; it

COFFEE 79

expresses a subtle conviviality that transcends relations of political domination, religious affiliations, and the country's incredible ethnic diversity.

In most Ethiopian languages, the first cup you are served is called *abol*, the second *tona*, and the third *bäräka*. One can recognize the words *awwal*, *thanwa*, *baraka*, that is "first," "second," and "blessing," in Arabic. We don't know how old these borrowings are, but they certainly date back to an earlier age, that of the use of coffee by the Sufi brotherhoods that propagated the second Islamization of the Horn of Africa from the sixteenth century onward. Although coffee was often proscribed by Muslim ulama, its ability to stimulate nocturnal vigilance and sharpen the mind was nevertheless sought after by mystical orders. This use originated in Yemen, where the drink had been introduced as early as the middle of the fifteenth century, and then cultivated from coffee trees planted on terraced lands in the middle of the sixteenth century. Yemen's place in the history of global trade in the modern age is well known. Yemen was the checkpoint at the mouth of the Red Sea, the hinge between the eastern Mediterranean and the Indian Ocean. From Mokha, a transit port and warehouse for Indian cotton, Indian spices, and Chinese porcelain, which gave its name to Yemeni coffee, the beverage spread from Egypt to Iran and the Mughal Empire. At the beginning of the seventeenth century European chartered companies, primarily the Dutch East India Company, took on some of this Islamic cargo on their own account before opening European markets to coffee. In the second half of the century cafés were set up in Venice, Marseille, Amsterdam, London, Paris, and Hamburg. To meet demand, plantations were established in the European colonies of Java and Bourbon Island in the early eighteenth century; then an industrial plantation system based on the deportation of Africans was instituted in the Americas in the 1720s.

The drink that is referred to in English as coffee is called *café* in French, *koffie* in Dutch, *caffè* in Italian, and *kahve* in Turkish. These are all borrowings from the Arabic *qahwa*. Behind the Arabic word one hears resonances of Kaffa, a region in southwestern Ethiopia where the coffee tree, *Coffea arabica L.*, grows naturally in the misty mountains at altitudes of between 1,000 and 2,500 meters (3,281–8,202 ft.). The vegetation is a shrub that may grow up to six meters (19.7 ft.) in height but is pruned to two meters (6.6 ft.) to increase its yield. These are hardly primal forests. Each plot is owned. Ethnobotanists have inventoried hundreds of species exploited for human food and animal fodder, for medicines, and for honey production. Surrounding trees cast shade over the coffee plantings. The Kaffa forest is an anthropized mosaic that has been cultivated for ages, for coffee was Ethiopian before it became a worldwide commodity. In Amharic, the drink is called *bunna*. The ancient history of this beverage is difficult to retrace.

However, even the most secular versions of the coffee ceremony have a religious air of altar tables, fumigations, sacrifices, and offerings. In the Oromiffa language, a preparation of roasted berries mixed with butter is called *buna qalaa*, or a "coffee sacrifice." That designation alone suggests the plant was consumed for liturgical purposes. It has also been noted that the ceremony bore some resemblance to apotropaic magic used to ward off or exorcise the *zar*, that is, the harmful pan-Ethiopian spirits that descend on individuals and straddle their bodies. It may be that before contributing to "nation-building" in the contemporary age, coffee was used to cure maladies and social ills. In any case, its uses are much broader in Ethiopia than in the rest of the world: in various regions, in addition to drinking the *bunna* of roasted beans, people chew the beans when they are still green, place the leaves of the shrub in the cheek, eat fortifying pellets of butter and crushed beans, and make infusions from the leaves and the bean shells.

François-Xavier Fauvelle

FURTHER READING

Eloi Ficquet. "Le rituel du café, contribution musulmane à l'identité nationale éthiopienne." In *O Islão na África subsariana*, ed. António C. Gonçalves, 159–65. Porto: Centro de Estudos Africanos da Universidade do Porto, 2004.

André Raymond. "Le café du Yémen et l'Égypte (xviie–xviiie siècles)." *Chroniques yéménites* 3 (1995): 16–25.

Feyera Senbeta, Tadesse Woldemariam Gole, Manfred Denich, and Ensermu Kellbessa. "Diversity of Useful Plants in the Coffee Forests of Ethiopia." *Ethnobotany Research & Applications* 11 (2013): 49–69.

Michel Tuchscherer. "Des épices au café: Le Yémen dans le commerce international (xvie–xviie siecle)." *Chroniques yéménites* 4–5 (1997): 102–3.

Bula Sirika Wayessa. "Buna Qalaa: A Quest for Traditional Uses of Coffee Among Oromo People with Special Emphasis on Wallaga, Ethiopia." *African Diaspora Archaeology Newsletter* 14, no. 3 (2011): 1–18.

FURTHER TRAVELING

Beet Sugar, Chicory, Condensed Milk (Sweetened), Cornflakes, Pepper, Salt, Tea

Condensed Milk (Sweetened)

Patented in 1856, milk concentration is one of those inventions that has marked the history of processed food and its complex relationship to good health. The process, developed by American businessman Gail Borden Jr., involves removing 50–60 percent of the water from milk through evaporation at very high temperatures. The liquid is then heavily sweetened up to 50 grams (1.76 oz.) per 100 to ensure its preservation, an addition that gives it its yellowish color and characteristic thick, viscous texture. Packaged in cans, the food soon graced the canteens of Civil War soldiers. But its consumption was propelled by the glass bottle and rubber teats, innovations through which it became a substitute for breastfeeding.

It must be said that industrialization and urbanization prevented many women from engaging in this practice at the same time that there was a shortage of wetnurses. Working in factories paid better than breastfeeding another's children. As for cow's milk, whose therapeutic virtues were recognized, it was relatively expensive, not always well digested, and difficult to transport and store. Moreover, its pasteurization, which became compulsory at the beginning of the twentieth century, did not prevent adulteration. The complex social and health issues at stake were undoubtedly conducive to the development of the agricultural-food sector. Two years after its birth, in 1868, the Swiss company Nestlé was already selling 374,000 units of its "condensed," a "natural source of energy" which, at half the price of its fresh equivalent, conquered the working classes.

While companies were quick to point out that many mothers breastfeed poorly, with disastrous consequences for infant mortality in cities like Paris or London, hygienists and pediatricians were annoyed by such slogans and by the popularity of "artificial milks." They condemned excessive dilution and the use of unboiled water for reconcentration and supported the establishment of supervised distribution centers offering postnatal consultations. The medicalization of maternal and child health increased in step with the development of nutritional knowledge, discoveries about vitamins, minerals, and proteins, and so-called deficiency diseases such as blindness, scurvy, rickets, and beriberi. And yet, while it provides up to 4,500 calories per liter, concentrate remains low in fat. In this sense it is nourishing without being nutritious.

While milk flours (mixtures of milk, cereals, and mineral salts) and evaporated milks (unsweetened dehydrated milks) struggled to carve out a share of the market, the first powdered products (by drying or complete dehydration) with added vitamins A and D or calcium, appeared in the 1930s. However, the quality of supply remained highly uneven at a time when the trade in these substitutes had become globalized. As a result, it was difficult to avoid the pitfalls of counterfeiting and misleading advertising as well as dubious imperialist intentions.

Beyond its propensity to buy up rivals and dairy companies across the globe, Nestlé in particular played the philanthropist, sponsoring hospitals and setting up offices and subsidiaries all over Asia from Istanbul to Singapore. In the columns of the leading women's magazines in Shanghai and Saigon, Nestlé's concentrate was seen as an indispensable aid in infant growth. The Swiss company also supported doctors stationed in sub-Saharan Africa who sought to neutralize the reproductive repercussions of "cultural" abstinence during the lactation period and were wary of "too rich" breast milk.

World War II seemed to put the brakes on this sprawling, aggressive food capitalism. The conflict led to glaring shortages of essential manufactured goods, and infant malnutrition was on everyone's expert lips. However, "natural" breastfeeding was not restored to its former glory. The democratization of the refrigerator meant that milk could be kept fresher for longer, and in the 1960s, women's movements advocated the more liberating practice of bottle-feeding, which underpinned a dynamic labor market. By 1967 only 25 percent of American newborns were breastfed.

In 1974, however, a report by a South African engineer commissioned by the British NGO War on Want and specializing in development issues threw a spanner in the works. In *The Baby Killer*, Mike Muller stressed the damaging effects of the undue influence of "Big Food," particularly infant formula and condensed milk, on the health of toddlers in the countries of the decolonized South. Nestlé was singled out as a master in the art of manipulating both mothers and health workers under the guise of human intervention. The book also highlighted their direct involvement in the campaign against kwashiorkor, an acute and lethal protein deficiency, led by several United Nations bodies in the Belgian Congo at the turn of the 1950s.

The target of an impressive boycott launched in the United States in 1977, before spreading to Australia and then Europe, Nestlé-branded products became subject to the International Code of Marketing of Breast-Milk Substitutes, introduced by the World Health Organization in 1981. This legal framework marked a growing awareness of children's rights and world hunger, as well as new knowledge on the functioning of the immune system, which scientifically supported the superiority of mother's milk over its competitors in the first months and even years of life.

The text echoed national initiatives, some of them long-standing, which did not necessarily have the desired effect—Great Britain imposed the words "unfit for babies" on skimmed milk labels in 1894, a warning extended to concentrate in 1923, without curbing sales. The subject of hundreds of violations a year, which regularly led to the resumption of the 1977 boycott suspended in 1984, it did not revolutionize the domestic habits of the most vulnerable, accustomed to affordable expedients to satisfy their hunger. The medical, legal, and ethical blacklisting of condensed milk also widened health and gender inequalities. Those who use it today, in Bangladesh and in the poor districts of major American metropolises, are regularly accused of being bad mothers, even though they are often unable to obtain the best infant formulas or to breastfeed.

That said, this accessible, convenient product was never used solely for (poorly) nourishing babies. A simple cultural marker, it has been adapted to suit culinary traditions. As the sole ingredient in Argentina's *dulce de leche*, an essential ingredient in Vietnamese *ca phe sua da*, used in pastries, in candies or as spreads on bread for a snack, it continues to satisfy epicures young and old alike.

Laurence Monnais

FURTHER READING

Rima Apple. *Mothers and Medicine. A Social History of Infant Feeding, 1890–1950*. Madison: University of Wisconsin Press, 1987.

Adel P. Den Hartog. "The Discovery of Vitamins and its Impact on the Food Industry: The Issue of Tinned Sweetened Condensed Skim Milk 1890–1940." In *Food and the City in Europe since 1800*, 131–42. London: Routledge, 2016.

Thomas David DuBois. "Branding and Retail Strategy in the Condensed Milk Trade: Borden and Nestlé in East Asia, 1870–1929." *Business History* 65 (2023): 902–19.

84 CONDENSED MILK (SWEETENED)

Tehila Sasson. "Milking the Third World? Humanitarianism, Capitalism, and the Moral Economy of the Nestlé Boycott." *American Historical Review* 121, no. 4 (2016): 1196–1224.

Lola Wilhelm. "Business et santé infantile mondiale: La stratégie médicale de Nestlé au sein des réseaux pédiatriques et humanitaires transnationaux." *Monde(s)* 20 (2021): 49–66.

FURTHER TRAVELING

Beet Sugar, Chicory, Coffee, Cornflakes, Tea

Cornflakes

Only half-awake and immersed in a bowl of crackling grilled flakes of corn, one could hardly imagine that this inaugural daily pleasure was invented in the United States in 1894 by a vegetarian Adventist doctor who pioneered dietetics and advocated sexual abstinence. The creation contributed to his vision of providing patients in his sanitarium with a healthy, bland diet in order to combine physical health and moral temperance. Around the same time in Europe, nascent psychoanalysis was demonstrating the intimate link between the act of eating and sexual desire. In other words, products like cornflakes sat at the crossroads of asceticism and pleasure from the start. A few decades later, anthropologists from the 1940s onwards would begin to analyze the central role played by food in structuring society. Or, as one of the leading anthropologists of the period, Marcel Mauss, would have argued, cornflakes were a total social fact. And like all total social facts, they evolved, traveled, and metamorphosed.

Cornflakes became a symbol of the American way of life and its affluent society for a significant part of the twentieth century. Invented by Dr. John Harvey Kellogg, they were marketed by his brother Will Keith, who founded the Battle Creek Toasted Corn Flake Company in 1906. The company grew rapidly. By the mid-1910s cereals mixed with milk had become part of the typical breakfast of the average American, who bought them from a variety of brands, of which Kellogg's was among the most important. The first international media launch of the toasted corn flake came at the San Francisco World's Fair in 1915. The fair featured a variety of prepared foods that already represented 20 percent of all manufactured goods in the United States. In a country with a fast-growing population and a burgeoning mass market, cornflakes were one of the products shaping new culinary practices, not only in the United States but also in many other countries around the world. As early as 1922 they were exported to England, before their success led the brand to build a factory there in 1938. In 1924 they also began to be sold in Canada and Australia. Entry into other European markets was slower. It was only in 1968 that Kellogg's established itself in France, helping to forge a new breakfast cereal market in which it became the market leader at the beginning of the twenty-first century.

Nor was internationalization confined to Europe. Further east, the presence of American machines for making cornflakes could be found in the USSR in the early 1940s. More recently, in 1994, Kellogg's opened its first factory in Mumbai. Kellogg's has been present in Africa since the early 2000s, particularly in Nigeria. In 2022, in addition to the United States, the brand had manufacturing plants in twenty-seven countries, including Mexico, Brazil, Nigeria, South Africa, Japan, Malaysia, Egypt, and Poland. Exports included the many variations of its cornflakes sent to 180 countries. While it is the world's leading producer of prepared cereals, it is hardly alone. As a sign of its international success, the term "cornflakes" has become distinct from the original product and brand to become a category encompassing, according to the United Nations classification, any type of puffed and/or toasted cereal.

Beyond its international success, the cornflake has been emblematic of many of the developments that took place across the food industry in the twentieth century. First and foremost, it testifies to the growing role of technological innovation and scientific research alongside the art of cooking. Toasted corn is a product of the agri-food industry, which developed formulas for preparing perishable products, mass-producing them at lower cost, preserving them, and then distributing them. At the end of the nineteenth century condensed milk, powdered milk, pasteurization, and sterilization were decisive instruments in the mass consumption of milk outside rural areas, in the United States as elsewhere. As for sugar, the development of the beet plant democratized its consumption and increased its production, which is said to have increased a thousandfold between the eighteenth and twentieth centuries! Without pasteurized milk and refined sugar, the worldwide success of cornflakes, inseparable from their crackling sound in the morning bowl, would probably have remained impossible.

Equally important has been the rise of hygienic concerns, for which the agrifood industry has been an often overlooked influence. Its machines enabled food to be processed without coming into contact with human hands, thus avoiding the circulation of microbes. In this respect, the corn flake, a dried product with a long shelf-life, is the culinary counterpart of the vaccine and Dakin's solution—one ingredient among others in a contemporary society

CORNFLAKES 87

aiming to keep infections, microbes, and diseases at bay once and for all. Finally, the cornflake bears witness to the evolution of eating habits, particularly breakfast, of which it fast became a central component. The growing importance of this first meal of the day from the end of the nineteenth century onward owes much to the changing relationship to time in industrialized societies, with the rise of a mathematical structuring of the day, where working hours, at the factory or at school, are punctuated by meals. From this point of view, the promotion of breakfast to the rank of a major meal of the day accompanied the generalization of salaried employment and schooling.

Like all products that travel, cornflakes are consumed differently in different places. And as with all cultural transfers, the plasticity of the transferred object is the key to its successful appropriation. The success of corn petals is largely due to the basic nature of the recipe, which makes them adaptable to a variety of culinary contexts. In Mexico in the 1940s, for example, they were eaten with shrimp. In addition, the principle of drying, grilling, and puffing, originally applied to corn, was rapidly extended to other cereals made of wheat or rice, making it possible to reach other markets according to consumer habits and the grains that served as the basis of their diet. This is where an elaborate marketing strategy developed, which is the other key factor in the success of cornflakes. As early as the 1910s, Kellogg's offered children's pictures to customers buying several packs, used figures from American mythology to illustrate packaging, from cowboys to housewives, and above all used media stunts to promote its product. For example, it served as breakfast for the Apollo 11 crew who walked on the moon in 1969. In addition, Kellogg's, like all American companies with an international vocation since the beginning of the twentieth century, has multiplied its localization strategies in order to adapt to the different national contexts in which it operates. This is the case in India, for example, where the first attempt to penetrate the market in 1994 ended in failure, because the Indian habit of consuming hot morning milk was incompatible with the classic cornflake, made for cold milk. A deep shift in the choice of products as well as their marketing and packaging, helped the company to finally gain a foothold in this market. As a result, concerns about its American origins slowly dissipated.

Cornflakes have become one of the emblematic products of the changes in eating habits that took place at the turn of the twentieth century. But while they are firmly established in today's culinary landscape, at the start of the twenty-first century we may well wonder whether they remain in step with contemporary transformations in food consumption. Does eating a prepared, processed, sweetened food wrapped in plastic still make sense at a time when the agri-food industry is increasingly criticized for its contribution to the global epidemic of obesity and environmental degradation? Paraphrasing the French philosopher Michel Foucault's work *The Order of Things*, one might suggest that if the conditions that presided over its appearance at the end of the nineteenth century were to disappear, then the cornflake might "fade away like a face in the sand on the edge of the sea."

Ludovic Tournès

FURTHER READING

Pierre François and Claire Lemercier. *Sociologie historique du capitalisme*. Paris: La Découverte, 2021.

Christian Grataloup. *Le monde dans nos tasses: Trois siècles de petit- déjeuner*. Malakoff, France: Armand Colin, 2017.

Howard Markel. *The Kelloggs: The Battling Brothers of Battle Creek*. New York: Pantheon Books, 2017.

Faustine Régnier, Anne Lhuissier, and Séverine Gojard. *Sociologie de l'alimentation*. Paris: La Découverte, 2009.

Ludovic Tournès. *Américanisation: Une histoire mondiale, xviiie–xixe siècle*. Paris: Fayard, 2020.

FURTHER TRAVELING

Beet Sugar, Chicory, Coffee, Condensed Milk (Sweetened), Tea

Couscous

In September 2016, Algeria announced that it would be applying to UNESCO for recognition of couscous as intangible cultural heritage. Protests were soon heard from neighboring Morocco, followed by Tunisia and Mauritania, all vying for the paternity of this emblematic dish of the Maghreb, composed of semolina, meat or fish, and spices. A few months later, experts from the four countries began working on a gastronomic and diplomatic compromise for the dish, the mere mention of which left no one indifferent, as witnessed by the numerous articles and tributes published at the time. Out of caution, the dossier submitted to UNESCO did not include recipes, preferring instead to emphasize the "knowledge, know-how, and practices associated with the production and consumption of couscous." For North Africans, couscous is at once a dish for the everyday and exceptional events. It evokes memories of childhood and recalls all the important moments of life. A central element of the diet, life, and culture of the men and women of the Maghreb, it is sometimes referred to by the Arabic term *ta'âm*, which in the broadest sense simply means food.

Like much of the material civilization of the Maghreb, couscous is Berber. The Arabic word *kuskusu*, which designates both semolina and the dish of which it is the basic element, derives from *seksu*, attested in virtually all Algerian-Moroccan Berber dialects. Long used in popular Arabic and appearing in cookbooks in the Islamic West from the seventeenth and eighteenth centuries, it wasn't until the nineteenth century that the word appeared in classical dictionaries. The history of the dish remains more controversial. Archaeological excavations have uncovered pottery with perforated bottoms in Roman tombs in the Tunisian Sahel and in burials dating from the time of King Massinissa in northern Algeria. No other source allows us to specify the use of these ancient objects. Couscous seems to have been developed later, in the Middle Ages, in the rural communities of western and central Maghreb, before reaching Al-Andalus Spain, Tunisia, and Muslim Sicily. It was also consumed in the Sahara and Sahel. The first references to it in sub-Saharan Africa date back to the fourteenth century, with Ibn Battûta's account of his voyage, but they remain allusive, even contradictory, until the seventeenth century. Finally, in the late Middle Ages, it could be found in the eastern Mediterranean, in Syria and Egypt, where sources mention its North African origins.

This wide area of dissemination explains the infinite variety of recipes. Different types and sizes of semolina were used: wheat, barley, millet, and sorghum in the Maghreb; cassava, findi, or millet in the Sahel. The dish is garnished with vegetables, meat or fish, spices, and herbs, depending on what is available, eating habits, and taste preferences. Couscous is also eaten sweetened, under the name *mesfouf* or *seffa*, in its Moroccan version with butter, raisins, orange blossom, and cinnamon, brought back by sailors from the Indian Ocean. It is eaten on a variety of occasions by rural and urban dwellers alike, from the lowest to the highest levels of society. A staple of festivals, often eaten in families on Fridays, it is also the invariable evening meal for many rural communities. Its preparation, which requires time and knowledge, is the exclusive domain of women. Knowledge, techniques, and recipes are passed down orally, from generation to generation, in families that jealously guard their secrets.

The intensification of trade in modern times has facilitated its circulation outside the world of the Muslim East. Known thanks to the accounts of travelers in the Maghreb, couscous spread to Italy, Spain, and then Portugal, which in turn exported it to Brazil in the sixteenth century. Brazilian *cuzcuz* is still prepared with corn semolina in the São Paulo region or with manioc in the northeast. It can be eaten savory or sweet, accompanied by coconut milk and served for breakfast. Rabelais mentions "coscosson" in his *Pantagruel* (1532) and "coscotons à la moresque" in the Fifth Book (1564), while travelers attest to its consumption in Provence in the seventeenth century. The "coussou coussou" appears in Alexandre Dumas's *Grand dictionnaire de cuisine* (1873) and was featured at the Universal Exposition in Paris in 1889.

Its consumption began in France with the arrival of North African workers and soldiers in the first half of the twentieth century. Cooked by men, with semolina brought directly from the Maghreb by the new arrivals, it was a festive dish. Soldiers in garrison were supplied with semolina or the dish already prepared, the recipe for which appeared in the *Manuel du cuisinier militaire* (The Military Cook Manual, 1940). During World War II, ration tickets marked with a crescent were reserved for "indigenous" North African populations. Until the 1960s couscous remained an "exotic" dish, whose ordinary consumption was associated with colonized populations, before becoming part of the French culinary and cultural universe with the arrival of repatriates and North African immigrants, which came at the cost of homogenizing and simplifying the dish.

The pied-noir version of couscous is close to its Kabyle form, served with lots of vegetables and a red sauce that is less varied than that of the rural regions of central Maghreb. The pieds-noirs (populations who returned from North Africa to France after decolonization) also brought merguez, which, in France found its way into couscous. Whereas, on the other side of the Mediterranean, it was served as an appetizer. With the arrival of the wives of Maghrebi workers, the dish was eaten by families and friends according to original recipes, despite the limited choice of products, particularly semolina. Both Maghrebi and pieds-noirs restaurateurs have helped to make couscous a popular dish with the French as a whole, thanks in particular to the couscous royal, which mixes different types of meat, even though in the Maghreb the broth is prepared with just one meat. The food industry transformed couscous into an everyday dish. Algerian independence meant a major loss of production for millers, who developed strategies to win over new consumers while adapting to the expectations of the time, especially by shortening and simplifying preparation. Manufacturers began offering precooked, medium-caliber couscous at the expense of fine semolina, as well as ready-to-eat meals that simply required mixing a variety of reheated ingredients. In 1962, Marseille-based Garbit introduced the first canned couscous. With advertising that played on the stereotypes associated with various Maghreb populations, actors wearing djellabas or turbans and speaking with a pied-noir accent promoted a version of couscous that was both sanitized and folkloric. It was also featured in popular song.

Couscous has been adapted and reinvented through migrations. It is regularly cited as one of France's favorite dishes, and in December 2020 it was awarded heritage status, confirming its success on tables the world over. A competition has been held in Italy since 1997. In 2017 an Angolan team won the prize, and then a Romanian chef was crowned world champion in 2021. Beyond this, a whole range of practices have been recognized. Its image remains associated with conviviality and a certain art of living. For example, during the Marseilles Kouss Kouss festival, participants gather all over the city to share versions proposed by top chefs as well as more humble interpretations alongside "kouss kouss bouillabaisse" or a "kouss'croute." The dish has lent itself to all kinds of culinary fusions.

Aurélia Dusserre

FURTHER READING

Marianne Brisville. "Et le Moyen Âge inventa le couscous." *L'Histoire* 471 (May 2020): 68–71.

A. Cour and C. Pellat. "Kuskusū." In *Encyclopédie de l'islam*, 5:531–32. Leiden: Brill, 1986.

Hélène Franconie, Monique Chastagnet, and François Sigaut, eds. *Couscous, boulgour et polenta: Transformer et consommer les céréales dans le monde.* Paris: Karthala, 2010.

Marin Wagda. "Le couscous: Nouveau plat national du pays de France." *Hommes et migrations* 1205 (January–February 1997): 142–43.

——. "L'histoire d'une migration culinaire." *Hommes et migrations* 1207 (May–June 1997): 163–66.

FURTHER TRAVELING

Chorba, Döner Kebab, Harissa

Curry

In 1747, Englishwoman Hannah Glasse published a recipe in one of her best-selling cookbooks entitled "Making an Indian Curry," echoing a long-standing tradition. Portuguese subjects arriving in India at the end of the fifteenth century had already noted this characteristic and widespread preparation of vegetable or meat dishes in a spicy sauce called *caril* or *caree* (from the Tamil *kari*). Now "currey" or "curry," the word has nothing to do with the Old English "cury" which was used in the title of a famous fourteenth-century recipe book, *The Forme of Cury*, or in modern English *The Book of Cooking*. That term is derived from the Middle French *cuire*, or simply "to cook."

In the sixteenth century the Dutch traveler Jan Huyghen van Linschoten spoke of the use of curry in Goa to cook fish, and the Italian Pietro della Valle described it in the seventeenth century as a broth made with butter, spices, ginger, turmeric, and other condiments. Edward Terry, chaplain to ambassador Sir Thomas Roe in India (1615–19), described the preparation in even greater detail. At the court of the great Mugha, he notes, meat was cut into small cubes, cooked with onions, herbs, roots, ginger, a few spices, and a little sauce, making the food adaptable to all tastes.

This sauce, prepared with different spices depending on the dish, appealed to Western taste buds to the point of raising doubts about the Indian origins of the curry powder now available in grocery stores. Could it be, as some Indian chefs claim, a pure invention of the British? Or simply the result of metropolitan adaptations of Indian culinary practices? One thing is certain: whether Indian, British, or global, its many uses have transformed it so much during its gastronomic journey that it no longer resembles the sauce that Portuguese merchants discovered in the 1490s. Persian influence, through the Mughal emperors, and the introduction of chilis from South America have enriched curry. But the British modified it the most, adapting it to their own tastes. It appealed to some employees of the East India Company who in the eighteenth century also took Hindu or Muslim wives and adopted some of their culinary and sartorial customs. From then on curry became an export commodity in the form of a powdered spice blend: back home, the nabobs, that is, the British who had lived and worked in India and were nostalgic for Indian flavors, grew fond of it. Despite its popularity, curry's conquest of palates was hardly linear. After the great revolt of 1857 against the East India Company, the era of accommodation between the British and Indians ended abruptly. The colonizers took refuge in a preference for canned salmon, jars of peas, and bland English food.

Nevertheless, fending off the taste for curry proved impossible. From then on, curry developed in two culinary worlds with distinct trajectories. When the British added curry powder to their repertoire of chutneys and pickles, Indian reactions to these new culinary practices were ambivalent. In Bengal, the first region exposed to colonization, the appearance of English restaurants and new dishes led to the defense of traditional dishes and a fascination with these new culinary horizons. As a result, curry found its way into Indian recipe books. In 1889 Bipradas Mukhopadhyay, a master of the art, asserted in one of his publications that what the British called Calcutta curry powder—a mixture of coffee, poppy seeds, turmeric, chili, cumin, and salt—was in fact not Indian at all. Europeans, he maintained, learned to cook curry from the Jews, and the Jews from the Muslims. This did not prevent him from proposing lamb curry, egg curry, shrimp curry, and other *firangi* (foreign) curry recipes. The indiscriminate use of the spice was clearly contrary to the delicacy of Bengali dishes. Yet curry powder became an essential ingredient in Anglo-Indian recipes such as mulligatawny soup, a creamy rice with chicken broth, or rice curry, a favorite of British residents.

Indians took it with them on their journeys to the Caribbean, Fiji, Guyana, the Maldives, Mauritius, Surinam, South Africa, and Trinidad. In North America, at the beginning of the twentieth century, the arrival of Sikhs from Punjab in Mexico and Southern California generated the chicken curry enchilada, a blend of Mexican and Punjabi culinary traditions. The name Curry Row, given to a street in Manhattan, New York, marked its culinary consecration. In Great Britain, thanks to Bengali immigrants from the Sylhet region, curries spread beyond small intimate circles; in the 1940s they became popular among students in London, rivaling fish and chips and hot pies. In the 1960s young people also became enthusiastic about curry rice, to be enjoyed with a beer or after a night in the pub. The unsophisticated Madras curry was the new order of the day. The sale of curry paste facilitated its introduction in a wide variety of dishes, with chips, to flavor fruit (*sultanas*) or with cold chicken and mayonnaise. Many ships of the traditionalist Royal Navy even adopted it for their Sunday lunches. More recently, fusion cuisine elevated it to the status of an ethnic alternative.

Elsewhere, curry has taken its place in many traditional dishes. In Germany, currywurst, a spicy curried sausage, has become one of Berlin's signature foods. Japanese *kari pan* is a kind of fried doughnut with a curry filling. In South Africa *bunny chow* is a bread stuffed with curry. It is also used in the preparation of Singapore noodles. What country in the world has not discovered the wonders of curry? Southeast Asia has developed Thai massaman curry or, more surprisingly, Thai curry pizza, and curries from La Réunion, Jamaica, and Nigeria proclaim their identity loud and clear. Imported from England to Japan in the nineteenth century, curry adds flavor to rice as *frog curry* or in little packets. Today curry is to Japan what the hamburger is to the United States.

More recently, curry has returned to India as a British product in an ironic new form of gastronomic imperialism. In 2010 the Taste of Britain festival in Calcutta presented curry as one of fifty typically British dishes at a time when a National Curry Week was being organized in Great Britain and several cities were vying to be recognized as "the curry city," such as London, Newcastle, or Birmingham, proud of their specialty, Balti curry, cooked in a small wok called a *balti*. While curry doesn't claim to have any medicinal virtues, it can be used to help people cope with difficult news, as in the film *The Fish Curry* (2017), directed by Abhishek Verma, where a fish curry, a father's favorite dish, is supposed to help him come to terms with the shock of his son's coming out.

In the face of such adaptations, Indians have reinvested curry with a strong national sentiment, denouncing the forms of dispossession inflicted on them by commercial practices such as the relocation of Basmati rice cultivation to California or the appropriation of turmeric by foreign pharmaceutical companies. Traditional Indian preparations do not use industrial curry powder according to Indian chefs. A real curry is a specific blend, adapted to each dish and used according to precise methods. In India thousands of curries exist, none of which may be likened to the generic powder sold around the world.

In the image of Great Britain, the world has now become "curryholic" far beyond the imperial space throughout which it first spread. Curry's many adaptions have divorced it from national traditions, customary practices, and a specific terroir. Despite calls from Indian chefs to reclaim its authenticity and integrate it into Indian soft power, curry embodies the cross-fertilization at work in a globalized, postcolonial world. Its worldwide success has made it a part of humanity's cultural heritage.

Arundhati Virmani

FURTHER READING

Shrabani Basu. *Curry: The Story of Britain's Favourite Dish*. London: Sutton Publishing, 2004.

Lizzie Collingham. *A Tale of Cooks and Conquerors*. Oxford: Oxford University Press, 2006.

Charlotte Hughes. "For Gourmets and Others, Curry Comes to the Table." *New York Times*, March 12, 1939.

Utsa Ray. *Culinary Culture in Colonial India: A Cosmopolitan Platter and the Middle-Class*. Cambridge: Cambridge University Press, 2015.

Morieda Takashi. "The Unlikely Love Affair with Curry and Rice." *Japan Quarterly* 47, no. 2 (2000): 66–74.

FURTHER TRAVELING

Beer, Chili Pepper, Fish and Chips, Naan, Pepper, Salt, Singapore Noodles, Tikka

Dafina

In his 1980 novel *Parcours immobile*, Edmond Amran El Maleh depicts a scene from the life of his protagonist, a political prisoner under the regime of Hassan II, written as an autobiography: "It was Saturday, and they had brought him a *skhina*.... A *skhina* to please him, since nothing could be more comforting to a Jew. What derision and irony! For a man who had hated it all his life!" *Skhina* is one of the many names given to the emblematic Sephardic Shabbat dish, dafina. Its preparation is adapted to Jewish religious law, which forbids the making of fires from sunset on Friday to nightfall on Saturday, and yet it is recommended that it be eaten hot during this time. It generally consists of meat in pieces or dumplings, vegetables, legumes (white beans or chickpeas), whole eggs cooked in their shells, and spices within a cereal preparation (wheat, barley, or rice). The ingredients are placed with water in an earthen dish, sealed and sent to the traditional oven, where it cooks overnight buried under the embers. It is from this cooking method that the dish takes its generic name, from the Arabic *dafana*, meaning "to hide, bury." This slow cooking of all the elements together, usually with a marrow bone or a veal or beef trotter, gives it a thick, confit-like texture. The ingredients, especially the eggs, turn brown after a night of simmering, providing dafina with its characteristic color.

The origin of dafina is uncertain. The oldest recipe book on the Iberian Peninsula, an anonymous book written in Arabic between the eleventh and thirteenth centuries on the cuisine of Morocco and al-Andalus during the Almohad period, mentions a "hidden stuffed Jewish dish" (*madfūn*) with a similar cooking method. In late medieval Spain, the preparation or consumption of this dish led to recurring criteria mentioned in manuals and instructions of inquisitors to unmask converts who were maintaining their original faith. In 1491 the Inquisition Court in the Castilian town of Soria recorded the deposition of Mari Sánchez: "She said that on certain Saturdays she saw Alfonso Sánchez, her employer, carrying dafina under his coat, and that he ate it alone in his house, and that she saw him do it. And this witness remembers bringing Alfonso Sánchez the said dafina two or three times, which she would pick up from her father, Oroçeta, a Jew, always on Saturdays." The new Christian was thus suspected of secretly "Judaizing" and risked being burned at the stake. From the fifteenth century onward dafina followed the Jews expelled from Spain into exile all around the Mediterranean. In 1528 Francisco Delicado reported its appetizing aroma in the streets of Rome in *La lozana andaluza* (The Kind Andalusian). A newly arrived prostitute converses with her guide, who takes her through the neighborhoods where she practices her trade: "It smells so good here!—Can't you see that everyone here is Jewish, that tomorrow is Saturday and they are preparing dafina? Look at the braziers and the pots sitting on them."

In Algeria and Tunisia spinach and turnips dominated the recipe, while in Morocco potatoes and sweet potatoes became more common after their introduction from South America in the sixteenth century. While mutton was the main meat used in Spain, it was gradually supplanted by beef or veal in the Maghreb, as part of a strategy to distinguish itself from its Muslim neighbors. In Iraq, chicken is cooked in this way, and the Jews of Baghdad who settled in India and Burma from the nineteenth century onward added turmeric. In Yemen millet is used, in Egypt wheatgrass; in Iran lentils and split peas are added to the recipe.

Reflecting this great diversity, there are many different words for the dish. It is also called *adafina* or *skhina* in Morocco; *t'fina* in Algeria, and *t'fina harissa* in Tunisia, where there is a version based on fried spinach and white beans, *pqaïla*, is popular on feast days; *t'bit* in Iraq; *khalebibi* in the Shiraz region of Iran; *ferik* in Egypt; *bourghoul di dfin* in Syria; *gillah* in Yemen; *khamin* in Calcutta; and the list goes on. In the Judeo-Spanish tradition of the Balkans, Eastern Europe, and Turkey the term *hamin*, "hot" in Hebrew, and its derivative *haminiko* are the most widely used. The Yiddish word *tcholent*, used by Ashkenazim to designate a stew prepared according to identical rules, is said to derive from the same Hebrew word, which has passed into Judeo-French *kalente*. Dafina is therefore a diasporic dish par excellence, adapted to the constraints of kashrut and the different regions which have been home to Jewish communities. For centuries it was central to the life of Jews in the Maghreb and the Middle East. An ode attributed to the great master of Andalusian music of the early twentieth century David Iflah, from Essaouira in Morocco, was even composed in its honor, the *qṣida skhina*. The verses in Judeo-Arabic celebrate its virtues: "The scent of its spices and fine saffron and its gold-colored appearance awaken those who suffer."

In the 1950s, at the Grand Arénas camp south of Marseille, employees of the Jewish Agency prepared whole pots of this dish for Shabbat for Jews from the Maghreb, especially Moroccans and Tunisians, en route to the new state of Israel. In this place of transit, where would-be emigrants stayed for weeks, months, or even years, the consumption of this dish was a way of re-creating the atmosphere of the country they had left behind, of re-creating social ties, and no doubt also of maintaining a symbol of continuity in an uncertain migratory journey. The mass exodus of Jews from the Arab and Muslim world, which began in the mid-twentieth century, has created a new geography for dafina. In Israel the dish has become part of the national cuisine, and some restaurants have made a specialty of preparing different types or offering new versions inspired by "fusion cuisine." In South America dafina has been present on the tables of families from northern Morocco, Tangiers, and Tetouan since the late nineteenth century; in Venezuela it even provided the title to a play published in 2002 and regularly performed ever since.

All of this is to suggest that dafina has a long, wide-ranging history. It is still prepared by many families around the world, each with its own recipe. Admittedly, the electric hotplate has replaced the embers of the traditional oven, the metal casserole, and the earthen dish. But dafina has become a true "realm of memory" for Sephardic Jews, who perpetuate the tradition, as well as for some of their former neighbors. In Morocco it is an object of nostalgia for those who remember watching it cook all night in the communal oven, and who brought it to Jewish families returning from the synagogue on Saturday lunchtime, or even smelling it as they passed. Today it is also prepared in many Muslim families. In Spain dafina is sometimes referred to as the "mother of all stews." For their own peace and quiet, the Jewish *conversos* are said to have begun replacing mutton with pork, giving rise to such emblematic dishes of peninsular cuisine as *cocido madrileño* and *olla podrida*.

Claire Marynower

FURTHER READING

Joëlle Bahloul. "Nourritures de l'altérité: Le double langage des juifs algériens en France." *Annales: ESC* 38, no. 2 (1983): 325–40.

Joseph Chetrit. "Délices et fastes sabbatiques: Édition et analyse d'une qasi—da judéo-arabe d'Essaouira/ Mogador sur le repas festif du sabbat." In *Autour de la langue arabe*, ed. Johannes Den Heijer, Paolo La Spisa, and Laurence Tuerlinckx, 87–117. Louvain: Presses Universitaires de Louvain, 2012.

Nathalie Deguigné and Émile Temime. "Le camp du Grand Arénas, l'étape française des émigrants du Maghreb en route vers Israël (1952–1966)." *Archives juives* 41, no. 2 (2008): 34–50.

Gil Marks. *Encyclopedia of Jewish Food*. Hoboken: Wiley, 2010.

Claudia Roden. *Le livre de la cuisine juive*. Paris: Flammarion, 2017.

FURTHER TRAVELING

Couscous, Feijoada, Harissa, Matzah

Dim Sum

According to a sign in the Pearl Pavilion dating from 1745 in the Guangzhou Tea House Association, which is considered the oldest reference to dim sum in the city, this culinary practice dates from the mid-eighteenth century. Teahouses accompanied their tea selections with dim sum. The founding in 1876 of one of the most famous teahouses still in operation, Glorious China, attests to the existence of this custom in the nineteenth-century capital Guangdong.

This Cantonese practice began to flourish in the 1920s–30s. Canton was urbanizing and becoming a hub of national and international trade, in which tea exports were an integral part. The trade favored the birth of a business community in its western districts which provided a ready-made clientele for this type of establishment. And they were not alone. Starting out as simple thatched sheds, teahouses gradually evolved into two- or three-story buildings. The first floor catered to passing workers who enjoyed a glass of tea with two or three simple cakes for a modest price. The rooms on the upper floors were intended for a less hurried and more demanding clientele who preferred higher quality and more choice of both tea and dim sum.

Today, the term *dim sum* is used to describe small, ready-made, steamed or fried bites, popularized and appreciated even beyond the Chinese-speaking world. Though this was not its original meaning. In Canton, Hong Kong, and in the Cantonese world of the Chinese diaspora in Southeast Asia and overseas, dim sum was considered an essential part of the "Cantonese breakfast," served with an infusion of *yamcha* tea (tea drinking). Even today, when one invites friends to share this first meal of the day, one simply says *yumcha dim sum*: "Let's go drink tea and eat dim sum!"

Outside the Maoist period, when restaurants were greatly diminished, the habit of having breakfast in a teahouse continued, especially following a revival in the 1980s. The ritual has become well established, particularly in Hong Kong, the second center of Cantonese food culture. As soon as you cross the threshold of the establishment, the tea you have chosen upon entering (usually pu'er or chrysanthemum) is already brewing in a large teapot on the table. You then select your dim sum by ticking off your preferences on a list printed on detachable sheets in a notebook. If there are many guests, the steam baskets quickly pile up on the table. But there always seems to be room for delicate fried ravioli made from lacy taro dough, or fragile darioles, tarts derived from the Portuguese tradition of *pasteis de nata*, whose recipe was developed to perfection in Canton, and has spread to Hong Kong, Singapore, Australia, and elsewhere. At the very least a decent breakfast should include the best-known of these steamed preparations, such as shrimp ravioli, juicy garlic ribs, famous chicken feet with black beans, bao rolls stuffed with Cantonese roast meat or custard, or sticky rice, stuffed with sweet-tasting pork and wrapped in lotus leaves. The choices are endless, each house serving its own variety.

In the room of Canton's famous Taotaoju one finds customers of all ages and walks of life, dressed simply or elaborately. Everyone seems to be doing as they please: chatting, reading the paper, consulting their cell phones. If teahouses are the place for the first quick, ordinary snack for workers before their daily grind, it is also par excellence the meeting point for the Sunday brunch for families gathered around a teapot and a range of the best dim sum. Since places are limited, Sunday brunch requires a reservation. Although Cantonese cuisine is the most renowned of Chinese cuisines, its repertoire does not in principle include dim sum specialties, which are enjoyed only as an accompaniment to tea for the first meal of the day. In this context they are designed solely for the pleasure of *yamcha* tasting. In this sense, they stand in stark contrast to the nourishing everyday diet of cereal-based, generally rice, menus of southern China.

The opposition between the need for formal meals and gourmet pleasure has blurred with the evolution of eating practices in China since the 2000s and the extraordinary spread of dim sum, now on the menu of restaurants in major cities around the world. The evolution began in China itself. Some of Guangzhou's best-known establishments, such as Dim Dou Dak, have responded to foreign tourist demand by offering the service any time of day. Dim sum has become distinct and is now eaten in lieu of a rice-based meal. It now forms part of an ordinary menu. Tea has also lost some of its importance in these meals, since herbal infusions are increasingly part of a more refined consumption in other venues.

Parallel to this evolution in southern China, small preparations, called dim sum in Cantonese, are known as *dianxin* in Mandarin. They are also part of a specific commercial tradition that has a long history in eastern coastal towns. In central and northern China *dianxin* has come to signify indulgence with no other purpose than pure gourmet pleasure, in contrast to ordinary grain-based meals. As such, these hand-eaten morsels or pastries are eaten any time of the day, even outside of mealtimes. Each region has its own set of offerings, shaped by local flavors. These little snacks are sometimes the local specialties that people bring back as souvenirs from their travels.

The fact remains that the Cantonese concept of dim sum has overtaken that of *dianxin* in culinary circles the world over. Dim sum has sparked the imagination of creative chefs in China and elsewhere who improve their compositions by adding vegetable colorings, noble ingredients such as truffles, or more unusual ingredients such as chocolate. These innovations are recent, and the dim sum boom in Paris, for example, dates back to only the 2010s, when it was recognized by gastronomic critics and even attracted the attention of the Michelin guide. While a few Chinese restaurants serving Cantonese cuisine in Paris have long had a dim sum menu for an amateur clientele, dim sum has now spread throughout the city to the point where some have made it their sole specialty, offering customers inventive tasting menus at all price points.

Paris restaurants are not alone in exploiting this vein. Similar menus can be found in Los Angeles, Tokyo, London, Berlin, Sydney, and Singapore. While many establishments remain faithful to the established list of dim sum, more or less inspired by Cantonese versions, others concoct various small dishes or ravioli, simply calling them dim sum. The original ritual has clearly been lost. Other establishments are careful to respect a certain tradition, sometimes beautifully reinvented, such as London-based Ding Song Dim Sum, which sells takeaway "dim sum boxes." These charming kits include an assortment of dim sum to be cooked, accompanied by their sauce, as well as a biodegradable steamer basket enabling you to prepare an authentic meal in less than thirty minutes. Like all culinary fashions, dim sum's popularity may be short-lived, but the name has entered the culinary vocabulary of Western languages and has found its way into most dictionaries, even if the definition varies widely from one lexicon to another. It refers to classic preparations in the tradition of Cantonese-style "breakfast," or, on the contrary, draws on the trend of aperitifs that have become so popular with young people, who compare these "small portions of sweet and savory, steamed, fried or baked culinary preparations" to Spanish tapas or the unpretentious finger foods that have now become so popular around the world.

Françoise Sabban

FURTHER READING

Sea-ling Cheng. "Eating Hong Kong's Way Out." In *Asian Food: The Global to the Local*, ed. Katarzyna J. Cwiertka and Boudewijn Walraven, 16–33. Honolulu: University of Hawai'i Press, 2001.

Jakob Akiba Klein. "Reinventing the Traditional Guangzhou Teahouse: Caterers, Customers and Cooks in Post-Socialist Urban South China." PhD dissertation, School of Oriental and African Studies, University of London, 2004.

J. A. G. Roberts. *China to Chinatown: Chinese Food in the West*. London: Reaktion Books, 2002.

David Y. H. Wu and Sidney C. H. Cheung. *The Globalization of Chinese Food*. Richmond, UK: Curzon Press, 2002.

FURTHER TRAVELING

Chili Pepper, Food Coloring and Preservatives, Singapore Noodles, Soy Sauce, Tea and Chai

Dogmeat

In April 2020 an employee of a Canadian clothing brand posted on social networks a photograph of a T-shirt design entitled "Bat Fried Rice." On the back of the T-shirt, a Chinese takeaway food box, complete with bat wings, carried the inscription "No Thank You"; on the other side was a pair of Chinese chopsticks with wings. At a time when the SARS-CoV-2 epidemic was causing an explosion of Sinophobic stereotypes and violence in the United States in the spring of 2020, this was far from an isolated attack on Chinese cuisine. Suspected of originating from the Wuhan animal market—where bats and pangolins remained the prime suspects for the transmission of the coronavirus to humans for several months—the pandemic immediately reactivated a long-standing mistrust based on tenacious myths.

These myths can be traced back to at least the sixteenth century. In 1614 the Portuguese Fernão Mendes Pinto published his *Peregrinaçam*, written between 1569 and 1578, based on his travels in Asia. In particular, he described the work of Chinese butchers cutting, salting, and smoking "ham, pork, bacon, ducks, geese" and then, in an increasingly fanciful enumeration, "cranes, bustards, ostriches, game, beef, buffalo, tapir, yak, horse, tiger, dog, fox, and the meat of every other species of animal that exists on earth."

In the travel narratives that became popular in the sixteenth century, food became a recurring motif, and human societies were gradually distributed along a scale of civilization descending from the European table to cannibalism, the suspicion of which accompanied European explorers around the world. In the second half of the eighteenth century, as growing Sinophobia pushed China further and further down this ladder of human civilization, the caricature of China's strange foods took hold in Western imaginations. The same descriptions of swallows' nests, sharks' fins, cats, dogs, rats, and sea cucumbers were tirelessly copied from book to book. This was true to such an extent that sinologist Jean-Pierre Abel-Rémusat denounced this shameless plagiarism in his "Lettres sur le régime des lettrés de la Chine" (Letters on the Diet of Chinese Scholars), published in 1843 in his posthumous *Mémoires*, before concluding playfully "that reheated dinners were always horrible." It is worth noting that the development of these caricatured accounts is not unrelated to the state of Sino-Western relations at the beginning of the nineteenth century. Until the 1842 Treaty of Nanking anyone wishing to trade in Canton had to play by the rules of the game set by the Qing dynasty to win the good graces of their Chinese interlocutors. The fear of having to taste dishes that one often struggled to identify at the table, lest one offend one's hosts, fed fantasies about Chinese eating habits.

One of these habits was particularly shocking: eating dogmeat. With the growing attention paid to animal sentience from the eighteenth century onward, the violence inflicted on man's best friend became increasingly unacceptable to European elites. The Royal Society for the Prevention of Cruelty to Animals was founded in England in 1824, and in France in 1845 it was renamed the Société Protectrice des Animaux (Society for Animal Protection). Over the course of the century laws were progressively passed to punish mistreatment of domestic animals, which were increasingly seen as an integral part of the family—do dogs not mourn their deceased masters, as edifying anecdotes so often suggest? After cannibalism, eating dogs became the ultimate dietary transgression and a veritable stigma associated with the Chinese population. The military attaché of the Chinese legation in France, Chen Jitong, better known under the name of General Tcheng Ki Tong, his pen name for his many amusing books on China in the last decades of the century, made several efforts to dispel this stereotype, from which he himself had suffered. When the first permanent Chinese legation was set up in Paris in 1878, a Polish countess, who lived next door to the legation and "kept a dozen little Chinese dogs in her house [which she] loved madly," reportedly informed her suspicious neighbors "that if she lost one of her dogs, she would set fire to the legation's hotel."

Against this tenacious prejudice, Chen Jitong points to the geographical and social richness and diversity of Chinese gastronomy. Though perhaps he goes a little too far when he claims that in China he had never "known or seen anyone eat cat or dog." Certain dogs are still bred for culinary purposes today, and the consumption of dogmeat is attested as far back as antiquity. In the form of soup (*geng*) or stew (*peng*) under the Zhou dynasty, dogmeat was a food even worthy of consumption by the Son of Heaven or emperor. According to the *Liji*, the sovereign must eat dog in autumn. It also appears in ancient medical treatises. Fragment 22 of the *Huang Di nei jing su wen*, a medical compilation attributed to the mythical Yellow Emperor, who lived in the third millennium BCE, recommends eating sour foods for heart disease: beans, plums, shallots, and dogmeat. Of the many uses of the dog in these ancient times, which also included hunting and ritual sacrifice, the only one to be ethically condemned was as a pet. Feeding a dog for the simple pleasure of its company was in fact a luxury denounced by authors during the Warring Kingdoms (between the fifth and second centuries BCE), who criticized the expensive lifestyle of the elite, particularly in times of famine.

What a contrast with the Dogs and Cats Regulations passed in Hong Kong in 1950, when the British colony banned the sale and consumption of dog and cat meat! This was the culmination of two centuries of attempts to establish European dietary practices and sensibilities in southern China, which began as early as the eighteenth century, when merchants from European charter companies tried to import and cultivate Western foods in Canton and Macao, and to adapt Chinese cuisine to their tastes and dislikes. It was no coincidence, moreover, that these efforts to reproduce tables close to European standards in southern China coincided with the development of Chinese food myths. Since the end of the fifteenth century, fear of the dangers of Europeans tasting local cuisines has focused anxious attention on such concerns, while at the same time stimulating food imports from Europe. This distrust persisted into the nineteenth century, with non-European foods being blamed for death, degeneracy, and indigenization. Such suspicion was not shared by all, however. As they discovered, contrary to stereotypes focused mainly on animal foods, that most Chinese were vegetarians or close to it, some doctors attributed the extraordinary resistance of Chinese populations to infection and climate to their diet. The vegetarian movement that emerged in Europe during the nineteenth century even advocated using it as a model for reforming Western dietary practices by the turn of the twentieth century.

Beware, then, of being misled by the apparent linearity of this story, which at first glance seems to run from Fernão Mendes Pinto to bat fried rice. From travel accounts to press articles, the same stories have been reproduced and the same stereotypes perpetuated from century to century. These food myths nonetheless reconfigure and change status as sensibilities, medical theories, and the modalities of Western presence in China evolve, and as Europe's conviction that it is the sole measure of civilization wanes.

Clément Fabre

FURTHER READING

Rebecca Earle. "'If You Eat Their Food . . .': Diets and Bodies in Early Colonial Spanish America." *American Historical Review* 115, no. 3 (2010): 688–713.

Lisa Hellman. *This House Is Not a Home: European Everyday Life in Canton and Macao, 1730–1830.* Leiden: Brill, 2019.

Thomas O. Höllmann. *The Land of the Five Flavors: A Cultural History of Chinese Cuisine.* Trans. Karen Margolis. New York: Columbia University Press, 2014.

Olivia Milburn. "Confucius and His Dog: Perspectives on Animal Ownership in Early Chinese Ritual and Philosophical Texts." 漢學 研究 (Chinese Studies) 29, no, 4 (2011): 289–315.

Victoria Vanneau. *Le chien: Histoire d'un objet de compagnie.* Paris: Autrement, 2014.

FURTHER TRAVELING

Hedgehog Stew

Döner Kebab

The first known photograph of a döner kebab in the Ottoman Empire was taken in 1855 by James Robertson, chief engraver at the Imperial Ottoman Mint. It shows a wandering cook waiting for his customers, roasting his meat on his mobile counter. The word *döner* means "turning" or "that turns" in Turkish. In Europe, the döner kebab, also known as gyros (in Greek) or shawarma (in Arabic, a word derived from the Turkish *çevirme*), consists of stacked pieces of meat placed on a spit in the shape of an inverted cone that turns on itself and is slowly grilled over a wood fire, or now more commonly in a turning gas or electric rotisserie. The outer layer of mutton, lamb, or veal is then cut into thin slices as the cooking continues.

Döner is a kind of kebab—the term actually refers to a preferred method of cooking all types of meat, directly over the fire, without adding water. According to Ottoman cookbooks there were two different ways of making kebab in the eighteenth and nineteenth centuries. Pieces of meat, mutton, poultry, and even game birds could be roasted on skewers over a charcoal fire. But kebabs could also be cooked in the oven or in a pan. The döner technique did not appear in cookbooks until the 1880s. In fact, the origins of the döner remains unclear. The first reference to the dish can be found in Evliya Çelebi's *Seyahatname*. The famous Ottoman traveler noted that in 1666, in the Crimea, he ate a type of horizontal roast kebab made by the Tatars: "They slaughter a whole fat sheep, then cut all the meat into pieces and skewer them so that they are thick in the center and thin at both ends. That way they do not fall off. Then a wagon wheel is broken off and placed under the kebab, which cooks as this piece of wood slowly burns away." This type of kebab has survived to the present day in northeastern Anatolia, notably in Artvin, Kerkük, Yusufeli, and Erzurum. It is the dish of choice for outdoor picnics.

To this day, two Turkish towns vie for the invention of the döner kebab on a vertical rotating spit: Kastamonu, where the famous cooking is attested in 1855, thanks to a cook named Hamdi Usta, and Bursa, in the 1880s, where İskender Efendi worked. However, Robertson's photograph and a color engraving of a döner kebab roaster demonstrate that Istanbul could also lay claim to the title. European travelers' accounts also report that döner kebab has existed in various cities since at least the second half of the nineteenth century. According to Eugène-Jacques Chesnel (known as Kesnin Bey), in Istanbul in the 1880s, mutton was grilled on small skewers (*şiş kebab*) or roasted on a vertical skewer and was called *deunèl kebab*. *La Maîtresse*, a cookbook published in Istanbul in 1883, describes the same dish as "kebab d'Izmir." Another English traveler attests to kebab cooked on a vertical rotating spit in Amasya (a town in northwest Anatolia) around 1915.

The arrival of the döner in Europe is full of legend. A young Turkish émigré, Mehmet Aygün, is said to have introduced it to Berlin in 1971, where he served the grilled meat in a pita with sauce. The story is undoubtedly more complex and follows the major waves of migration. The first spread of döner outside the Ottoman Empire began in the 1920s with the arrival of Anatolian Greeks in France. From the 1930s onward they opened restaurants offering döner kebabs, which took the Greek name of gyros. Following the first bilateral labor agreement between Turkey and Germany (in 1961), followed by France, Belgium and the Netherlands, hundreds of Turkish workers arrived in Europe. Turkish immigrants launched fast-food kebab restaurants. Small restaurants (called *Dönerbuden*) sprang up, particularly in Germany, and especially in Kreuzeberg, Berlin's Turkish quarter, where they began selling döner. Between the 1980s and 1990s the number of kebab shops run by Turkish immigrants grew remarkably in Germany, but also in France, Belgium, Holland, and England.

Initially eaten mainly by Turks, döner kebab fast became a popular fast-food dish. Served as a sandwich filled with strips of grilled meat (lamb, veal, or chicken), garnished with salad, tomatoes, onion, and various sauces (yogurt, harissa, or even hummus) and accompanied by French fries, it has become a sought-after dish. Originating in Ottoman cuisine and representing the Turkish identity in Germany and Europe, it has been denationalized. The final stage in the spread of kebab around the world came with the Lebanese, who introduced it under the name of shawarma to South America and Africa. In Mexico, the döner "*al pastor*" (literally "of the shepherd") is a kind of corn-based taco tortilla filled with grilled pork, and sometimes a sandwich made with flat bread (called *pan arabe)*. The pork, marinated in a blend of spices, chili, pineapple juice and sometimes achiote, captures local Mexican tastes.

Once handcrafted in small batches of twenty or thirty kilos (44–66 lbs.) and slow-roasted over a charcoal fire, döner has become a quasi-industrial fast food dish adapted to local tastes. The meat is marinated with salt, spices, onions, milk, or yogurt and placed on the spit. Originally made with mutton, it is now combined with beef, while modern variants include chicken, turkey, or pork. Produced in the form of long oval blocks of meat weighing between twenty and two hundred kilos (44–441 lbs.), industrial manufacturers now produce up to several thousand tons a day in Europe, mainly in Germany. All over the world they supply small döner restaurants run by Turks, Kurds, Armenians, Greeks, Cypriots, Lebanese, and Iranians. The affordable price of kebabs makes them ideal for small budgets (students and workers). Döners also have a practical dimension since they can be eaten quickly in the street and adapted to different palates thanks to their many variations. They have become a best-seller in a globalized world of taste.

Özge Samancı

FURTHER READING

Ayşe S. Çağlar. "Mc Kebap: Döner Kebap and the Social Positioning Struggle of German Turks." In *Changing Food Habits: Case Studies from Africa, Latin America and Europe*, ed. Carola Lentz, 263–83. New York: Gordon and Breach, 1998.

Musa Dağdeviren. "Dönerin Fırıldağı Nereye Dönüyor." *Yemek ve Kültür* 19 (2010): 108–31.

Stéphane de Tapia. "De Berlin à la conquête du monde: L'irrésistible expansion du döner kebab." *Anthropology of the Middle East* 15, no. 2 (2020): 194–204.

Priscilla Mary Işin. "Döner Kebabın Geçmişi." In *Osmanlı'da Mimari, Sanat ve Yemek Kültürü*, ed. Mükerrem B. Zülfikar-Aydın and Ravza Aydın, 337–57. Istanbul: Osamer, 2018.

Pierre Raffard. "Döner Universel." *Alternatives Internationales* 15 (May 2014). https://www.alternatives-economiques.fr/ doner-universel/00076236.

FURTHER TRAVELING

Chili Pepper, French Fries, Harissa, Hummus, Salt, Sandwich, Yogurt

Feijoada

In 1977, the young songwriter Chico Buarque wrote a samba entitled "Feijoada completa" (Complete Feijoada) for the soundtrack of Hugo Carvana's comedy filmed in Rio, *Se segura, malandro!* (Be sure, punk!). The malandro, a common figure in the Brazilian social imaginary, is a man of many tricks. The film's broad popular appeal was captured in the song from the soundtrack: the malandro asks his wife to hurry up and prepare a feijoada for the many friends invited for dinner.

> Woman
> You're going to fry
> Lots of rind to accompany
> The white rice, farofa, and chili
> The orange-*baía* or *seleta*
> Throw the sausage, dried meat, and bacon into the pot
> And we'll add water to the black beans.

In these lyrics, alongside their share of sexism, the spirit of camaraderie and festivity of feijoada is brilliantly embodied, reflecting the dish's popular and traditional origins. This has also generated the figurative meaning of feijoada in Portuguese, which is synonymous with festive gathering, confusion, or disorder.

Each of the song's stanzas details the many long stages involved in preparing feijoada, which brings together ingredients dating from the arrival of the first settlers in America. For it was the circulation of animal and plant species hitherto unknown on either side of the Atlantic that gave rise to this dish, which was to become a symbol of Brazil in the twentieth century.

Farofa refers to manioc flour. It is a term of Tupi origin used to describe a variety of root vegetables, the consumption of which is the result of centuries of domestication. After harvesting, manioc must be peeled and grated and the toxic juice squeezed out before cooking. As early as the sixteenth century the Portuguese colonists adopted farofa as a substitute for bread-making cereals; they also used it to feed the slaves forcibly transported from Africa to work on the plantations. Black beans, also of American origin, were consumed by the Tupi-Guarani tribes, as attested by Jean de Léry, who visited Guanabara Bay in 1557–58. Feijão (beans), whose nutritive virtues and preservative properties were equally appreciated by the Portuguese, was a key foodstuff in the conquest of the interior, the *sertões* of Brazil. As for rice, the cultivation of which was introduced by the Portuguese, it wasn't until the twentieth century that it became a staple food. Finally, meat, so important in guaranteeing the flavor and creaminess of feijão, followed the introduction of pig and beef to America by the colonists.

It was in Recife and Rio de Janeiro, capital of imperial Brazil (1822–89), that hotel restaurants published the first advertisements in daily newspapers informing readers that they were serving feijoada. In 1853 an advertisement informed Rio residents that a restaurant would be serving "a good feijoada cooked in the Brazilian style" every Thursday lunchtime, to distinguish it from the Portuguese feijoadas, the stews of white or red beans cooked with meat that were served at restaurant tables in Lisbon or Porto. Other ads suggest that the dish was eaten with *cachaça* (a drink made from fermented sugarcane) or accompanied by a cigar, proof that the feijoada is an atypical meal, long and festive, that breaks with everyday meals, as is the case in Chico Buarque's samba. Later in the century, with the first democratization of the press, hotels and restaurants vied with each other to attract clients for this robust dish. In 1881, the *Revista illustrada* reported on the new fashion for eating feijoada on Thursdays in the province of Rio de Janeiro, as was the case, for example, at the Colegio Pedro II, a renowned public establishment in the capital. From then on there were numerous references to feijoada in the press that were presented as "complete," "Brazilian-style," "tasty," "healthy," "famous," or "appetizing."

The diversity of recipes, depending on the quantity and quality of meat used, makes feijoada a dish to be enjoyed by all, as the American Elizabeth Cary Agassiz noted in her 1865 travelogue. A favorite of hotel and restaurant guests in Rio, feijoada is also a poor man's and a slave's dish, still most often eaten by hand, by mixing cooked feijão and farofa into a thick paste. As a famous columnist for Rio's *Gazeta de noticias* noted, the dish thus acquired a strong identity, its reputation comparable to that of the most famous verses by the poet Gonçalves Dias, where the romanticism of Brazilian identity is echoed in gastronomy. Also in 1877, the *Revista illustrada* published a series of drawings on Emperor Peter II's visit to the pope. The two are seated over a feijoada and a plate of "macaroni," and the cartoonist hopes that the emperor will have demonstrated "the superiority of a good feijoada."

Although feijoada had already won a place on the tables of imperial society by the nineteenth century, it was not until the following century that a legend suggested that it originated in the huts of slaves in colonial times, where they may have taken up the habit of cooking the meat left behind by their masters with black beans accompanied by farofa. Slaves rarely had access to fresh meat, and the less desirable parts of the pig, such as ears, tails and feet, were highly prized by the Portuguese masters. Was this a myth meant to attenuate the legacy of slavery in the 1930s when Brazil, under the impetus of Getúlio Vargas, finally recognized itself as a country of mixed race? At the same time, feijoada was elevated to the status of "national dish," embodying the ideal of "racial democracy" so dear to anthropologist Gilberto Freyre, symbolized here by the meeting of white (rice) and black (beans).

The dish is made not only in Brazil. It can be found in different recipes in Portugal and Portuguese colonial countries, such as Mozambique and Angola ("Feijoada de Luanda"), as well as in Cape Verde, where *cachupa* is a bean and corn-based dish garnished with vegetables, banana, or fish. It has nonetheless contributed to the international promotion of an exoticized image of Brazil. Like carnival, capoeira, and samba, feijoada reflects a way of life of which Rio, although stripped of its status as capital in 1960, remains the finest incarnation. For at least a century, feijoada has been a typical dish served in Brazilian restaurants around the world, as part of the Brazilian diaspora.

However, in a society still deeply marked by inequality and discrimination, feijoada can also be a mark of resistance, even of negritude, because it is associated with slavery. At the end of the 1990s, filmmakers founded the Dogme Feijoada group to defend the legitimacy of "black Brazilian cinema." The aim was to counter "European dogma," still dominant on big and small screens behind the facade of a mixed-race, inclusive Brazil that this dish symbolizes.

Sébastien Rozeaux

FURTHER READING

Luís da Câmara Cascudo. *História da alimentação no Brasil.* 2 vols. São Paulo: Ed. Itatiaia/Ed. da Universidade de São Paulo, 1983.

Amir El Kareh. *A vitória da feijoada.* Niterói: Ed. da Universidade Federal Fluminense, 2012.

Rodrigo Elias. "Breve história da feijoada." *Revista nossa história* 4 (2004): 33–39.

Jane Fajans. *Brazilian Food: Race, Class and Identity in Regional Cuisines.* New York: Berg, 2012.

Olivia Ware Terenzio. "Feijoada and Hoppin' John: Dishing the African Diaspora in Brazil and the United States." *Southern Cultures* 25, no. 4 (2019): 158–75.

FURTHER TRAVELING

Cassoulet, Chili Pepper, Noodles and Macaroni, Rum

Fish and Chips

On September 26, 1968, the British Minister of Agriculture, Fisheries, and Food presented a plaque to Denis Malin, recognized by the National Federation of Fish and Chip Vendors as the owner of the oldest fish and chip shop, said to have opened in London's East End in 1860. A Lancashire man attending the ceremony protested loudly. According to his account, the oldest store in the trade was Lee's, in Mossley, near Manchester. Dundee, Scotland, and Dublin, Ireland also claimed paternity. In reality no one really knew, and the dispute reflected above all the importance of the famous dish in British culture, a prominence examined by historians John K. Walton and Panikos Panayi.

This controversy over the origins of fish and chips is partly due to its composite nature. Fish has been eaten in Britain for thousands of years. Cod caught in the cold waters of the North Atlantic was at the heart of the first imperial expansion in the seventeenth century. In 1781 a famous cookbook by Hannah Glasse mentioned frying as a Jewish technique for preserving cod or salmon. Charles Dickens, in his novel *Oliver Twist* (1838), describes a London alleyway with its barber, café, beer garden, and fish and chips store. Victorian transformations made fresh fish widely available. By midcentury the railroads made it possible to bring goods overnight from coastal ports to London and other major cities. The second half of the nineteenth century saw the rise of shops selling fresh fish as well as salted fish. But the dish would not be complete without potatoes. Potatoes were first cultivated in Ireland before making inroads into Great Britain in the early nineteenth century as the price of potatoes fell and the price of wheat rose. Chips, probably imported from France and Belgium, began to be eaten around midcentury. It is possible that the frying of potatoes evolved

FISH AND CHIPS 117

simultaneously in these countries. That said, "chips" are thicker than their Continental counterpart "french fries" and when served with fish are seasoned with vinegar.

The two products became street food staples and in the last quarter of the century, stores began to offer them together: fish and chips were born. The popularity of fish and chips among the working classes was spectacular. By 1888 there were already ten thousand to twelve thousand distributors in the country. By 1913 there were 25,000, consuming at least a quarter of the fish caught at sea. The golden age of the profession was undoubtedly between the world wars when most industrial towns could boast at least one shop on every street. In 1917 a working-class town like Bradford had 303 stores. By 1927 the industry had formed a national federation boasting 35,000 shops and publishing its own journal, the *Fish Friers' Review*.

Fish and chips became a staple of the working-class diet and an object of condescension in bourgeois circles, who saw its success as a reflection of the working classes' inability to cook. It remains a simple dish, made with just five ingredients (oil, potatoes, flour, fish, and water). Because of the large quantity of oil required to prepare it, it is eaten mainly away from home. It can be bought in stores and, from the interwar years onward, in restaurants. Inexpensive, the fact that it was filling was long considered an asset before the days of obesity epidemics and the fight against fried foods. Its one thousand calories and fifty grams (1.75 oz.) of fat per portion did not help.

Cod remained the king ingredient of fish and chips. Its high price has led some sellers to fall back on haddock, pollock, whiting, dogfish, skate, or plaice. Behind its British identity, fish and chips is at the crossroads of a certain globalization. The fish is caught in the North Atlantic, off Norway or even Russia, and the potatoes are generally homegrown. The oils, such as Egyptian cottonseed or palm oil, are often imported, while the packaging is often made in China. Fish and chips also offer a market for lower-quality flours and eggs used for breading.

Fish and chips were widely exported. Its rise coincided with massive British emigration, particularly to the United States and the Empire. Since the 1930s fish and chips have been consumed in Canada, Australia, New Zealand, and South Africa. Between the wars, it also spread to the European continent, including Germany. The Harry Ramsden's chain opened stores in Hong Kong, Singapore, and the Persian Gulf. In Scandinavia, Paris, Turkey, and Spain, fish and chips were sold as a British specialty, with its name often written in English. In Singapore, Japan, Vietnam, and India, pomfret fish often replaced cod, served with pepper and chili sauce.

In the space of a few decades fish and chips supplanted roast beef, which had hitherto embodied British cuisine. In 2019 a poll, admittedly commissioned by British Fisheries, showed that 85 percent of people considered it a national dish, far ahead of chicken tikka masala (4 percent). This symbolic construction dates to the 1950s. It may be attributed in some ways to the poverty of Britain's culinary heritage.

After World War II the consumption of fish and chips seemed to decelerate. Today, the National Federation of Fish and Chip Vendors claims UK sales of £1.2 billion and 10,500 sellers. This figure is difficult to verify, for it is now common for the same shop to sell fish and chips and other takeaways at the same time. However, while the trend is toward concentration of the sector around chains, overall volumes are far from declining. Since the end of the nineteenth century fish and chips have enabled many people with limited capital and ordinary culinary skills to acquire financial security and social mobility. Over the past half century, Cypriot and Turkish kebabs, as well as Chinese and Indian takeaways, have replicated the model established by fish and chips.

In recent decades it has found itself at the heart of several political conflicts. Between 1958 and 1976, several "cod wars" pitted Iceland, which wanted to extend its territorial waters, against the United Kingdom, whose trawlers fished Iceland's rich waters. In the early 1970s the Royal Navy was mobilized, several collisions occurred at sea, and a British trawler was boarded. The conflict, which resulted in one death, laid the foundations for the notion of an "exclusive economic zone," formalized in 1982. Fish and chips also found themselves at the heart of debates on Brexit, the agreement for which was sealed in 2019: How could British fishermen continue to catch cod big enough to fry if the Europeans raided their seas? While fishing counts for little economically, it was an important symbolic issue in the divorce negotiations between the European Union and the United Kingdom.

Finally, fish and chips have been mobilized in debates on immigration and multiculturalism. When in 2008 Panikos Panayi explained that this national symbol was undoubtedly the result of a marriage between a Jewish preparation of fish and a Belgian or French cooking of potatoes, he was attacked by a far-right website as an enemy from within. Thus, this dish of foreign import, which became part of working-class cuisine, and ultimately of all Britons, has been the centerpiece of a political battle. Its history, though still relatively short, reminds us that the identity of a dish and its modes of consumption, even when they seem fixed, are constantly being reinvented.

Fabrice Bensimon

FURTHER READING

Mark Kurlansky. *Cod: A Biography of the Fish That Changed the World*. New York: Penguin Books, 1998.
National Federation of Fish Friers website: https://www.nfff.co.uk/.
Panikos Panayi. *Fish and Chips: A History*. London: Reaktion Books, 2014.
John K. Walton. *Fish and Chips and the British Working Class, 1870–1940*. Leicester: Leicester University Press, 1992.

FURTHER TRAVELING

Beer, Chili Pepper, Döner Kebab, French Fries, Mayonnaise, Palm Oil, Pepper

Fish Sauce (Nuoc Mam)

The first Vietnamese restaurant opened in France in 1889 at the Paris World's Fair. It was an ephemeral restaurant offering visitors a chance to discover the culinary subtleties of the French colonies of Indochina. Since then, Vietnamese cuisine has spread across the world, with nuoc mam gracing supermarket shelves from Seoul to California. It is the Vietnamese condiment of choice among the many fish brines and pastes used in Asian cuisine for cooking, sauces, and garnishes. Obtained by fermenting fish and/or shellfish, these preparations are particularly useful for making up for the lack of animal proteins in Asian peasant diets, which are largely dominated by cereals and legumes. They play a role similar to salt in the imaginations and practices of consumers, a vital ingredient whose absence is tantamount to deprivation. Nuoc mam and its Cambodian (*tek trei*), Thai (*nam pla*), or Malay (*kecap*) avatars were not initially developed for export. Brown in color, with a pronounced odor, they repelled Westerners who conquered Southeast Asia from the sixteenth to the twentieth century. In Indochina, nuoc mam represented indigenous food par excellence in the eyes of the colonists, while the Vietnamese, Cambodians, and Laotians compared the rejection of nuoc mam in French kitchens to their disgust for cheese. Like durian, nuoc mam embodies the extremes of the spectrum of olfactory and gustatory sensibilities: the former is still forbidden on public transport in many postcolonial societies in Southeast Asia; as for the latter, Vietnamese refugees in the 1980s sometimes prefer to substitute it with Maggi sauce or soy sauce lest its scent upset their French, American, or Australian neighbors.

The story of the globalization of nuoc mam began in 1915. The General Government of Indochina had the brine shipped from Saigon to supply metropolitan France. It was deemed essential to the diet of the 93,000 Indochinese soldiers and workers called up to serve in World War I. With peace restored, from Cochinchina to Marseille, nuoc mam traveled even more as the flow of migrants from Indochina intensified. In particular, bottles of nuoc mam made by craftsmen or early industrial producers were carried in the luggage of the 5,000 Indochinese soldiers stationed in Europe and North Africa, and the 2,500 workers, sailors, servants, and students—mainly Vietnamese—living in France. While they frequented the capital's Chinese restaurants, the Vietnamese also set up their own supply networks for Asian products. Anticolonial activist Tran Le Luat, who came as a laborer during World War I, became a trader in exotic products. He used his store in Paris to host political meetings of Vietnamese associations and parties in France. He sold nuoc mam and distributed newspapers and leaflets on his rounds, particularly among Vietnamese riflemen.

Among those Indochinese servants who moved between the metropolis and Asia, it was the cooks who contributed to spreading nuoc mam across Western dining tables. Trained in French cuisine in Indochina, they also offered to cook "Chinese," by which they meant "Vietnamese." After rejecting it, however, Westerners then rediscovered and adopted this condiment as they acclimatized to the colonies. Chinese (*ke-tsiap*) and Malay (*kecap*) fish sauces were distant relatives of ketchup, the famous tomato sauce, having been adapted to the palates of the British in North America. As for nuoc mam, it has become the marker of a mixed Franco-Indochinese identity and gastronomy. In metropolitan France, its consumption has become a colonial Proustian madeleine. Nuoc mam figured prominently in the cuisine of the French novelist Marguerite Duras, who was born in Vietnam in 1914 and moved to France in 1933. In the 1920s and 1930s, Indochinese cooks were also employed by the many Americans living in Paris. Some Vietnamese chefs also tried their luck in the United States. Across the Pacific, Vietnamese workers made their way to New Caledonia. Although still modest in scale, nuoc mam is already making its way around the world.

From national product to cosmopolitan condiment, nuoc mam has followed in the footsteps of the Vietnamese diaspora from the twentieth to the twenty-first century, consisting of 4.5 million people in 2018. The wars in Indochina (1946–54) and Vietnam (1965–75) and then the tragedies of reunification drove them into exile. The Vietnamese used nuoc mam to enhance the dishes of the countries to which they had fled and to adapt to new culinary cultures. The Franco-Vietnamese families repatriated from Indochina and billeted after 1955 in Noyant d'Allier, Auvergne, gradually converted their Bourbonnais and Polish neighbors to the subtleties of nuoc mam. Vietnamese women have been

FISH SAUCE (NUOC MAM)

particularly active in perpetuating their culinary traditions. The trade in exotic products, catering businesses, and restaurants all popularized nuoc mam among Western audiences. They relied on their transnational support networks, their expertise in the food trade, and their ability to innovate in foreign lands. In the 1960s Vietnamese restaurants sprang up near American military bases where soldiers of the South Vietnamese army were trained. American, Korean, and Australian servicemen and women, as well as journalists, came to these restaurants to nostalgically rediscover the flavors of the front lines. Later, in the 1980s, North American, European, and Australian metropolises saw the opening of restaurants run by refugees. Out of a million displaced Vietnamese, 110,000 arrived in Canada, and Montreal's Côte-des-Neiges district became a veritable little Vietnam. Popularized by city dwellers thanks to their affordable prices, fast service, and fresh produce, Vietnamese restaurants soon won over young workers, who were in a hurry but also concerned about their diets and curious for new taste experiences. Proud of their gastronomy, the Vietnamese used food to create social and economic opportunities in their host societies. In the 1990s Vietnamese businesses—like their Chinese predecessors—became key players in small and medium-scale distribution in the Indian Ocean, Oceania, the Caribbean, the West Indies, and French Guiana, where they even spread into distant rural areas.

As for nuoc mam, however, it has long been necessary to rely on substitute products. Indeed, the most popular brines in international trade—in Asian grocery stores from the 1980s onward, and today in supermarkets—are made in Thailand. Less salty, with a less pronounced taste and a lighter color, *nam pla* has all the qualities of nuoc mam without some of its drawbacks, and it has served as a link between all the diasporas of Asia and the Pacific. It is in this industrial form, with the addition of lemon, vinegar, and spices, that this condiment has become a success in international cuisine, which initially associated it with eggrolls and retained its Vietnamese name. It has recently found its way into the cupboards of home-cooking enthusiasts, with culinary blogs extolling its use in a wide range of Asian dishes. In the culinary world it is particularly common in the fusion recipes that have sprung up on the West Coast of the United States, combining references to Japanese, Hawaiian, and Vietnamese traditions and symbolizing the Asian-American melting pot. Vietnamese families, for their part, have long complained about not having access to real nuoc mam. Subject to an embargo after 1975, Vietnam began exporting it to the Western world only after joining the World Trade Organization in 1997. Since then, some of the best nuoc mam, made on the island of Phu Quoc, has been available. In 2013 it became the first of the Southeast Asian products to receive a Protected Designation of Origin (PDO) from the European Union.

Marie Aberdam

FURTHER READING

Wanni Wibulswasdi Anderson and Robert G. Lee, eds. *Displacements and Diasporas: Asians in the Americas*. New Brunswick, NJ: Rutgers University Press, 2005.
Marguerite Duras and Michèle Kastner. *La cuisine de Marguerite*. Paris: Benoît Jacob, 1999.
Solène Granier. *Domestiques indochinois*. Paris: Vendémiaire, 2014.
Nelly Krowolski and Ida Simon-Barouch, eds. *Autour du riz, le repas chez quelques populations d'Asie du Sud-Est*. Paris: L'Harmattan, 1993.
Philippe Rostan. *Le petit Viêtnam*. Documentary film. France, 2007.

FURTHER TRAVELING

Dim Sum, Ketchup, Mayonnaise, Pepper, Pho, Salt, Soy Sauce

Food Coloring and Preservatives

In 1896, in the provincial French district of Lorraine, Émile Moench began producing a white powder that he sold in a small pink ten gram (.35 oz.) bag: baking powder. The worldwide career of *Alsa* yeast, with its famous Alsatian maiden, had been launched and with it a new way of making cakes in kitchens. It also played a part in the meteoric rise of food additives on an international scale that started at the end of the nineteenth century.

Four major groups of additives are generally distinguished according to their function. There are those that ensure preservation (preservatives and antioxidants); that modify organoleptic properties (colorants, flavors, flavor enhancers, sweeteners, and acidifiers); those that affect texture (gelling agents, thickeners, emulsifiers, stabilizers, and so on); and those that influence manufacturing, either permanently or temporarily (enzymes, clarifying agents, flocculants, and the like).

The use of additives in food is an ancient practice, the initial aim of which was to preserve food as long and as well as possible. Honey, salt, and brine have been used since antiquity. Vegetables have also been colored for centuries, such as the greening of vegetables with Egyptian nitrate reported by Pliny the Elder. These practices continued into modern times and cases of adulteration were commonplace, such as coloring butter with buttercup flowers or asparagus seeds. The aim was to make the product more attractive to consumers, just as marketing campaigns insisted on their desirability. The large-scale movement of rural populations to cities amplified the food needs of the new urban dwellers, who were now cut off from any possibility of raising their own food. The issue of food safety became crucial from the Enlightenment to the mid-nineteenth century, when transport and storage conditions were still unsuitable and food fraud was rife.

The transition from alchemy to chemistry, with its new tools and paradigms, was a major turning point. Whereas in 1800 around 550 organic chemical substances were known, a century later, in 1900, the number of substances derived from organic chemistry was estimated at around 150,000. Advances in organic chemistry and food packaging accompanied the growth of the agri-food sector. It was against this backdrop that the use of food additives began, followed by a phase of acceleration between the world wars and then intensification from the 1950s onward. Aniline, for example, identified in 1826 from an analysis of indigo, was not industrially produced until 1856 by chemist W. H. Perkin, who patented mauveine and set up the first synthetic dye factory near London. Used in particular by confectioners because of its high coloring power, aniline and its derivatives proved toxic and were banned for food use in France as early as 1856.

The use of synthetic additives by agri-food companies was introduced early on, accompanied by the emergence of a category of newly trained chemists whose initial functions, focused on production control, were extended to research and development of new products.

Food chemistry research focused on the development of new preservatives at a time when long-lasting cold preservation was impossible. Three types of substance were studied: boric acid, which is used in milk and meat products; salicylic acid, which is used in wine and fruit juices; and formaldehyde. Benzoic acid (E 210) is a food preservative naturally present in certain plants, whose chemical properties were discovered in 1837 by the Germans F. Wöhler and J. von Liebig, from the amygdalin contained in bitter almonds. These scientists' work on the benzoyl radical opened a vast field of new discoveries. Benzoic acid spread rapidly in the food industry, and in 1879 Pasteur and the prefect of the Seine discussed its potential authorization. Boric acid, sodium borate, and salicylic acid were also tested for food preservation in France in the 1870s.

In the United Kingdom, controversy over their use dominated much of the debate in the scientific community. The medical press, notably *The Lancet*, questioned the health effects of salicylic acid (1877), borax (1879), and benzoates (1886). In 1900, a survey by the Society of Public Analysts showed that 39 percent of marketed foods contained preservatives or antiseptics. The interwar years saw an acceleration in research into antioxidants, substances capable of stopping the oxidative action of oxygen on foodstuffs. These molecules were even added to packaging materials to stop food products from going rancid, as in the case of cellophane developed by Du Pont de Nemours. Widely used in our daily lives beyond the food industry, these substances were the subject of ongoing toxicology research, notably to understand "cocktail effects," the unforeseen reactions of substances with one another. Boric acid is now recognized as a reprotoxic substance by the European Community, as is formaldehyde, which is also carcinogenic and genotoxic.

The issue of using preservatives has caused major divisions within both the scientific and industrial communities. Pure Food advocates in the United Kingdom and United States reject their use. In 1906, the Pure Food and Drug Act was passed by the U.S. Congress in the name of the risks associated with food additives, the beginning of a long series of consumer protection laws.

Faced with the uncontrolled growth of these new substances, Western countries reacted with appropriate and increasingly restrictive regulations. The first food laws were passed from the nineteenth century onward as part of a broader international movement: the Penal Code of 1810 and the law on adulteration in 1909 in France; the Adulteration Act in 1860 and 1872, followed by the Sale of Food and Drugs Act in 1875 in Great Britain; the Meat Act in 1868 as well as the first law on trade, food, and utensils in 1879 in Germany; and in 1906 in the United States, the Meat Inspection Act, which completed the Pure Food and Drug Act. Everywhere, regulators met with resistance from manufacturers and relied on scientists. Some countries such as France have opted for a positive list of authorized substances: only certain products may be used. In other contexts such as the United States a list of prohibited substances has been provided. These laws are regularly strengthened in line with toxicological research and new practices.

After 1945 the question of food purity and its definition became a central issue. The stakes went beyond public health to shape the international market. National states were primarily concerned with protecting their markets and businesses, but the construction of the European Union required standardization of food production, preservation, and labeling practices. The creation of the World Health Organization (WHO) and the Food and Agriculture Organization of the United Nations (FAO) marked an important step. The question of food additives was raised at the sixth session of the World Health Assembly in Geneva in May 1953, with the suggestion of coordinating the work and standardizing the methods of public health laboratories worldwide. The idea gained ground. In September 1955 the first joint FAO/WHO conference on substances added to foodstuffs was held in Geneva. This conference proved essential for original exploration on the question. At the end of 1956 a Joint Expert Committee on Food Additives (JECFA) was set up in Rome to assess the safety of food additives. Its first recommendations aimed to define the use of additives according to three types of criteria: technical usefulness, consumer protection against fraud and faulty preparation methods and, above all, data establishing the substance's harmlessness. Collaboration and solidarity between countries has enabled those less advanced in the regulation of food additives to benefit from the scientific progress of others. But the debate is not over, as the issue of nitrites in charcuterie demonstrates.

Florence Hachez-Leroy

FURTHER READING

Warren Belasco and Philip Scranton, eds. *Food Nations: Selling Taste in Consumer Societies*. New York: Routledge, 2002.

Martin Bruegel and Bruno Laurioux. *Histoire et identités alimentaires en Europe*. Paris: Hachette Littérature, 2002.

John Burnett and Derek J. Oddy, eds. *The Origins and Development of Food Policies in Europe*. Leicester: Leicester University Press, 1994.

Florence Hachez-Leroy. *Menaces sur l'alimentation: Emballages, colorants et autres contaminants alimentaires, xixe–xxe siècles*. Tours: Presses Universitaires François-Rabelais, 2019.

Ai Hisani. *Visualizing Taste: How Business Changed the Look of What You Eat*. Cambridge, MA: Harvard University Press, 2019.

FURTHER TRAVELING

Charcuterie, Salt, Wine

Freeze-Dried Foods

The year is 1953, and the Food Technology Laboratory at the University of California has achieved a scientific breakthrough that will, according to the *New York Times*, soon put preserved but succulent steaks in soldiers' mess tins. But this is only a first step. While the Department of Defense has funded these studies, because a diversified food supply is good for troop morale, research into industrially processed foods has aimed at developing a market in which households will be the primary consumers.

Military strategists and quartermasters had always dreamed of foods that did not deteriorate at room temperature and that, in small volumes, retained their nutritional profiles and eating qualities (including appearance, taste, and texture). During the Korean War (1950–53), the U.S. military extended to the food industry the technique of cryodesiccation that had been used to ensure the stability and transport of blood plasma and penicillin during World War II. The technique involves the rapid freezing of biological products and then passing them through a vacuum chamber where slight heating causes the ice crystals to sublimate. Evaporation removes the fluid state of water. Liquids and purées are transformed into granules, flakes, or powders, forms suitable for pharmaceutical and medical use, while solid foodstuffs retain their physical structure, minus 60 to 95 percent of their weight. Freeze-dried products require airtight packaging to protect from humidity and oxygen. They may be reconstituted with water or any other liquid. The aim of experiments in military laboratories went beyond the simple logistics of calories. The aim was to make GIs' rations more gastronomically pleasant by turning, for example, tough dried beef into a tender steak through the rehydration of choice freeze-dried cuts.

Ten years on, engineering cleared the hurdle of single-serving packaging. Shrimp, chicken, mushrooms, and freeze-dried peas were added to food reference catalogs. The 1962 International Packaging Exhibition in London heralded a new era in food production by offering journalists a banquet of freeze-dried foods—fruit, seafood, vegetables, fish, and meat. Scientific American magazine identified freeze-drying as the "new frontier" in food technology. The press was full of superlatives: freeze-drying would be the greatest technological innovation since the tin can, a significant contribution to reducing daily domestic servitude, a revolution with prodigious consequences in the kitchen, in short (because family nutrition was presented as their responsibility), a giant step in women's liberation. In 1964 *Le Monde* asked: "Will we soon be eating freeze-dried food?" The advertising touted the practical advantages of these products: light to transport, easy to prepare, quick to serve, identical to the original, while reducing waste. With so many advantages, the price seemed secondary.

Freeze-drying requires heavy, sophisticated, and expensive equipment. Nevertheless, agri-food giants saw a profit-making opportunity. Armour & Co in the United States worked closely with an entrepreneur who in 1956 bought a federal blood plasma production site with facilities that would be used to freeze-dry food. In 1960 Unilever acquired the experimental research station in Aberdeen that had been funded by the UK government for ten years. According to American specialist Kermit Bird, as early as 1963 it became the source of much of what we know about the possibilities of cryodesiccation. The scientific team was relocated to Ireland, where the National Development Agency helped finance a factory near Cork, whose production was exported under the Liebig brand. At the same time, the nationalized Irish Sugar Company invested in the research and development of freeze-dried products under the Erin brand. The American company Heinz, known for its condiments and ketchup, joined in the effort in 1967 as the Irish government pursued its policy of supporting agriculture. Since the automation of production was a constant target of investment for freeze-drying factories, Heinz rarely employed more than a hundred workers, but its demand for agricultural raw materials sustained many farmers. Erin alone had thirty thousand farmers under contract in 1965, while the area of land cultivated with seeds developed in its laboratory to obtain more standardized products (the homogeneity of raw materials facilitated the application of large-scale processes) doubled by 1968.

Growth was more rapid in the United States, where the volume of freeze-dried foods quintupled between 1962 and 1964. The army remained the most important customer for the twenty or so companies manufacturing them.

Despite tasting sessions at the Massachusetts Institute of Technology and the U.S. Department of Agriculture, sales were confined to niche markets. "Useful in air-raid shelters and for emergency food aid," concluded one analysis, before targeting extreme sportsmen and women as primary customers and sports stores as an essential distribution channel. If this new mode of consumption faced serious constraints, marketing turned them into selling points. News reports never failed to mention that freeze-dried food supported mountaineer Edmund Hillary, the first man to climb Everest with Tensing Norgay and that it had enabled a British nuclear submarine to break the record for the distance covered in a dive in 1967, or that it helped feed astronauts from 1965 onward.

Consumers, nonetheless, preferred fresh or frozen alternatives due to the high prices—often more than double—of freeze-dried products. The unusual appearance of the dishes—often compared to desiccated sponges—also slowed down consumption. In France, where only one factory had been freeze-drying mushrooms since the late 1960s, the unappetizing nature of these products and the impression of "buying air" may have generated a certain reluctance to this innovation. These foods have become most widely accepted as an accompaniment by a public that is often unaware of their presence in packet soups (vegetables and spices) and breakfast cereals (fruit). From 1967 onward only freeze-dried coffee enjoyed an undeniable success, thanks to the chain stores that distributed it with heavy advertising.

These niche markets remain buoyant. While their steady growth followed that of endurance sports, crises and disasters have propelled purchases of freeze-dried foods. The 1973 oil crisis fanned the flames of anxiety and boosted the sale of "survival foods." Every cataclysm has brought its share of new buyers: the nuclear accidents at Chernobyl in 1986 and Fukushima in 2011, the "great recession" of 2008, Brexit, and Covid-19 all encouraged the stockpiling of freeze-dried foods. Meanwhile, NASA has had less luck. Looking for a return on investment in the civilian sector, in 1976 it failed to place freeze-dried meals designed to send men into space on the plates of senior citizens.

Martin Bruegel

FURTHER READING

Kermit Bird. *Freeze-Dried Foods: Palatability Tests*. Washington, DC: U.S. Department of Agriculture, 1963.

Deborah Fitzgerald. "World War II and the Quest for Time-Insensitive Foods." *Osiris* 35 (2020): 291–309.

Bernard Palanché. *La lyophilisation dans les industries alimentaires.* Paris: Compagnie française d'éditions, 1975.

Gérard Rabot. *La lyophilisation dans les industries de l'alimentation: Avenir économique.* Lyon: Imprimerie Bosc Frères, 1964.

FURTHER TRAVELING

Coffee, Cornflakes, Ketchup

French Fries

In 1986 photographer Martin Parr published *The Last Resort*, his series of photographs of the British middle class in the English seaside resort of New Brighton. One photograph may be considered to have closed a cycle opened a century earlier with Van Gogh's painting *The Potato Eaters* (1885). The Dutch painter had depicted a poor Dutch peasant family devouring hot tubers in a dark interior. Parr records the end of a popular culture with the image of women and children eating french fries seated in front of a pile of trash. Whether served on their own in a tray, in a kebab sandwich, as an accompaniment to fried fish in newspaper, next to a steak on a plate, in a bowl with mussels or covered in tomato sauce, french fries are ubiquitous on tables across the world. But their abundance paradoxically conceals their disappearance. The way fries have been prepared for two centuries has become a mere fraction of their production: of the more than eleven billion kilos (24.2 billion lbs.) consumed in 2011, the overwhelming majority were frozen. Freezing has radically altered the nature, taste, and political and social image of this food.

In August 1999, in Millau in the southern Aveyron region of France, members of the Confédération Paysanne, led by French activist and politician José Bové, dismantled a McDonald's restaurant a few days before it was due to open. This spectacular action was part of a campaign to defend Roquefort cheese, which the United States had decided to overtax through new tariffs. The action was aimed at fast food, that is hamburgers and what are now known even in France as *french fries*, sold in small, medium, or large conical containers in a continuous stream from morning to night. Since the eighteenth century these potatoes, cooked in an oil bath, were a luxury product because the oil was so precious. They became an object of desire and were reserved for the wealthiest consumers until the 1950s. But in less than fifty years they became the emblem of junk food, a treat that makes children obese, a food of malaise and misery. Worse still, in the twenty-first century, eating and feeding your children frozen french fries has become an irresponsible act, almost a health and political "crime."

This condemnation is no doubt related to the fact that the potato was the main remedy for famine, particularly in rural Europe in the nineteenth century. During the conquest of the New World the Spaniards discovered this plant, which had long occupied a central place in the diet of indigenous cultures, along with corn, notably among the Chimu on the Peruvian coast. In 1560 King Philip II of Spain brought back around a hundred of these tubers, which then spread rapidly throughout continental Europe and North America. Historians of agronomy have been quick to point out that their primary European use was medicinal and that a certain mistrust surrounded their consumption. Did the Spanish monarch not first send the pope a potato sample to treat his gout? In France, the name Parmentier is closely associated with the potato, because this pharmacist who joined the army discovered the power of potatoes during his captivity in the Seven Years' War (1756–63) by the Prussians, who had made them the staple food ration for their prisoners. So, when France was in the grip of famine after his release, he entered a competition held by the Academy of Besançon on "plants that could replace those commonly used for human consumption in the event of famine" and won first prize with the potato. Parmentier fought all his life to promote the potato to Louis XVI and the court, to the academies, but above all to the people, who remained suspicious. In Saxony and Russia, where the powers that be had forced peasants to grow potatoes on pain of execution or condemnation, changing one's diet was not a common occurrence. This was even more the case as wealthy consumers fried their potatoes in fat, giving them more flavor than when boiled. The result was the potato of the poor and the potato of the middle class. It was precisely this inequality that the inventors of french fries sought to bridge.

One of them was Frédéric Krieger, born in Bavaria in 1817. The son of fairground musicians, he was introduced to rotisserie cooking on the rue Montmartre in Paris, where he learned to cook roasted potatoes in slices. Upon his return to Belgium, he adopted the pseudonym Fritz and introduced the fried potato. He cut them into sticks for greater convenience and brought them to fairs, places of social mixing, and other places where people made exceptional expenditures. Adopting the codes of the travelling show, he made french fries a feast and their consumption a pleasure. In the years that followed, Monsieur Fritz settled down and opened a brick-and-mortar restaurant where tubers were cut by a machine. Krieger had many competitors: these cones of french fries were soon eaten all over Europe's major cities, usually standing up. Krieger's french fry cones were part of the construction of an urban modernity, along with omnibuses, advertising, and lampposts. They also testify to the emergence of an unprecedented democratization of food. For a century, fries embodied a European way of life. Along roadsides, on beaches, or in city centers, the french fry stand became part of the landscape. Moreover, fries made their way onto our plates, becoming a staple of communal dining. In France they have given birth to an entire imaginary world of accordions, greasy paper, and the froth of a glass of beer.

Paradoxically, their gradual disappearance has been the main consequence of their proliferation. French fries have entered households on a massive scale. People worried about the dangerous oil bath that could catch fire if left on the gas stove, or which, if too hot, threatened to burn the stove itself. Yet they became the most common side dish on the family table: in the 1960s–70s, *poulet-frites* (chicken and french fries) were as popular as beef and carrots. Despite their popularity, fries depend on the daunting chore of peeling potatoes. The task became even more burdensome as prefried potatoes cut into thin slices could be bought in packets and merely heated in the oven.

Despite efforts across the industry to develop a plethora of household appliances to limit unpleasant odors, the deep-fat fryer has become a thing of the past, and the fry shack is no more than a vestige of regional folklore. Fries are now industrialized, bagged, and frozen. It has become the equivalent of Ikea furniture, the symbol of a global village. Whether you are in Moscow or Santiago de Chile, these standardized "matchsticks" make you forget that they came originally from potatoes of different shapes. To be fried, the stick must be immersed in an oil with the same characteristics, at the same temperature, for the same length of time. This agri-food chain, from producer to distributor to fast-food outlet, isolates fries from all other foods. It is the model for a neoliberal food economy far removed from the vision of the Belgian artist Marcel Broodthaers, who saw fries, mussels, and eggs as perfect forms.

The story of french fries would not be so tragic if they had not become a staple for poorer populations that have suffered the most in our affluent societies, and thus the marker of what sociologist Robert Castel called disaffiliation.

Philippe Artières

FURTHER READING

Hubert Bonin. "Les frites, profondément ancrées dans la culture européenne." *Cahiers de nutrition et diététique* 45, no. 6 (2010): S74–S79.

Patrick Rousselle, Daniel Ellisseche, and Françoise Rousselle. "La pomme de terre." *Cahiers d'outre-mer* 179–80 (1992): 303–14.

FURTHER TRAVELING

Beer, Döner Kebab, Hamburger, Ketchup, Roquefort

Gin

On February 27, 1734, Judith Defour, a spinner by trade, was sentenced to death for the murder of her two-year-old daughter Mary a month earlier. She admitted taking the child to a field near Bethnal Green, on the outskirts of London, "strangling her with a handkerchief, after having entirely undressed her," then leaving her for dead in a ditch. With the sixteen pence from the sale of the child's "coat, corset, petticoat and socks," shared with her accomplice, Sukey, she then bought a quarter pint of gin. The story caused considerable stir, particularly among the temperance leagues and associations then flourishing in Great Britain, as well as in the American colonies, Belgium, Germany, and the Netherlands. In the collective imagination, the word "gin" evoked an evil power leading to madness, suicide, and infanticide. In the 1750s, the use of the concept of madness went hand in hand with accusations of moral degeneration leveled at women who indulged in the beverage. A gin craze had spread throughout Northern Europe, wreaking havoc everywhere. Moral indignation prompted the authorities to introduce a series of legislative measures on a scale comparable to the present-day fight against drug use. No less than five Gin Acts were passed in England between 1729 and 1751 to regulate the consumption of this beverage, which was compared to opium in the East. Cheaper than beer, often of mediocre quality, and frequently adulterated (it could contain sawdust, turpentine, or sulfuric acid), gin was particularly popular among the working classes of large northern European cities. The most numerous victims seem to have been sedentary workers and women, while agricultural workers remained faithful to beer.

"Mother's helper" or "Mother's ruin" was originally appreciated for its therapeutic virtues in the fight against illnesses as diverse as indigestion, bile, and the

Black Death. In his famous diary of October 1663, Samuel Pepys recounts how he was treated for constipation with a brandy made from juniper berries imported from the Netherlands. Gin, then known as jenever, is said to have been created by Flemish monks in the thirteenth century, even though the medicinal virtues of juniper berries had been known since antiquity. The monks recommended drinking it in the morning before going to work in order to help "thrust you into your work." In 1575 the Bols distillery in Amsterdam was the first to manufacture and sell gin. The Dutch East India Company, founded in 1602, supplied it with exotic spices and aromatics from all over the world in exchange for spirits and brandies. Distillation took off to meet the needs of long-distance trade. Distilled alcohol is a stable product that does not suffer from long sea voyages, unlike wine and beer, which travel less well. The port of Schiedam, near Rotterdam, became the jenever capital of the world, with some four hundred distilleries and fumes blackening the city walls, which gave it its nickname, Black Nazareth. Up to a million liters (264,172 gal.) of jenever left the port every week. In the American colonies, the Caribbean, and West Africa, "Atlantic consumers" such as colonists, sailors, and slaves became key figures in an expanding Atlantic economy and expanded the markets for any alcohol distilled on either side of the ocean.

It was in the seventeenth century that gin became, so to speak, an authentically British spirit. During the Thirty Years' War, Englishmen fighting alongside the Dutch against Philip of Spain discovered the origin of Dutch courage. When William of Orange came ashore from Holland to become king of England in 1689, it is said that he restored liberty and introduced jenever. The war with France and the ensuing embargo on cognac opened a new market to British distillers. In 1690 the king abolished the monopoly of the London Distillers' Guild, allowing any citizen to become a distiller. Gin was easy to produce and inexpensive to sell, with little tax and no licensing requirements. Made from grain alcohol (barley, wheat, or oats) rather than grape must, it enabled farmers to dispose of their surplus grain of inferior quality. This marked the beginning of a consumer revolution.

In the nineteenth century, new distillation processes based on the steam infusion of plants and spices transformed gin production. Technological advances such as the introduction of column distillation by Irish inventor Aeneas Coffey in 1830 brought a quantum leap in the quality of grain brandies. The number of distilleries increased, mainly in port cities, where distillers had direct access to spices and a thriving urban market.

Meanwhile, gin consumption had spread across the globe. Legislation in England in 1760 encouraging the export of spirits contributed to the development of a gin industry for colonial trade. Gin became a significant source of income in the Empire. In the second half of the nineteenth century, the soldiers of the East India Company took to mixing it with quinine as a stimulant against malaria. Imported from the Andes, quinine was diluted with soda water, but its bitter taste made it unpleasant. Winston Churchill famously said, "Gin and tonic has saved more British lives and minds than all the doctors of the Empire put together."

A craze for gin-based cocktails spread throughout Europe in the Belle Époque. The first recipe for the dry martini was published in a book in Paris in 1904. James Bond's favorite cocktail, made with Old Tom gin, was also very popular in the United States. Between 1880 and 1914 gin imports to West Africa exploded, reaching almost 85,000 hectoliters (2,245,462 gal.) a year. After that, due to war and economic depression, they declined to 1,620 (42,795 gal.) hectoliters in 1939. In Nigeria in the 1930s, temperance leagues and pro-alcohol lobbies agreed to prohibit locally produced gin, which was dangerous both to public health and to the British Empire's revenues. After World War II, imports stabilized at between five thousand and seven thousand hectoliters (132,086–184,920 gal.) a year.

The image of gin changed with decolonization. In West Africa, advertisements emphasized its place in ancestral rituals, depicting chiefs in traditional dress drinking gin at funeral ceremonies, for example. In Europe and the United States, gin was associated with the aristocracy, with Queen Victoria serving as its icon. From Canadian Empress Gin to the American Bombay Dry Gin the beverage was reinvented, leaving behind the repulsive and sordid image of the infanticidal mother to become the shining symbol of aristocracy and empire. According to published accounts, the Queen loved a blend of eight ingredients—juniper, coriander, licorice, lemon, iris, blackcurrant, almonds, and angelica—the recipe for which was invented by Thomas Dakin in 1761. In 1997 Bombay Dry Gin was acquired by Bacardi and became Bombay Sapphire Gin, in homage to the British Raj and the 182-carat "Star of Bombay" sapphire mined in Sri Lanka. Two ingredients were added: cubeba berries and paradise seeds.

Gin is made with a wide choice of ingredients. The selection of herbs and spices macerated with juniper berries not only allows for different tastes, but also a variety of colors, with the addition of flowers resulting in pink or violet gins, for example. These innovations explain the revival of gin since the late 1990s and early 2000s. A relatively neutral and versatile beverage, it can be used to establish an identity. In Brittany it is now iodized with seaweed; in Oregon it is scented with lavender and Indian sarsaparilla; in Japan it is prepared with yuzu, kabosu, amanatsu, and shikuwasa. If Her Queen Majesty's spy liked his dry martini "shaken, not stirred," the French humorist Alphonse Allais could retort in advance: *"Par les bois du Djinn, Parle et bois du gin?"* (When in the woods of Djinn, would you speak and drink of gin?).

Clarisse Berthezène

FURTHER READING

Daniel Defoe. *A Brief Case of the Distillers and of the Distilling Trade in England, Shewing How Far It Is the Interest of England to Encourage the Said Trade. . . .* London: T. Warner, 1726.

Patrick Dillon. *The Much-Lamented Death of Madam Geneva: The Eighteenth-Century Gin Craze.* London: Headline Review, 2002.

Henry Fielding. *An Enquiry Into the Causes of the Late Increase of Robbers, and Related Writings.* Ed. Malvin R. Zirker. Oxford: Clarendon Press, 1988.

Lesley J. Solmonson. *Gin: A Global History.* London: Reaktion Books, 2012.

Jessica Warner. *Craze: Gin and Debauchery in the Age of Reason.* London: Random House, 2003.

FURTHER TRAVELING

Beer, Sparkling Water, Wine

Guacamole

In 2015, the recipe for guacamole became a subject of national debate in the United States, after the *New York Times* proposed a recipe that included peas. When asked about the issue, President Obama himself affirmed his support for the "classic" recipe: onions, garlic, and chili (in addition to avocado, of course).

In just a few years, guacamole has become a staple among U.S. dipping sauces, especially during the Super Bowl. Since its creation in 2013, the Avocados from Mexico consortium has paid a hefty price ($4 million for thirty seconds) for advertising space during the country's most-watched sporting event, promoting an association that is now self-evident. No American football night is complete without a bowl of guacamole. By 2021, 100 million kilos (220 million lb.) of avocados had been imported from the Mexican state of Michoacan to the United States for this occasion, not counting the ready-made preparations available for purchase in supermarkets. Yet this "green gold" only belatedly entered mass consumption, following a long global history of Mexico and Mexicans.

Guacamole is an ancestral recipe of the Aztecs, whose name comes from the Nahuatl words *ahuacatl* (avocado) and *molli* (sauce). It has been prepared since at least the thirteenth century, and its origins can be found in the legends of this people. Avocado pulp is crushed in a stone mortar, along with chili pepper and sometimes tomato, two other fruits native to the Americas. At the time, the avocado tree only grew in Central America.

The Spanish conquistadors discovered guacamole as they discovered Aztec civilization, which they defeated in the early sixteenth century. Thanks to the exchange of plants, animals, and microbes, avocado trees began to be cultivated on the Iberian Peninsula, and the recipe was adapted by the Spaniards, who added lemon, onion, and other spices, all ingredients that had come from the Orient. The preparation became known and noted by travelers but did not conquer Europe, unlike another culinary discovery from the same region, chocolate.

At the turn of the twentieth century the avocado was one of the tropical plants studied in colonial publications. In the United States avocados became more prominent as the country increasingly moved economically and politically into Cuba and Mexico. The U.S. Department of Agriculture, inspired by the success of bananas and coffee, sent expeditions to Central America and the Caribbean to find new tropical products and develop their cultivation there. Up to that point botanical travelers had paid tribute to Mexican know-how and traditions concerning the fruit. But the situation changed as new room was made for American scientific and industrial progress in its development. Hundreds of samples were sent north. Some species were patented for their specific qualities, such as frost resistance.

In the process, the surprising fruit found defenders who sought to stimulate American taste, which was traditionally accustomed to more sugar than fat, and might have an aversion to its color. This was no easy task. But real estate speculation was rife in Southern California at the time. The region was ideally suited for such cultivation and provided serious allies for the promotion of what was also known as the "alligator pear." The possibility of having a few avocado trees in one's garden became a selling point and a driving force behind higher prices, since such a crop could be an income supplement. At the same time, the avocado lobby (made up of early growers, real-estate speculators, researchers, and local elites) succeeded in banning the import of Mexican production for supposedly carrying pests. The competition from cheaper fruit due to the lower cost of labor and land south of the border was thus permanently eliminated.

Beyond the financial aspect, California's citrus, avocado, and other orchards have fueled the Edenic image of a land of abundance, where one simply lifts a hand toward the sky to taste nature's simple, delicious foods. The image of a "California lifestyle" was relayed by Hollywood stars such as Frank Capra and Boris Karloff, who between two horror films prepared guacamole according to his own recipe, including a drop of sherry.

Thanks to the support of the Ministry of Agriculture and local universities, research was undertaken to prove the nutritional value of the fruit. At the same time, chemical analyses established a harvesting protocol, as avocados do not ripen on the tree. In 1924 Calavo, a cooperative of producers pooling their advertising efforts, was founded. Initially the association targeted wealthier classes, through the women who presided over family purchases and menus, investing in the magazines dedicated to them. It was a relative failure. Despite the hope that it would take the place of meat, due to its high fat content, the link between this fruit and salad remained too strong. For most meat lovers it was neither masculine enough nor in keeping with an "Anglo-Saxon" identity. This is paradoxical when you consider that the Aztecs apparently did not allow women to pick this fruit, whose name means "testicle." Conversely, the fat content was an obstacle to its inclusion in slimming diets. It thus became a priority to prove that avocado fat was not bad for the body.

Though the initial trend was to associate it with Spain rather than Mexico, after World War II sellers began capitalizing on the exotic, ethnic character of guacamole. As in California, whose Spanish heritage was valued, European and Mediterranean roots were preferred to an ethnic identification tied to the south of the border. Soon, however, ethnic forms of consumption gained ground, driven by the demographic growth of immigrant populations and by various developments in culinary industrialization. In the 1960s the Calavo cooperative succeeded in producing frozen avocado pulp that did not deteriorate in appearance and taste when thawed and marketed its own guacamole in the 1970s. Further research was carried out to improve the sauce's preservation (it had an unfortunate tendency to darken over time) and to create less expensive recipes, that is, containing as little avocado as possible since prices were rising with demand. It was also the time of the first fast-food outlets offering Mexican dishes, such as Taco Bell or Chipotle. Against this backdrop the avocado once again became an issue in trade negotiations between the United States and Mexico, which led to the progressive opening to Mexican imports under the North American Free Trade Agreement in 1997. Avocado consumption in the United States quadrupled between 2000 and 2014, and the vast majority of products came from Mexico, so much so that the country would have run out of the commodity in three weeks if imports had stopped, as was a risk during the Trump presidency in the second half of the 2010s. The increase in consumption was not confined to the United States, however, and Europe also imported avocados (grown in Spain as well) on a massive scale from Israel and Africa.

In opposition to its image as a healthy product, the avocado is now responsible for serious social and environmental damage, due to its increased production to meet globalized demand. Avocado trees are major consumers of space and water (1,000 liters per kilo/264 gal. per 2.2 lb.). In Kenya their intensive cultivation has led to a drastic reduction in elephant habitat, for example around Amboseli Park. In Andalusia they have exacerbated water stress. In Mexico, the avocado's homeland, deforestation has been compounded by other problems. Its export to the United States has become so lucrative that drug cartels have made controlling its trade a business in its own right, particularly in the Michoacan region. In February 2022 intimidation by U.S. phytosanitary inspectors caused a temporary halt to the trade, but negotiations ensured that supplies were available in time for that year's Super Bowl.

Emmanuelle Perez Tisserant

FURTHER READING

California Advisory Board. *The Avocado Bravo: Spain's Legacy to California Cuisine*. Newport Beach, CA: CAB, 1978.

Jeffrey Charles. "Searching for Gold in Guacamole: California Growers Market the Avocado, 1910–1994." In *Food Nations: Selling Taste in Consumer Societies*, ed. Warren Belasco and Philip Scranton, 131–55. New York: Routledge, 2001.

Guy N. Collins. *The Avocado, a Salad Fruit from the Tropics*. Washington, DC: U.S. Government Printing Office, 1905.

Donna Gabacci. *We Are What We Eat: Ethnic Food and the Making of Americans*. Cambridge, MA: Harvard University Press, 2000.

FURTHER TRAVELING

Chili Pepper, Coffee, Maki

Hamburger

In 1982, Andy Warhol agreed to be filmed by Danish director Jørgen Leth for his *66 Scenes from America*. In the longest scene, filmed in a single take, the pop art icon unwraps a Burger King Whopper, adds ketchup and chews it in silence for four minutes and twenty seconds. The sequence ends when Warhol pronounces his name, suggesting that in the United States, celebrities and anonymous people alike are equal before food. It is certainly this democratic dimension of the burger that has contributed to its international success. Eminently American, but named after a German city, hamburger has many ancestors in Europe and other parts of the world. The hamburger is the epitome of globalized food. Whether in Los Angeles, Moscow, Beijing, or Lagos, it is easy to eat and cheap to buy.

Because meat was so difficult to preserve for centuries, it was seasoned with a minced version of salt or brine—*Frikadelle* in Germany, forcemeat with herbs in England. The city of Hamburg was renowned for its beef sausage, which was adopted in England in the eighteenth century before crossing the Atlantic. "Hamburg sausage" appeared in the American edition of Anna Glass's cookbook *The Art of Cookery Made Plain and Easy* in 1805, and was transformed into "Hamburg Steak" on the menu of the recently opened Delmonico restaurant on William Street, New York, in 1834. From the mid-nineteenth century onward the conquest of the American Great Plains brought beef in abundance and at lower prices. It became accessible to the working classes when the mincer appeared around 1850. Butchers recycled the less noble parts of the meat, eventually adding cartilage or fat without the consumer noticing. In 1876 the "Beefsteak à la Hamburg" or "Hamburg Steak," still without bread, was the talk of the town at the Centennial Exhibition in Philadelphia.

In the age of industrialization, the "Hamburg Steak" left restaurants to be cooked on the grills of mobile stands next to factories and eaten in a bun. The fact that it was so unanimously adopted by workers made it suspect in the eyes of high society. Ground beef was suspected of coming from putrid meat that was excessively matured and cut with chemical preservatives. In Wichita, Kansas, J. Walter Anderson embraced its proletarian character while deciding to improve the food's image. He flattened the meat and placed it in a bun, cooked it on the grill in full view of customers by uniformed waiters, and sold it for five cents apiece. His most audacious idea was to offer only a few items on the menu— hamburgers, coffee, Coca-Cola, and pie—to be taken away and consumed immediately. In 1921 he teamed up with Edgar Waldo Ingram, who redesigned the sales stands as small castles and renamed the company White Castle. Ingram applied the main features of the Fordist model to the gastronomy business: standardization of production and service, aggressive marketing to a popular, male clientele, and establishment in city centers.

In the consumer society of the post–World War II era, beef replaced pork. Fast-food restaurants and drive-ins became commonplace. The conditions were set for the hamburger's take off. In 1940 the McDonald brothers opened a small octagonal restaurant on E Street in San Bernardino, California. With red and white walls and two golden arches supporting the restaurant, they invented the visual identity of the company that, sixty years later, would become a multinational with almost 30,000 branches and 250,000 employees worldwide. Ray Kroc, who bought the family business in 1961, came up with the recipe for success: cater to middle-class families in restaurants in residential suburbs, further rationalize production by dividing it into simple tasks that require no special skills to master, and ask customers to do some of the service. By 1963 McDonald's was selling a million burgers a day. In 1966 its shares were listed on the New York Stock Exchange. The company was so successful that it could begin to export its burgers abroad.

In fact, burgers had already begun their gastronomic conquest of the world some forty years earlier. As early as the 1920s Jack Baker was serving them to American expatriates in his Parisian restaurant. After the war, military bases in Europe and Asia offered them to homesick GIs. Outside the camps, local restaurateurs put them on their menus to attract Americans to their tables. The first international franchises of American fast-food chains benefited from this taste and curiosity. To facilitate their adoption, these chains endeavored to source their beef and bread locally and to adapt their products to local eating habits. For example, the burger became vegan in India and could be eaten with beer in Germany or espresso in Italy.

Despite its popularity, the hamburger was seen by the far left as a Trojan horse for U.S.-led liberal globalization. In 1986 the London branch of Greenpeace distributed a six-page brochure outside McDonald's restaurants: "What's wrong with McDonald's? Everything you don't want to know," accusing the company of producing poverty, exploiting workers, torturing animals, and destroying the Amazon rainforest to create pasture for cattle. In 1999 José Bové's Confédération Paysanne responded to the U.S. imposition of import duties on Roquefort cheese by dismantling a fast-food restaurant under construction in the town of Millau. During his trial, thirty thousand people demonstrated behind a sign reading "No to McMerde" (McShit).

More than the hamburger itself, it is the multinationals that sell it as a standardized commodity and are targeted for their disastrous economic and environmental model. Nostalgists fear the standardization of tastes as well as the disappearance of regional and local culinary traditions. Food scandals have given them ample arguments. In *Fast Food Nation*, published in 2001, Eric Schlosser recalls that in 1982 dozens of children fell ill after eating contaminated McDonald's hamburgers. In 1993 more than seven hundred people suffered from hemorrhagic diarrhea in four American states. Doctors blamed it on the *E. coli* 0157:H7 bacteria found in hamburgers sold by the Jack in the Box chain. In his book, which shook up the agri-food industry and struck a blow to the hamburger industry, Schlosser also denounced inhumane working conditions in slaughterhouses, the role of hamburgers (which are too fatty and addictive) in obesity, the use of antibiotics to accelerate the growth of cattle, the race for supersized quantities, packaging waste, the employment of young, female workers at insufficient wages, and much more. The best-selling book sounded the death knell for the Big Mac sold in Styrofoam, but it did not prevent more elaborate gourmet versions, served on wood-fired buns and eaten with a knife and fork from appearing on menus across the world's major cities.

Pauline Peretz

FURTHER READING

"Fast Food" and "Hamburger." *Encyclopedia of Food and Culture*. New York: Scribner, 2003.
Josh Ozersky. *Hamburgers: A Cultural History*. New Haven, CT: Yale University Press, 1996.

Eric Schlosser. *Fast Food Nation: The Dark Side of the All-American Meal*. Boston: Houghton Mifflin, 2001.

Andrew F. Smith. *Eating History: 30 Turning Points in the Making of American Cuisine*. New York: Columbia University Press, 2009.

——. *Hamburger: A Global History*. London: Reaktion Books, 2008.

FURTHER TRAVELING

Beer, Coca-Cola, Coffee, French Fries, Ketchup, Mayonnaise

Harissa

In 1946, in the small village of Grombalia at the entrance to Tunisia's Cap Bon, two entrepreneurs, Bakha Gastli and Hecot Borge, founded a company that would conquer the world within a few decades. The aim of the Société des Conserves Alimentaires des Producteurs du Cap Bon (SCAPB), which created the famous Le Phare du Cap Bon brand of harissa, was to sell the region's agricultural produce, mainly tomatoes and peppers, on an industrial scale. It was part of the development of the food canning industry in Tunisia, and in the Tunis region in particular, from the interwar period onward, focusing in particular on tomatoes, artichokes, green beans, peas, and even cooked dishes such as *chakchouka*. In the following decades, various companies developed around French, Italian, and Tunisian industrialists, producing 3,000–4,000 tons of canned goods per year in the last years of French colonization. Here a new product gradually emerged: harissa.

The word *harissa* is derived from the Arabic word *harss*, meaning crushing or grinding an ingredient. In medieval texts it was used to designate a mixture of pounded fatty meat and soaked, crushed wheat, cooked for a long time at a moderate oven temperature. In modern and contemporary Tunisia, and more generally in a vast area stretching from Morocco to Libya, it refers to at least two products: harissa with red chili pepper and harissa with fresh green chili pepper. The term harissa can also refer to a preparation made from crushed almonds and sugar syrup. Generally used as a condiment, this chili puree is thought to be a result of the Spanish occupation of the region between 1535 and 1574. Other traditions report that this product originated from Jewish and Muslim communities expelled from Spain at the end of the fifteenth century, who found refuge in present-day Tunisia. In both cases this culinary transfer took place via the

Iberian Peninsula. It was itself the result of the Spanish conquest of the Americas and Colombian trade between Europe and the Americas in the sixteenth and eighteenth centuries, involving tomatoes and chilis.

Both harissa preparations are made from peppers, generally harvested in spring and dried in summer. They are ground and mixed with various ingredients, such as caraway seeds, coriander seeds, garlic, coarse salt, and above all olive oil, which preserves the paste. The proportions of the various ingredients vary from family to family and community to community. It was the red chili-based harissa that became widely available on an industrial scale, no doubt because it was less strictly seasonal than green chili paste. Since then, the geography of harissa production has been closely linked to that of chilies in the northern and central regions of the country, the provinces of Nabeul, Sidi Bouzid, and Kairouan. Le Phare du Cap Bon therefore refers first and foremost to the essential agricultural products of a region that has historically been one of the poorest in Tunisia. However, the production remained limited to a few hundred tons at the end of the protectorate and during the first years of independence.

After decades of stagnation, harissa conquered the world in the 2000s. Exports reached half of total production, and quantities increased sevenfold over the decade from 2,800 tons in 2002 to 15,000 tons in 2011. The Tunisian diaspora facilitated this transformation. By the end of the 2000s Tunisian harissa was being exported to some thirty countries, mainly in the Maghreb, Europe, and North America, following a similar pattern to that of the Tunisian community abroad. France is the main market, absorbing up to two-thirds of the exports in some years. Moreover, the condiment is gradually becoming popularized in cultural production as an identity marker of Maghrebian culture through, for example, Frédéric Dantec's film *Harissa mon amour* (2011) or the novels by Yamina Khodri (*Les gaufrettes à l'harissa*, 2011) and Sonia Medina (*Rouge harissa*, 2008). Logistical and technical improvements have also facilitated its globalization. Retailers have diversified the product, and it is now available in canned form, as well as in tubes and jars.

The 2010s saw a return to the heritage of Tunisian harissa against a backdrop of increasing international competition, particularly from production in Morocco. Tunisian exports stagnated or fell slightly over the decade, forcing producers to shift upmarket. In 2014 the Harissa Food Quality Label Tunisia was created under the authority of the Ministry of Industry, in conjunction with the United Nations Industrial Development Organization (UNIDO), which five companies joined, representing a third of national production. Production is becoming increasingly standardized, in terms of the types of chilis to be harvested, the time of harvest, and the processing procedures. Cultural heritage identification has also developed in connection with tourism issues. The town of Nabeul, south of Cap Bon, organizes a harissa festival every autumn, with the 2016 edition even welcoming delegations from Croatia, Hungary, and North Korea. Above all, Tunisia applied for it to be recognized by UNESCO as intangible cultural heritage in October 2020. Over and above the tourism possibilities, harissa also has the advantage of being a dish from Muslim, Berber, and Jewish cuisines, as well as being a consensual product and particularly consistent with a Tunisian national narrative, based on the kaleidoscope and meeting of cultures with a common heritage.

In the late 2010s, harissa from the Phare du Cap Bon represented an important economic niche. The Grombalia-based plant employs around one hundred people and four hundred seasonal workers and produces thirty thousand tons of harissa every year on a twenty-thousand-hectare (49,421 ac.) site. The condiment's nutritional virtues (digestion, prevention of certain infectious diseases) are gradually being incorporated into international standards, with *Time* magazine in 2015 ranking harissa among the fifty healthiest products of all time. As a result of globalization, world-renowned chefs such as Britain's Jamie Oliver, through his roast chicken with harissa, and Anglo-Israeli chef Yotam Ottolenghi have contributed to its popularization. In France the raspberry sorbet dessert with harissa by Alexandre Mazzia, a newly declared triple Michelin-starred chef in 2021, brought harissa into the realm of haute cuisine, helping to turn this chili puree, consumed by a few thousand Tunisians just two centuries ago, into a globalized product of the twenty-first century.

Nessim Znaien

FURTHER READING

Marianne Brisville. "Plats sûrs et plats sains dans l'Occident médiéval: La harissa comme contre-exemple?" Conference of the CTHS de Rennes, April 2013.

Sihem Debbabi-Missaoui. *Mâ'idat Ifriqiya Dirâsa fî Alwân al-Ta'âm*. Carthage: Académie Tunisienne des Sciences, des Lettres et des Arts, 2017.

Sihem Debbabi-Missaoui and Kilien Stengel, eds. *La cuisine du Maghreb n'est-elle qu'une simple histoire de couscous?* Paris: L'Harmattan, 2020.

Annie Hubert. *Le pain et l'olive: Aspects de l'alimentation en Tunisie*. Paris: CNRS Éditions, 1984.

FURTHER TRAVELING

Chili Pepper, Chorba, Couscous, Olive Oil, Salt

Hedgehog Stew

On July 4, 1985, the local newspaper from Auvergne, France, *La Montagne*, reported on the sentencing of Mr. Jean Reinhart to a 220-franc fine for eating a hedgehog. The name was not without a certain resonance: he may have been a "cousin" (albeit a distant one) of Django Reinhardt, the famous Roma guitarist. The meal was not exactly a newsworthy story—"Gypsies" were already known to eat hedgehogs—had it not been for the fact that a fine had been imposed by the local court. Since a ministerial decree of April 17, 1981, the animal has been classified as a protected mammal, the hunting (and therefore consumption) of which constituted an offence. The journalist ended the story on a humorous note: "Since hedgehogs weigh around 200g, Gascon gourmets were quick to deduce the price per kilo: 1,000 F, which was more expensive than foie gras."

The author of the article did not specify how the hedgehog was prepared: grilled, barbecued, or boiled in a hedgehog stew, as was customary. In the recipes, it was not hedgehog but *"niglo,"* a term that comes from Romanes (the language of the "Gypsies"). This is a Sinti/Manouche adaptation of the German word *igel*, hedgehog. Other Romanes variants do not use a specific term for the hedgehog, which is often associated with the badger. This is the case of the French Roms, called Zongrois among Travelers who have adopted the Manouche word *niglo*.

This etymological tradition reflects a reality to which Jan Yoors's story bears witness. Before World War II the twelve-year-old Dutch boy went to live with nomadic Roma from eastern Romania and Hungary who occasionally passed through his village. He stayed with them for five years (1934–39), then joined them again during the war, when they engaged in the Resistance. He reports that one day, forced to flee from the police, the *kumpania* or group found refuge in the woods. The Roma came across two "brightly colored" covered wagons: "A little further on we met some young Sinti. . . . They were returning from a hedgehog hunt. We bought two of them. For a few silver coins more, they agreed to kill, clean, and cook them over an improvised fire." In other words, these Roma from the east did not know how to hunt or prepare hedgehogs.

Yoors clarifies an important point: the consumption of niglo is the work of those who call themselves Sinti, a group of families who in France identify themselves as "Manouche." In Romany, *manush* means man, human being. So these Gypsies consider themselves distinct from Roma, with whom they share a "family resemblance," as well as distinct from *gadjé* (non-Gypsies).

The ancestors of these *niglo*-consuming Manouches lived in German-speaking areas on both sides of the Rhine. But the Thirty Years' War (1618–48), which shook Europe, forced many families to live in the woods as far away as possible from the warring armies. Among them were Zigeuner/Bohemians, as well as other rural populations who learned from the former the art of survival in the woods (protecting themselves from the cold and rain, feeding themselves, escaping, finding each other, and so forth). These ancestors of the Yenish were assimilated to the Zigeuner/Bohemians, reinforcing the distinction between "blond Gypsies" and "black Gypsies." From then on, their destinies were intertwined, through the administrative and police treatment that their descendants still confront. The wars of the nineteenth century, in particular those of 1870 and 1914, led them to flee Germanic areas on both sides of the Rhine to find refuge in central France, where they form the largest community of Travelers.

Nesting in gardens, ditches, and woods, the hedgehog was a source of protein and fat for these forest-dwelling families, as it was for the *gadjé* who lived in the same conditions. In fact, the consumption of hedgehogs has been characteristic of periods of famine in Europe for many centuries. From the mid-nineteenth century onward, many of these Sinti and Yenish families migrated from German-speaking areas to central and western France, taking their eating habits with them. Some moved closer to urban centers while others chose rural areas. It is primarily "bush people," as ethnologist Patrick Williams calls them, who maintain the tradition of eating *niglo*.

Initially, consumption was a necessity for a people involved in a wide range of activities: weavers, tinsmiths, repairers, as well as occasional labor on farms for seasonal work. Up until the 1970s the farmers who relied on them supplied only potatoes. The source of meat available through hunting was therefore limited to hedgehogs, all the more so as hunting took place after nightfall, while harvesting and grape picking was carried out from morning to night.

Two seasons are ideal for catching *niglo*. In spring, as they emerge from winter, they are lean and best prepared on the barbecue. In summer one needs to be careful not to catch *nigli*, pregnant females that are difficult to distinguish from the large edible male. In autumn, the *niglo* becomes fat after a season of building up reserves. One must know how to track it. A dog, or *djoukel*, is indispensable for this. Once caught, it needs to be killed, and a strike to the nose is all it needs to be bled. This is followed by the removal of the quills with a sharp knife. Its flesh is strong, and an autumn *niglo* can give taste to three to five kilos (6.6–11 lb.) of potatoes. Depending on the region, the broth is enhanced with local herbs: thyme, bay leaves, onions, shallots, and garlic. But one month of such a diet can result in jaundice. The meat is so rich in fat that it saturates the liver.

Nowadays *niglo* is no longer eaten as a stopgap. It has evolved into a festive collective meal that affirms one's belonging to *menchi*, or the "gypsy world." To do this, one must collect hedgehogs in large numbers, gather an assembly of "real Manouches" around a fire, and set up a vast "grill." This is illegal, as everyone knows, but the transgression brings a certain energy to the "community." The hedgehog is a protected species. Its consumption seems to have died out in Germany, Austria, and Italy, where Sinti also live. In France, the daily news section (as well as videos on YouTube) attests to the fact that *niglo* are still occasionally hunted for the holidays. This is no longer a simple eating habit but an act of shared identity. Common in Germanic-speaking areas and in eastern France at certain times of the year, the consumption of hedgehogs has gradually marked a distinction with the *gadjé* but also, sometimes, between "gypsies" themselves. In Spain, while the Moros (Moroccans) eat hedgehogs, the Gitanos of Andalusia declare the animal to be "dirty" and abhor it. And the only market stalls where hedgehogs are known to be displayed and sold are in Maghrebi countries.

Though hedgehog stew has existed elsewhere and has not always been the sole preserve of "Gypsies," it remains, along with its history, intimately linked to these populations. And beyond the dish, the animal itself. A man once explained to Patrick Williams, smiling out of the corner of his mouth that Manouches shared something with hedgehogs: "Look at the hedgehoggess [*sic*] and her little ones, they are like us in a convoy with our camping cars [caravans], if you touch us we curl up into a ball and sting!"

Marc Bordigoni

FURTHER READING

Françoise Burgaud. "Du hérisson honni au hérisson blason de la nature." *Journal d'agriculture traditionnelle et de botanique appliquée* 38, no. 2 (1996): 21–41.

Latcho Raben Collective. *Cuisine tzigane*. Serres-Castet, France: Faucompret, 1994.

Alain Reyniers. "Les compagnons du buisson." In *Des tsiganes en Europe*, ed. Michaël Stewart and Patrick Williams, 141–62. Paris: Éditions de la Maison des Sciences de l'Homme, 2011.

Patrick Williams. "Nommer, connaître, faire connaître." In *Roms en Europe: Sous le regard de trois ethnologues*, ed. Patrick Williams, Martin Olivera, and Victor Alexandre Stoiochită, 7–18. Nanterre: Société d'Ethnologie, 2016.

——. *Nous, on n'en parle pas: Les morts et les vivants chez les manouches.* Paris: Éditions de la Maison des Sciences de l'Homme, 1993.

FURTHER TRAVELING

Barbecue, Dogmeat

Hot Dogs

In June 1939 the British royal couple made an official visit to the United States. George VI's aim was to secure North American support in the face of the deteriorating situation in Europe. On June 11 President Franklin Delano Roosevelt and his wife invited their visitors to Hyde Park on the Hudson River in New York for a traditional American picnic. On the menu there were potato salad, beer, and hot dogs. The next day a *New York Times* headline read: "King tries hot dog and asks for more," making this culinary success a symbol of the strengthened alliance between the United Kingdom and the United States.

Although the hot dog entered diplomatic history on the eve of World War II, it had been the embodiment of the close relationship between Europe and America for at least fifty years already. The symbol that emerged in 1939 was all the stronger since the sausages enjoyed by the future allies originated in the German city of Frankfurt-am-Main. The sausage is said to have been invented by a rural butcher, Johann Georghehner, who settled in Frankfurt at the end of the fifteenth century, where his trade flourished, leading the city to commemorate the five hundredth anniversary of this culinary invention in 1987. But it was migrants from Central Europe who carried the austere sausage on their transatlantic journey, transforming it into a symbol. In 1929, when Walt Disney introduced talking pictures with his animated cartoon *The Carnival Kid*, among the first words his Mickey Mouse character uttered was "hot dogs." The history of this sausage is directly linked to its role as a mainstay of mass culture and the various venues where it is served. In 1964 Roy Lichtenstein doubled Disney's gesture in his multiple works on sheet metal soberly entitled *Hot Dog (Food and Drinks)*, definitively associating it with the idea of entertainment. The pop art artist took a comic-book image of the sausage smiling broadly, surrounded by two pieces of bread, and turned it into a metonymy for fun.

It was at Coney Island, on the beach and along Surf Avenue in particular, in the world's first permanent amusement park, that the hot dog became the food symbol of popular culture. It was part of the invention of this new form of entertainment, produced by the very singular mix of the screams of visitors on roller coasters such as the famous Cyclone, the mechanical din of the rides, the music of the booths where people literally shot at each other, and the speeches of those trying to win over the onlookers to discover the human torso and other "freaks." Accompanied by Coca-Cola for the young ones, it mitigated the effects of beer for others. But caution was necessary: hot dogs lead to their own form of inebriation (one may not want to eat more than one). At the turn of the century, amid the merry-go-rounds and tattoo parlors, the little sausage stands became veritable institutions. Charles Feltman, who seems to have been the first to dedicate himself to selling them at a stand in 1871, was followed by numerous merchants who competed fiercely with each other. One of Feltman's old Polish employees, Nathan Handwerker, dominated the market from 1916 onward, selling his Nathan's Famous Hot Dogs at half price. Eating became a game, and in July, to celebrate the national holiday, Coney Island held a contest for the fastest hot dog eater.

In 1893, at the Chicago World's Fair, the world discovered what European migrants had done to the little red sausage. At the foot of the first monumental Ferris wheel, there was another event: a tiny kiosk run by two Austro-Hungarian émigrés, Emil Reichel and Sam Ladany, selling a hot beef and pork sausage surrounded by a soft bun that could be swallowed in three bites as one gazed up to admire the extraordinary giant rotating wheel. The mouth hanging open, one could only satisfy their hunger through finger food.

With the development of spectator sports in the United States, one of the most symbolic venues for the hot dog became the baseball stadium or the velodrome. In New York, whether in Yankee Stadium in the Bronx or inside Madison Square Garden in Manhattan, where the cyclists rode endlessly around a track, people ate hot dogs, their eyes hypnotized by such athletic ballets. The sandwich was perfectly in tune with the temporality of these sporting events that could drag on for long hours, freeing the working classes for an evening from the infernal pace of the factories. Each trip to the hot dog stand allowed them to take in the spectacle, make it their own, and find their place in it.

But the sale and consumption of the hot dog burst far beyond these places, for New Amsterdam (an early name for New York) was itself a huge amusement park, as the French author Céline pointed out in *Voyage au bout de la nuit* when the lead character, Bardamu, arrives in the great metropolis. The hot dog set the stage for the temporality of the modern city as it reorganized time, starting with the great division of day and night as well as three daily meals. From the 1910s onward the inexpensive little sandwich, garnished to one's taste with cooked cabbage, fried onions, mustard, and other condiments, became the appetite suppressant of a hurried America that mocked a staid old Europe.

The very name of the sausage was entertaining. Some specialists have pointed out that the sausage shape reminded women and men of the 1870s of a dog breed, the dachshund, that it was often used by French press cartoonists to represent Germany. However, given the challenge of shouting such a name to attract hurried customers, and since the sausage was to be consumed hot, the term "hot dog" was preferred. Another, more prosaic explanation recounts that before the hot dog, cooked sausages were already one of the least expensive foodstuffs from the mid-nineteenth century onward in the booming metropolises like New York. "Sausage carts" were springing up everywhere, selling a variety of takeaway foods on street corners. Sausages were also perceived as safer than the "fresh" meat served in local restaurants, which was too expensive and risked spoiling if not consumed quickly. As the ingredients of sausages were not well known, it was also rumored that they contained rat, dog, or cat flesh as well as pork or beef, and the street began to refer to these rolling kiosks as "dog carts." The hot dog's immense success was never undermined by such rhetoric since the actual hot dog connotes more than just the sausage within it. The oblong bun is equally essential. This distinctive bread wrapping is also an all-American product and the work of another first-generation migrant, Austrian Ignatz Frischman, who opened a bakery in New York's Coney Island in the mid-nineteenth century. And if the recipe for the Frankfurter hot dog undoubtedly lost some of its subtle nuances (garlic, cardamom, coriander, ginger, chili, pepper, and salt) over the course of the twentieth century, this singular sandwich remained garnished, according to personal or family histories, with numerous condiments and accompaniments: ketchup, mustard, sauces, relish, fried onions, and sauerkraut. As a result, the hot dog has also been exported with new variations outside the United States. In Canada it is known as the *Guédille*, with the sausage replaced by a lobster or crab salad. In Chile the *Completo* is topped with crushed tomatoes and avocado. But the hot dog has remained remarkably stable since it first appeared over 140 years ago, as if in its modest container, it embodies a moment in history, that of the massive arrival of European migrants anxious to invent a new way of life together, with new temporalities and collective rituals.

Philippe Artières

FURTHER READING

Sean Basinski. "Hot Dogs, Hipsters, and Xenophobia: Immigrant Street Food Vendors in New York." *Social Research* 81, no. 2 (2014): 397–408.
Bruce Kraig and Patty Carroll. *Man Bites Dog: Hot Dog Culture in America*. Lanham, MD: AltaMira Press, 2012.

FURTHER TRAVELING

Beer, Chili Pepper, Coca-Cola, Dogmeat, French Fries, Ketchup, Salt, Sandwich

Hummus

On March 14, 2006, Sabra Foods, an American food company backed by Israeli capital, entered the Guinness Book of Records for the largest hummus dish ever made, weighing almost 400 kilos (882 lb.) in a container 3.5 meters (11.5 ft.) in diameter, triggering what is now known as the hummus war. Hummus is a puree of chickpeas mixed with tahini, a sesame seed cream, a hint of garlic, and a squeeze of lemon juice onto which a drizzle of olive oil is poured. The recipe is simple, but the search for balance and excellence of taste is delicate. Yet this seemingly banal and inexpensive dish is loaded with symbolic, political, and economic implications.

The word *hummus* means chickpea in Arabic. The term has since come to designate one of the flagship dishes made with this vegetable, whose origins, both geographical and historical, are obscure. This lack of knowledge has given rise to much speculation and dispute. Chickpeas, on the other hand, undoubtedly originated in the eastern Mediterranean, where they were domesticated between the seventh and sixth millennia BCE and spread to the West and East. In the Indian subcontinent, it is the main legume crop and plays an important role in cooking. As for today's hummus, its definitive origins remain a mystery, though it may well have been invented for the Turkish elite in eighteenth-century Damascus or in Beirut. Be that as it may, the idea of pureeing chickpeas is old and recipes for it can be found in Arab cooking treatises as early as the tenth century, albeit in far more sophisticated formulas than the current recipe. The latter, no doubt because of its simplicity, has become a contemporary staple of Middle Eastern cuisine. Hummus takes pride of place among the *mezzés* for which Syro-Lebanese, Palestinians, Jordanians, and Turks, unified under the Ottomans, are renowned. It can also be found in Egypt, though it is often less flavorsome. Cleverly arranged in a small red earthenware bowl with raised sides, it is served with a piece of pita bread. It can also be topped with a warm garnish of small pieces of lamb, liver, pastirma (pastrami), or sujuk (sausage).

However, the conviviality surrounding hummus has been curtailed by the arrival of a new actor in the region, Israel, which also claims to be the originator, since the dish is, according to some, mentioned in the Hebrew Bible. In reality, the consumption of hummus, borrowed from the Palestinians, developed only after the creation of the state of Israel in 1948, but since then it has been so popular with the Israeli population that they have come to regard it as their own, and even as a symbol of their identity. In Israel, as in the occupied Palestinian territories, one finds a multitude of *houmousiyât* (in Arabic) or *hummusiyot* (in Hebrew), small restaurants serving nothing but hummus, always fresh daily and prepared in many varieties. Israel has been marketing industrial hummus internationally since the late 1950s, as has Lebanon. The recent hummus war sits precisely at the crossroads of these economic interests and demands for identity and patriotism. Irritated by Israel's claims over hummus, and considering that the neighboring country, with which it remained virtually at war, was usurping its culinary heritage, Lebanon retaliated with two dazzling actions. At the end of 2008, at the initiative of the president of the Association of Lebanese Industrialists, Lebanon unsuccessfully applied to the European Union for the creation of a Geographical Indication and Quality status for hummus, which would then be labeled as a specifically Lebanese dish, as Greece had obtained for feta cheese in 2002. In 2009, to support this initiative, 250 Lebanese apprentice cooks produced a hummus dish weighing more than two tons, enabling Lebanon to enter the Guinness Book of Records, erasing the record previously held by Sabra. The following year, in January 2010, an Israeli Arab restaurateur from the village of Abu Gosh, Israel, replied by filling a satellite dish with four tons of hummus, not made for the occasion but from tin cans. His record entered in the Guinness Book of Records nonetheless. In May of the same year, three hundred Lebanese cooks gathered near Beirut to shatter the record by making a hummus dish weighing 10,452 kilos (23,042 lb.), a figure equivalent to the surface area of Lebanon in square kilometers.

In 2012 an Australian filmmaker, himself a great fan of the hummus he enjoyed on Bondi Beach near Sydney, took up the subject of this other Middle Eastern war in a documentary entitled *Make Hummus, Not War*. In 2015, an Israeli filmmaker, Oren Rosenfeld, set out in *Hummus, the Movie* to follow three hummus restaurant owners in Israel: one Jewish, another Christian, the third a Muslim woman who was victorious in a televised competition for Israel's best hummus maker and has become a symbol of female success. After a phase of denial, the Arab identity of hummus has become increasingly recognized by Israelis. This is humorously confirmed by Israeli Arab director Sameh Zoabi's film *Tel Aviv on Fire* (2018), in which the Israeli hero asks his Palestinian counterpart for "good Arab hummus" in exchange for his help. Hummus has thus gone from being a disputed foodstuff to a form of "gastromediation," to use the term coined by Israeli anthropologist Nir Avieli.

The hummus war came at a time when the economic stakes reached new heights. In the 2000s the wave of vegetarianism and veganism gave hummus a new lease of life. Legumes like chickpeas that are rich in fiber and vegetable proteins were being rediscovered. Agronomists invested in chickpea cultivation in the semiarid regions expanding with global warming. The context was therefore propitious for the globalization of the hummus market. In 2006 Sabra took the initiative to conquer the huge North American market. In 2008 a partnership signed with PepsiCo gave Sabra control of the lion's share of the industrial hummus market, which exploded in the United States from $100 million in the early 2000s to $230 million in 2009. Nowadays it is not only Israelis and Lebanese who produce hummus industrially. It can be found on supermarket shelves the world over. Nutritious, convenient, and relatively inexpensive, it has become a popular choice for an aperitif or a starter. Penniless students who want to get away from junk food transform it, with bread, into a complete meal. Such is its success that the term hummus is used for purées made from other legumes or vegetables, which have nothing to do with the chickpea to which the name refers. These innovations have alarmed purists, and in the face of global market competition, quality and authenticity have acquired an added value. On the initiative of an Israeli-American businessman in 2012, May 13 has become World Hummus Day, an event that receives an echo especially on social media. And in February 2018 Lebanese students organized a hummus festival in Manchester, England, to promote "authentic Lebanese hummus" in the face of industrial products. Could this be considered a euphemistic revival of the hummus war?

Sylvia Chiffoleau

FURTHER READING

Ari Ariel. "The Hummus Wars," *Gastronomica: The Journal of Food and Culture* 12, no. 1 (2012): 34–42.

Nir Avieli. "The Hummus Wars: Local Food, Guinness Records and Palestinian-Israeli Gastropolitics." In *Cooking Cultures: Convergent Histories of Food and Feeling*, ed. Ishita Banerjee-Dube, 39–57. Cambridge: Cambridge University Press, 2016.

Robert Bistolfi and Farouk Mardam-Bey. *Traité du pois chiche*. Arles: Actes Sud, Sindbad, 2019.

162   HUMMUS

Rafi Grosglik. "Le houmous et le bio en Israël: Comment un plat national devient cosmopolite." *Ethnologie française* 45, no. 2 (2015): 257–67.

Dafna Hirsch. "'Hummus is best when it is fresh and made by Arabs': The Gourmetization of Hummus in Israel and the Return of the Repressed Arab." *American Ethnologist* 38, no. 4 (2011): 617–30.

FURTHER TRAVELING

Chorba, Dafina, Matzah, Olive Oil

Ice Cubes

In 1965, at the end of a hard day's coring in the Antarctic ice, glaciologist Claude Lorius, a member of the French mission wintering at the Dumont-d'Urville base in Adélie Land, was enjoying an aperitif with his team. He poured himself a glass of whiskey, took an ice cube from a thousand-year-old ice core on the white continent, and observed the air bubbles released in the Scottish beverage. Lorius had a premonition that led to a revolution in the history of the climate. These bubbles were as old as the ice that had trapped them, and this ice cube—and its gas—was a precious witness to the atmosphere of the past. Polar ice became the world's climate memory. But if this small cube of ice could tell a story that went back millions of years, an impressive enough accomplishment in the history of food, it also and above all resulted from a global history and a world geography of cold drink consumption.

The quest for cold or freshness, through the preservation of ice or snow, was at the origin of an ambitious commercial enterprise, long before the democratization of the refrigerator. Cold production and preservation were virtually universal, and the choice of lukewarm or cool beverages, based in particular on the constraints of geography, may be considered as essential as the division between raw and cooked, popularized by Claude Lévi-Strauss. As far back as antiquity, in the Han Empire, Persian Empire, or Roman Empire, winter or mountain ice was transported to cities and palaces and stored in wells or *yakhtchāl* (in Iran) until the height of summer. The *Shijing*, or "Classic of Verses," an anthology of Chinese poetry from the first millennium BCE, already described the harvesting and storage of ice. Requiring abundant manpower and costly infrastructures, it was reserved for a social elite, whether it came from the Andes for the Incan aristocracy, the Sierra Nevada for the Umayyad caliphs, or the Hindu

Kush for the Mughal emperors, who in the sixteenth century used horse relays to transport the ice to Agra or Delhi. In early modern Europe aristocratic châteaux were equipped with icehouses, as in the gardens of the Château de Versailles.

But the real boom in the ice business dates from the nineteenth century, and with it the massive use of crushed ice and small ice cubes. The industrialization of block ice harvesting and distribution began in North America and Western Europe. From there the market went global. By midcentury, steamships were transporting American ice as far as India and Australia, and the advent of railcars and refrigerated ships made it possible to transport meat and fruit and vegetables over long distances, and even to export them. In Europe, Norway became a leading ice producer at the end of the century and a giant in the international cold trade. This activity played a key role in the emergence of a specific Norwegian identity, emancipating the country from Danish and then Swedish tutelage. Collected with a saw, the blocks were then extracted with ice tongs and stored in a warehouse. In summer, ice merchants sold ice in the form of small blocks that people placed in their domestic coolers, in a compartment above the food. Small pieces of ice were often placed in porcelain buckets, which were originally designed to maintain a low temperature for desserts, without coming into contact with the food.

In East Asia, on the other hand, perhaps long before the ice cube, grated ice had been used for centuries in desserts, creating such delights as Japanese kakigōri or Korean patbingsu. According to an apocryphal Japanese tradition, Sei Shōnagon, a court lady of the Heian period (ninth to eleventh centuries) and author of *Makura no sōshi* or "Pillow Notes," a masterpiece of world literature like the *Tale of Genji*, first had the idea of pouring syrup over ice. But it was in the nineteenth century, at the end of the Edo period, that this dessert became widespread, with, as in the Western world, the rise of the ice trade. From the time of the forced opening up of the country following Commodore Perry's expedition in 1853, kakigōri were often made with American ice imported into Japan (Boston ice), after more than six months' travel, and then, as in Europe, with local ice from the northern island of Hokkaido, transported from the port of Hakodate to the port of Yokohama near Tokyo (Hakodate ice). As early as 1870 the famous Japanese entrepreneur Kahe Nakagawa, a pioneer of trade with the West, made his fortune in this trade and helped democratize ice cream consumption in the country. The Japanese colonization of Korea (1910–45) also contributed to the democratization of Korean bingsu, previously reserved for the elite Choseon dynasty, for whom the "government office of the royal icehouse," Seobingo, was created. Patbingsu, which literally means "red bean paste on ice flakes," now holds a unique place in Korean culinary culture. Further east, the immigration of Japanese workers to the sugarcane and pineapple plantations in the Hawaiian archipelago between 1868 and 1907 led to a local adaptation of the Japanese dessert into "Hawaiian granita" (shaved ice).

The invention of industrial ice was a turning point in the history of the ice cube. As early as 1845, Floridian physician John Gorrie patented a machine for making ice cubes to treat his patients suffering from tropical diseases, particularly yellow fever. And in 1913 Chicago-born Frederick William Wolf Jr. became the first inventor to place an ice cube tray in a refrigerator (the DOMERLE, or DOMestic ELectric REfrigerator). The small cube became the heart of domestic consumption of artificial ice. The first flexible trays, which could be bent sideways to crack and eject ice cubes, were produced in the 1930s. After World War II aluminum trays with a removable cube divider and release handles became widespread, before the advent of molded plastic ice cube trays, which for the last thirty years have been able to take any possible shape. The "Titanic and Icebergs," for example, offers the "coolest" version, allowing you to dive into the glasses of ocean liners and ice giants with a surprising taste that borders on the sublime. In the 1960s, automatic icemakers began to proliferate in North American motels, before manufacturers began offering them in fridge-freezers and even in door-mounted dispensers.

The advent of the ice cube has created a global geography of the pure and the impure. In some countries where tap water is not treated for pathogens, it is advisable to avoid drinks and food in contact with ice cubes or crushed ice. The history of the ice cube began in the West, accompanying British imperialism and colonialism in the nineteenth century, followed by the advent of the American way of life. Ice became the essential ingredient of one of the first typically American drinks, the cocktail. Charles Dickens, in his 1842 account of his stay in North America, *American Notes*, mentions the pleasures of sipping iced cocktails in summer. Cocktails on the rocks, in particular whiskey and bourbon, became a classic of triumphant American masculinity, supported by literature and the Hollywood film industry. More recently, the fashion for "swimming pool" cocktails, served in large glasses with lots of ice, has become a staple of extremely simplified mixology. Although rosé and other spirits can be served in a "piscine," a large glass with ice cubes, the standard mix contains champagne, which has remained particularly "gendered." Women have been targeted as the preferred consumers of these lighter, more diluted cocktails. Despite criticism from purists, champagne houses have sought to capture this new market. In 2010 Moët et Chandon created Ice Impérial, with a higher sugar content, the world's first champagne to be enjoyed over ice—and unfortunately almost undrinkable without it!

Fabrice Argounès

FURTHER READING

Xavier de Planhol. *L'eau de neige: Le tiède et le frais—Histoire et géographie des boissons fraîches*. Paris: Fayard, 1995.

Luke Fater. "How American Gunboat Diplomacy Helped Democratize Japanese Shaved Ice." *Atlas Obscura*, September 5, 2019.

Per G. Norseng. "The 'Last Ice Age' in Maritime History: An Introduction." *International Journal of Maritime History* 34, no. 1 (2022): 101–12.

Jonathan Rees. *Refrigeration Nation: A History of Ice, Appliances, and Enterprise in America*. Baltimore: Johns Hopkins University Press, 2013.

Aline Rousselle, ed. *La glace et ses usages*. Perpignan: Presses Universitaires de Perpignan, 1999.

FURTHER TRAVELING

Champagne, Whiskey

Indomie

In 1988 Tolaram, a Singapore-based holding company, decided to diversify its activities in Africa and took a gamble on selling a product previously unknown in Nigeria: instant noodles. In less than forty years, a commercial initiative from Southeast Asia turned the country upside down, making noodles sold by the Indonesian brand Indomie one of the most widely consumed food products in the country. At the beginning of the twenty-first century, Nigeria became the world's eleventh-largest consumer of instant noodles, all brands combined.

It all began in 1958, when the Taiwanese-Japanese Ando Momofuku commercialized a process that enabled dried ramen to be preserved and cooked in just a few minutes by adding boiling water. Ramen are wheat noodles of Chinese origin, the consumption of which was encouraged by the United States, eager to sell its wheat in postwar Japan. Momofuku, since known as Mr. Noodle, gave thousands of Japanese a speedy way to cook ramen at home. Neighboring countries quickly adopted the idea. In the 1980s Indonesia became the world's biggest producer, thanks to a state monopoly in a country with a booming population. The success of instant noodles is due not only to their low manufacturing costs but also to the ease with which they can be transported and stored. As a result, their selling price remains easily accessible. If Indomie (a cross-breed of *Indo* for Indonesia and *mie* for noodles) is a proof of success, it is above all the triumph of Nigeria's agri-food companies. Ten large factories now produce millions of bags for Dufil, a subsidiary of the Tolaram group. The result of a conglomerate between a Singaporean and an Indonesian company, Dufil symbolizes a certain globalization of capital and tastes between Asia and Africa. The success of its flagship product is that of a food model that is both capital-intensive and adapted to the demands of rapidly growing populations (Nigeria was expected to have two hundred million inhabitants by 2022). So it is no surprise to find Indomie in Saudi Arabia, Sudan, and Kenya.

In Nigeria, this brand is so popular that the word Indomie is now synonymous with noodles, despite the arrival of other Nigerian instant noodles. Even if a dozen companies such as Honeywell or Dangote (owned by Nigerian billionaire Aliko Dangote) coexist, Indomie controlled approximately two-thirds of the market by 2020. Demographic and social factors may explain this success. As in other fast-growing countries around the world, instant noodles have caught on with an ever-younger population. Nigerian workers are short of time, and long working hours prevent them from cooking full meals. The economic argument is also fundamental to understanding how Indomie has established itself in Nigeria, where the poverty rate remains very high. But this cannot be the only explanation.

In a country renowned for its geographical differences, Indomie can now be found in almost every region. Added to this is a veritable advertising blitz modeled on Coca-Cola or Maggi cubes. In every Nigerian town and village, there are billboards, parade grounds in the markets, and red paint on the walls of houses in Indomie colors. Public space is thus visibly marked by the transformation of Nigeria's food supply. Aggressive marketing has also extended the brand's influence, whether on television or radio. The different pack sizes are suitable for a family meal or for the appetite of a single adult. Gendered ads promote the "Hungry Man" pack, while there's a "Full Belly" pack for the hungriest. It can be eaten by all faiths, and the company also promotes it for Ramadan. In a flurry of advertising, Indomie appears to be the perfect example of unbridled Nigerian capitalism.

Since the early 2000s, children in particular have become the target of Indomie's advertising campaigns. By entering schools, the company gambled on transforming the dietary habits of an entire generation, and thus of a country. Twenty years on, Indomie products are no longer found only in schools; Nigerians now eat them at home in a variety of forms. Today the brand would like to appeal to everyone, even if the older generations remain perplexed by this fashion, which has little to do with more traditional Nigerian food and dishes. How can a dish prepared in a few minutes compete with yams, manioc, or rice and the rich soups for which Nigerian cuisine is so famous?

Yet, as in many countries around the world, Indomie has adapted to local tastes. In Nigeria instant noodles are not prepared as soups as in China. Instead, they are first boiled with the spices or flavor packets included in the package. Once boiled, Indomie is cooked with palm oil and chilis. They are served with whatever vegetables are available at the time: chilis are always included, green onions are common, and occasionally there are tomatoes. For breakfast they are best eaten with an omelet on the noodles. For lunch or dinner one can replace the omelet with chicken. There is no exhaustive list of the different ways to cook the noodles. The possibilities are endless. Indomie noodles are constantly being reinvented, whether in the home or in Nigeria's countless street kitchens.

Although not a "national dish," these noodles have almost reached the status of jollof rice in the eyes of Nigerians. And their omnipresence means that the dish is considered as such by the inhabitants of neighboring countries. Prepared according to the same recipes in street kitchens from Benin to Ghana, over the past half century Japanese instant noodles sold in Indonesia have found a new identity in Nigeria.

Vincent Hiribarren

FURTHER READING

Yemisi Aribisala. *Longthroat Memoirs: Soups, Sex and Nigerian Taste Buds.* London: Cassava Republic Press, 2016.
"How Indomie Became Insanely Popular in Nigeria." https://www.vice.com/en/article/3d9p5y/how-indomie-became-insanely-popular-in-nigeria.
Mutiara Sri Dewi Mulyaning. "Instant Noodle Boom in Indonesia: A Commodity Chain Analysis Study." 2016. https://thesis.eur.nl/pub/37266/.
"World Instant Noodles Association." https://instantnoodles.org/en/.

FURTHER TRAVELING

Chili Pepper, Coca-Cola, Palm Oil, Ramen

Injera

In September 1974 Emperor Haile Selassie I of Ethiopia was deposed by a revolutionary government. Many refugees fled the country in the months and years that followed. Among them were families linked to the former regime, who found their way to North America and occasionally to Western Europe. In 1987, at a time when Ethiopian restaurants were flourishing in the United States, Daniel Jote Mesfin, himself from one of these families living in the suburbs of Washington, published his first cookbook in English. Drawing heavily on the banqueting skills of his mother and other exiled "ladies" (*weyzero*), he set out to present a refined Ethiopian cuisine, based on the contrast between *injera*, a subtly sour flatbread, and spicy *wat* (sauce).

Ethiopian injera is a soft, spongy bread made from a dough of water and cereal flour, fermented for twenty-four to forty-eight hours. In a few minutes, injera is cooked on one side on a *metad* (in Amharic) or *magogo* (in Tigrinya), a large earthenware plate placed on the stove under a lid. A daily staple for tens of millions of Ethiopians and Eritreans, injera is most often eaten fresh with one or more sauces or other preparations and served on a platter. Injera is at the heart of what is known as "Ethiopian cuisine," but it is the central element of a more narrowly defined food culture, that of the Ethiopian highlands—the mountain range to the west of the Rift Valley and the Afar Triangle. This region is inhabited by a predominantly rural, cereal-growing population, most of whom speak Amharic and Tigrinya (two relatively closely related Semitic languages). Despite some deep-rooted political divisions, these populations cultivate a strong sense of cultural unity. Over the centuries they have formed part of the various avatars of the "Christian kingdom of Ethiopia," whose rulers claimed to be related to King Solomon and the Queen of Sheba (or Makeda). They call themselves *habasha* (from which the French term "*abyssin*" derives), are predominantly Christian (of the Tewahedo Church, the Ethiopian Orthodox Church), and see their way of life as distinct from that of their immediate neighbors.

Injera makes the meal and determines its order. The meal is eaten with the right hand, seizing with the flatbread food that has been prepared in a common round dish and ideally placed on a *mesob* (a small wickerwork table). The injera can in turn be transformed: *firfir* (torn into pieces and mixed into the sauce), *fitfit* (chopped and served like moistened porridge), or *derkosh* (small, dried pieces which are then rehydrated). Injera is still largely prepared at home, its production has been modernized through the limited urban distribution of electric heating units called *metad*. The making of injera is exclusively a woman's job, and men purchase it from women sellers. In North America and Europe, Ethiopian grocery stores sell injera, which is more or less industrially produced and sold in plastic packaging. The inimitable taste of "real" injera is an inexhaustible source of nostalgia for exiles.

In the highlands, injera is closely associated with a local cereal, teff (*Eragrostis tef*), whose flour is used almost exclusively. Ethiopians and Eritreans share the idea that the best injera is made with teff flour (preferably white) and that injera made with anything else is just a poor substitute. But this ideal often comes up against the reality of the unavailability of teff flour, depending on the region or farm, and above all its high price. This forces farmers to sell their produce on the market. Barley, wheat, corn, sorghum, and finger millet flours are therefore often used as well. Daniel's cookbook includes these variants, since exiled communities often need to manage despite the absence of teff. Nevertheless, teff remains the most important grain in the recipe. Because it is gluten-free, it lends itself specifically to the preparation of flatbreads, and its use seems to have conditioned the shape of the *metad*, on which most other Ethiopian breads are also baked (there are no traditional bread ovens in the highlands). It is probably because teff is an endemic plant of this region that the injera has become a specific cultural marker for its inhabitants.

Historians have questioned how closely injera has been related to bread over the long term. The first appearance of the word in an Ethiopian text (otherwise marked by the appearance of vernacular terms in Amharic rather than in Guez, the classical language) dates from the fifteenth century. Sources up to the nineteenth century reveal a food culture in which (wheat) bread and injera coexisted, but the nature of this documentation—Ethiopian royal chronicles and accounts by primarily European travelers—tends to give greater importance to exceptional consumption. Nevertheless, the importance of injera is revealed indirectly, and many authors have noted the preeminence of teff seed. As early as the fourteenth century, the Syrian al-Umari, using his own value system, compared teff to the "wheat" of the *habasha*, from which they made their "bread." Teff does indeed seem to be the "wheat" of the rural and political imagination of the highlands, as traditions evoking the origins of the Ethiopian kingdom closely associate its domestication with the birth of the state. In 1909, during a visit to a monastery in Tigray, Johannes Kolmodin was able to copy the manuscript of a "short chronicle," a list of kings preceded by an account of the reign of the serpent, Arwe, whose destruction marked the birth of the kingdom. Teff appears for the first time on the monster's remains and is described as "food for the people of Ethiopia." An oral tradition collected by Michel Perret and Michel Denais in 1983 develops the anecdote that white teff grew on the remains of the snake before being replanted by man.

Far from Tigray, in the Choa region (Addis Ababa), it was not until the writings of Gabra Selasse, minister to the king of kings Menelik II (r. 1889–1913), that a "discourse of gastronomy" emerged, highlighting for the first time the qualities of the cuisine served at banquets organized by Empress Taytu. Particular attention was paid to injera, as the author praised the exceptional sifting of teff flour, especially white teff. The banquet, to which each subject was invited in the order of his or her rank, united the people with their sovereign around the same cuisine and the same culinary ideals. This idea of an Ethiopia united by its cuisine, and therefore by quality injera, was forged in a specific context. Just as Abyssinia (Al-Habbash) was being unified at the end of the nineteenth century, Menelik II began the conquest of a vast empire and created modern administrative institutions. This expansion marked the first time injera was exported beyond its native soil. In the conquered territories, dotted with military camps that became cities, injera traveled with the settlers from the high plateaus, leading to the cohabitation of their cuisine with other food cultures—bread and banana porridges from the tropical hills of the southwest, agro-pastoral foods from the Afars and Somalis in the east, sorghum and leaf dumplings from the far south, and so on—and to the export of injera to other countries. Injera, in this context, became for the first time the constitutive element of an "imperial cuisine" soon to become a national symbol, fixed in writing for the first time in 1945 by the cookbook of the country's first girls' school. A symbol that successive political crises and tragedies in the Horn of Africa subsequently helped to export, with Ethiopian restaurants and their injera becoming important socialization tools for "Little Ethiopias" around the world.

Thomas Guindeuil

FURTHER READING

Abebe Kifleyesus. "The Construction of Ethiopian National Cuisine." *Ethnorêma* 2 (2006): 27–47.

Johannes Kolmodin. *Traditions de Tsazzega et Hazzega*. Uppsala: E. Berling, 1914.

Diane Lyons and Catherine D'Andrea. "Griddles, Ovens, and Agricultural Origins: An Ethnoarchaeological Study of Bread Baking in Highland Ethiopia." *American Anthropologist* 105, no. 3 (2003): 515–30.

Daniel Jote Mesfin. *Exotic Ethiopian Cooking*. Falls Church, VA: Ethiopian Cookbook Enterprises, 1987.

Michel Perret and Michel Denais. "La mort du serpent." In *Guirlande pour Abba Jérôme*, ed. Joseph Tubiana, 117–52. Paris: Le Mois en Afrique, 1983.

FURTHER TRAVELING

Chili Pepper, Chorba, Dafina, Naan, Pizza

Ketchup

On October 11, 1924, at 6:30 p.m. in Pittsburgh; at 3:30 p.m. in San Francisco; and at 11:30 p.m. in London, sixty-two banquets began that spread across sixty-two cities in the United States, Canada, and the United Kingdom. They were accompanied by several radio speeches, including one delivered from the White House by the president of the United States, Calvin Coolidge. More than ten thousand people took part in this spectacular event. Each person was offered the same menu, starting with tomato soup.

The idea for this large-scale banquet had sprouted from the minds of Heinz Company executives five years after the death of the company's founder, Henry J. Heinz, whose statue had been unveiled that very morning. The occasion was a celebration of the company's fifty-fifth anniversary (which was not quite true: Henry J. Heinz had founded his first company in Pittsburgh in 1869, but it had gone bankrupt, and the current Heinz Company dated back to 1876). The speeches went on and on. At the time of the banquet, Heinz had fifty-three sites in the United States, five in the United Kingdom, and four in Canada. The future was full of promise. Pages of advertising in English-language newspapers showed two cuts of a globe populated by workers of all races, some in traditional dress, linked to a central blue dot adorned with fruit and vegetables, which read: "57 varieties of good things to eat." The slogan then stated: "From the world's gardens to the world's markets."

One of the goods marketed by the Heinz Company was "tomato ketchup," produced in excess of ten million bottles a year by the 1900s. Consumers are inevitably familiar with the product, which arrived in France after World War II. Today, Kraft Heinz alone sells 650 million bottles a year worldwide, to which must be added the countless fast-food packets invented by the Heinz Company in the late 1960s, which have inextricably linked ketchup to fries and hamburgers. The octagonal bottle of Heinz ketchup has become almost as famous as Coca-Cola, and like Coca-Cola it has often been made a symbol of the Americanization of the world. In 1999, when "Heinz tomato ketchup" was included by NASA on the list of foods that could be eaten on the International Space Station, it was commented on as the completion of the conquest of the world by the little glass bottle filled with red sauce. (The fact that in the same years Heinz was the first Western company to advertise on Chinese television was also significant.)

This conquest was the result of a remarkable industrial process. Around 1900, the Heinz plant in Pittsburgh had already pioneered the automation of production, including that of its own glass bottles. The model developed at the same time by Henry Ford in the automobile industry comes to mind. Yet there was one notable difference between the two: in line with the prejudice that food preparation was a woman's business, the fledgling food industry employed a majority of female workers to fill cans and bottles. Although only men spoke at the banquet for the Heinz Company's ten thousand employees in 1924, women were undoubtedly in the majority at the tables.

Ketchup is not just a metaphor for the Americanization of the world. The legend of Henry J. Heinz recounts how this son of German immigrants began his professional life helping his mother make tinned horseradish before he had the idea of adding sugar to the sauce he would market, from 1876, under the name "catsup." While partly original, this preparation was merely a variant of the many sauces adapted since the end of the seventeenth century by the British on their return from Southeast Asia and then imported into the North American colonies. It is highly likely that these fish-based brines, known as *ké-tsiap* in southern China and *kicap* or *kecap* in Malaysia, gradually became known in English as "catsup" and then ketchup, at the same time that fish ceased to be a fundamental ingredient. By the time Henry J. Heinz created his own recipe, anchovies had been replaced by tomatoes in "catsup" for several decades.

It is remarkable, then, that after traveling from Southeast Asia to Great Britain and the United States and establishing itself as one of the most global products of our time, ketchup was made from one of the most symbolic fruits to emerge from the meeting of the New and Old Worlds (it should be remembered that "tomato" is one of those full-flavored words that, like "avocado" and "chocolate," come from the Nahuatl language). The small, green, sometimes purplish, not always edible fruit, native to northwestern South America, had been acclimatized in Spain by the 1520s and then in Italy around 1540. In a way, ketchup is the heir to the first forms of tomato consumption, which Europeans used from the end of the seventeenth century as a condiment to spice up sauces. But ketchup is above all the result of two major, more recent transformations.

The first is the process by which the fruit is peeled, deseeded, heated, and crushed. Water is then removed by evaporation to produce an easily transportable concentrate. The process is not new. As early as the first decades of the nineteenth century, people in Sicily were making large black loaves of sun-dried tomatoes in this way: *pani neri*. The method was industrialized in Emilia-Romagna in Italy with the appearance of canning factories (the first to specialize in tomato derivatives was inaugurated in Parma in 1888). By the end of the twentieth century Italian companies had become the world's largest producers of small cans of tomato paste. In the United States, where the use of tomato paste became the rule at the Heinz Company around 1970, the industry initially focused on California, since its climate lent itself to tomato cultivation.

This involved a second major transformation: the development of the industrial tomato derived from a variety from the Galápagos Islands, whose gene was identified in the 1940s by a botany professor at University of California, Davis, Charles M. Rick. In 1957 the Heinz Company began to produce its own tomato seeds (Heinz Seeds is now the world's leading producer of industrial tomato seeds). They produced dense, thick-skinned fruit that could be transported without being crushed and yielded maximum juice. The first machines to harvest this type of tomato were developed in California in the early 1960s. Ten years later the entire harvest was mechanized. Huge companies such as Morning Star, which today accounts for 12 percent of the world's tomato concentrate, began supplying the industry. Today, Kraft Heinz alone consumes 5 percent of the world's industrial tomato production, or 450,000 tons of tomato paste.

Things have changed since, however. The Chinese government decided in the early 1990s to invest massively in industrial tomato production. Today China is the world's second-largest tomato producer, behind California and ahead of Italy, and the world's leading exporter of tomato concentrate. Italian companies, which had helped build the first Chinese factories in Xinjiang, soon found themselves competing on their own turf. While Chinese concentrates were initially sent to Italy for repackaging and shipment to non-European markets, they are now exported directly to these markets, from Algeria to Ghana, where concentrates with Italian names (Gino, Pomo) are commercialized from Chinese tomatoes and often mixed with various additives (starch, soy fiber, dextrose, and so on). In Europe Heinz ketchup, like many other ketchups, is now made from concentrate produced partially in China, where the cultivation of industrial tomatoes also serves to repress the Uyghurs of Xinjiang, who are forced to work and harvest the fruit, often in very difficult conditions. This is not always fresh in one's mind when dipping fries into the lush red sauce.

Sylvain Venayre

FURTHER READING

David Gentilcore. *Pomodoro! A History of the Tomato in Italy.* New York: Columbia University Press, 2010.
Jean-Baptiste Malet. *L'empire de l'or rouge: Enquête mondiale sur la tomate d'industrie.* Paris: Fayard, 2017.
Quentin R. Skrabec. *H. J. Heinz: A Biography.* Jefferson, NC: McFarland, 2009.
Andrew F. Smith. *Pure Ketchup: A History of America's National Condiment.* Columbia: University of South Carolina Press, 2011.
Ludovic Tournès. *Américanisation: Une histoire mondiale (xviiie–xxie siècles).* Paris: Fayard, 2020.

FURTHER TRAVELING

Coca-Cola, Fish Sauce (Nuoc Mam), French Fries, Hamburger, Mayonnaise

Lato

In 1952, on the island of Mactan in the central Philippines (Visayas), a fish farmer mixed fragments of the *Caulerpa lentillifera* algae into the food he was feeding to the *bangus* (milkfish) in one of his tidepools. A few days later he realized that the unintentionally introduced cuttings had flourished. He then had the idea of devoting part of his farm to the exclusive production of a green seaweed known in Visayas as *lato*. This seaweed, like others previously harvested from the sea, was soon in great demand in the markets of nearby Cebu. Seemingly accidental, this discovery was the result of a meeting between two features common to the populations of East and Southeast Asia: the banality of seaweed consumption and the accumulation of practical knowledge of aquaculture, unrivaled anywhere in the world.

The appearance, texture, and taste of lato are unique. These small, fish-egg-sized, emerald green and translucent spheres cling to the seaweed like a bunch of miniature grapes. They are almost crunchy and release a fresh gel that is neither too salty nor too algae-like. To enhance the subtle taste, a few drops of one of the local vinegars (rice, coconut, nipa, cane), a little sauce (*patis*), or paste (*bagoong*) of fermented fish or shrimp is sufficient. Today it is often served on a salad (*ensaladang lato*), in multiple combinations such as with onion rings, tomato wedges, or slices of green mango. These colorful combinations are an eyecatcher for gourmets. But lato also has enough organoleptic intensity that it can go without such trappings.

For the Filipino population, seaweed is an ancient and widespread nutritional complement to a diet based on cereals, greens, and root vegetables. The silence of colonial sources speaks volumes about the status of seaweed within Western culinary values. A product of gathering rather than working the land, it could be eaten raw without elaborate preparation. Moreover, in European eyes lato was considered a nonfood item and even used as further proof of indigenous backwardness. By the end of the colonial period, the locals' passion for raw seafood was suspected by travelers and doctors alike of being responsible for certain illnesses in coastal populations and even for the physical deficiencies—some of them irreparable—of these "races." Under U.S. colonial rule (1898–1946), new advances in shipping, agronomy, food preservation, and processing methods facilitated access to Western products and made it possible to model the diet of the colonized on that of the colonizers. This project of "civilization through the fork" further marginalized the consumption of edible seaweed, both socially and culturally, although some coastal populations did not give it up, either out of necessity or taste.

Consumption of lato did not begin to spread throughout the archipelago until the 1950s due to several factors. The first was an increase in supply thanks to Asia's "blue revolution" in the second half of the twentieth century. The domestication of lato benefited from advances in scientific aquaculture, in particular that of red algae, which, transformed into gelling agents, thickeners and other stabilizers, entered the food industry on a massive scale. The Philippines became one of the world leaders in this sector, thanks to the close collaboration between elite Filipino scientists, international experts in phycology, particularly from the United States, and local fishermen-farmers whose practical knowledge was often decisive. In addition to snorkeling and mariculture in ponds, caulerpa thus became, in the 1990s, an open-sea crop and a valuable resource supplement for thousands of families. Second, the metropolis of Manila played a key role in disseminating lato. From the 1960s to the 1970s the capital's markets were regularly supplied to satisfy the immigrant clientele from the provinces, who were traditional seaweed consumers, as well as serve a broader demand. The diversity of regional cuisines, street food, seafood products and the custom of eating them raw or lightly marinated in vinegar or citrus juice (*kinilaw*) were gradually reasserted as part of a movement to exalt "authentic" Filipino values. The rediscovery of lato was part of this food nationalism and participated in a culinary revenge against the colonial period. Finally, from the 1980s onward Philippine production was sustained by exports to Japan, where the craze for "sea grapes" (*umi-budō*) from the Ryukyu Islands made it difficult to meet domestic demand. Today, Vietnam, Malaysia, Indonesia, and Australia produce lato for their domestic markets and for export to Japan, as well as Taiwan, China, and Korea.

Apart from a few eccentric lost settlers far from Manila, the first Westerners to "discover" and appreciate lato were the backpackers of the last decades of the twentieth century, who frequented some of the spectacular beaches located in the cradles of lato production in Boracay (Panay) or El Nido (Palawan). These unwitting pioneers of mass tourism did not play a direct role in the popularization of lato, since its spread came up against a major obstacle: fresh seaweed can only be kept for a few days, which limits its transport by cargo, and it does not tolerate the temperature variations of costly air transport. However, a method of preservation was soon perfected: the seaweed is dehydrated, then preserved in brine and vacuum-packed. Afterward it is simply soaked for a few minutes in fresh water, and the seaweed regains its original appearance and texture. The transformation is spectacular. This is the form through which lato is currently conquering the world, especially thanks to online sales. While supply and distribution chains remain tenuous outside Asia, marketing has adapted the food to the expectations of a globalized gastronomic elite. Promotional marketing emphasizes visual or gustatory analogies that are more or less well-founded but always enticing: "sea grapes," "green/sea/vegetal caviar," even "sea gooseberries." Lato has benefited from the exoticization of eating habits and a passion for Asian cuisines, all of which privilege seaweed. More generally, seaweed is the object of changing appetites. Well-known and influential chefs are giving it pride of place. Though lacking scientific confirmation, promoters transform seaweed or seaweed-based dietary supplements into a panacea. Thanks to the many preventive and curative benefits attributed to its low caloric value, lato features prominently on the list of health-friendly algae. Last but not least, cultured lato satisfies two of the world's most pressing food concerns. Even if it presents some ecological risks, its production is sustainable: it is energy-efficient (the algae reach maturity forty-five to sixty days after planting); it pollutes little or not at all; it requires no fertilizers, unlike industrial agriculture, and no feed, unlike fish and shrimp farming. Since it is plant-based, lato also appeals to consumers keen to limit, or even abolish, the use and consumption of animal proteins.

Will the ubiquitous Filipino diaspora be the driving force behind the globalization of lato? Probably not, given the lack of international visibility of the archipelago's culinary traditions. Likelier the globalization of lato will be driven by the worldwide influence of Japanese cuisine. In turn, and paradoxically, it may be that its growing popularity around the world will encourage its spread across the Philippines, as was the case in the past for many dishes now identified as "national" when they were originally regional products.

Xavier Huetz de Lemps

FURTHER READING

Ole G. Mouritsen. *Algues marines: Propriétés, usages, recettes*. Trans. Denis Richard. Paris: Delachaux et Niestlé, 2015.

Peter Neushul and Lawrence Badash. "Harvesting the Pacific: The Blue Revolution in China and the Philippines." *Osiris* 13 (1998): 186–209.

Alexander Nützenadel and Frank Trentmann, eds. *Food and Globalization: Consumption, Markets and Politics in the Modern World*. Oxford: Berg, 2008.

René Alexander D. Orquiza Jr. *Taste of Control: Food and the Filipino Colonial Mentality Under American Rule*. New Brunswick, NJ: Rutgers University Press, 2020.

Gavino C. Trono Jr. *Manual on Seaweed Culture, Pond Culture of Caulerpa and Pond Culture of Gracilaria*. Manila: ASEAN/UNPD/ FAO, 1988.

FURTHER TRAVELING

Maki

Maki

In 1981 a series of articles in the *New York Times* brought a California invention, initially aimed at a local clientele of Japanese businessmen, to a national audience: the California roll. This American adaptation of maki, was to become a staple of Japanophilia in the 1980s.

The maki (or *makizushi*), which means "roll," is a particular form of sushi, where vinegar-coated rice, raw fish, and other ingredients are rolled up in a sheet of Porphyra seaweed (*nori*) either by hand or using a small mat of bamboo stalks called a *makisu*. The manufacture of these seaweed sheets was made possible by adapting the technologies used in the paper industry in the nineteenth century. The roll prevented the rice from drying out, so it was only cut when served. Invented shortly after raw fish sushi, it was a less common and popular variation.

Japanese culinary tastes spread through the Japanese migration in various forms based on the diversity and evolution of flavors and practices. The destruction of Tokyo in the 1923 earthquake, with its subsequent exodus, and Japanese expansion helped popularize raw fish sushi elsewhere in Asia, notably in Korea, where maki became *gimbap*, for example.

In the United States, Japanese immigration began mainly on the West Coast as early as the nineteenth century (from 1868, in Hawaii, then to the mainland) when Japan reopened to the world. Immigrants opened restaurants and organized the importation of ingredients that could withstand the transpacific journey. Raw fish sushi, maki, and sashimi remained a rarity on the menus of these establishments. While the forced internment of Japanese and Japanese Americans during World War II was a blow to the community, the American occupation of the archipelago (1945–52) and then the Cold War helped to strengthen ties between Japan and the United States. Los Angeles's Little Tokyo district became a focal point for Japanese culture in America, especially from 1965 onward, when immigration laws once again legalized the arrival of immigrants from Asia and Japanese companies began sending their executives to the West Coast to develop their businesses. The population sought local access to Japan's then-fashionable specialties, including sushi, sashimi, and raw fish maki. The first sushi bars opened in Los Angeles in 1964, serving only Japanese customers at first.

It was in this context that the California roll was invented, probably in Los Angeles, although several stories exist, at least one of which traces its origins to Vancouver. This new type of maki was undoubtedly a response to two recurring problems: obtaining fresh fish in all seasons and converting American palates. The fish most used in maki, because of its texture, was tuna. However, tuna was only available in California in summer, during its migration across the Pacific from the coasts of Mexico. Air transport and freezing were not as developed at the time. So Japanese chefs in Los Angeles restaurants came up with the idea of replacing tuna with an ingredient that was relatively common in Southern California, with its fatty, creamy flesh: avocado. Initial attempts were inconclusive. The sushi version (*nigiri*) did not work largely because the avocado was visible above the rice bed and the greenish color was unappetizing. On the contrary, hidden within a roll, it proved a convincing substitute. The recipe then set out to conquer Americans, who were reluctant to taste raw fish and more accustomed to the canned tuna used to making "tuna salad" through the addition of mayonnaise.

The dark green sheet of seaweed paper still had to be accepted. Some Americans tried their luck at removing it, and Ishita came up with the idea of inverting the maki assembly by putting the seaweed inside, thus creating an "ura-maki." To these ingredients were also added shrimp, sometimes replaced by locally available crab claw meat, and mayonnaise. The popularity of rolls soon led to the introduction of surimi (made with fish, wheat, and egg white), an invention patented in Japan in 1974 and exported via San Francisco in 1977.

This proposal came at a propitious time in the evolution of Californian and American tastes, when people were advocating a return to simple, fresh foods, in line with the growing hippie movement and a new fad for slimness, particularly among women. Indeed, California rolls found an audience, first locally thanks to the businessmen who worked with Japanese companies, then nationally thanks to *Gourmet Magazine* and the *New York Times* in the early 1980s. The wave was also driven by the media coverage of consumption by Hollywood stars. Some were even named in their honor, such as the Christina Aguilera roll.

Other makis were subsequently invented. Variations on the success of a first wave to flatter the American palate and beyond: the New York roll with apple (Big Apple) or mango as in Brazil or Singapore. These makis are often hand-rolled and conical in shape (*temakizushi*), a technique that makes it possible to incorporate these new ingredients from the unbridled imagination of chefs, Japanese or otherwise. The invention of these varied rolls ensured their success in Europe in the 1990s.

This freedom also had its excesses. With the possibility of multiplying ingredients and flavors also came the possibility in some of restaurants of concealing the use of frozen fish of lesser quality. Such is the case with the popular "spicy tuna," in which chili seasoning has benefited from the Tex-Mex craze. Distinction now depends on product quality, with the development of air transport and refrigeration enabling high-end establishments to import fresh fish from Japanese seas.

From the Japanese point of view, the evolution of maki is quite exotic and even liberating. The Japanese oscillate between pride in such globalization of their gastronomy and horrified amusement at such inventions. Tasting these reincarnations is an unmissable part of any trip across the Pacific. In fact, these proposals are now partly reimported, appearing on the menu of sushi restaurants in the archipelago.

Emmanuelle Perez Tisserant

FURTHER READING

Sasha Issenberg. *The Sushi Economy: Globalization and the Making of a Modern Delicacy*. New York: Gotham Books, 2014.

David Kamp. *The United States of Arugula: How We Became a Gourmet Nation*. New York: Broadway Books, 2006.

Robert Ji-Song Ku. *Dubious Gastronomy: The Cultural Politics of Eating Asian in the USA*. Honolulu: University of Hawai'i Press, 2016.

Andrew McKevitt. *Consuming Japan: Popular Culture and the Globalizing of 1980s America*. Chapel Hill: University of North Carolina Press, 2017.

FURTHER TRAVELING

Chili Pepper, Mayonnaise, Poke, Sushi

Margarine

In 1869, Napoleon III's Second Empire was still buoyed by the gigantic success of the Universal Exhibition, which two years earlier had attracted more than ten million visitors to Paris in celebration of industry and agriculture. The emperor launched a competition to provide the navy, as well as the working classes, with a product that could replace butter and that could be preserved without acquiring the pungent taste and strong odor that butter quickly acquired in a larder.

Chemist Hippolyte Mège-Mouriès was at the height of his career as an inventor, "known for his eminent work on wheat and bread-making." After observing that slimmed-down cows continued to give fat-rich milk, he imagined he could artificially reconstitute the process that led to the production of butter. He achieved this by creating an animal-based fat from tallow, skimmed milk, and water, which he boiled with pieces of cow udder. He gave it the beautiful name of "margarine," inspired by the color of the pearl in ancient Greek, registered patent 86,480, and set up a factory in the French town of Poissy. He sold his patent in Germany, Great Britain, and the Netherlands, where it was bought by a butter merchant, Anton Jurgens, who called the invention "steam butter." Arriving in the United States in 1873, it provoked the same enthusiasm as in Europe.

This inexpensive fat has a color similar to butter. This "fake butter," as it was renamed, gave off an air of being counterfeit which was used by the defenders of authentic French agriculture as a pretext for resistance. In the United States butter manufacturers attacked it for its yellow-orange color, obtained from a natural coloring agent, annatto. In some states, margarine had to be colored pink to distinguish it from butter, a decision ultimately rejected by the Supreme Court. It was part of the birth of the agri-food industry. But the days of regrating—selling secondhand food scraps salvaged from restaurants and supermarkets and seasoned to restore their taste—were not over. So in the last third of the nineteenth century, two worlds coexisted: the galloping progress showcased at the Universal Exhibitions cohabited with the fear of trafficking of which wholesale food merchants were so often accused. Mouriès margarine paid the price of this coexistence, and the *"margariniers"* who improved the recipe once its inventor had disappeared, were transformed by the press and farm lobbies into unscrupulous traffickers peddling their wares to people who could not afford real Normandy butter.

In a short text published in 1874, two years after margarine was first sold, the polygraph Léo Lespès, one of the editors of the popular French newspaper *Le petit journal* who signed his name as Timothée Trimm, defended what he dubbed "fresh butter for everyone." He opened by pointing out the mistake made by the invention's promoters: allowing it to be described as "artificial butter." For "the public confuses 'artificial' with 'fake.' . . . And yet, it makes no sense to apply an adjective that is so widely misunderstood to a product made absolutely and exclusively from the materials used to make butter."

In every country where margarine was introduced, complaints and lawsuits rained down. Representatives and senators were called upon to legislate throughout the 1880s. In France the law of March 14, 1887, prohibited the use of the name butter to sell, display, or import margarine or oleomargarine. This was followed within a few weeks by similar laws and ordinances in Great Britain, Germany, Denmark, Norway, and Russia.

But the fraudsters continued to trade. In May 1891, during a visit to the central market in Paris's central market, Les Halles, the city's chief of police unexpectedly descended into the basement of a retail pavilion where butter handling took place and discovered a vast counterfeiting workshop in which up to half of the butter incorporated margarine. The margarine makers had drifted some distance from the spirit behind Mège-Mouriès's invention, that is, helping the poor to feed themselves. Throughout the 1890s the French Assembly and Senate tightened regulations and condemned fraud, without success, even more so as the increasingly stringent legislation put the country that gave birth to margarine at a disadvantage compared to Northern Europe and the United States, where sales of "poor man's butter" reached record levels. In the mid-1930s, the French consumed four hundred grams (14.1 oz.) of table margarine per person per year, while the Belgians bought nine kilos (19.8 lb.) and the Danes twenty-four (53 lb.).

The invention of the hydrogenation of oils and fats in 1902 by German chemist Wilhelm Normann turned the industry upside down. It made it possible to produce vegetable margarines that avoided suspicions of food tampering. After

World War I they were made with palm kernel, peanut, copra, or coconut oils, produced in the colonies of European powers. Unilever, born of the merger of soap manufacturer Lever and United Margarines, founded earlier in the Netherlands by Anton Jurgens, invested massively in huge plantations in the Belgian Congo to provide the raw material for its soaps and margarines. European imports of peanuts from colonial Africa, Senegal, and Nigeria in particular, increased between the wars, and colonial exhibitions in Marseille and Paris featured oil manufacturers importing these new fats from the empire, which cookie and pastry makers incorporated into their preparations.

Nevertheless, margarine remained the "poor man's butter" during the economic crisis of the 1930s. In Germany, Great Britain, and France margarine became a kitchen staple. Against the backdrop of the crisis, Germany even started making whale margarine. But it was not until World War II that margarine fully entered the public consciousness. Requisitions and shortages made the product indispensable during the war years, both in London and Paris, while prisoners of war in Germany reported the importance of margarine and the black bread that accompanied it, sometimes adorned with molasses. The civilian population also had to contend with butter shortages and black-market prices. Margarine took over and became an everyday kitchen staple. However, its use did not end with the German surrender. Rationing continued after the war in Germany's "Year Zero," when adults in Hamburg in 1945 were entitled to only 250 grams (8.8 oz.) of butter and 250 grams of margarine per month. The situation was similar in Great Britain and France. In 1948 the newspaper *Le Monde* explained that thanks to its digestibility, this "very pure vegetable oil emulsion is one of the most nourishing foods you can find."

But once rations returned to normal, the fatty substance that had helped people muddle through these difficult times once again faced attacks from the dairy industry. These attacks were confronted with the constant reinvention of margarine which benefited from a new image far removed from the original accusations of fraud and food tampering. It profited from the proliferation of butter-free diets and even became a health product. At the turn of the new millennium, manufacturers incorporated omega 3 and sterols, supposedly to lower cholesterol.

While the consumption of butter has never been totally globalized, that of its substitute, margarine—produced from animal or vegetable fats, made of phytin from olive oil in Greece, or made from crushed peanut, palm, copra, or cottonseed oil elsewhere—has been adapted to markets worldwide, making it both a global and local product like pizza or hamburgers.

Emmanuel Laurentin

FURTHER READING

Madeleine Ferrières. *Histoire des peurs alimentaires du Moyen Âge à l'aube du xx* siècle*. Paris: Seuil, 2002.
Florence Quellier, ed. *Histoire de l'alimentation de la préhistoire à nos jours*. Paris: Belin, 2002.

FURTHER TRAVELING

Food Coloring and Preservatives, Hamburger, Olive Oil, Palm Oil, Pizza

Mate

It was a first. On November 30, 2015, Argentina celebrated "National Mate Day" to "promote the lasting recognition of [its] customs," of which the drink is said to be the symbol. Annual consumption of mate now exceeds 250 million tons, in a country where, according to a 2009 survey, the drink is consumed in 98 percent of households. The date is also chosen to honor the memory of Andresito Guacurarí, a caudillo who was the first and only Indigenous governor in Argentine history, in the famous frontier province of Misiones, at the beginning of the nineteenth century. It was a way of recalling the Indigenous origins of a drink which, ironically, became a national symbol after Argentina decimated the last Indigenous peoples following the conquest of the "desert."

Mate's local roots explain why the drink is still consumed today in several neighboring countries, starting with Paraguay, where yerba mate was harvested, prepared, and circulated through trade routes even before the arrival of the first settlers. Archaeology attests to the ancestral use of mate by the peoples of the Americas, in various forms. In colonial times, it became customary to drink the hot infusion from a calabash called a "mati," from which the term "mate" is derived. The earliest colonial chronicles also describe the round object of the Guarani, in connection with ritual and funeral practices, notably in Guayrá (present-day Paraná in southern Brazil).

During an exploration in Brazil in the early nineteenth century, Frenchman Auguste de Saint-Hilaire produced the first analysis of the tree from which mate is derived and named it *Ilex paraguariensis*. The "medium-sized tree, twiggy at the top [and] very leafy," whose leaves and young twigs are harvested, then dried, and roughly ground at intervals of at least three years to guarantee the sustainability of the resource. In colonial times, "Paraguay grass" circulated throughout the vast viceroyalty of Peru, from Lima to the Rio de la Plata, passing through the Cerro Rico de Potosí and following the course of the Paraná River. In an economy that had yet to be monetized, *yerba* was often used as a substitute currency. Its consumption grew in South America, but not in Europe, where mate, unlike coffee, had been known since the seventeenth century. In fact, some religious figures tried to prohibit its consumption, arguing that mate, likened to drugs and other stimulants such as coca or alcoholic beverages, corrupted souls. The attempt was unsuccessful, however, and it was other clerics who on the contrary promoted its use. The Jesuits hoped to turn the "Pampas" Indigenous populations away from brandy consumption and encourage them to work harder and better in their missions. Indeed, in addition to its many choleretic, diuretic, and antioxidant virtues, mate is very rich in caffeine.

But the *yerba* trade accelerated the demographic collapse of the Guaraní populations of Paraguay. As tributaries, the indigenous peoples were subjected to *mita*—six months of forced labor that exhausted both body and soul. The creation of the first mate plantations in the Jesuit "Mission Province" in the seventeenth century aroused the ire of the Spaniards, who had built up a monopoly for the exploitation of this natural resource in their vast *haciendas* and *encomiendas*. After the expulsion of the Jesuits in 1767, the native populations of the missions were once again subjected to the *mita*, which had been suspended for a time under Jesuit authority. They were thus exposed to terrible working conditions to increase production and profits. The powerful colonists also counted on free populations, Creoles or mestizos, to make up for the lack of native labor.

By the end of the eighteenth century, Buenos Aires, the new viceroyal capital and future capital of Argentina, had established itself as the principal trading port for *yerba* produced in Paraguay and the southern provinces of Brazil. In the pampas, mate consumption even spread to rebellious populations. Unable to find *Ilex paraguariensis* in its natural state, they resorted to stealing or bartering with settlers to obtain supplies of mate, as they did for tobacco, sugar, or alcohol.

It was after independence in 1816 that mate, widely consumed in Argentina, gradually gained the status of a common tradition, in a country where national identity was slow to emerge due to the internal wars that broke out in the nineteenth century. Omnipresent in private circles as well as in public ceremonies and events, mate was particularly prized by the gauchos, who extended their hold over the immense pampas as the native populations were driven out. Tense relations with the now-independent Paraguay forced Argentina to source mate from Brazil, where it disputed sovereignty over the mission provinces. When this territory was recognized as Argentinean by international arbitration (1876), the cultivation of new plantations enabled the country to establish itself as the world's leading mate producer. Both sides of the border paid tribute to the French botanist Aimé Bonpland, who, after accompanying Humboldt on his long journey through Spanish America, played an important role in the province's exploration, two centuries after the Jesuits, of the germination mechanism of *Ilex paraguariensis*.

Alongside *asado* (grilled meat) and soccer, mate has become a marker of "Argentinianness," even though it is also common in Uruguay, Paraguay, and southern Brazil, where gauchos enjoy *chimarrão*. In Chile, on the other hand, the mate craze faded after independence in favor of tea and coffee. Its almost universal consumption in Argentina, with which millions of migrants from across the Atlantic in search of a better future have also become familiar, symbolically compensates for sharp social inequalities that have become even more pronounced since the military dictatorship and the structural adjustment plans under the aegis of the International Monetary Fund. Thus, mate remains deeply rooted in custom, whether consumed alone or in a group. Gathered in a circle under the supervision of the *cebador*, in charge of preparing the infusion, the calabash is passed from hand to hand, and each person in turn drinks the beverage through the *bombilla*, the straw fitted with a filter. Even the arrival of COVID-19 in 2020 did little to change the practice, though the government tried to prevent a rapid contagion by popularizing the new slogan among Argentines: "Share the water, not the *bombilla*." Thus, the collective use of mate remains firmly rooted in America's southern cone, just as it also spread to certain regions of the Middle East, following the great migrations that have connected South America to Lebanon and Syria. Indeed, mate consumption spread to the Levant with the return of migrants hit by the many economic and political crises that shook Argentina in the twentieth century.

Sébastien Rozeaux

FURTHER READING

Fernando Bouza. "El arbitrio de la hierba 'provechosa' del Paraguay de 1637: Experiencia y práctica en la construcción de saberes locales de Indias a través del Atlántico." *Años 90* 24–45 (2017): 73–100.
Juan Carlos Garavaglia. *Mercado interno y economía colonial: Tres siglos de historia de la yerba mate*. Mexico City: Grijalbo, 1983.

Juan Francisco Jiménez and Sebastián Alioto. "*Excitantia* en las pampas: Difusión y apropiación de la yerba mate (*Ilex paraquariensis*) entre las sociedades nativas de la región pampeana en la segunda mitad del siglo XVIII." *Cuadernos del sur—Historia* 49 (2020): 81–112.

Barbosa Lessa. *História do chimarrão*. Porto Alegre, Brazil: Sulina, 1950.

José Natanson. "En Argentine, le maté en dépit du covid-19." *Le monde diplomatique*, February 2021.

FURTHER TRAVELING

Coffee, Tea and Chai

Matzah

In 1838, Isaac Singer, an Alsatian Jew, invented the first machine for rolling matzah. The machine marked a revolution in the manufacture of this product, also known as unleavened bread, which is eaten during Passover, the feast commemorating the exodus of the Hebrews from Egypt. Fleeing the Pharaoh and Egypt, where they were enslaved, the Hebrews had no time to wait for the dough to rise, so they made unleavened bread. This "bread," as flat as it was tasteless, accompanied the Hebrews as they crossed the desert and became the Jewish people, from Egypt to Canaan, from ancient Palestine to the contemporary diaspora.

To be considered kosher for Passover, a time when leavened foods are forbidden, matzah is prepared according to a strict recipe. Made from flour and water, without salt or sugar, it can be made for no longer than eighteen minutes (a symbolic number in Judaism, signifying life).

Made locally and by hand around the world until the mid-nineteenth century, Singer's invention led to controversy. The process was perfected in the United States by Behr Manischewitz, an Orthodox Jewish immigrant from Prussia, who set up his own manufacturing company in Cincinnati in 1888. In addition to mechanization, Manischewitz also innovated the shape of the matzah, traditionally round. To facilitate distribution and transportation in boxes, he produced square matzah, even though lively rabbinical debate in Europe attests to their presence long before the company was founded.

The controversy surrounding mechanization and this change of form provoked a stir throughout the Jewish world. Although historians date it back to the late 1850s, twenty years after Singer, the changes brought about by Singer did not leave the rabbinate in France and the German-speaking countries indifferent, as they tended to favor its development. On the other hand, the arrival of this innovation in Hungary and Poland toward the end of the 1850s, and in Jerusalem in 1863, gave rise to deep discussions that were renewed at the end of the nineteenth century and resurfaced in Jerusalem ten years later. Over and above kosher requirements, the debate raised the social question so prevalent in industrializing societies: Was it permissible to replace the jobs of the poor with machines? Would opening up to modernity not lead to assimilation? The most orthodox rabbis saw mechanization as a breach that could lead to the abandonment of Judaism. Sensitive to the demands of the most traditional and to its own success, the Manischewitz company won votes by financing a house of study (a yeshiva) in Jerusalem in 1914, where the rabbis endorsed industrial matzah. By the 1920s, however, the company was boasting that it supplied 80 percent of North American Jews. Some continued to advocate handmade, round *matsot shemurot*, at least for the seder.

Long before the controversies surrounding their mass production, matzah fueled anti-Jewish myths in Christian Europe, according to which their manufacture required the blood of Christian children. This may account for the Jewish tradition, from eastern France and Germany to as far afield as Tunisia, of offering them to Christian and Muslim neighbors at Passover as a gesture of friendship and as a sign of fragile coexistence. Could this reminder of friendship not also be a sign of deeper anguish? Matzah also animates moments of sharing. A case in point is the Mimouna feast, celebrated in Morocco, North Africa, Israel, and throughout the Sephardic diaspora at the end of Passover. This meal, which marks the return of leavened dishes, is traditionally shared with neighbors and friends. Depending on the place, Muslims take an active role in this rite of friendship: since Jews cannot make bread during Pesach, they bring it, often after having kept the food forbidden to their neighbors during the holiday.

During the Holocaust and in the immediate postwar period, Jewish organizations did their utmost to distribute matzah. During the Occupation, the Consistoire Central in France drew up lists of names and addresses—easily misappropriated by Nazi and Vichy authorities—to deliver them. Such lists provide a rare insight into the demography and geography of the Jewish population, hidden from view but eager to observe its religious rites. After World War II the American Joint Distribution Committee took on this responsibility to ensure that Passover, so symbolically important after the Holocaust, could be celebrated with dignity. All this for a food that the vast majority of Jews dislike.

Yet culinary creativity emerged from this early globalized food. In the Ashkenazi world, matzah is mixed with eggs and fried in butter to make *Matze brei*, served with cream, or ground into flour to make matzah balls, the dumplings that accompany chicken soup. These dishes are as comforting as they are delicious. In North African Judaism, matzah flour is used to make cakes and fritters served in honey syrup or scented with orange blossom. The list goes on and on, accentuating the discreet charm of this typically Jewish delicacy. Available in supermarkets in industrialized countries, "unleavened bread" now attracts above all those who avoid leavened bread for dietary or medical reasons.

Today matzah production is limited to a dozen companies worldwide. Few have managed to maintain a family production model. While the Manischewitz company remained in the hands of the founder's heirs until 1990, it has since been passed from hand to hand through a series of takeovers. Other companies are resisting this trend. In France, Ashkenazi Jews are fond of square matzah, manufactured by the Heumann company in Alsace since 1907 or Rosinski in the Paris region since 1929, while Sephardim (and some Ashkenazim) prefer the sturdier round matzah, manufactured "according to the formulas used in Algeria" by the Bitone family in Agen since 1956. A true symbol of the Jewish condition, between lament and creativity, is it possible that such a fragile wafer could be strong enough to contain 5,782 years of history?

Laura Hobson Faure

FURTHER READING

Laura Manischewitz Alpern. *Manischewitz: The Matzo Family. The Making of an American Jewish Icon.* Jersey City, NJ: Ktav, 2008.

Meir Hildesheimer and Yehoshua Liebermann. "The Controversy Surrounding Machine-made Matzot: Halakhic, Social and Economic Repercussions." *Hebrew Union College Annual* 75 (2004): 193–262.

Norman Kleeblatt, Larry Rivers, and Anita Friedman. *Larry Rivers' History of Matzah: The Story of the Jews.* New York: The Jewish Museum, 1984.

Catherine Munsch. "Une des dix dernières fabriques de pain azyme dans le monde se trouve en Alsace." *France 3*, September 25, 2020, https:// france3-regions.francetvinfo.fr/grand-est/dix-dernieres-fabriques-pain- azyme-monde-se-trouve-alsace-1876740.html.

Jonathan Sarna. *How Matza Became Square: Manischewitz and the Development of Machine-Made Matzah in the United States.* New York: Touro College, 2005.

FURTHER TRAVELING

Salt

Mayonnaise

In 1885, the American veterinarian D. E. Salmon described for the first time a bacterium of the *Enterobacteriaceae* family, present in the stomachs of animals, particularly birds, that contaminates the environment. Named after its discoverer, the *Salmonella* bacteria, causing the eponymous disease salmonellosis, resists cold and is found in raw foods, particularly eggs, dairy products, and meat. According to the World Health Organization's definition, salmonellosis is usually characterized by a sudden onset of fever, abdominal pain, diarrhea, nausea, and sometimes vomiting. It is also known to be life-threatening in young children and the elderly. However, our familiarity with this food poisoning today may be due to the extraordinary success of mayonnaise, which is often blamed for it. Although its recipe has undoubtedly been used since the end of the eighteenth century in the courts of several European rulers which were hotbeds of culinary innovation, it was in 1806 that chef André Viard recorded a new way of preparing remoulade, one of the sauces developed to accompany fish and meat, in his collection of 950 recipes entitled *Le cuisinier impérial*. Rather than cooking a time-consuming, ingredient-intensive velouté to make his sauce creamy, Viard suggested adding an egg yolk and mixing it for a long time with oil and mustard. At the beginning of the nineteenth century, the chef, who had survived the French Revolution without harm, unwittingly revolutionized cooking by inventing a stable emulsion that was not yet called mayonnaise but that closely resembled it.

What Viard failed to appreciate was not so much that he had separated the two components of the egg—the yolk and the white—as that he favored the yolk. Until then, whites had been more popular. They were used to make meringues, so appreciated at the table of King Stanislas of Poland, and they were still the basis of macaroons and other financiers. From this point forward, the remaining egg whites would be used to prepare these little sweets. Mayonnaise reversed the hierarchy of the egg, so much so that in the following period one of Europe's most popular starters became egg mayonnaise. It was a veritable coup d'état of yolks over whites.

But the importance of mayonnaise could hardly be limited to this inversion. With its spread into bourgeois cuisine and then to the working classes in the twentieth century, it went from being an accessory to an essential ingredient. Since its official recognition in 1815 by Antonin Carême, cold chicken could not be consumed without mayonnaise. In the twentieth century, "mayo" became a central condiment on our plates. No whelks, shrimp, or avocados could be served without it, and no club sandwich or, in some places, hamburgers either. Mayonnaise could be served with chicken fritters in the United States, merguez in North Africa, or fried potatoes in Spain. Mayonnaise was a subversive force for modern cooking, taking on meat and fish as well as eggs and vegetables. There was nothing mayonnaise could not tackle so much pleasure did it bring.

Mayonnaise also comforts. It is hardly a coincidence that before it became a ubiquitous global delicacy, some historians traced its origins back to the history of medicine and health care. Indeed, it seems that during the medieval period, pharmacists recognized the virtues of a stable egg-yolk emulsion. It was recommended in the case of burns or wounds, and eighteenth-century treatises indicated its proper use was to relieve suffering. Rather than imagine a transfer of knowledge from medicine to the kitchen, it should be noted that a similar gesture is used to correctly prepare both ointments or plasters and for mayonnaise. To achieve its characteristic creaminess, the oil must be poured in gently and evenly while beating an egg yolk at room temperature. It is a question of articulating two types of movement together, the difficulty of which is hard to measure with today's electric mixer. In Europe, from the nineteenth century onward, a mother's skill in the kitchen was judged by her ability to "make mayonnaise set." A young woman who did not know how to make mayonnaise was considered incapable of running a household.

The injunction was so powerful that it went beyond the confines of the kitchen and the domestic sphere. It referred to someone's ability to bring different parties together, to federate a group of people who might not enjoy each other's company. The history of mayonnaise is as much the history of a metaphor as it is of marketing. From tubes to jars and bags of industrial mayonnaise, the product has undoubtedly been emptied of much of its original meaning. Having become an international product, mayonnaise softens the edges of a North American schoolboy's sandwich. At the same time, the presence of a jar of mayo has become essential to a pleasant picnic, which from the beginning of the twentieth century played a part in the development of leisure activities. In London's great urban parks, people share a lunch of cold meats accompanied by mayonnaise.

One might think that the limitation of egg content in the mid-twentieth century, which has the effect of increasing its whiteness, was fueled by hygienic concerns. However, if the famous Heinz mayonnaise contains fewer and fewer egg yolks, it is in fact for economic reasons. The sauce's main enemy is oxygen in the air, which produces oxidation reactions in the emulsion. When mayonnaise became an industrial product after World War II, it had to be made in an air vacuum. Glass jars were also preferred to help limit the speed of these reactions, which tended to spoil the mayonnaise. This phenomenon, which occurred during storage or transport, was no longer noticeable by sight but through its unpleasant flavors. Such reactions were accelerated by high ambient temperatures, which forced a radical modification of the recipe in countries with warm climates. Adding sugar was one solution to countering this adulteration. Nevertheless, before the advent of refrigeration, the appropriation of this recipe into culinary traditions was limited to temperate or cold climates. Depending on the ingredients added, it became Béarnaise, Gribiche, Hollandaise, Tartare. Only refrigerators and chemical preservatives could transform it into an all-purpose sauce capable of withstanding temperature variations.

Despite the extraordinary longevity of its name in French, the use of mayonnaise in English is attested as early as 1815. This internationalization is not unrelated to the sauce's prehistory. Historians of the Hispanic world point out that in 1850 a cookbook entitled *Art de la Cuina, llibre cuina menorquina del s. XVIII*, written by a Menorcan Franciscan monk of the eighteenth century named Fra Francesc Roger, appeared. Under the name "Aïoli Bo," the mayonnaise sauce attributed to Viard was found in twenty-five recipes. So it was not in French kitchens but on the island of Menorca that the emulsion was created? This remains a mystery. But what we do know is that mayonnaise helped carry meals out the door, leaving the dining room table behind as it headed into the great outdoors on excursions in baskets, on beaches, in parks, and mountain clearings.

Philippe Artières

FURTHER READING

André Viard. *Le cuisinier impérial, ou L'art de faire la cuisine et la pâtisserie pour toutes les fortunes, avec différentes recettes d'office et de fruits confits et la manière de servir une table depuis vingt jusqu'à soixante couverts. . . .* Paris: 1806.

Jean Vitaux. *Les petits plats de l'histoire.* Paris: Presses Universitaires de France, 2011.

FURTHER TRAVELING

Hamburger, Sandwich

Naan

In 2019 a video of Korean pop group BTS eating naan, a bread of Indian origin, went viral within hours. The fascination was hardly new. As early as 1300, the Indo-Persian poet Amir Khusro, a keen observer of the royal court as well as popular practices, already mentioned the common consumption of this type of bread. His distinction between *naan-e-tunuk* (light bread) and *naan-e-tanuri* (baked in a clay oven called a *tandoor*) testified to its geographical and social mobility, facilitated by trade routes, frequent conquests, and fluid borders. Originally from Persia, but undoubtedly known in ancient Egypt and arriving in India with invaders from Central Asia, it was transformed by using yeast. Preferred by travelers for its durability and ease of transport, it was also perceived by Persians as a symbol of high culture and refinement.

In the sixteenth century, this oblong wafer was a dish reserved for Mughal aristocrats. Accompanied by minced meat, the bread became the preferred breakfast food of royalty. With the wars and expansion of empires in Central and South Asia, it entered dietary practices more broadly, from Iran to the Arabian Peninsula, from Anatolia to Tajikistan, from the Balkans to Burma, all the way to China's Xinjiang region. Its name varied from region to region—*naan balochi*, *parthiane*, *sogian*, *pashto*, *kash-miri*, *peshwari*, *punjabi*—as did its shape, from small in Punjab to a meter long in Iran or Afghanistan. In Uzbekistan, the bakers used a specific tool, the *nonpar*, to shape it, allowing each bakery to imprint its own motif or even its telephone number. Today it can be found in the Balearic Islands as *ceviche naan*, in Sikkim as *phaley*, or in Peru. Depending on the country, it can include ingredients as varied as grapes, garlic, cheese, coriander, olives, or even be gluten-free or low-carb.

Naan has remained relatively stable amid its travels. True to its origins—crispy on the outside, soft in the middle—it naturally became associated with the key foods of national cuisines such as minced meat in Central Asia, cabbage in Tibet, peanut butter in the United States, cheese in Korea or, more broadly, curry, pesto, or butter. Take, for example, the popular "merguez-Vache qui rit" naan offered by some kebabs in Marseille. These peregrinations sometimes had a surprising effect. An Italian cooking channel, Cookist, shared a video on the preparation of naan under the name of "balloon bread," provoking debate on its specificity compared to other forms of bread such as pita, pupusa (enjoyed in El Salvador and Honduras), or Turkish or Lebanese bread, giving rise to novel terms such as naan-pizza. Nationalist or purist reactions aside, it remains the bread best suited to contemporary tastes, lending itself as much to the culinary advice of popular British chefs like Jamie Oliver as to the recipes of a Madhu Jaffrey, spokesperson for good Indian food abroad.

Its popularity among the Indian, Pakistani, Afghan, and Iranian diasporas recalls what French philosopher and literary critic Roland Barthes referred to as an "attitude," linked to certain customs that go beyond food. Naan is not a marker of an ethnic group, a national identity, or a social class. It is eaten and shared equally within the family, without hierarchy, between father, mother, sons, or daughters. It is part of every meal, daily or festive, and sets aside taboos and distinctions between rice and wheat regions, just as it easily coexists with other cereals. Contrary to current trends, it has not become closely identified with one particular terroir, like Parma ham or Camargue rice.

Although it belongs to the large family of breads and shares the same ideal qualities—crisp, soft, warm, supple—its appearance sets it apart from pita, chapati, baguette, or pizza. Despite the competition with these foods, it has made a name for itself, thanks to the possibilities of preparing it in the traditional clay or modern oven as well as in the frying pan. Naan is a way of sharing common values. The popularity it enjoys among the various diasporas has ensured its presence in supermarkets across the world. In the United Kingdom naan is found in the bread aisle, in mini or large sizes, stuffed or plain. In France, on the other hand, the preponderance of baguettes and the role of bakeries limit its distribution to Indian, Pakistani, and Bangladeshi restaurants. The proliferation of websites offering recipes for making naans at home, from the simplest to the most sophisticated, is an indicator of its widespread success. The questions asked are many and varied, including the fundamental ones of the proportion of whole grain flour and white flour, the merits of adding yogurt, egg, or milk, the use of yeast or baking soda, which may or may not classify it as a vegan recipe. For some, however, naan is a way of rediscovering their national past, reviving the memories and practices of a social and cultural world they have left behind. For others it is a way of displaying their participation in a cosmopolitan culture and expressing ease and familiarity with global gastronomic cultures.

Some restaurants even use it in their advertising, such as Naan Street Food in Mallorca, Spain, or the astonishing Bar à Naan in Saint-Malo, France. Its appropriation by such diverse culinary traditions does not, however, prevent it from remaining essentially identified as Indian, within the vast global range of wheat-based breads.

Outside its homeland naan has found its place, without significant transformation or adaptation, among the multiplicity of breads of different shapes, textures, or sizes. Its discreet origins do not give rise to conflict, perhaps because, like any other bread, it is eaten, without formality, with one's fingers.

Arundhati Virmani

FURTHER READING

Roland Barthes. "Vers une psycho-sociologie de l'alimentation moderne." *Annales ESC* 16, no. 5 (1961): 977–86.
Carole M. Counihan. "Bread as World: Food Habits and Social Relations in Modernizing Sardinia." *Anthropological Quarterly* 57, no. 2 (1984): 47–59.
Jean-Philippe de Tonnac, ed. *Dictionnaire universel du pain.* Paris: Robert Laffont, 2010.
Matt Garcia, E. Melanie DuPuis, and Don Mitchell, eds. *Food Across Borders.* New Brunswick, NJ: Rutgers University Press, 2017.
Ilaria Porciani, ed. *Food Heritage and Nationalism in Europe.* London: Routledge, 2021.

FURTHER TRAVELING

Baguette, Curry, Matzah, Pizza, Tikka, Yogurt

Noodles and Macaroni

In September 1788 Thomas Jefferson, who in 1785 had succeeded Benjamin Franklin as head of the U.S. legation to the king of France, instructed his private secretary William Short to procure a macaroni press like those in Naples. The coauthor of the Declaration of Independence had not developed a taste for this product during his trip to the Po Valley in 1787. On that trip he had been focused on the quality of Italian rice, and he brought back seeds to test their cultivation in Virginia. It was actually in Paris that he discovered these "Italian pastas," which were enjoying a certain success in the capital's fine restaurants. Local production had developed using techniques and equipment perfected by Neapolitan artisans. Received in the summer of 1789, the order was shipped in 1790, at the height of the French Revolution, to his estate in Monticello, Virginia, to be installed in a wooden press made on the spot. This initiative probably made Jefferson the introducer of macaroni production in the United States, almost a century before the great Italian migrations and the expansion of popular consumption across the North American continent. Naples, Paris, and Monticello, followed by Washington, were among the first steps in the global spread of this singular cereal-based preparation, which keeps well and remains part of Italian culinary identity even as it has undergone a wide variety of local adaptations.

These preserved foods, which were consumed after drying, unlike other pasta preparations, were distinct from domestic preparations found in virtually all food cultures that made use of cereals, especially in comparison to preparations typical of Asian or Central European culinary cultures. They originated in the Near East, where a variety of pasta shapes have been found since ancient times: short, threadlike or laminated, and dried in the open air. As a food for sailors and travelers, they spread throughout the Mediterranean and at the same time they progressed among Arab populations. The Iberian tradition of *fideos*, a term derived from Arabic, and the Italian tradition of *vermicelli*, and later macaroni, all have a common root. They were enjoyed in sweet, honey-based preparations, directly inspired by Oriental pastries. A relatively expensive product, their use remained limited until the eighteenth century. They also had a pronounced taste of preservatives, making them a crude food to be reserved for emergencies for city dwellers and travelers. However, the cuisine of the French Enlightenment elite developed a new interest in them and encouraged their use.

Joseph Menon, who marked French court cuisine from the 1730s onward, encouraged the use of canned vermicelli and macaroni imported from Italy, which he recommended blanching before use to remove their coarse taste. He appreciated their neutral flavor and cooking properties for his "vermicelli soup," which established a culinary tradition that continues to this day. Vermicelli thus became a major ingredient in broths, the preparation of which became a central element among the skills of French chefs, who used it to show their ability to obtain a balance of flavors. The institution of the "bouillon restaurant" in Paris in the mid-eighteenth century, where people could eat at any time and according to their desires, also contributed to making this dish a benchmark for both gastronomy and health cuisine. Macaroni, on the other hand, was eaten in timbales, entremets, and gratins. These preparations differed from older Italian recipes, which used juices loaded with meats, truffles, and condiments and emphasized the use of cheese, preferably Parmesan, that made it "stringy."

Initially imported from Italy or Provence, "pasta from Italy" gave rise to a Parisian craft industry that began to flourish in the 1760s around the rue des Prouvaires, near the Halle aux Grains. The initiative came from Dr. Paul-Jacques Malouin, who in 1767 wrote a complete description of the art, based on his observations in Naples. Neapolitan production set the standard from the turn of the sixteenth century, since the dough was worked with presses rather than by hand and knife. The characteristic hollowing of macaroni, which makes it easy to dry, facilitates cooking, and allows it to absorb the flavor of the broths in which it is prepared, was achieved by ingeniously designed presses, rather than by winding each piece of dough around a straw or wire. The development of partially hollowed dies allowed the dough to wrap around a central core and then close up at the end while remaining hollow. However, dexterity and the use of high-quality wheat was required to obtain satisfactory results. This was the device Jefferson ordered, in the form of a machined bronze mold nearly sixty centimeters (2 ft.) thick.

In fact, it was the reputation of French cuisine, rather than Jefferson's efforts, that led to the worldwide spread of recipes for vermicelli broth and macaroni gratin in the nineteenth century. Both trade and local production followed this craze. In

France, Parisian vermicelli production outstripped Italian imports from the Napoleonic Empire from the beginning of the nineteenth century onward. From the 1830s, the business developed into a veritable industry, capable of producing the more difficult macaroni format thanks to Ukrainian wheat arriving in the port of Marseille. French production even set the standard for the Anglo-American world until the Belle Époque and for a time outstripped Italian production in world trade. The Italianization of these products and uses only came about following the migrations of the turn of the nineteenth century, with the Italian diaspora working to link these products to the peninsula alone, and to make them, along with pizza, one of the world-renowned emblems of Italian cuisine. Antoine Zerega and Vincenzo La Rosa in New York, Luigi Nicolini and Eugenio Corgono in Lima, Ferrari in Paris, Scaramelli in Marseille and Jean Panzani in Niort, all contributed to this development, establishing local brands with an Italian flavor and promoting a wider range of uses than macaroni and cheese and chicken with vermicelli. In New York in 1928, Ettore Boiardi helped create the joint sale of spaghetti and ready-to-use tomato sauce in a form known as "spaghetti dinner," forging an association considered emblematic of Italian cuisine, even though it was far removed from the infinite diversity of preparations specific to the peninsula. It was not until the turn of the twentieth century that Barilla and its Italian counterparts promoted globalized brands and practices under the banner of Italian cuisine, marked by ready-to-use sauces such as pesto and arrabbiata. This globalization has not, however, eliminated the infinite diversity of local appropriations of a product that has become universal, such as the coquillettes gratin served in French school cafeterias or the popular Peruvian *spaghetti a la huancaina*.

Pierre-Antoine Dessaux

FURTHER READING

Pierre-Antoine Dessaux. *Vermicelles et coquillettes: Histoire de l'industrie des pâtes alimentaires en France.* Tours: Presses Universitaires François Rabelais, 2022.
Paul-Jacques Malouin. *Description et détails des arts du meûnier, du vermicelier et du boulanger; avec une histoire abrégée de la boulangerie et un dictionnaire de ces arts.* Paris: Saillant et Nyon, 1767.
Françoise Sabban and Silvano Serventi. *Les pâtes: Histoire d'une culture universelle.* Arles: Actes Sud, 2001.

FURTHER TRAVELING

Indomie, Parmesan Cheese, Pizza, Ramen, Singapore Noodles

Olive Oil

In November 2013, UNESCO inscribed the Mediterranean diet on the Representative List of the Intangible Cultural Heritage of Humanity, consecrating the international success of a diet based on the abundant consumption of olive oil, fruit, vegetables, legumes, cereals, and little meat. Since the 1950s, following in the footsteps of American physiologist Ancel Keys, numerous medical studies have emphasized the health benefits of this "Cretan diet," particularly in the prevention of cardiovascular disease. However, we now know that if the population living in Crete in the 1950s consumed very little meat or dairy products, it was not because of some thousand-year-old tradition but because of the disruption of food supplies during World War II.

The constructed and mythologized concept of the "Cretan diet" is thus the vector of an imaginary vision of the Mediterranean, which is in fact traditionally the land of olive trees and olive oil. The climate of the Mediterranean basin is perfectly suited to this tree, which, like ash and lilac, belongs to the *Oleaceae* family. Its fruit can be pressed to obtain oil by cold separating the four components: stones, fiber, water, and oil, the latter representing between 15 percent and 25 percent of the total weight. For the Greeks and Romans olive oil was the only oil (*oleum* means olive oil). It was an essential part of the lifestyle in all social circles, used for cooking, lighting, anointing athletes, producing makeup, and therapeutic balms.

But by the Carolingian era olive oil was only available in very small quantities outside the regions where it was produced. Rare and expensive, it was mainly used for liturgical purposes. Up to and including the modern era, fat was generally absent from the ordinary diet of the rural masses. It could take the form of small amounts of olive oil in the southern provinces of the kingdom of France. Olive oil circulated widely throughout the Mediterranean basin, with olive cultivation spreading massively in certain regions, such as the Venetian colonies of Crete and Corfu. Demand came from soap factories—those in Venice, Savona, and Genoa competed with those in Marseille, which came into its own in the seventeenth century. In the food sector, where a gastronomic and geographical imaginary began to take shape in Europe in the second half of the eighteenth century, Lucca olive oil was one of the regional specialties alongside Bayonne and Westphalian hams, Dijon mustard, Gruyere cheeses, and Bologna mortadella.

In the nineteenth century olive oil was used as a foodstuff, but also for lamps and lighthouses, lubricating machinery, and performing various washing operations in the textile industry. Around 1880, it was excluded from most nonalimentary uses by the arrival on European markets of large quantities of animal fats and oilseeds (peanuts, for example) from America, Africa, and Asia. Nevertheless, new opportunities arose with the emigration across the Atlantic between 1880 and 1913 of more than ten million Italians, Spaniards, Portuguese, and Greeks, all of whom were accustomed to its consumption. U.S. imports increased tenfold between 1880 and 1914, outstripping requests from fish canneries in Northern Europe. In Andalusia, the sharp rise in demand led to an extension of olive-growing areas and an intense development of oil export activity, which rose from 7,000 tons to over 36,000 tons between 1860 and 1900. In 1912–14, 70 percent of olive oil shipped from Catalonia went to Italy and Argentina.

The Catalan industry has adapted to the needs of consumers on the other side of the Atlantic, who prefer finer, low-acid olive oils for cooking and seasoning. Olive varieties, such as arbequina, have been homogenized and are now hand-picked before being crushed in hydraulic presses to reduce the time between harvesting and pressing. Export firms have adopted modern marketing strategies: brand registration, diversified packaging forms, and new modes of advertising. From 1896 onward, in Buenos Aires, Manuel Porcar y Tió had all the containers of olive oil sold by his company from Tortosa (Barcelona) labeled with the following words: "Gatherer and supplier to the kings of Spain. Awarded 56 gold and silver medals. Special preparations for the West Indies, Mexico, Venezuela, Ecuador, Central America, Chile, and Uruguay." Many companies were quick to grasp the benefits of promoting a cultural identification between olive oil and immigrants' homelands and used brand names or symbols designed to evoke famous olive-growing regions of the Mediterranean basin. In Brazil in

1916, the Chamber of Commerce and Industry of Portugal in Rio de Janeiro reported that olive oil was being sold in Brazil under brand names evoking Portuguese origin when in fact it had been produced, packaged, and labeled in Spain.

After a golden period in the 1930s, the Spanish olive oil economy, like other sectors, was isolated from international trade under the first Franco regime. The economic opening opted for by the dictatorship from 1959 onward enabled Spain, and Andalusia in particular, to export a large volume of production to Italy. In Provence and the French Maritime Alps, olive growing was gradually abandoned: the severe frost in 1956 accentuated the decline in production that had begun in the late nineteenth century due to competition from North African olive oil. But by the end of the 1970s a new revival was underway. In an article published in 1979 in the French magazine *L'Histoire*, Marie-Claire Amouretti noted with astonishment that "in a Mediterranean countryside invaded by concrete and brush fires, young olive shoots have sprouted from old trunks thanks to the work of a few men." In fact, during the last quarter of the twentieth century, French olive growing was rekindled with the production of quality olive oils that were soon recognized by several AOCs (the first was from Nyons in 1994). In Spain, integration into the European Economic Community and the mechanisms of the Common Agricultural Policy (CAP) enabled the development of intensive olive-growing with the help of irrigation. Since 1985 "the olive tree has risen again from the mare nostrum." The world's olive-growing area has steadily increased. In 2017, 3.3 million tons of olive oil were produced in forty-seven countries. Spain, Tunisia, Italy, Morocco, Greece, and Turkey head a ranking that now also includes Argentina, Chile, and Australia. Although the countries of the Mediterranean basin remain the leading consumers, the International Olive Oil Council has highlighted the globalization of demand, with olives now sold in more than 150 countries. The future of Andalusian olive growers "is not in Brussels, Madrid or Seville, but in kitchens the world over."

Amélie Nuq

FURTHER READING

Marie-Claire Amouretti and Georges Comet. *Le livre de l'olivier.* Aix- en-Provence: Édisud, 2000.
Marinella Katsilieri. "Au coeur de la diète méditerranéenne: L'huile d'olive." In *Le grand mezzé*, ed. Édouard de Laubrie, 37–41. Marseille: MUCEM/Actes Sud, 2021.

Juan Francisco Zambrana Pineda, ed. "Olivos y aceites: Una historia milenaria." *Andalucía en la historia* 69 (2020).

Florent Quellier, ed. *Histoire de l'alimentation: De la préhistoire à nos jours.* Paris: Belin, 2021.

Ramon Ramon-Muñoz. "The Expansion of Branding in International Marketing: The Case of Olive Oil, 1870s–1930s." *Business History* 62, no. 1 (2020): 98–122.

FURTHER TRAVELING

Margarine, Palm Oil, Sardines (Canned)

Orangina

In 1951, Jean-Claude Beton founded the Compagnie Française des Produits Orangina. Though it bears a French name, its history has followed the contours of colonization and decolonization in the Mediterranean across Algeria, Spain, and France. The Orangina recipe has several ingredients. First, there is its Algerian heritage with its elaborate culture of refreshment. When Beton founded Orangina in Boufarik, a small farming town in the Mitidja region south of Algiers, it was but one among many cold drinks. A local clientele had come to rely on it during the hot summers. Boufarik was already famous for his *sharbat*, an iced lemonade consumed during the evenings of Ramadan. Although this was a colonial society marked by strong divisions and inequalities, everyone—children, adults, Muslims, Jews, and Christians—appreciated good lemonade. Unlike alcoholic beverages such as wine, which was the main colonial product in Algeria, sodas appealed to a very wide audience.

The second ingredient is of course oranges, whose abundance in the Mitidja is a product of French colonization. Although the region produced oranges long before 1830, the violent redistribution of land by the French army disrupted local agriculture and led to the intensive cultivation of citrus fruits for export. Most farms were controlled by European settlers, while the workforce was primarily Algerian and occasionally Spanish. Algerian oranges were the fruit of this unequal coproduction.

Finally, a third component was needed to produce Orangina, a Spanish recipe. In the 1930s, Algerian citrus growers were looking for new outlets for their produce against a backdrop of global economic protectionism following the Great Depression. In 1935 entrepreneur Léon Beton, born in Boufarik in 1899 to a Jewish Algerian family, visited his brother in Marseille. At the Foire Internationale et Coloniale he met the pharmacist Agustín Trigo Mezquita, a well-known figure in his country and former mayor of Valencia. There, he promoted his flagship product, Trinaranjus, a small bottle of orange syrup for mixing. Beton bought the recipe from him. From the start, Orangina had a noncarbonated sister, the Spanish Trina, which is still consumed today. Orangina was born of Mediterranean trade during of the colonial era, when people moved easily from Algiers to Marseille or Valencia. Many of the farm workers in the Mitidja were themselves Spanish, often from the coast between Valencia and Alicante.

When Léon Beton returned from Marseille, he didn't immediately develop his patent. It was his son, Jean-Claude, an agricultural engineer, who launched the brand in 1951. But he faced tremendous challenges. How could the brand expand beyond the (small) Algerian market? The entrepreneur developed partnerships in metropolitan France to set up secondary production plants on the other side of the sea. Hence came the fourth ingredient necessary for the spread of Orangina: the Algerian War of Independence. Following the Front de Libération Nationale uprising in 1954, the French government responded with mass mobilization. Conscripts flocked to Algeria (400,000 men in 1956), where they discovered and began shaking the beverage in its famous little round container. When they returned to France, they brought the drink back with them, making it an integral part of French drinking habits.

In France's postwar three-decade economic boom known as the "Trente Glorieuses," Orangina became the symbol of summer, of vacations in the South along the Mediterranean, and of a youthful thirst for freedom. The final ingredient in this success was marketing, supported from 1953 by posters designed by Villemot. The product's original weakness (one must shake the pulp that accumulates at the bottom of the bottle) became its strength in advertising campaigns that played up this dynamic drink, shaking up the habits of café-goers.

While the beginnings of Orangina were built on trips back and forth across the Mediterranean, the story became French in 1962. Like most Algerian Jews who had been French citizens since 1870, the Beton family headed for France. The fate of the Orangina company followed that of the pieds-noirs, the French who returned to the metropole after Algerian independence. Production moved to Vitrolles in the Bouches-du-Rhône, not far from the port where boats arrived from Algeria, while in Boufarik the historic factory was nationalized by the new Algerian government, continuing to produce orange juice and other related drinks.

Yet it would be too simple to describe Orangina as a drink reserved for pieds-noirs. In many respects its history is similar to the prized drink of Algerian nationalism, Hamoud Boualem lemonade, whose company was also founded, or more accurately refounded, in 1951. Like Léon Beton, Youcef Hamoud had crossed the Mediterranean to learn a new siphoning technique in Marseille in the nineteenth century. Like him, he relied on the production of citrus fruits in Algiers—lemons, not oranges—to develop his drink, and as with Orangina, its success was the work of a single family spanning several generations. Despite a nationalist facade, there is no such thing as a French Orangina and an Algerian Hamoud. Both drinks were the work of Algerian entrepreneurs (one Jewish, one Muslim, both naturalized French) who seized on technological innovations in the context of the colonial economy and managed to keep their companies within the family fold. Above all, they bear witness to the local industrialization at work in colonial Algeria, through the processing of agricultural products on the initiative of a few families, such as the Tamzali or the Ferrero families, who developed pasta and industrial couscous.

Despite the land and economic transformation brought about by colonial settlement, innovation and entrepreneurship remained possible, albeit difficult, in a colonial situation. With the war of independence, however, political choices had to be made: Orangina sided with French Algeria by supplying soldiers, while Hamoud financially supported the FLN's struggle. Hamoud was one of the few companies to resist collectivization after independence.

So, is Orangina French? In fact, the drink defies any purely national framework. Rather than plant flags in oranges, the simple bottle offers an unexpected archive, containing a history on a human scale that traces how colonization violently shaped a volatile geography.

Arthur Asseraf

FURTHER READING

Thierry Lefebvre. "Un pharmacien espagnol à l'origine d'Orangina." *Revue d'histoire de la pharmacie* 348 (2005): 595–96.

José María de Jaime Lorén. "Nuevas noticias sobre el farmacéutico valenciano Agustín Trigo Mezquita y sobre el Trinaranjus." *Revista de la Societat Catalana d'Història de la Farmàcia* 13 (2019): 145–56.

Claire Moyrand. "Hamoud Boualem, le goût de l'Algérie depuis 1878." *Histoires d'entreprises* 7 (July 2009): 44–49.

George Mutin. "L'Algérie et ses agrumes." *Géocarrefour* 44, no. 1 (1969): 5–36.

"Orangina, une épopée algérienne." *France-Culture*, August 27, 2015.

FURTHER TRAVELING

Coca-Cola, Coffee, Noodles and Macaroni, Tea and Chai, Wine

Oyster

March 1834. As every year since the end of the Napoleonic Wars, a flotilla of some one hundred English fishing sloops entered Granville Bay in scattered order, dredging the vast reefs of wild oysters. But this winter, a drama worthy of a Jack London story took place in this disputed region of the English Channel. On March 12 a Portsmouth skipper accustomed to poaching in French territorial waters was shot by fishery guards after offering armed resistance when he docked. Threatening to sour relations between Paris and London, this affair put the question of the limits of these international waters back on the diplomatic agenda and led to the signing of the Franco-English convention of August 2, 1839, one of the first international conventions on fishing and the conservation of fishery resources, which governed the exploitation and sharing of the natural oyster beds located between the mainland and the Channel Islands.

This tragic episode testifies not only to the violence of conflicts over access to the sea's resources, but also to the economic and cultural importance of the oyster, a mollusk prized since antiquity for its many culinary, dietary, and aphrodisiac virtues. Their ancient heritage has been demonstrated by excavations at numerous archaeological sites, the most impressive of which are undoubtedly the gigantic shell mounds built over the centuries by Indigenous North American populations on the Atlantic and Pacific coasts. In vogue at European courts in the seventeenth century, consumption of this luxury foodstuff gradually democratized during the modern period, culminating in a global boom in the nineteenth century. Oysters became a fashionable product, transcending social barriers and national borders. Sometimes considered a "poor man's dish" due to their low cost, oysters remained a delicacy of choice, associated, for example, with the rise of the first seaside resorts. Throughout the Western world, they were readily available in most towns with rail links to the coast and could be enjoyed just about anywhere, whether at a restaurant table, a tavern counter, or a street vendor's stall.

In New York, which became the oyster capital of the world in the nineteenth century, annual consumption ran into the hundreds of millions, and it was not uncommon to eat oysters several times a week. Oysters were eaten in a variety of ways: fried, roasted, candied, marinated, or smoked; in soups, stews, hot-dogs, on crackers, or simply raw, on the half shell, seasoned with a little vinegar and a pick if you wanted to look modern and distinguished. This culinary trend also benefited from the development of new preservation processes that spread in the industrial era. In Europe and the United States, oysters appeared in grocery stores in the form of canned goods, while in China's Guangdong Province bottled oyster sauce production took off in the late 1880s and rapidly became one of the defining condiments of globalized Asian cuisine, alongside soy sauce.

However, the consequences of this oyster boom were significant. By the middle of the century, the same damning observation was being made every-where: nature's oyster beds were declining, and resources were dwindling. The cause? The indiscriminate use of dredgers, which devastated the seabed, as well as overfishing, which gradually exceeded the natural reproductive capacity of a mollusk long thought to be inexhaustible. As is so often the case, the history of food intersected with environmental history. To halt the decline in the resource, conservation measures were introduced by fishing authorities, but they were often difficult to enforce, particularly by foreign fishermen who did not always respect the restrictions imposed by states in their territorial waters. On both sides of the Atlantic the nineteenth century was peppered with fishing incidents that sometimes degenerated into full-blown clashes at sea. The most violent of these were undoubtedly the famous oyster wars that broke out in the Chesa-peake Bay from 1865 onward, following the imposition by Maryland authorities of a fishing license designed to restrict access to its marine riches to residents of that coastal state.

It was in this context that some people began devising a definitive solution to the problem of depleting natural oyster beds, using science to cultivate the sea like they did the land. It was a question of mastering the reproductive cycle in order to multiply oysters artificially. Oyster farming was already being practiced around the world, involving the collection of baby oysters (spat) from one bed and their subsequent replanting on another, or the creation of a new one. Though oyster farming has been documented in China, Japan, and Mexico,

Victor Coste (1807–73), a scientist and professor of comparative embryology at the Collège de France, has long been credited with "inventing" the process. According to historians, he made this discovery on his return from a scientific observation trip to the shores of Lake Fusaro, near Naples, where the spat collection technique, inherited from Roman times, had already been tried and tested. In reality, his contribution consisted mainly in perfecting this technique and convincing Emperor Napoleon III of the usefulness of applying it on a large scale. But the details matter little in this case, since the experiments he conducted throughout the 1850s and 1860s, with the support and subsidies of the French navy, aroused keen interest in coastal communities and led to the development of an oyster industry in France, whose success was made abundantly clear to the rest of the world at the 1867 Paris World's Fair—to such an extent that many countries, including Belgium, Norway, Canada, and Austria-Hungary, set out in the following years to copy this model and establish it on their own coasts.

Just as the new industry began to flourish, the first in a long series of crises occurred that have continued to shake it to its foundations ever since. As filter feeders, oysters are extremely sensitive to the quality of the water around them, which is why biologists today regard them as "sentinel" species. From the 1890s onward this newfound property made them suddenly suspect in the eyes of consumers, leading to a sharp drop in demand. Food panics broke out in France, Ireland, the United Kingdom, and the United States, following virulent press campaigns linking the consumption of unsanitary oysters to tens of thousands of cases of typhoid fever. Better management of wastewater discharges and the introduction of sanitary control procedures restored confidence, but the crisis dealt the oyster-farming industry a severe blow, especially in 1920–21, when an epizootic disease suddenly affected the European flat oyster (*Ostrea edulis*). Completing the work already begun by a century of overexploitation, it led to the almost total destruction of the natural beds necessary for spat collection. Like winegrowers confronted with phylloxera a few decades earlier, European oyster farmers took the gamble of growing another, more resistant species, the Portuguese oyster (*Crassostrea angulata*). Introduced by accident to the waters of the Tagus during the time of the great discoveries, this hollow oyster, probably originating from the Taiwan Strait, was established in the Arcachon Basin since the 1860s, gradually replacing the flat oyster. And then a new epizootic caused its sudden disappearance in the early 1970s. It was after this episode that the Japanese oyster (*Crassostrea gigas*) became common. Already successfully introduced in the United States and Canada in the 1920s and in Australia and New Zealand in the 1950s, the Japanese oyster quickly acclimatized in European waters and still reigns almost unchallenged throughout the world's oyster industries.

Romain Grancher

FURTHER READING

Mark Kurlansky. *The Big Oyster: History on the Half Shell*. New York: Random House, 2007.
Olivier Levasseur. *Histoire de l'huître en Bretagne*. Morlaix: Skol Vreizh, 2006.
Jack London. *Patrouille de pêche: Les pirates de San Francisco et autres nouvelles*. Paris: Éditions Phébus, 2000.
Bonnie J. McCay. *Oyster Wars and the Public Trust: Property, Law and Ecology in New Jersey History*. Tucson: University of Arizona Press, 1998.
Robert Neild. *The English, the French and the Oyster*. London: Quiller Press, 1995.

FURTHER TRAVELING

Caviar, Ceviche, Fish Sauce (Nuoc Mam), Hot Dog, Poke, Soy Sauce, Sushi

Palm Oil

In 1887 the British consul in the Niger Delta apprehended Jaja, a former slave who had become a powerful commercial intermediary in the export of palm oil to Opobo. He was tried in Accra for obstructing free trade and breaching a protectorate treaty signed in 1873. The story of Jaja d'Opobo, exiled for resisting British political and commercial domination, offers an entry point into understanding the roots of palm oil production in the region, its links with slavery, and the conflicting relationships between local producers and companies who sought to control the entire chain from plantation to consumer on a global scale.

Jaja's arrest coincides with the end of a cycle in the palm oil trade on Africa's coasts. The oleaginous product extracted from the fruit or kernel of the *Elaeis guineensis* palm, a West African species whose use as a foodstuff is attested as far back as 5000 BCE, entered global commerce with the Atlantic slave trade. Slave ships carried a few barrels of this red oil to supplement the rations allocated to their human cargo. But the abolition of the slave trade by European nations at the beginning of the nineteenth century gave it a new legitimacy: it became the substitute product par excellence in the eyes of the abolitionists. African countries such as Dahomey and the city-states along the "oil rivers" of the Niger Delta, which were developing their production for export, used the slaves they could no longer sell to Europeans for this purpose. Moreover, this trade provided cover for a clandestine trade that continued until the early 1860s.

Slaves in Opobo harvested the fruit at the top of the palm trees, crushed and boiled the pulp to extract the oil, and transported it in large canoes to the coast, helping set the wheels in motion for the Industrial Revolution. Indeed, until the 1880s, Europeans focused on nonfood uses for palm oil: soap, stearin, and machine lubrication. The African populations provided an unrefined, acidic, and odoriferous product for export, unsuitable for consumption, while reserving the "sweet" oil for themselves. In the 1840s Samuel Herring, born a slave in Virginia and settled in Liberia, discovered the use of palm kernel oil. This white, solid vegetable fat seemed to him closer to Western tastes. He invented a machine to extract it and promoted it under the name of "African lard," without success. Palm kernel was first used in Europe as livestock feed, particularly in dairy farming. In Germany and Denmark it was used to make fatter butter. In the 1880s the British firm Loders patented a process for deodorizing palm kernel oil, enabling it to be used in margarine and industrial pastries. In 1896 a firm in Marseille combined it with coconut oil in its Végétaline breads. By 1900 palm kernels outstripped palm oil in African exports. From 1920 onward Malaysia and Sumatra became the land of choice for oil palms. European entrepreneurs converted the plantations set up for rubber trees at the beginning of the twentieth century, using large numbers of Chinese and Indian coolies. In Africa, with the exception of the Belgian Congo, where Unilever obtained large land concessions, the colonizers preferred small-scale farming. Their efforts to standardize quality and impose mechanical extraction met with resistance from farmers, who shunned the big mills. At the end of the 1930s, 65 percent of the palm oil produced in Nigeria was consumed locally; in Côte d'Ivoire and Dahomey, mills exported only the kernels.

In parts of the world where palm oil was not yet part of the diet, its arrival caused controversy. In India it appeared in the 1920s as a cheap substitute for ghee (clarified butter). Like margarine in Europe, this product met with mistrust from consumers worried about the "impure" ingredients that manufacturers might add to it, such as tallow or whale fat. Renamed *vanaspati ghi*, it became associated with the positive image of the tutelary divinity of the vegetable kingdom, under the aegis of the popular Dalda brand. The company orchestrated advertising campaigns in the mid-1930s, highlighting its exclusively vegetable composition and good preservation in airtight tins adorned with a palm tree. At the time of independence, the Cow Protection League saw it as an anti-cow product and mobilized Indian patriotism against its import.

In the United States, from the 1970s onward, fear of competition led soybean producers to campaign against palm oil, which drove down prices as the plantations in Malaysia expanded. This launched an "oil war." In a globalized economy where protectionism necessarily posed a threat, health-related arguments were mobilized: medical research established a correlation between consumption of fats and cardiovascular disorders. The distinction between saturated and unsaturated fatty acids, initially aimed at animal fats, was used in the 1980s to disqualify the more saturated "tropical oils." In the following decade, the spotlight fell on oils transformed by hydrogenation (trans fats), in particular soybean oil, which had the saturated oil consistency sought by margarine manufacturers. When deodorized and bleached, palm oil becomes invisible. Concealed under the generic term of "vegetable fat," it could replace cocoa butter in chocolate and be incorporated into any preparation concocted by the agri-food industry: pizzas, cookies, sweets, crackers, and even ice creams. In Côte d'Ivoire it was sometimes substituted for peanut oil. In China it is a staple in instant noodles. In Indonesia and Malaysia it has gradually replaced coconut oil, which has become too expensive. Malaysia promotes it as a halal product in Muslim countries and GMO-free for consumers in northern countries. Though it is processed and rich in saturated fats, the latest research does not allow us to settle the debate on its supposed harmfulness. As the most widely consumed vegetable oil in the world, it is said to increase both "good" and "bad" cholesterol.

However, it is in the name of environmental protection that palm oil is increasingly criticized. Clearing fires release huge quantities of CO_2, as in Sumatra and Borneo during the El Niño episode of 2015–16. The orangutan became the symbol of this deforestation, which has destroyed its natural habitat. In 2010 the NGO Greenpeace caused a sensation with a false advertisement in which an employee unwrapped a Kit-Kat that revealed two fingers of the famous primate, and after he took a bite, blood spurted onto his horrified colleagues. These targeted campaigns were designed to launch boycott movements with the aim of revising production standards. However, they were aimed indiscriminately at small planters and large globalized agribusiness complexes. The new standards offered no guarantees against deforestation, and certification continued to rely on unverified traceability. Today Greenpeace is working to ensure a "zero deforestation" strategy, without taking a stand on the exploitation of plantation workers, or the spoliation and violence suffered by small-scale producers and the populations evicted from their homes.

A symbol of "junk food," which has been rendered invisible, odorless, and tasteless, palm oil is produced under conditions that must not go unnoticed. These problems are still debated, especially as its nonfood uses increase in areas such as biofuels.

Isabelle Surun

FURTHER READING

K. G. Berger and S. M. Martin. "Palm Oil." In *The Cambridge World History of Food*, ed. Kenneth F. Kiple and Kriemhield Coneè Ornelas, 397–411. Cambridge: Cambridge University Press, 2000.

Sylvanus John Sodienye Cookey. *King Jaja of the Niger Delta: His Life and Times, 1821–1891*. New York: NOK, 1974.

Valeria Giacomin. "The Emergence of an Export Cluster: Traders and Palm Oil in Early Twentieth Century South-East Asia." *Enterprise & Society* 19, no. 2 (2018): 272–308.

Martin Lynn. *Commerce and Economic Change in West Africa: The Palm Oil Trade in the Nineteenth Century*. Cambridge: Cambridge University Press, 2002.

Jonathan E. Robins. *Oil Palm: A Global History*. Chapel Hill: University of North Carolina Press, 2021.

FURTHER TRAVELING

Margarine, Olive Oil, Pizza

Parmesan Cheese

The year 1928 marked the start of a revolution in Parmesan production. The Reggio Emilia–based Consorzio del Grana Reggiano was founded and soon extended to neighboring provinces. Its aim was to combat imitations and blends, and to defend the identity of a cheese that, under the proprietary name of Parmigiano Reggiano, was soon to conquer the world.

Parmesan's success dates to the eleventh century, and stems from its preservative qualities, which ensured that it circulated more easily than other dairy products. The Cistercian monks of Chiaravalle Abbey, near Milan, are said to have inherited its production methods from Switzerland. At the end of the Middle Ages, the pastures of the Po Valley were put to good use once it was realized that cattle could be used not only for their labor and meat but also for milk, which until then had been limited to sheep and goats. Far from the mountains and hills, the qualities of the grass and cows at the origin of Parmesan cheese opened new possibilities for its production, transport, and consumption. Boccaccio had already associated it with opulence. In his work, the eighth day of the Decameron (1350–53) dedicated to the misadventures of the painter Calandrino recounts that in the land of Bengodi, that is, of Cockaigne, there was a mountain made of grated Parmesan cheese and inhabited by people who did nothing but make macaroni and ravioli. It became a staple of princely tables. Among salted cheeses, distinct from fresh cheeses, Parmesan was continually praised in Italian cookbooks of the Renaissance, from the *Liber de coquina* in the fourteenth century to the *Summa lacticiniorum* by the physician Pantaleone da Confienza (1477) and the recipe manual of Pope Bartolomeo Scappi's cook (c. 1570). An engraving by Annibal Carrache shows a vendor holding half of a

Parmesan cheese under his arm ("Vende Formaggio Parmigiano," *Le arti di Bologna*, 1646).

The culinary relay was soon taken up by European travelers, who celebrated the abundance of Parmesan cheese despite the crisis affecting the Duchy of Parma in the seventeenth century. The rich meadows of Lombardy were described by Lalande (1769), Arthur Young (1789), and Lullin de Châteauvieux (1812–13). By the fourteenth century Parmesan cheese had already been exported to the rest of Europe and to Constantinople, first by the Pisans and then the Venetians. According to the diary of Samuel Pepys, during the great fire of London in 1666, the inhabitants put parmesan cheese in a safe place along with some of their most prized possessions. Later, in Stevenson's *Treasure Island* (1883), Doctor Livesey confides in young Jim: "You've seen my snuff-box, haven't you? And you never saw me take snuff, the reason being that in my snuff-box I carry a piece of Parmesan cheese—a cheese made in Italy, very nutritious." Even in the twentieth century, Parmesan cheese continued to fill imaginations. In episode seven of the ninth season of the American TV series *Columbo* (1989), the assassin is betrayed by his taste for the cheese. After biting into a piece of Reggiano cheese on his victim's desk, the culprit leaves traces of his teeth, enabling the famous lieutenant to follow the trail.

A product of the Po Valley, Parmesan has contributed to the region's history, but also to history much further afield. If it has become an exportable item and a piece of cultural heritage for every Italian, it is because it was quickly appreciated outside its place of origin. While asiago, Bitto, and Gorgonzola—all cheeses from the north—face competition from Marzolino and caciotta from central Italy, or cacciocavallo and burrata from the south, the history of parmesan is first and foremost that of a link between the different territories of the peninsula. Its success with Italians is based on a paradox: to contribute to national cohesion, it needed to be bound to a specific region, distinct from other cheese-making regions.

Dairy products were not widely consumed at the end of the eighteenth century, but they spread to European tables in the nineteenth century with the industrialization of production. Parmesan cheese was no exception. After 1850 it became the flagship of Lombardy's agricultural industry, from Codogno to Casalpusterlengo and Lodi. Marketing led from Milan as well as imitations throughout Italy and the rest of the world made it necessary to protect the more artisanal production of Parmigiano Reggiano in southern Lombardy and Emilia. This area took on a status of its own, leaving the rest of northern Italy to produce Grana Padano, previously known as Parmesan, whose qualities producers were no less careful to preserve.

Between 1928 and 1954 pride in the distinctive character and traditions of the territory of Parmesan cheese gradually created a divergence from Grana Padano. Six years after its appearance in Reggio Emilia, the consortium for the defense of Grana Reggiano extended to the provinces of Parma and Modena and to part of the province of Mantua south of the Po (Grana Tipico), before including the western side of the province of Bologna in 1937. In 1954 this quadrilateral formed the Consorzio del Formaggio Parmigiano-Reggiano. Parmesan cheese in its current form was born and duly protected by a 1996 European directive against imitation. Produced in these five provinces alone, it is an object of visceral attachment among producers and consumers alike.

A hard cheese with flavors that vary according to the length of its maturation period, from twelve to seventy-two months, Parmesan owes its worldwide popularity to the prestige of its local identities. Parmesan should not be confused with Grana Padano, another hard cheese—hence the name Grana, meaning grain— with an ancient tradition, but it matures for less time, from nine to twenty months, and is therefore not as hard as parmesan. Ricotta is produced all over Italy. And while Pecorino Romano is made from 90 percent Sardinian sheep's milk from the island, there also exists a Tuscan version. Parmesan, on the other hand, is an exclusive cheese. At least 50 percent of its milk comes from cows fed on the meadows of Emilia-Romagna and Lombardy. For Italians it is the king of cheeses. Taking its name from a town, which is rare for a cheese, it is a matter of local and even national pride, much like opera, which also has a strong connection to region of Emilia-Romagna.

Parmesan can be eaten on its own, in the form of prepackaged pieces. It is only since the 1930s that cheese has been assigned a place of its own within the meal, creating a moment of pause between the appetite-satisfying meats and the "soft voluptuousness" of dessert. But it is often combined with other ingredients through which it is transformed. As an aperitif with a dry or sparkling white wine and charcuterie (*salumi*), or by scraping and sprinkling on both "solid" and "liquid" dishes such as pasta, salads, or soups, which it enhances like truffles or saffron. The pleasure of tasting it in small blocks (*incisum*) complements that of the gratinated powder (*gratatum*) obtained by grating it or buying it in prepared sachets distributed to the four corners of the globe. Like grana, parmesan delights the palate with its soft, grainy substance.

Parmesan is also a word marked by oppositions: on the one hand, it has its place as a fine food with all the opulence and self-confidence characteristic of a globalized economy, as evidenced by supermarket shelves, freeway service areas, and airport stores; on the other, it connotes the frail elegance of the pink or violet color in the Mannerist paintings of Mazzola, known as Parmigianino. And although the novel *The Charterhouse of Parma* does not mention the cheese, Stendhal did evoke it in the *Life of Napoleon*. It thus reflects a proximity between the pleasures of eating and the arts, which transcends material pleasures. The aesthetics of Parmesan cheese are also echoed in the architecture of the places where it used to be made, monuments that are often surrounded by colonnades and can be circular like some Romanesque baptisteries or quadrangular in the neoclassical spirit. The labyrinthine mausoleum of the famous art publisher Franco Maria Ricci in Fontanellato, near Soragna, is another example of cheese as a work of art. Located in the heart of the Parmesan countryside, it helps us understand how a local product was able to conquer the world.

Gilles Bertrand

FURTHER READING

Claudio Besana. *Tra agricoltura e industria: Il settore caseario nella Lombardia dell'Ottocento*. Rome: Vita e Pensiero, 2012.

Alberto Capatti and Massimo Montanari. *La cuisine italienne: Histoire d'une culture*. Paris: Seuil, 2002.

Enzo Dieci. *Parmigiano reggiano: Viaggiatori stranieri e storia padana*. Reggio Emilia: Istituto Agrario Statale A. Zanelli, 1980.

Stefano Levati. "Cibo sano, comodo a conservarsi e al trasporto, di squisito gusto: Il commercio del parmigiano nello stato di Milano tra Sette e Ottocento." In *Oro bianco: Il settore lattiero-caseario in Val Padana tra Otto e Novecento*, ed. Patrizia Battilani and Giorgio Bigatti, 67–98. Lodi: Giona, 2002.

Mario Zannoni. *Il parmigiano-reggiano nella storia*. Collecchio: Silva, 1999.

FURTHER TRAVELING

Charcuterie, Noodles and Macaroni, Roquefort, Tofu, Wine

Pepper

Between 1989 and 2016, nine volumes of the Indian government's *Ayurvedic Pharmacopoeia* were published, listing a variety of plants. Among them was long pepper, or *pippali* in Sanskrit and several Indian languages, which was described as treating respiratory disorders (*śvāsa*), coughs (*kāsa*), and fevers (*jvara*) like black pepper, or *marica* in Sanskrit.

The peppercorn, which originated in India, has been used therapeutically for thousands of years. In the nineteenth century pepper was partly adopted by British colonists in India, who consumed pepper water to combat fevers and cholera. A pharmacopoeia preserved in English archives even recommended it against madness: to do this, it must be boiled with turmeric and a frog—whose skin is now known to contain active chemical molecules, notably antibiotics. Pepper also has a long history in Chinese medicine. It is a valuable remedy for stomachaches, kidney problems, or, mixed with radish, epileptic seizures. Since the end of the twentieth century, allopathic medicine has been examining the efficacy of *piperine*, one of pepper's components, in combating convulsions. In Europe, pepper is used in the form of an essential oil to soothe inflammation.

But it is above all for its gustatory properties that pepper is renowned. Peppercorns are used to spice up vegetable, meat, and fish dishes. Eaten as black pepper (picked before ripening and then dried), green pepper (picked before ripening and preserved in brine), or white pepper (picked when ripe and immersed in water for removal from their black husks). Thanks to its worldwide success, it is now cultivated in Africa, South America, Asia, and Oceania, sometimes as part of high-quality production schemes combining a specific terroir and variety. In 2013 white pepper from Penja, a coastal region of Cameroon, became one of the first three Protected Geographical Indications in West and Central

Africa, modeled on the European Protected Geographical Indications or Protected Designations of Origin.

Pepper is one of the most widely traded spices in the world, but this is nothing new. It was one of the first global food commodities. As far back as antiquity it was traded from India to the Mediterranean, via the Silk Road or, by sea, via the Gulf of Aden and Egypt. A costly product, it was stored in the treasuries of Roman emperors alongside precious metals. It was even part of the ransom demanded by the Visigoth king Alaric during the siege of Rome in 410 BCE.

In the Middle Ages pepper consumption spread throughout Europe. Spices became extraordinarily popular, sought after by the wealthy for their digestive properties, their supposed aphrodisiac virtues, and above all their function as a marker of social distinction. The stakes of the spice trade were so high in the Mediterranean in the fifteenth century that Christopher Columbus set out to find a new route to India in order to bring back "Christians and spices." Columbus brought chili pepper back from the Americas, and his counterpart Vasco de Gama returned to Portugal with a precious cargo of black pepper. He then began an intense trade from India, the main exporter of the spice. At the turn of the sixteenth and seventeenth centuries, when pepper was the leading spice traded in terms of volume, the merchants' supplies extended to Southeast Asia, particularly the Indonesian island of Sumatra. While Portuguese merchants, like the Muslim merchants of Java and Malaya, remained active, Chinese merchants made their presence felt in the region, just as the English and Dutch of the East India companies also entered the market. The Dutch founded the port of Batavia (now Jakarta) in 1619, which in the eighteenth century became the hub of the pepper trade in Southeast Asia. The spice was bought there by Chinese and Portuguese merchants bound for the Chinese market, as well as by Portuguese, Spanish, Armenian, and Muslim merchants chartering ships for Manila, the starting point for the Pacific crossing to the Americas.

In the eighteenth century increasing trade volumes drove down the price of pepper, as it was eclipsed in East India company ships in the highly lucrative opium trade. Tastes were also changing. Spice fever began dying out in Europe while demand was growing for new colonial consumer products such as tea, coffee, sugar, and tobacco. The pepper trade remained nonetheless a source of enrichment, and therefore a desired commodity. In 1739, a "pepper scandal" broke out in the small French trading post of Mahé, located on the south Indian coast in present-day Kerala. Administrators hijacked a French East India Company ship to send their personal cargoes of pepper to Mocha, in present-day Yemen, and profit from the illicit operation. A few years later other French merchants obtained pepper from rebels in the kingdom of Banten, north of the island of Java, supplying them with barrels of gunpowder for their fight against the sultan and their Dutch colonial competitors. At the end of the century, competition between merchants was reinforced by the arrival of American ships chartered from Salem or Boston, which obtained their supplies from the northwest coast of Sumatra, nicknamed the "Pepper Coast," despite the presence of Malay pirates. In the nineteenth century pepper cultivation continued to develop in Southeast Asia, driven by Chinese merchants and planters, particularly in Singapore.

Today pepper in all its forms can be found in a wide variety of the city-state's culinary specialties, a legacy of the many flows and intermingling of populations. A cosmopolitan product par excellence, at the beginning of the twenty-first century pepper featured in cookbooks throughout the world. At the same time, it formed part of the identity of dishes considered typically national. In France this is the case with steak au poivre, a recipe for which chef Raymond Olivier first published in a cookbook in 1957. Simple and fast, the recipe has adapted to the changing lifestyles of the French, who spend less time at the table and have adopted the single-course menu. Other transformations have also shaped its consumption. Since the 1970s spices have been used not just for their own sake, but to enhance and bring out the taste of products. In this culinary movement, pepper is now associated with chocolate. Chef Alain Ducasse has made it one of his signature desserts, served at the Hôtel de Paris restaurant in Monaco in 2021, *"Chocolat Java de notre manufacture, poivre sauvage"* (house-made Java chocolate with wild pepper). From India to China, from Indonesia to Monaco, via Yemen, pepper continues its millennia-long journey.

Julie Marquet

FURTHER READING

Ota Atsushi. "Banten Rebellion, 1750–1752: Factors Behind the Mass Participation." *Modern Asian Studies* 37, no. 3 (2003): 613–51.

Lizzie Collingham. *Curry: A Tale of Cooks and Conquerors.* Oxford: Oxford University Press, 2006.

Catherine Manning. *Fortunes à faire: The French in Asian Trade, 1719–1748.* London: Routledge, 1996.

Anthony Reid. "An 'Age of Commerce' in Southeast Asian History." *Modern Asian Studies* 24, no. 1 (1990): 1–30.

Jean Vitaux. *La mondialisation à table.* Paris: Presses Universitaires de France, 2009.

FURTHER TRAVELING

Charcuterie, Chili Pepper, Coffee, Curry, Salt, Tea and Chai

Pet Food and Treats

Around 1861, James Spratt founded Spratt's Patent Limited in England, a company that produced animal biscuits and marketed them with public health arguments. From the 1870s onward the company expanded production to the United States, Canada, and Russia, but demand remained limited due to household habits. Indeed, the composition and preparation of animal feed remained a predominantly private affair. For livestock this remained the case as long as rural economies relied on both breeding and polyculture. For pets, food was available as long as the domestic economy mobilized raw products that produced waste and meal scraps, which could be used to feed them. Moreover, many animals grazed on common land (pigs), hunted (cats), or found their food in waste dumps (dogs in particular).

The pet food industry, from dog biscuits to cattle pellets, began to develop in northwestern Europe and North America in the second half of the nineteenth century. It sat at the crossroads of changes in production and consumption patterns that were bound to demographic, urban, and industrial growth as well as public health biopolitical programs that combined the disciplining of stray animals and the centralized management of food waste, particularly meat. It also benefited from developments in zootechnics and nutritional sciences, as well as a growing taste for companion animals. While several English and American companies specialized in the production of bird food at the beginning of the nineteenth century, the industrialization of the livestock and dog biscuit sector developed slowly during the second half of the century, as Spratt's company illustrates.

At the same time, the sharp rise in meat and milk consumption and the resulting quest to improve livestock productivity prompted agricultural experiments in Germany and then the United States on the composition of livestock rations. This work led to the development of optimal standard formulas, refined through research in chemistry and physiology. It also highlighted the value of high-energy feeds such as press cakes, as well as micronutrients, following the discovery of vitamins in 1913 and trace elements in the 1920s. Advances in nutritional science were inseparably linked to human and animal nutrition in a constant dialectic embodied by nutritional experiments on laboratory animals.

While this scientific approach to food was developing at the beginning of the twentieth century, American meat industries were developing the mass production of canned dog food. This enabled them to take advantage of products that were unsuitable for human consumption, difficult to sell—such as horse or whale meat—or parts that were no longer used, such as tripe. The market expanded from the interwar years onward, thanks to demand fueled by the increased value of leisure time and the standardization of human food, which reduced the amount of domestic waste. At the outbreak of World War II, around 20 percent of American dogs were fed commercially, and production of these canned foods doubled between 1947 and 1954. They were also used for cats, for which the industry was slow to develop a specialized market, reflecting their later integration into households and their marginalization in laboratory experiments.

The development of industrial livestock breeding after World War II was based on increased collaboration and transfers of knowledge between public research and the private sector, including the food industry. The latter developed more concentrated feeds to meet the demands of breeds selected for their productivity, encouraging new forms of organization and division of agricultural labor, which excluded breeders from the development of rations. The use of feed additives intensified in the context of stall breeding, and from the 1950s included antibiotics, for prophylactic and growth purposes as well as to use up pharmaceutical surplus. This was followed by introduction of growth hormones. By the mid-1960s around 85 percent of industrial livestock feed in the United States contained additives or drugs, raising public health concerns that were mitigated by timid restrictions.

The industrial standardization of animal feed was both a product of, and a driving force behind, the expansion of agriculture and the globalization of trade, including the movement of animals. From the eighteenth century onward, as the quest for productivity encouraged the production of more efficient hybrids, Chinese breeds of fast-fattening pigs, raised in cowsheds and fed mainly on agricultural waste and by-products, were imported to England and then to the United States, enabling the development of intensive pig farming. Public agricultural experimental research labs were set up in Europe, the United States, China, and Japan from the second half of the nineteenth century onward, as well as agroindustrial companies, universities, and later research and development centers. They encouraged the circulation of animals, breeding practices, and agronomic guidelines. In recent decades, these asymmetrical exchanges have had the side effect of contributing to the disappearance of local breeds. Companion animals have also been subject to long-range circulation. Among many examples, the elites and middle classes of the Ottoman Empire in the late nineteenth century who were eager to adopt European culture imported pedigree dogs as a sign of social distinction.

Animal food has been a part of these international trajectories, even as its development and trade have followed certain specificities. In the late nineteenth century, Danish imports of low-cost cereals from European settler colonies were used to feed livestock. Today multinationals produce kibbles and pellets using ingredients imported from several continents, from Thai cassava to Brazilian soy. The complexity of these transfers, combined with the industrialization of livestock farming, has led to health crises of global proportions, such as those involving meat and bone meal consumed by mad cows in Europe or Japan, or the addition of melamine to animal rations in China. Such practices open windows onto the biopolitical stranglehold exerted on animals, as well as the anxieties and health risks raised by the nondomesticated part of the living world.

Violette Pouillard

FURTHER READING

Delphine Berdah. "Pour une autre histoire de la 'modernisation' des pratiques d'élevage." In *Histoire des modernisations agricoles au xxᵉ siècle*, ed. Margot Lyautey, Léna Humbert, and Christophe Bonneuil, 101–14. Rennes: Presses Universitaires de Rennes, 2021.

Katherine C. Grier. "Provisioning Man's Best Friend: The Early Years of the American Pet Food Industry, 1870–1942." In *Food Chains: From Farmyard to Shopping Cart*, ed. Warren Belasco and Roger Horowitz, 126–41. Philadelphia: University of Pennsylvania Press, 2010.

Cihangir Gündoğdu. "Dogs Feared and Dogs Loved: Human-Dogs Relations in the Late Ottoman Empire." *Society & Animals* (2020): 1–22.

Brendan Matz. "Nutrition Science and the Practice of Animal Feeding in Germany, 1850–1880." In *New Perspectives on the History of Life Sciences and Agriculture*, ed. Denise Phillips and Sharon Kingsland, 163–81. New York: Springer, 2015.

Sam White. "From Globalized Pig Breeds to Capitalist Pigs: A Study in Animal Cultures and Evolutionary History." *Environmental History* 16 (2011): 94–120.

FURTHER TRAVELING

Food Coloring and Preservatives

Pho

In the early hours of January 31, 1968, Communist forces launched the famous Tet offensive. A major turning point in the Vietnam War, this offensive had been secretly planned by regional Communist forces on the second floor of the Pho Binh restaurant in Saigon. It had been the HQ of the F100 secret cell as early as 1965 under the noses of American and South Vietnamese policemen and soldiers who gathered on the first floor to enjoy *pho bac*, the "soup of the North," which had become an improbable link between culinary heritage, national history, and identity.

Since then, pho restaurants have proliferated across the world, from Hanoi to Hollywood, from London to Johannesburg and from Paris to Canberra. Difficult to pronounce for foreigners because of the interrogative *hỏi* tone on the "ơ," the Vietnamese pronunciation of the word *phở* alone suggests the ripples of flavored steam that emanate from its meticulous cuisine. The success and notoriety of Vietnamese soup, now a worldwide phenomenon, can be explained first and foremost by the visceral attachment of the Vietnamese to one of the monuments of their national gastronomy, and by the ability they have demonstrated to preserve it at all costs, even in the darkest hours of their history, under the bombs and in poverty, even in the most modest villages. Today, Vietnam's most prized broth, with its voluptuous rice noodles, powerfully aromatic herbs like láng mint, whispering ginger, onions, and light spices, is enjoyed from morning to night by Vietnamese of all classes and ages. Still served in the street "*bouis-bouis*" that delight locals and tourists alike, it offers a unique concentration of Vietnamese character. Even more than the national identity promoted by the Vietnamese authorities, it reflects an exceptional cultural and culinary wealth, nourished by the history of interactions with foreign empires—Chinese, Khmer,

Cham, French, or American—as well as contacts between the fifty-four ethnic groups that make up this people.

Just over a century old, pho is rather young in Vietnam's long culinary history. A hypothesis often repeated on French-language tourism blogs, perhaps inherited from the colonial authorities' desire to extol the merits of great French cuisine as an element of national prestige to be regained after the defeat of 1870, notes that beef had been absent from traditional Vietnamese cuisine, that it was introduced into pho during French colonization, and that pho may even derive from pot-au-feu. This ignores sources that attest to the consumption of slices of buffalo in Vietnamese dishes cooked at the imperial court, particularly in the late eighteenth century. It also ignores the Asian roots put forward by various specialists—Chinese (the soup is said to have been brought back by Vietnamese nationalists returning from the Chinese province of Yunnan in the late nineteenth century), Mongolian, Polynesian, or even exclusively Vietnamese.

The geographical origin of pho is more consensual. It was born in the north at the end of the nineteenth century, in the region the French called Tonkin, and more precisely in the old quarter of Hanoi, capital of French Indochina and a veritable commercial hub at the heart of interactions between Vietnamese, French, and Chinese. Popular with workers whose livelihood depended on the French and Chinese merchant ships that sailed the Red River, pho quickly caught on. It spread as the town urbanized by street vendors, who were depicted as early as 1909 in colonial administrator Henri Oger's book *Technique du peuple annamite*, and then, from the 1920s onward, through small shops built on the model of those in Van Cu. This poor village in Nam Dinh province, some one hundred kilometers (62 mi.) from Hanoi, is sometimes presented as the soup's true place of origin, because it has produced so many pho masters. From 1939 onward chicken was introduced due to restrictions imposed on the sale of beef by authorities anxious to control the slaughter of draft animals for food, a situation that was exacerbated by Japanese occupation. Initially shunned, *pho ga* (chicken) eventually became just as prized as *pho bo* (beef).

Pho subsequently survived the vicissitudes of war and spread with migrations. Soon to become the symbol of a hindered national unity, it gradually spread to the south of the country, starting in the early 1950s and even more so after the signing of the Geneva Accords in 1954, when hundreds of thousands of inhabitants migrated north of the seventeenth parallel. While the nationalization of businesses in the north made life more difficult for pho merchants, pho restaurants spread rapidly in the south. Among them, Pho Binh had been opened by Ngo Toai after his departure from the north in 1955. Three days after the start of the Tet offensive in 1968 he was arrested by the Americans and thrown into prison, where he underwent long sessions of torture and attempted suicide. Finally released, he took advantage of the signing of the Paris Agreement on January 27, 1973, to resume his restaurant business. Later, in the 1990s, he and his son-in-law Nguyen Kim Bach began serving the "pho of peace" to visiting American tourists, while Mr. Nguyen's son moved to Houston. And it was in a similar restaurant, renamed Pho 2000, that U.S. President Bill Clinton came to seal the reconciliation between the United States and Vietnam, twenty-five years after the end of the war.

Abandoned for a time in the 1980s by the Vietnamese population due to shortages of all kinds, pho quickly returned after the *Doi moi* ("revival") in 1986. It was shaped by regional tastes (with spicier soups in the south, for example) and enriched with numerous variants, such as vegan pho, despite the danger of antagonizing purists.

But this magical concoction would not be so famous today if it had not been exported to the four corners of the planet by Vietnamese who, having left or fled their country in the 1970s–80s, sought comfort amid their nostalgia for the motherland. They marketed pho, their pho, in efforts to rediscover the flavors of the mythical soup and share them with as many people as possible, while cookbooks proliferated, especially in the United States and Australia. Thus, the spread of pho seems to have followed the migratory trajectories of some five million Viet Kieu, the overseas Vietnamese. While it does not necessarily carry all the authenticity or flavors found in the homeland, globalized pho is clearly an iconic element of Vietnamese identity, whatever the ethnic and regional origins of the Vietnamese who cook it. In North America, Europe, and Australia, within a resolutely globalized Vietnamese diaspora, a symbiotic relationship is maintained between language, culinary practices, and national identity, a fusion willingly encouraged by the authorities in post–Cold War Vietnam. The internationalization of "Vietnamese cuisine," driven by diasporic migration, economic globalization, and the growth of Vietnam's tourism industry, should not, however, overshadow efforts to preserve the richness of local and regional culinary traditions. For example, French chef Didier Corloux, the first foreign chef to arrive in Hanoi after the war in 1991 and soon convinced that Hanoi pho constituted "the best soup in the world" was quick to respond to the exhortations of the poet Vu Quan Phuong that it should be protected while also evolving through inspiration.

Pierre Journoud

FURTHER READING

C. Annear and J. Harris. "Cooking up the Culinary Nation or Savoring Its Regions? Teaching Food Studies in Vietnam." *ASIANetwork Exchange: A Journal for Asian Studies in the Liberal Arts* 25, no. 1 (2018): 115–48.

Alexandra Greeley. "Phở: The Vietnamese Addiction." *Gastronomica* 2, no. 1 (2002): 80–83.

Andrea Nguyen. *The Pho Cookbook*. Berkeley: Ten Speed Press, 2017.

Erica J. Peters. "Defusing Phở: Soup Stories and Ethnic Erasures, 1919–2009." *Contemporary French and Francophone Studies* 14, no. 2 (2010): 159–67.

——. "Power Struggles and Social Positioning: Culinary Appropriation and Anxiety in Colonial Vietnam." In *Food Anxiety in Globalising Vietnam*, ed. Judith Ehlert and Nora Katharina Faltmann, 43–76. New York: Palgrave Macmillan, 2019.

FURTHER TRAVELING

Banh Mi, Chorba, Fish Sauce (Nuoc Mam), Ramen, Soy Sauce

Pizza

The creation of Pizza Hut in 1958 in Kansas, later relocated to metropolitan Dallas, Texas, marked the entry of pizza into the era of globalization. Behind its apparently simple shape, pizza combines the singularity of its Italian origin with the multiplicity of its geographical variations. The great variety of descriptors used by sellers testifies to how far it has come from its origins. Attested already in Gaeta in 997 to designate a *fouace* or galette, present in the Neapolitan dialect in 1535, it entered the Italian language in 1549 in two forms: pizzella was described by Giovanni Basile in a collection of tales in 1634 (*Lo cunto de li cunti*) as either salted for the common people or sweetened with almonds for the elite. A typical dish for the poor Neapolitan, the *lazzarone* whose creative ingenuity Alexandre Dumas celebrated in *The Corricolo* (1841), pizza broke the monotony of daily routines before eventually being embellished with tomatoes along the same lines as macaroni.

By the end of the 1950s, pizza had generated only a limited market on the Italian peninsula. It had left its Neapolitan cradle to become familiar to the inhabitants of both the north and south, while the crunchier, less codified Sicilian pizza was embarking on its own migration. It represented the family home, thanks to its wood-fired oven and the figure of the *pizzaiolo*, brother-in-arms to the baker and skillful man who kneaded the dough, lined it with an ever-diversifying list of ingredients, put it in the oven, oversaw the cooking, and finally placed it on the customer's plate.

Its influence was based on the combination of craftsmanship and the ease with which it could be marketed. It was marked by the material and symbolic warmth of cooking, as well as by the convivial space generated by the oven. Although a restaurant, a pizzeria doesn't necessarily require major investment.

As a result, it has evolved into a mobile restaurant in food trucks, can be found in any place that sells food, and even places where food is not usually sold. In such places pizza is served as fast food or in a more traditional restaurant style, while frozen pizzas have conquered markets in global consumption.

The global spread of pizza owes much to Italian emigration around the world. The Italians did not create colonial empires like those of the Portuguese, French, or Dutch, with the fleeting exception of Libya and Ethiopia. On the other hand, they migrated widely, particularly to the rest of Europe and to North and South America. The fact that migrants settled in so many "Little Italy" districts explains the initial success of pizza, which offered a means of preserving their identity. The national colors of green, white, and red can be seen in the tomatoes, mozzarella, and basil that are the basic ingredients of the pizza Margherita, named in 1889 after Queen Margaret of Savoy.

The widespread success of pizza is paradoxical. In the post–World War II era of "McDonaldization," a model of industrialized, high-volume production and rapid distribution of pizza was established in the United States. Subjected to new hygiene standards, its development benefited from the myth of the self-made man who needed to eat during his working hours with as few interruptions as possible. By the 1940s Chicago pizza was based on a synchronic rather than sequential conception of the meal: loaded with a rich, layered topping, it became a meal in itself. The power of American companies like the fast-food chain Pizza Hut helped spread this model far beyond North America. Bought by PepsiCo in 1977 and then by Yum! in 1997, Pizza Hut now has thirteen thousand restaurants in more than a hundred and ten countries on every continent. Other companies compete with Pizza Hut, such as Domino's Pizza, which appeared in Michigan in 1960 and now boasts eleven thousand restaurants in seventy countries. Yet, despite the thick layers of cheese and the economic power of these networks, pizza has not suffered from the same reprobation as the hamburger. It has tended to avoid accusations of impoverishing our eating habits.

This may be because pizza has not conquered the world by imposing a single mode of consumption. Despite recurring features (pizza Margherita, Napoletana, or Romana), it has adapted to cultures that have reshaped it, if not in its appearance, then at least in its cultural meanings. Far from an ostensible American homogenization, different countries have reappropriated pizza in a variety of "nationalized" forms. From the hamburger in the United States to the *galette-saucisse* in Brittany and the *tarte flambée* (or *flammenkuchen*) on the Rhine, pizza's distribution methods have been diversified. This plasticity may account for its prestige. It combines with local customs, may include meat or not, or may respect Muslim law. It can be enjoyed in the warmth of a restaurant or in the street, in the car or at home, alone or with friends. It can be eaten as part of a meal with drinks and dessert, or simply picked up, delivered, or even cooked at home.

In France, the Americanized model of pizza consumption has led to the emergence of a countermodel embodied by the pizza truck. Arriving in Marseille at the end of the nineteenth century, the pizza of Provence was initially white, topped with cheese, pig fat, basil, and occasionally anchovies. In the 1920s it turned red as Provençal tomatoes were added to its toppings. In the 1930s Neapolitans, Piemontese, and locals joined the ranks of street vendors, before the 1960s saw the emergence of several hundred pizza trucks, still typical of Marseille today. Gradually spreading throughout France, particularly in Brittany in the 1980s, they substituted for bistros, thanks to the values of artisanal production and bonding and sharing around a wood fire. As for pizzerias, they have sometimes come to define entire neighborhoods, as in Grenoble, where they line the banks of the Isère.

In Italy, pizza has become an indigenous model that is distinct from its origins. It is marked by the pleasure of being together around a table, or having a slice (*pizza al trancio*) eaten standing outside. Adapted to different generations, it offers meals with little preparation time and within everyone's reach. The rise in restaurant prices over the last thirty years explains why many people have returned to its consumption. By contrast, since it is usually eaten hot and on the run, pizza is at the heart of a strange Italian idiomatic expression, "*che pizza!*," which alludes to a dough that is difficult to digest. The expression is used to denote the boredom of an interminable film or any situation that seems to go on without end.

Is pizza, after all, a badge of Italy in every corner of the globe? A return to its birthplace seems impossible, as revealed by the failure of the Neapolitans' application for a protected designation of origin in 1997. Today pizza is neither Neapolitan nor Italian, nor is it American. It is par excellence a versatile product, respecting the requirements of a multiplicity of cultures, even if it means continually introducing reinventions and varieties into each of them.

Gilles Bertrand

FURTHER READING

Marie-Claude Blanc-Chaléard, Antonio Bechelloni, Bénédicte Deschamps, Michel Dreyfus, and Éric Vial, eds. *Les petites Italies dans le monde*. Rennes: Presses Universitaires de Rennes, 2007.

Claude Fischler. "La 'macdonaldisation' des moeurs." *Histoire de l'alimentation*, ed. Jean-Louis Flandrin et Massimo Montanari, 725–47. Paris: Fayard, 1996.

François-Régis Gaudry. *On va déguster l'Italie*. Vanves: Marabout, 2020.

Stéphane Mourlane. "Pasta et pizza," In *Marseille l'italienne: Une passion séculaire*, ed. Jean Boutier and Stéphane Mourlane, 120–23. Marseille: Arnaud Bizalion, 2021.

Sylvie Sanchez. *Pizza connexion: Une séduction transculturelle*. Paris: CNRS Éditions, 2007.

FURTHER TRAVELING

Hamburger, Injera, Naan, Noodles and Macaroni

Poke

In 1991, in the town of Waimea on Hawai'i's Big Island, Hawaiian chef Sam Choy launched his Poke Festival and Recipe Contest, a celebration of poke recipes and competitions, under an army tent. The event marked both the twenty-year development of poke in the archipelago and the start of international expansion for a type of cuisine with a bright future. The poke bowl can be seen as a culinary and gastronomic example of a reinvented tradition. The rediscovery and popular appeal of the dish are relatively recent. A legend, now widely circulated, has it that the great navigator James Cook was invited to eat poke by Hawaiian chefs during his time on the islands. Yet the detailed logbooks of the Briton and his first mates make no mention of this.

In the Hawaiian Islands, before their encounter with James Cook and Westerners, fishermen would set out to sea carrying fish, garnished with condiments, and cut into cubes, or *poke*, meaning "cut," "sliced," or "piece" in several Polynesian languages. This poke was not, however, the object of any particular publicity or attention. Significantly, the American historian Ralph Simpson Kuykendall, a professor at the University of Hawai'i, makes no mention of it in his monumental three-volume history *The Hawaiian Kingdom*, published between 1938 and 1967.

In fact, the present Hawaiian form of poke became popular in the archipelago only around 1960–70. The term itself was introduced at that time to designate preparations based on raw fish. It does not appear in the writings of the European travelers who visited the archipelago in the nineteenth century, nor in those of the American Puritan missionaries who imposed Christianity with an iron fist from the 1820s onward and who left an abundant literature on Polynesian habits and customs.

The original poke consists essentially of raw fish, most often tuna, from which the bones have been removed, marinated with or without the skin, and

POKE

241

served with Hawaiian salt, seaweed, and sometimes ground, toasted, and roasted kukui or other nuts. Beginning in the mid-1800s, various waves of Chinese, Japanese, Filipino, Korean, and Portuguese migrants introduced soy sauces, sesame oils, and other condiments, leading to diversification in poke preparation. From the 1960s onward, poke became even more complex, and its many recipes began to be written down. Japanese and Japanese-inspired chefs such as Alan Wong were working to synthesize Japanese and Polynesian gastronomy. The openness to culinary traditions from elsewhere heralded a success story that, for the time being, was confined to Polynesia. In 1979 an official report from Hawaiʻi's Department of Agriculture and Natural Resources noted a sharp increase in demand for tuna and lemon for poke.

In 1991 Sam Choy, "the king of Island food," launched his competition. His numerous cookbooks and TV show helped poke gain widespread popularity. In the late 1990s he invented the fried poke, something of a culinary oxymoron. Another Hawaiian chef in Waikiki created a poke served with oyster sauce. Avocados, onions, pineapple, and other fruits and vegetables were combined with the raw fish, while Hawaiian Airlines featured it in its advertising. Poke was becoming one of the archipelago's tourist attractions.

The variations of this dish, in line with contemporary aspirations for healthier eating, soon met with international success. Some twenty years after the first poke festival, poke crossed the Pacific. Sam Choy's promotion of poke has even been compared to McDonald's promotion of the hamburger as an extraordinary culinary ambassador to the world. It was around 2010 that poke became popular in North America, first in California. In New York, legend has it that it all started at the Sons of Thunder hamburger joint. When the oven for the tuna steaks broke down, one of the cooks, of Hawaiian origin, suggested serving poke. None of the customers had heard of it, and they resisted, but a *New York Times* food critic, herself a native of Honolulu who was present that day, praised the dish. In just a few years, the number of Hawaiian poke restaurants in the United States grew from three hundred to seven hundred.

However, while the very principle of Hawaiian poke is to marinate condiments for at least a quarter of an hour so that the fish can absorb all the required flavors, the continental American version ignores this step. Instead, it is served with sauces added on demand. Moreover, they now include ingredients that would never be found in a traditional poke, such as quinoa and chicken. All these regional variations demonstrate the syncretism of gastronomy in general, and that of the islands in particular.

In Europe's capitals and major cities, poke remains the reserve of the young urban elite who have been quick to follow the poke craze. In Paris poke bowl spots, almost all located on the right bank, are adorned with Hawaiian-sounding names:

Koko, Pokawa, and so forth. In 2018 the first poke festival was held there. And now, in New York as in the City of London, bankers, executives, and students are lining up for their poke lunch break. It has thus far made few inroads into rural areas.

The success of poke in the West is based on many factors. It contains "good" fats, is rich in fresh produce and low in processed foods, is nourishing, exotic, and cheerfully colorful, and is a quick, tasty, easy-to-take-away dish that is practical for business lunches or friendly get-togethers. Unfortunately, since it is usually made with salmon and/or tuna, it can be loaded with heavy metals that are easily overlooked. Vegans and gluten-free eaters have seized upon it, expelling all nonvegetal elements for some, all traces of wheat for others, and transforming it into a raw vegetable salad. Indeed, fish is not an essential ingredient. One of Sam Choy's signature recipes is based on tofu and avocado. Poke also has many cousins in the Pacific and elsewhere, including one by sailors in Samoa and Fiji who prepare raw fish in much the same way, while Japanese and Korean gastronomies have dishes that are also similar. Some even find a parallel in Italian carpaccio, French tartare, or Peruvian ceviche. Unlike sushi, which obeys strict rules, poke leaves plenty of room for creativity. In this sense, too, it embodies the absolute freedom of the island worlds of the Pacific.

Claire Laux

FURTHER READING

Florence Fabricant. "Poké, a Hawaiian Specialty Emerges in Chelsea." *New York Times*, January 26, 2016.
Rachel Laudan. *The Food of Paradise: Exploring Hawaii's Culinary Heritage.* Honolulu: University of Hawai'i Press, 1996.
Kristin McAndrews. "Incorporating the Local Tourist at the Big Island Poke Festival." In *Culinary Tourism*, ed. Lucy M. Long, 114–27. Lexington: University Press of Kentucky, 1998.
Nancy Piianaia. "Poke: The Survival and Evolution of a Traditional Native Food in a Changing, Multi-Cultural Society." In *Fish: Food from the Waters—Proceedings of the Oxford Symposium on Food and Cookery 1997*, ed. Harlan Walker, 234–47. Totnes, UK: Prospect Books, 1998.
Margaret Titcomb. *Native Use of Fish in Hawaii.* Honolulu: University of Hawai'i Press, 1972.

FURTHER TRAVELING

Ceviche, Hamburger, Oysters, Salt, Soy Sauce, Sushi, Tofu

Port Wine

In 1833, Cyrus Redding noted in his *History and Description of Modern Wines* that "our taste for port wine was imposed on us by our sovereigns, out of jealousy against France." The English journalist and French wine enthusiast emphasized a phenomenon that was already centuries old: since the early eighteenth century, the British monarchy had conceded considerable tax advantages to port wines to put an end to the English elite's preference for claret, a light, colorful, young, and fruity Bordeaux wine.

Even more than the smell of alcohol, the figures of imports from France made the English government dizzy. In 1704, at the height of the War of the Spanish Succession, thirteen hundred tons of Bordeaux wine were smuggled in, despite the embargo officially declared that same year. At a time when commerce, to paraphrase Clausewitz, was conceived as the continuation of war by other means, this massive consumption of an "enemy" product was described as harmful to the interests of the state. An alternative had to be found to these wines, which goaded English patriotism.

The Methuen Treaty of 1703 between England and Portugal granted customs privileges to Portuguese wines over their French competitors. From then on, "port wines" from the Alto-Douro region, which until the 1670s had been destined only for local consumption, began to conquer the English market. In 1686 five hundred barrels were imported into England. Numbers continued to rise thereafter, while at the same time the share of French wines dwindled. Between 1750 and the early 1800s Portuguese wines accounted for 70 percent of wine imports into Great Britain, with port taking the lion's share.

To stabilize and transport the wine, producers increasingly blended their production with brandy. By 1750 the proportion had risen to 9 percent, rising to over 20 percent by the nineteenth century. The success of port wine also contained the seeds of disaster. With the Douro producing too few grapes to meet demand, winegrowers and merchants systematized processes of mixing their production with other spirits, or selling clever concoctions of cider, elderberry, blackberry and turnip juice, which became port in name only. Unsurprisingly, demand fell, and prices collapsed in the 1750s.

This crisis explains the Portuguese government's policy of economic interventionism, under the aegis of the prime minister, the future Marquis de Pombal, who created the General Company of Viticulture of the Upper Douro in 1756. To guarantee wine quality, this organization reduced production zones to two narrow hillside strips along the Douro River. The General Company regulated the fortification (the process of mixing wines with brandy), controlled transport by barge on the river, and inspected drinking establishments. It also set annual production quotas, decided on selling prices and assumed the role of key intermediary between Portuguese producers and English buyers. Quality improved rapidly, and wine exports to England picked up again, reaching record levels by the end of the eighteenth century. The composition of port wine continued to evolve, however, to keep pace with the changing tastes of English consumers, who were fond of strong spirits.

Before the General Company was founded, port production was controlled by English firms based in Portugal. By the early 1780s there were around forty of them, involved in grape selection, wine preparation and transport, storage, and export. In the second half of the eighteenth century, as demand continued to grow and stocks fluctuated with the harvest, competition raged between English merchants. And so, in 1790, tempers flared and blood was spilled. Climatic factors, in a region where summers are dry and scorching and winters very cold, added further complications. Once it arrived in Porto the wine was processed and generally exported within a year to save on storage costs, even when aging was insufficient.

Port's success across the Channel was largely due to the politicization of its consumption. The Whig Party, which had pushed for the signing of the Methuen Treaty, saw in this agreement an opportunity to open the Portuguese market to English fabrics, and even more, to outdo France. Port thus took pride of place in English and then British patriotism. In eighteenth-century caricatures, the port drinker was portrayed as a "true Englishman," a prosperous, laconic merchant with sturdy legs and a taste for roast beef, in contrast to the claret drinker, who was portrayed as a silk-socked, effeminate, verbose, Francophile aristocrat with a preference for wild game.

During the eighteenth century taste spread up and down the social hierarchy. From the beginning of the century aristocratic houses were buying port wine in large quantities; however, it still had the reputation of a rustic wine, generally consumed by servants. It soon became the preferred wine of the middle classes. According to the diary kept by James Woodforde, the sixth son of a vicar and a student at New College, Oxford University, he consumed an average of one bottle a day between 1759 and 1763. Port had two essential advantages. As the Prussian traveler Johann von Archenholz reported in 1788, "it is the taste for strong drinks that makes the English drink port wine with such pleasure, and at a very good price indeed." Yet it was neither the moderate price nor the high alcohol content of Portuguese wine that made port so popular with the British elite. Since the 1750s, criticism of aristocratic corruption, effeminacy, and lack of patriotism had been mounting. The triumph of port was that of the middle class and its values. A sign of this evolution was the emergence, at the end of the eighteenth century, of vintage port of superior quality, which began to be aged in the bottle. For British society, drinking this Portuguese wine from the foothills of the Douro became a marker of national identity.

The history of this fortified wine changed greatly over time. In 1831, the United Kingdom abrogated the Methuen Treaty. The first half of the nineteenth century also saw a new wave of criticism of port wine, which was accused of dumbing down the middle and working classes rather than, like lighter French wines, civilizing the soul. Nevertheless, port consumption remained high across the Channel, and for a long time: in the 1930s, 50 percent of port produced was still destined for the United Kingdom. In Portugal the turn of the twentieth century was a period of profound change. The phylloxera crisis, which first affected France, had a knock-on effect on port in the 1880s. Then the onset of dictatorship in Portugal in 1907 put an end to a new period of extreme growth. It wasn't until the 1930s that the wine sector was thoroughly reorganized, under the impetus of António de Oliveira Salazar, who became prime minister in 1932.

However, like the rest of the Portuguese economy, the port trade stagnated after the Second World War. In the Douro of the 1950s, people still traveled by mule or on foot rather than by car. The situation changed drastically again in the 1960s. A process of concentration began, with mergers and acquisitions that saw most British companies absorbed by multinationals. At the same time, markets were reorganized and divergent. The growing Americanization of tastes in the twentieth century knocked port wine off its pedestal among the British. New markets emerged in countries where lower cost and lower quality port was consumed as an aperitif. In 1963 France became the leading consumer market for this wine, followed by the Benelux countries. In 1965 the economist Jacques Rueff regretfully pointed out that "every time a Frenchman drinks a glass of port or a glass of whiskey, he contributes to the debt on France's balance sheet." Ironically, the world's best-selling port brand today, Porto Cruz, is part of a French spirits group.

Renaud Morieux

FURTHER READING

Norman R. Bennett. "The Golden Age of the Port Wine System, 1781–1807." *International History Review* 12, no. 2 (1990): 221–48.

Henri Enjalbert. "Comment naissent les grands crus: Bordeaux, Porto, Cognac." *Annales: Economies, sociétés, civilisations* 3 (1953): 315–28; 4 (1953): 457–74.

Charles Ludington. *The Politics of Wine in Britain: A New Cultural History.* Basingstoke: Palgrave Macmillan, 2013.

Richard Mayson. *Port and the Douro.* Oxford: Infinite Ideas, 2013.

Johan von Archenholz. *Tableau de l'Angleterre et de l'Italie*, vol. 2. Gotha: Chez Charles-Guillaume Ettinger, 1788.

FURTHER TRAVELING

Beer, Gin, Raki, Rum, Sake, Vodka, Whiskey, Wine

Raki

Officially, it was only in April 2009 that raki (in Turkish, *rakı*) became Turkey's "national drink," when the institute responsible for patents in Turkey reserved the term for the local product. However, it had already been considered as such in all kinds of publications, tourist and otherwise. "Lion's milk," as it is colloquially known in Turkish, is the product of the double distillation of grape must, with at least 40 percent alcohol. To this a certain quantity of aniseed is added, giving it a particular taste and whitish color when water is added. It is almost identical across countries that were once part of the Ottoman Empire, such as *ouzo* in Greece or *arak* in Syria and Lebanon. In the Balkan countries, however, *rakija* is most often used to designate a non-aniseed alcohol, similar to Italian grappa, or plum brandy, normally known as *slivovica* (slivovitz). French pastis, another aniseed-flavored drink, is much more recent, dating back to the First World War.

Following the spread of distillation techniques and the use of alcohol as a beverage rather than a medicine, raki made its historical debut in the early sixteenth century. After wine and *boza*, a kind of thick beer made from millet, it was the third alcoholic beverage consumed in the Ottoman Empire. Produced and sold by non-Muslims, it was enjoyed mainly by non-Muslims, but also by Muslims who did not fear transgression. In fact, while the Quran formally condemns wine, the state's official legal school of authority, Hanafism, tolerated other alcoholic beverages on condition that one is never inebriated, thus opening the door to moderate consumption of raki among the faithful. Nevertheless, raki production and consumption had its ups and downs, depending on the policies of the sultans. While some sultans were abolitionists, in other instances the financial needs of a state won over since it relied on alcohol taxes to balance budgets burdened by wars or reforms. The production of raki, whether familial or artisanal, was limited and costly. Until the nineteenth century raki lovers remained relatively few and far between. Raki was mainly consumed by Greeks, who added a resin produced on the island of Chios, giving the drink the name *mastika*.

The popularity of raki began with the Ottoman Tanzimat reforms. Throughout the century, the price of raki continued to fall, thanks to improved stills, the transition to industrial production, the use of imported grain spirits, competition from small producers, and the fact that it was now preferred without resin. While still vigorously condemned by religious and conservative circles, alcohol consumption was partly legitimized by the more tolerant behavior of sultans and political elites. New legislation, inspired by European law, became more flexible. At the same time, the civilian and military bureaucracy grew and became more open and took a liking to the "lion's milk." From there it spread to members of the new liberal professions—journalists, publishers, lawyers, and doctors, not to mention students at elite institutions, intellectuals, writers, and poets. From the mid-1860s, they were joined by the first political opponents, the Young Ottomans, who dreamed of freedom over a bottle of raki. For these middle classes, drinking alcohol had become part of the panoply of the ideal image of modernity, proof of their adherence to "civilization." Despite the hostility of the ulama, the state's concern for public order, the condemnation of doctors, and the criticism of intellectuals concerned with strengthening the family and even the "race," consumption continued to rise, reaching eighty million liters (21 million gal.) in the Ottoman Empire in 1914.

From the second half of the nineteenth century onward raki, rather than wine or beer, became the focus of what one Turkish historian has called a "tavern culture." The setting for this was modern establishments, with tables and chairs replacing the low trays and banquettes of the past, where people sat Turkish style. Previously confined to neighborhoods populated mainly by Greeks, Armenians, or Jews or relegated to the outskirts of large cities, taverns began to penetrate more mixed urban areas, shopping districts, leisure areas, around railway stations, and even, despite regulations, near certain mosques. Like cafés, they became part of the public space.

This tavern culture brought with it a sophisticated drinking culture. Raki gave rise to a specific ritual involving decors, furnishings, objects (glasses, carafes), company of one's choice, wait service, and refined conversation. Above all, there was a specific way of drinking. Unlike the Russian practice of swallowing vodka in one shot, raki was sipped from a tall glass filled half raki, half water and served with a variety of hors d'oeuvres (*meze*), dominated by chickpeas, pickled vegetables, stuffed produce, seafood, melons, cheeses, and fruit. It was better enjoyed with friends than alone. Consumed slowly, alcohol was prized for the sociability that it facilitated. Knowing how to drink also meant controlling the effects of alcohol. Hence the various ways in which drunkenness could be masked, such as a tripe soup consumed after a drunken evening or a last glass of raki seasoned with lemon juice in the early hours of the morning, or of course chewing on parsley to cleanse one's breath.

A sign of social distinction, raki gradually became an identity marker. If indulging in an alcoholic beverage was considered "modern," consuming raki emphasized the choice of a "local," "indigenous" alcohol, unlike beer, newly introduced into the empire. Around 1900, whether in Salonika, Istanbul, or Smyrna, the raki drinker was both a modern man and an Ottoman, dressed in European style with a fez. Indeed, it wasn't until the republic was established that raki was directly associated with Turkey. The use of raki became so widespread in the empire's major cities that the *Revue commerciale du Levant*, which defended French interests in area, took issue with this "national drink," which was accused of hindering the penetration of foreign alcohols into the Ottoman market. The Young Turkish Revolution of 1908, the Ottoman Empire's repeated wars from 1911 onward, and the occupation of Istanbul by the Allied armies after World War I all augmented alcohol consumption, particularly of raki. After a brief abolitionist episode encouraged by American prohibition, the Turkish Republic, founded in 1923, lifted restrictions and gradually moved towards a monopoly, especially since its founder and first president, Mustafa Kemal Atatürk, was known for his addiction to "lion's milk."

Despite this, in secular Turkey, whose population is 95 percent Muslim and Turkish, consumption remains moderate. On average, two liters (half a gallon) of alcohol are consumed per inhabitant per year, a far cry from the French, who consume six times as much. In recent years, Turkey's ruling conservative party has launched a new war on drinkers, considerably raising taxes on alcohol. The president of the Turkish Republic, Recep Tayyib Erdogan, has gone so far as to declare *ayran* (a drink made from yogurt and water) the "national drink" instead of raki. The attempts seem futile, however, since they run up against policies designed to encourage tourism, which is a major source of foreign currency. Above all there is the resistance of raki enthusiasts, including female drinkers, who are never short of imagination when it comes to indulging in their favorite pleasure against all odds. Turkey remains the land of raki.

François Georgeon

FURTHER READING

Sylvie Gangloff. *Boire en Turquie: Pratiques et représentations de l'alcool.* Paris: Éditions de la Maison des Sciences de l'Homme, 2015.

François Georgeon. *Au pays du raki: Le vin et l'alcool de l'Empire ottoman à la Turquie d'Erdogan, xive– xxie siècle.* Paris: CNRS Éditions, 2021.

Christoph K. Neumann. "Rakı Consumption and Production in Istanbul in the Nineteenth Century and To-day." In *From Kebab to Ćevapčići: Foodways in (Post-)Ottoman Europe*, ed. Arkadiusz Blaszczyk and Stefan Rohdewald, 224–40. Wiesbaden: Harrassowitz, 2018.

Rakı Ansiklopedisi (Encyclopedia of Raki). Istanbul: Overteam yayınları, 2010.

Erdir Zat. *Rakı: The Spirit of Turkey.* Istanbul: Overteam yayınları, 2012.

FURTHER TRAVELING

Beer, Gin, Raki, Rum, Sake, Vodka, Whiskey, Wine, Yogurt

Ramen

Known for centuries in China and popularized in Japan since the late nineteenth century, ramen became an everyday dish in 1958, following the invention of freeze-dried ramen, which made it possible to cook it at home for the first time. Of all the dishes in Japanese cuisine, it is certainly among the most comforting. Simple, nourishing, and warm, it can be eaten perched on a simple wooden stool, leaning against a bar, in a local joint near the station on the way home from work, side by side with strangers with whom, in the time it takes to eat a bowl, a peaceful silence is shared interspersed with the habitual noise of noodle suction. It can also be eaten alone, in its freeze-dried version, by simply heating a kettle. Here the pleasure lies in the almost magical transformation of the small, dried ingredients, which regain their natural shape in hot water.

With its salty, fatty broth, its copious ingredients, and its noodles—prepared through a special process of being soaked in *kansui*, an alkaline mineral water to retain their firmness in the soup—ramen is often accused of being unhealthy, the antithesis of the delicacy of sophisticated Japanese cuisine. Nevertheless, it does have a certain claim to nobility: two museums are dedicated to it in Yokohama, the dish's reputed birthplace, and its popular simplicity has been celebrated in major films, such as Juzo Itami's celebrated *Tampopo* (1985).

Every region of Japan has "its" ramen. From the island of Hokkaido in the north, with Sapporo ramen made with *miso* (fermented soybean paste) and seafood, to Kyushu, where Hakata ramen is famous for its pork-bone soup called *tonkotsu*, and Tokyo with its chicken broth and soy sauce. The basic ingredients, however, remain the same: a broth, the recipe for which is sometimes jealously guarded by the chefs, a seasoning (salt, soy sauce, *miso*, sometimes even curry) and toppings, often elaborated according to the customer's taste: *chashu* (a slice of roast pork), half a hard-boiled (marinated) egg, bean sprouts, seaweed (*nori* or *wakame*), black mushrooms, marinated bamboo shoots, corn kernels, seafood, *narutomaki* (a type of sliced surimi), sesame oil, *umeboshi* (salted plum). The combinations are endless, and all add to the customer's enjoyment.

Despite its central place in Japanese culinary culture today, this dish has only been truly popular for a little over a hundred years. Paradoxically, there is nothing Japanese about it at all. Its first name betrays its origins: *nankin-soba* is one of the specialties of Yokohama's Chinatown, Nankin-machi. It later became known as *shina-soba*, or Chinese noodles. It was only after 1945 that the term *ramen*, derived from the Chinese *lāmiàn* (hand-stretched noodles), entered widespread consumption.

Japan's perception of China probably influenced the dish's early popularity. After the Meiji Restoration (1868), the archipelago, officially opened to foreign trade and imported numerous culinary innovations. Among these, meat, bread, and cakes from the West were very fashionable but remained reserved for elites, since they were reputed to be expensive and difficult to eat. On the other hand, especially after Japan's victory over China in 1895, Chinese dishes were considered inexpensive pleasures and associated with *yatai*, the small mobile stalls that sprang up every evening in the new entertainment districts.

In the 1920s and 1930s Chinese noodles became as central to the new mass consumer society as cafés, cinemas, and department stores. The manufacturing process itself seemed appropriate for a rapidly industrializing society: the broth, while time-consuming to prepare, was perfectly suited to preparation in large quantities. Noodles, which had previously required lengthy kneading and, above all, stretching by hand, have been machine-prepared since 1883. The various ingredients, added at the last minute, enabled the dish to be quickly customized to individual tastes. Yet in the 1930s ramen was far from having achieved its status as an institution of Japanese culture. First and foremost, it was the fast food of the day: modern, rapid, very inexpensive, but tainted by a hint of sleaze.

From the 1920s onward ramen also reflected a growing anti-Chinese sentiment in Japan. The dish was even called "chankoro soba," or "chan soba," *chankoro* and *chan-chan* being two of the most insulting terms for the Chinese at the time. In fact, it was to avoid these offensive terms for her Chinese-born cooks that Ohisa Tatsu, wife of the owner of one of Sapporo's first ramen restaurants, the famous Rai-rai-ken, probably first offered the dish under its current name. The first ramen restaurant to open in Kyushu in 1938 bore the name "Nankin senryo," a dubious pun, since in Japanese these words can refer to both a decorative plant and the capture of Nanking by the Japanese army in

1937, made infamous by the appalling massacre of Chinese civilians and soldiers that accompanied it.

The American occupation of Japan after the defeat of 1945 contributed to the restoration of ramen's image through a combination of circumstances. Devastated by fifteen years of war and American bombing, the Japanese population desperately needed food. The loss of the colonies, which had been the main sources of rice, led to famine in the ruined cities. The American occupation government needed to distribute food to its former enemy. However, the Americans did not distribute rice but instead wheat flour, much to the consternation of Japanese housewives who didn't know what to do with this strange ingredient. Despite an extensive campaign to interest them in baking bread, a large proportion of the flour rations were traded on the parallel markets controlled by the yakuza, where *yatai* sold all kinds of cheap food. American flour was transformed into Chinese noodles and became an acceptable source of food for the Japanese population. *Yatai ramen* also benefited from propaganda. One could hear the radio repeating throughout the day that wheat was preferable to rice, that it was more nutritious and healthier. What could be more logical than turning to a big bowl of hot ramen to recover from the deprivations of war?

A few years after the end of the American occupation, an invention enabled the dish to conquer households: freeze-dried ramen, launched by entrepreneur Ando Momofuku in 1958, who based his marketing on the official recommendations of the Ministry of Health. The Japanese were not eating enough wheat or meat, they argued. Momofuku's first freeze-dried noodles, Nisshin Chikin Ramen, with their chicken broth, effectively compensated for all these shortcomings at a reasonable price.

But it was the unbridled affluence of the 1980s bubble economy and the ensuing period of very high growth that gave birth to the gourmet ramen phenomenon. As with other popular dishes, the ravenous demand led to greater and greater refinement. Ramen restaurants have been exalted in magazines and cooking shows, highlighting the complexity, excesses, and decadence of this everyday dish. At a time when Japan is suffering from a profound identity crisis linked to its extreme urbanization, ramen, which reminds the postwar generation of their childhood in the ruins of defeat, is served with gold flakes to decorate slices of Kobe beef.

A dish emblematic of a bygone era, ramen has been embellished by this nostalgia. Symbolizing both a lamented economic superiority and a warm, imaginary popular past, it may have lost its power to restore health, but it retains its power to warm hearts.

Constance Sereni

FURTHER READING

Batak Kushner. *Slurp! A Social and Culinary History of Ramen—Japan's Favorite Noodle Soup.* Boston: Global Oriental, 2012.

George Solt. *The Untold History of Ramen: How Political Crisis in Japan Spawned a Global Food Craze.* Berkeley: University of California Press, 2014.

FURTHER TRAVELING

Chorba, Curry, Freeze-Dried Foods, Macaroni and Cheese, Salt, Singapore Noodles, Soy Sauce

Rooibos

In the summer of 2021 the European Union finally recognized rooibos as a geographical indication. The announcement concluded the slow process of labeling a local plant on the international market. This red derivative of *Aspalathus linearis*, a plant that can be infused in hot water and added to teas and herbal infusions, officially entered the pantheon of South African flavors, symbolizing a new way of drinking thanks to its theine-free, anti-allergenic properties. However, its origins did not predispose this product to becoming the emblem of a new dietary practice, but on the contrary referenced its original home in the Cape Colony.

Rooibos belongs to a very common genus of bush teas, a wild-growing aromatic plant. There are at least twenty-five types in South Africa. Its specific characteristics, however, mean that it is not acclimatized outside the Cederberg Mountains, north of present-day Cape Town. Its history is therefore initially linked to this area. The presence of the plant and its use have been attested since at least the seventeenth century, with the first mention in 1691 by Leonard Plukenet, an English botanist. Carl Thunberg, one of the first botanists to record the nature of the Cape Colony in 1772, noted its use by local communities. These communities belonged to the Khoisan, a composite group of populations that survived the European colonization that spread from Cape Town. In the mountains they used this plant without necessarily having domesticated it. Regular contact with the new Afrikaner farmers over the next two centuries led to the identification of this tea for its gustatory properties.

In 1904, at the end of the first Anglo-Boer war, a young Russian migrant arrived in the Cederberg region. His family had traded tea in other parts of the world. During his stay he discovered the red infusion, which was offered to him at every stop. Understanding the product's commercial potential, he began buying and reselling the leaves. He developed his first processing method, which involved bruising, hammering, and fermenting the leaves before leaving them to dry in the sun. Without any major deviation from the Khoisan methods of production, Benjamin Ginsbert introduced this product to the region's markets under the name "mountain tea." In 1912 he opened his first shop in Clanswilliam, just as the Union of South Africa was created under the British. Ginsbert immediately encouraged white farmers to collect the product from local communities, integrating it into the new machinery of segregation that separated white, colored, and black land ownership.

In the aftermath of World War I, in partnership with naturalist Pieter Nofras Nortier, the company founded by Ginsbert developed a new, more resistant variety that was easier to grow and market. The first results were obtained in the 1920s. This new type became the main variety of the product currently referred to as rooibos. From contact with Boer farming groups, the product derived its current name, meaning "red bush" in Afrikaans. In the 1930s seeds were distributed and the cultivation of a product that became part of the local diet began. His discovery earned Nofras Nortier a doctorate from the University of Stellenbosch in 1948 for contributions to South African agriculture.

Then World War II changed everything. The demand for black tea could no longer be satisfied by the supply lines and the relative disorganization of cultivation. South Africa, largely unaffected by military developments, took an active part in the war effort through its industry, supplying a range of products. Among these, rooibos met with great success among the troops of the British Empire and was internationalized for the first time. In 1944 Benjamin Ginsbert died, and his son Charles took over. He branded his product under a new name, the "Eleven o'Clock" pack.

Agricultural development and the establishment of the system of segregation came together after the war. With the adoption of the apartheid system in 1948 and rooibos consumption plummeting with the end of the war, the first cooperative was set up between farmers, the Clanswilliam Tea Corporation. Finally, in 1954, the government created the Rooibos Tea Control Board (RTCB), institutionalizing production and sales in white South Africa. The product's popularity drove production to 850 tons, with 14 tons exported abroad. Charles Ginsbert successfully marketed the product, distributing it in cinemas, for example. However, the control of the state office slowed down commercial expansion.

Nevertheless, in 1963 in South Africa at the height of the apartheid era, rooibos was recognized as the national drink.

In 1968 a mother from Pretoria, on the other side of South Africa, gave the product a new identity. From a substitute for tea, it became an anti-allergenic product, particularly appreciated by children. While Charles Ginsbert sold his company, Annetjie Theron founded her own and developed a series of rooibos-based cosmetics. The innovation marked a turning point, and there was a shift in where rooibos was produced from the Cape Town region to South Africa's business hub, the Johannesburg-Pretoria conurbation, where Rooibos Ltd. was marketed. Although the product had a national base, it was still not fully integrated into the world market, especially as sanctions multiplied at the end of the 1970s to force the end of apartheid.

The year 1994 was an important milestone for the product. Like its country of origin, rooibos suddenly entered the international arena. The brand was registered in the United States. At the same time, the state-owned RTCB was dismantled and privatized. The land reform initiated by the new ANC government favored the redistribution of rooibos-producing lands. Khoisan descendants reclaimed the land for cultivation. These transformations participated in the reinvention of South African product identities. To boost the plant's local and international popularity, NGOs and local communities began a slow battle to label it a local product. Geographical identity was promoted on a 40,000-hectare (98,842 ac.) terroir. At the same time, harvests and sales tripled between 1990 and 2003, testifying to the rooibos boom on European and North American markets.

In the 2000s and 2010s the product spread to Western and emerging markets. In 2005 the American Board of Trade recognized the appellation as a generic trademark and no longer the property of Rooibos Ltd. Locally, its cultivation enabled a marginalized region to return to high value-added production. However, price fluctuations and ecological growing opportunities have meant that production remains variable. To promote full recognition of this product there have been new marketing efforts. After two decades of initiatives involving producers, associations, civil society activists, and international organizations, the recent European recognition of a geographical indication for rooibos has completed the internationalization of a product that has gone from the slopes of the Cederberg Mountains to the kitchens of the world.

Matthieu Rey

FURTHER READING

Estelle Biénabe, Maya Leclercq, and Pascale Moity-Maïzi. "Le rooibos d'Afrique du Sud: Comment la biodiversité s'invite dans la construction d'une indication géographique." *Autrepart* 50, no. 2 (2009): 117–34.

Sarah Fleming Ives. *Steeped in Heritage: The Racial Politics of South African Rooibos Tea—New Ecologies for the Twenty-First Century.* Durham, NC: Duke University Press, 2017.

Maya Leclercq. "Le rooibos: Dynamiques locales autour d'un produit marchand à succès, révélatrices d'une société sud-africaine plurielle." PhD thesis, Muséum National d'Histoire Naturelle, 2010.

FURTHER TRAVELING

Beet Sugar, Chicory, Coffee, Mate, Tea and Chai

Roquefort

The *Journal officiel de la République française* of July 31, 1926, published a law passed five days earlier by the French legislature, making Roquefort the first food product to be granted an Appellation d'Origine. Since 1905 this had only been given to wines and spirits, designating its production not only to a given region but also to specific ingredients and a restricted geographical area. The law safeguarded production. It was no longer possible to sweeten it by mixing cow's milk with sheep's milk, or to imagine it being produced outside Roquefort-sur-Soulzon, a village on the edge of the Larzac plateau in Aveyron. The law both protected the cheese and prevented the small agri-food complex from multiplying the number of production sites for this "king" of cheeses, which is appreciated throughout Europe, as well as in Tokyo and New York, thanks to the invention of electric refrigeration. It is impossible to imitate this symbol of French "gastronomy," which pairs beautifully with wine, whether Californian or Chilean. It was equally impossible for Aveyron emigrants to Argentina to produce it in their new homeland. The fact that the factory was assigned to the town also marked the concentration wrought by capitalism and denounced by Jean Jaurès in 1896: "Little by little, the most important of these factories was transformed from a small family-owned factory into a publicly owned manufacturing facility to bring in more capital." With this capital, other factories were gradually ruined. In 1896, in fact, the last cheese cellar, Carrière, was absorbed; the powerful Société Anonyme des Caves, founded in 1881 with 213 shareholders, held the world monopoly.

Thanks to a very active promotion policy, SAC made this cheese known throughout the world, with its unique taste resulting from a specific mold, *Penicillium roqueforti*, which sometimes offends delicate palates as it did the hygienism or public health movement that prevailed throughout the second half of the nineteenth century. Despite many crises, from the outset the company pursued a strategy of distinction to promote it on the model of certain spirits, champagne in particular. One of the first of these actions took place in 1867 at the Exposition Universelle in Paris, where Roquefort had its own pavilion, which it was supposed to share with other Aveyronnais cheeses. It was, however, not just a cheese that was presented, but rather the microsociety from which it came. On the Champ-de-Mars, a visit to the pavilion was a must. It included a reconstituted cellar occupied by two workers, the *"cabanières,"* specially brought up from the region where it was produced. A few ewes and rams of the Larzac breed could be found in an adjacent enclosure. This was the beginning of the remarkable story of Roquefort production that has continued since. While the first source documenting its existence is attested in the archives of the abbey church of Sainte-Foy de Conques around 1070, under the reign of Philippe I, a "charming" legend has taken precedence over historical fact. The cheese is said to date back to the beginning of the common era, when a shepherd who had abandoned his flock in pursuit of a beautiful maiden forgot his snack of bread and ewe's curd in a cave. Disappointed, he returned to the cave later to find his piece of bread covered with mold and the cheese miraculously transformed into Roquefort.

While this legend reinforces a certain rusticity, the figure of the sheep lends some authenticity. An iconography featuring a flock of sheep around a watering hole is thus associated with the cheese, echoing biblical pastoral images. Roquefort is the cheese of shepherds and the food of kings. The other side of the distinction is the technical feat of making such a delicate product which is available from Moscow to Chicago, especially considering it has such a precise period of maturation and comes from such an isolated place. The Larzac is a plateau at an altitude of eight hundred meters (2,625 ft.), on the border between the Massif Central and the Mediterranean coast. The transport of cheese loaves wrapped in tin foil benefited from the railroads. The company linked the small village of Roquefort to the national rail network. On the eve of World War I, the company ranked ninety-third among private French companies and was the only one in the food industry. Production rose from 250 tons to almost 10,000 tons between 1801 and 1914. The first decades of the twentieth century saw the emergence of stiff competition, from cow's milk blue cheese in France to Gorgonzola cheese in Italy. Meanwhile, the mistreated *cabanières* of the Causse lived in dormitories, worked in difficult conditions in the cold for long hours and repeatedly fought for better pay and shorter working hours.

The shareholders in the Société Anonyme des Caves had to give in, aware that Roquefort should remain the champagne of cheeses and that participating in the luxury industry came at a price. This was all the truer given that the AOC label was obtained at the same time as a small family-run cheese dairy in the French Jura region invented a new product that was to become a worldwide success. While the cellars of Aveyron produced the cheese of the rich, in the cheese dairies of the Jura, Bel frères produced the cheese of the poor, La Vache Qui Rit (The Laughing Cow). On his return from the war, Léon Bel had the idea of taking up the idea of the single-serving and combining it with the processed cheese technique perfected in Switzerland by Gerber in 1907. In 1924, modern machines in Lons-le-saunier increased production to some twelve thousand boxes a day, pouring the processed cheese into triangular portions, which were then wrapped in tinfoil and placed in cardboard boxes. The first foreign market was England. From 1933 onward production units and marketing companies were set up in Belgium, and gradually in other European countries and across the Atlantic. Whereas Roquefort did not travel well, The Laughing Cow took over the world with its mild, medium-bodied taste, and above all its resistance to high temperatures. A factory was opened in Tangiers. Both cheeses played on a strategy of embodying two friendly animals: the sheep and the cow.

They also share a military history, albeit in different ways. While it was the mirthful ox drawn in 1914 by poster artist Benjamin Rabier on the fresh meat supply trucks of his RVF B70 regiment that inspired Léon Bel to create the logo for La Vache Qui Rit, it was the announcement by Defense Minister Michel Debré in the autumn of 1970 of an extension to the Larzac military camp, and the mobilization that this entailed, that put Roquefort back in the spotlight. The military project, part of a policy of nuclear deterrence, threatened the farms on the Causse where milk was collected by SAC. The Millau Chamber of Commerce and Industry mobilized alongside the threatened farmers to have the project canceled. Industrialists made their voices heard in high places without much success. Eating Roquefort became an act of resistance only when, thirty years later, at antiglobalization forums, the cheese was erected as a symbol of eating well in opposition to consuming junk food. In 2009 Roquefort was once again at the forefront of the international stage when the United States tripled its import taxes in response to the European Union's ban on American hormone-treated beef. So it should be of little surprise that while barbecue, curry, and mayonnaise sauces accompany burgers in fast-food restaurants, Roquefort sauce is offered at an extra charge in luxury Madison Avenue brasseries.

Philippe Artières

FURTHER READING

Philippe Artières. *Le peuple du Larzac, une histoire de crânes, sorcières, croisés, paysans, prisonniers, soldats, ouvrières, militants, touristes et brebis. . . .* Paris: La Découverte, 2021.

Robert J. Courtine. *Larousse des fromages.* Paris: Larousse, 1998.

Sylvie Vabre. *Le sacre du Roquefort: L'émergence d'une industrie agroalimentaire (fin xviiie–1925).* Tours/Rennes: Presses Universitaires François-Rabelais/Presses Universitaires de Rennes, 2015.

FURTHER TRAVELING

Champagne, Curry, Hamburger, Mayonnaise, Parmesan Cheese, Tofu, Wine

Rum

A few drops of rooster's blood, a pinch of gunpowder, a dash of burial soil, and a lot of rum... this was the mixture consumed by Jamaican rebel slaves before confronting the British colonists in 1760. During the Caribbean revolts of the eighteenth and nineteenth centuries, this magical beverage gave courage and, above all, enabled communication with the spirits of the ancestors who inspired the combatants. The word "rum" itself, *rhum* in French and *ron* in Spanish, is said to derive from "rumbullion," or tumult and chaos. How did this revolutionary spirit become the essential ingredient in cocktails enjoyed by the Western middle classes in the twentieth century?

First known as tafia and guildive, rum undoubtedly originated as a form of resistance against the oppression of European owners on plantations of the West Indies. As early as the seventeenth century slaves were in the habit of collecting molasses, the viscous residue left over from sugarcane production, to extract alcohol. From then on rum became a centerpiece of sociability and a vector of spirituality for populations of African origin. Rum provided a temporary escape from the appalling working conditions in the European colonies of the Caribbean. Moreover, alcoholism, like running away, could be considered a form of disobedience, since it deprived the owners of part of the production capacity of their "movable property." As a result it was severely repressed, like theft. In exceptional cases, however, the colonists tolerated excessive rum consumption during festivities—every major harvest, Easter, Christmas, and New Year's Day—when captives symbolically and temporarily overturned the social order and sometimes took advantage of the occasion to spark major rebellions, as in Barbados in 1816 or Jamaica in 1831. As a sacrament, libation or medicine, rum played an essential role in the rituals of Afro-Caribbean religions such as Jamaican Obeah, Cuban Santería, and Haitian Voodoo.

The beverage was thus popular among the very slaves who were caged and traded across the Atlantic. Captives were bought by the British on the coasts of the Gulf of Guinea with rum distilled in New England from molasses produced in the West Indies. To obtain more and more slaves to expand their cane plantations, Portuguese traffickers flooded the Angola region with millions of liters of Brazilian cachaça, made from the extract of fresh sugarcane. By the eighteenth century then rum became the main fuel for a transatlantic trade and production circuit on a scale that was hitherto unprecedented in human history. In the thirteen colonies, this inexpensive beverage enjoyed a reputation of health improvement that won over workers, who often agreed to be paid partly "in kind." It was not until the American War of Independence against Great Britain (1775–83), which deprived the early American republic of molasses from the West Indies, that rum was dethroned by whiskey, which had the advantage of being distilled from a local grain, corn. West Indian and Latin American settlers remained loyal to rum, however, and considered it a remedy for all the ills of tropical climates: it "cools when hot, warms when cold, dries when wet and wets when parched," wrote British diplomat Richard Francis Burton in 1869 during his explorations of the Brazil Highlands.

Sugarcane was introduced to Hispaniola (Haiti) in 1493 during the second voyage of Christopher Columbus, whose father-in-law owned a plantation in Madeira. The plant, which originated in New Guinea, had gradually spread from Asia to the Mediterranean, where the Portuguese and Spanish developed the first plantations in Madeira and the Canary Islands respectively in the fifteenth century. But cultivation was labor-intensive. As a result, during the seventeenth and eighteenth centuries, malnourished and harshly treated slaves—primarily women—produced sugar in unspeakable conditions, six days a week from dawn to dusk. They were sometimes forced to continue into the night in order to process the cane cut during the day. On top of the corporal punishment and sexual violence inflicted by white foremen was also the exploitation of slaves newly arrived from Africa by Creole slaves born in the colony. In short, it was hell on earth for those who produced this precious nectar that warmed hearts and minds.

From the seventeenth century onward, rum appealed to sailors. The Royal Navy distributed a half pint of rum to sailors every day as a substitute for stagnant water and vinegary wine in ships' holds. Its success lay in its low production cost, high alcohol content, and consequent need for less storage space. In the 1740s Admiral Edward Vernon, nicknamed "Old Grog" because of his waterproof grogram overcoat, ordered rum to be cut with water to limit the effects of alcohol. This led to the invention of the grog when lemon juice was added to combat the scurvy that ravaged crews. The spirit remained an essential fuel for the Royal Navy until 1970, when the daily ration was abolished. Unlike their uniformed counterparts, pirates and buccaneers consumed rum without restrictions. Rum flowed freely on black-flag ships in the early eighteenth century, a golden age epitomized by the famous Blackbeard, who became the symbol of the perpetual inebriation associated with buccaneering, where it was not the abundance of rum but its absence that posed a disciplinary problem.

At the beginning of the nineteenth century, the boom in rum consumption resulted from the early industrialization of Antillean and Latin American sugar plantations. It was here that prototypes of the "modern" factory appeared: an enclosed productive space where large numbers of bonded laborers worked in an intensive, highly disciplined, and coordinated manner. The plantation turned out to be one of the main birthplaces of industrial capitalism, based on the disjunction of the worker and his tools, the separation of production and consumption, and the rationalization and division of tasks, all of which considerably increased productivity. As a result, by the early 1830s there were more steam engines on Bourbon Island (La Réunion) than in any other French department.

From then on, the share of industrial rum, made from molasses, grew steadily at the expense of agricultural rum, made from fermented sugarcane juice. Easier to produce and less dry, industrial white rum benefited from the cocktail craze that seduced Western consumers from the 1920s onward. In 1941 the young anthropologist Claude Lévi-Strauss, who fled Nazi Europe for the West Indies and Brazil, depicted this transformation that has generated a profound dilemma among consumers to this day:

> The rums of Martinique, tasted before old wooden vats covered in garbage, were sweet and fragrant, whereas those of Puerto Rico were vulgar and crude. Could it be that the finesse of the former was precisely the result of the impurities that persisted within such archaic modes of preparation? To my mind, this contrast illustrates a paradox of civilization, whose charms reside precisely in the residues carried into the present that we constantly strive to filter out. By being right twice over, we confess to being wrong. For we are right to be rational in seeking to increase production and lower costs. But we are also right to cherish those very imperfections we strive to eliminate.

Pierre Singaravélou

FURTHER READING

Jean-François Géraud. "Des habitations-sucreries aux usines sucrières: La 'mise en sucre' de l'Île Bourbon (1783–1848)." PhD dissertation, La Réunion, 2002.

Alain Huetz de Lemps. *Histoire du rhum*. Paris: Desjonquères, 1997.

Paulin Ismard, ed. *Les mondes de l'esclavage: Une histoire comparée*. Paris: Seuil, 2021.

Claude Lévi-Strauss. *Tristes Tropiques*. Paris: Plon, 1955.

Frederick H. Smith. *Caribbean Rum: A Social and Economic History*. Gainesville: University Press of Florida, 2005.

FURTHER TRAVELING

Beer, Gin, Port Wine, Raki, Rum, Sake, Vodka, Whiskey, Wine

Sake

In 1873 sake was officially presented at the Universal Exposition in Vienna by the new Meiji regime (1868). At a time when the "reopening of the country" (*kaikoku*), imposed by the arrival of Western gunboats from 1853 onward, was accompanied by the introduction or reintroduction of foreign beverages into the archipelago, a new phase in the global history of sake began. Although sake appears to be a typically Japanese beverage, its development is linked to a series of globalizations.

In Japanese, the term *sake* initially referred to all alcoholic beverages but gradually came to designate just one of them: the often translucent liquid resulting from the complex fermentation of a mixture of four ingredients including water, polished rice, a priming wort called koji, and a yeast called kobo, identified today as *nihonshu* (Japanese sake).

Sake has been known since antiquity, coming from tropical China and/or populations from Southeast Asia, where rice was masticated to produce a fermented beverage. Considered sacred, particularly by the Shinto religion, during the Middle Ages it became the subject of doctrinal disputes among Buddhist thinkers and monks, who opposed it to tea and its traditional ceremony. The various Buddhist sects, including Nichiren, Ikko, and Tendai, were deeply divided over the issue. This quarrel reached its zenith at the dawn of the "Christian century" (1549–1650), as the arrival of new foods and beverages from Europe stimulated reflection on the best substance to promote exchanges with the divine. Sake then came into competition with wine since it was introduced to celebrate mass.

According to a letter dated June 22, 1549, Francis Xavier, the first Jesuit to be sent to Japan, had brought with him "everything necessary to say Mass," including wine for Holy Communion. As he discovered, vines were not cultivated in the archipelago. Wine was imported at great cost from Europe via Macau in the form of a sweet liquid and in small quantities. Lord Hosokawa Tadatoshi (*daimyo*) of the fiefdoms of Kokura and Kumamoto in the northern part of Kyushu, soon acquired a taste for it. In frail health, he also saw medicinal virtues in the beverage, which was laced with opiates. His interest was probably also aroused by his mother, Hosokawa Gracia, a baptized woman and almost an emblem of the virgin Mary among Japan's new Catholic elite.

In 1627 Tadatoshi inaugurated a vineyard in the Kokura region. But during a visit to the capital Edo in 1630, he was told by the shogun authorities that he was forbidden to grow, sell, or consume wine because it was considered "Christian." The repression of Christianity, banned in 1614, impacted everything linked to it. At the same time, as Japan withdrew into isolation, sake exports ceased to Batavia, where it had been appreciated for its higher alcohol content than wine as well as to the "Japanese cities" (*nihonmachi*) of Southeast Asia which were left to their own fate.

With the elimination of both wine and beer following the first globalization of the "long sixteenth century," sake and tea became popular beverages in both sacred and secular domains in Japan. Japanese Christians who escaped repression and went underground replaced bread with raw fish and wine with sake, as their descendants still do today. The structural elements were thus in place to make sake, which also benefited from technical progress from the sixteenth century, a spirit with a strong and exclusive national identity, an image that remains powerful today. It was the country's most widely consumed beverage until 1959, when it was dethroned by beer.

When it was presented at the 1873 World's Fair, it seemed less successful than the pavilion architecture and their paintings. Western travelers to Japan at the end of the nineteenth century had contrasting views on the subject. Some considered it to be beer, others wine—a debate that is not entirely closed, since sake is similar to beer in its water base and brewing process but differs in that it does not produce foam. Some erroneously referred to it as brandy. Some found it insipid (Raymond de Dalmas in 1885), others "quite pleasant" (Villaret in 1889). This ambiguity along with its unique taste has ensured the beverage's association with being typically "Japanese."

Production increased thanks to its use by the armed forces during the compulsory men's military service introduced in 1872. But between 1919 and 1945 average annual per capita consumption of alcoholic beverages (90 percent sake) fell sharply, by a ratio of ten to one. Several factors led to this outcome: increased taxes; the rise of anti-alcohol campaigns embodied by the 1922 prohibition law; the influence of American prohibition in the name of sanitationist, rigorist, and modernist values; and the priority given to using rice for food to the detriment of sake-making, symbolized by the 1938 draft mobilization law, which was not offset by rice imports from the colonies (Taiwan, Korea).

After the defeat of 1945 sake, which was considered rural, peasant, and archaic, fell out of favor. By contrast, beverages such as beer, whiskey, and wine were assimilated with triumphant Western modernity and gained in popularity and market share. In the mid-1990s the rediscovery of local products became fashionable, initially among a trendy urban elite. Sake makers, whose numbers had dwindled considerably, particularly among small local brewers, took advantage of this to improve their production, diversify their range and refine their quality. "Country sake" (*jizake*) is the most popular. This revival is embodied by a woman, Obata Rumiko, who has taken over the family brewery (*kura*) on the island of Sado. Her vintages have won several trophies.

The year 2013 was when "traditional Japanese gastronomy" (*washoku*) was designated by UNESCO as a world cultural heritage, following a long process initiated by the institution's previous director general, Japanese diplomat Matsuura Koichiro, who served from 1999 to 2009. It was also the year Japanese sake exports began to grow significantly in value, and then in volume from 2017 onward.

Another factor in this success is the increase in the number of Japanese restaurants worldwide. Between 2006 and 2019 they multiplied by seven. Many are actually run by Chinese, and the sake served is not necessarily Japanese sake (*nihonshu*). This is not fraudulent, since the generic term *sake* and its ideogram, in both Chinese and Japanese, refer to any alcoholic beverage. The ignorant consumer may be fooled, but the return to the generic meaning reflects the all-purpose, regionalized, and globalized hybridization of an East Asian product, whatever its taste.

The countries concerned by exports of "authentic" sake are mainly those with Japanese communities or Japanese tourists. The United States leads the way, followed by China (now catching up), Hong Kong, Taiwan, South Korea, and Singapore. Sake's cultural success in former Japanese colonies and former enemies is one of the hallmarks of Japanese soft power in the third age of globalization.

Philippe Pelletier

FURTHER READING

Nicolas Baumert. *Le saké, une exception japonaise.* Rennes: Presses Universitaires de Rennes, 2011.

Claire-Akiko Brisset. "*La disputation sur le saké et le riz* (*Shuhanron emaki*): Une controverse parodique dans le Japon médiéval." *L'atelier du Centre de Recherches Historiques* 12 (2014). https://journals.openedition.org/acrh/5937.

Katarzyna J. Cwiertka and Miho Yasuhara. *Branding Japanese Food, from Meibutsu to Washoku.* Honolulu: University of Hawai'i Press, 2020.

Noriko Goto. "Kokura-han Hosokawa-ie no budoshu tsukuri to sono haikei" (Wine-making by the Hosokawa Clan, Fiefdom of Kokura, and Its Context). *Eisei bunko kenkyu* (University of Kumamoto), March 2018.

Philippe Pelletier. *L'invention du Japon.* Paris: Le Cavalier Bleu, 2020.

FURTHER TRAVELING

Beer, Gin, Port Wine, Raki, Rum, Tea and Chai, Vodka, Whiskey, Wine

Salt

On December 31, 1945, salt became a product like any other in France. The *gabelle*, the most unpopular of all taxes, had been abolished by the Revolution, but Napoleon's costly wars forced him to reintroduce a heavy tax on salt in 1806 that was out of all proportion to its cost. The product remains charged with symbolic value, and contemporaries still recall the image of Gandhi taking a handful of salt in defiance of British imperialism and in favor of Indian independence. In Russia and other countries, bread and salt were offered as a sign of welcome to foreign guests. The New England settlers, supplied by European vessels, feared that they would not find salt beyond the Appalachians, and thus hesitated for a long time to cross over them until they discovered the tracks carved by the hooves of thousands of buffalo transiting to the salt springs through the territories of the southern plains. Reassured, they reached the Great Plains and began the conquest of the West in the nineteenth century.

Salt, a unique and nonsubstitutable product, is an essential foodstuff for both humans and animals. It gives flavor to food and plays an important biological role in digestion. Since it is hygroscopic, it attracts water, dries products, and prevents bacterial proliferation. For a long time it was the main preservative for fish, meat, and vegetables, eggs and dairy products, butter and cheese, and animal feed. Salt consumption is used in medical prescriptions and is subject to a variety of dietary fashions. Brittany remains attached to its gray salt, while others prefer black salt from the volcanoes of Hawaii or pink and white colored salt from the lakes of Tibet. Under the ancien régime in France, a distinction was made between "pot and saltshaker," that is, coarse cooking salt and fine table salt. Today, gourmets place on their tables the fine, expensive *"fleur de sel,"* patiently harvested from the surface of the salt marsh, while the saltmaker then loosens the salt crystals from the floor of the saltworks. Some people will buy only salted butter, while others prefer it unsalted. Today salt is bought by weight, packaged, and placed on shelves. We pay little attention to its provenance. It would seem all the same, rough, white, fine, sea or gem, French or foreign. Yet, with advances in ecology and more sophisticated marketing, Atlantic salts harvested "the old-fashioned way" without the aid of machinery are becoming more common, bringing flavor to a host of industrial products.

Salt production, trade, and taxation reveal the inequalities between wealthy countries and poor populations. The resources are exploited using three techniques: farmed harvesting of sea salt, mining to extract rock salt, and industrial production by digging wells or introducing water into salt layers to dissolve it and produce brine, which is transported by pipeline to salt works. Salt production is a lengthy process requiring evaporation, during which two phases follow one another: concentration produces the raw material or brine, and crystallization delivers the finished product. Evaporation is done naturally, including sun and wind, or, in climates with cool, humid summers, it can be achieved artificially, using fuel (wood, coal, and electricity).

The importance of salt to mankind from the earliest times—the Bible mentions it, and Homer considered it a divine substance—is evident in world toponymy. It has found a name everywhere, from Salzburg to the Celtic Halls (Hallstatt or Hallein), from Salins to Salies or the Scottish Salt-Coats, from the Prussian Salzkotten to the Indian Lavanápura, from the Spanish Río Salado to the Maghrebian *melah*, from the Turkish Tuzla to the Russian Solikansk or Soligorsk and Usolye or to the Aztec names Ixtapan and Ixcateopan derived from the Nahuatl *iztati* (salt), *iztatlero* being someone who extracts or sells salt.

Salt is consumed daily. Production has always taken place across the planet, but there are some European regions, such as Italy, the Netherlands, and Scandinavia, that lack salt or are in deficit. Elsewhere, along coastlines for example, production is abundant, even if it is absent in the interior. So, for centuries, transportation has made salt a weighty product, the cost of which determines its price. Harvested along the coast under the ancien régime in France, salt traveled only by sea for fishing and salting. Supplying inland populations could only be done by transporting up rivers against the current. The last stages of this capillary salt trade were achieved as salt was peddled on the backs of men or animals along the paths. Salt was considered a public good, and the trade was organized by the state as a monopoly to combat speculation and shortages. The monopoly was unable to manage heavy economic operations such as production and transportation that required abundant human resources and a capable administration, and therefore focused on distribution. The state made the monopoly pay by introducing an increasingly heavy tax, the *gabelle*.

Humans need .75 gram (0.026 oz.) per day, but this intake is usually doubled because of the pleasure from eating moderately salty rather than bland foods. The gustatory system seems programmed to make people appreciate its taste: the tip of the tongue is lined with salt-sensitive buds. A salt-free diet weakens the body and harms health by preventing us from eating. Salt is an agent that creates flavors, stimulating sweetness and attenuating the bitterness of certain dishes.

The hunger for sodium is spontaneously felt by herbivores, who seek out the salt cure that elephants, camels, bison, yaks, and llamas crave. By the end of the nineteenth century the industry was supplying licking blocks for farmers' herds. In the United States, dairy cows consume over fifty pounds a year, beef cattle twenty-two pounds. Even today, hunters sprinkle salt on rocks to attract chamois and ibex, while Himalayan mountaineers use it to herd goats and sheep. At the beginning of the twentieth century a German geographer attempted to interpret the history of the African continent, still poorly known to Europeans, through the hunger for salt that forced certain populations to find a substitute in the blood and urine of animals.

Medicines make extensive use of salt, recognizing its qualities as a spa treatment, in bathing, wound healing, and as an aid for burn victims. For a long time, salt was reputed to cure or, better still, prevent all kinds of ailments. In the theory of humors, salt's hot and dry qualities gave it a fundamental role in resisting putrefaction and was recommended against the plague which it was believed came from excess humidity in the air. Medical science has also determined that too much salt is toxic. This justifies its use in fungicides and bactericides. Salt has rendered the greatest service to mankind as a food preservative, where it was for a long time without rival, until the creation of industrial refrigeration. The preservation of proteins, meat, and fish meant that everything did not have to be consumed immediately, and this often led to the building up of reserves for times of famine. Used in the transformation of hides into leather or in breadmaking, where it binds the dough and controls the activity of yeast, it has been one of the main factors in the economic and demographic development of Europe, its multiple uses having encouraged the birth and development of the chemical industry, of which it is, along with petroleum, the main constituent. It is difficult to say exactly how much salt is produced worldwide. Production is divided between sea salt and rock salt, the former subject to the elements, the latter being more stable. Salt in brine for electrolysis is also the main product of inorganic chemistry. The most populous countries are the main producers, led by China (around seventy million metric tons) and India (thirty million metric tons). Other producers include industrialized countries such as the United States (forty million metric tons) and Germany (fourteen million metric tons), and countries with dry tropical climates such as Australia and Mexico. France produced six million metric tons on average from 2015 to 2020.

Jean-Claude Hocquet

FURTHER READING

Jean-Claude Hocquet. *Le sel, de l'esclavage à la mondialisation*. Paris: CNRS Éditions, 2019.
——. *Venise et le monopole du sel: Production, commerce et finance d'une république marchande*. 2 vols. Venice and Paris: Les Belles Lettres, 2012.

FURTHER TRAVELING

Chili Pepper, Fish Sauce (Nuoc Mam), Food Coloring and Preservatives, Pepper, Soy Sauce

Sandwich

On November 24, 1762, Edward Gibbon recorded a seemingly ordinary but noteworthy event in his diary. While he had gone to the theater that day to see a performance of *The Spanish Fryar*, what struck him most of all was his meal at the Cocoa Tree, a Tory headquarters established on Pall Mall since 1746, where the novel and still quite rare sandwich was being served. The name already enjoyed a certain reputation, thanks to the practice of John Montagu, fourth Earl of Sandwich and first Lord of the Admiralty, who was fond of placing slices of grilled beef between two slices of toast so as not to leave the gaming or worktable. Contemporaries credit the word with entering cookbooks at the end of the eighteenth century. Charlotte Mason presents it as such in *The Lady's Assistant for Regulating and Supplying the Table*, published in London as early as 1773: very thin slices of beef, or sliced veal or ham, served between thin slices of buttered bread cut off at the ends. The word was new, but its use less so. A similar dish, *Belegde broodje*, was widespread in the Netherlands in the seventeenth century, as attested by naturalist John Ray in his travels in 1673. Peasant meals taken to the fields provided similar examples, even if the ingredients were less expensive.

The increased publication of cookbooks during the nineteenth century adapted the recipe for bourgeois kitchens. Eliza Leslie, trained at the first American culinary school, Goodfellow's Cooking School in Philadelphia, wrote cookbooks, including *Directions for Cookery, in Its Various Branches*, which she published in 1837. This bestseller, which sold more than 150,000 copies in the United States, describes the sandwich as two pieces of bread, possibly covered in butter or mustard, with a slice of cold-cooked ham between them, served for supper or lunch.

Such terse presentations were followed by increasingly sophisticated compositions. In 1847, the same writer mentioned "Biscuit sandwiches," prepared using small cookies or loaves of white bread, halved, buttered, filled with grated ham or smoked tongue, then cut into six pieces and presented in a pyramid on a dish, decorated with watercress leaves or flat-leaf parsley. Sandwiches acquired a privileged place on reception buffets. In his 1879 manual for bourgeois households in town and country, Émile Dumont described his ham sandwiches, made from stale bread sliced to "the thickness of a penny," with the crust removed, covered with fresh butter and "an excessively thin blade of ham cooked au naturel" placed on top. The foodstuff became increasingly common, drawing inspiration by English fashions. Sandwiches were served for snacks, in the evenings, and at tea time, with Italian cheeses, foie gras pâté, and smoked tongue. Escoffier devoted an entire paragraph to them in his 1934 guide *Ma cuisine*. Looking to impose new standards, the chef indicated that they should be rectangular, measuring eight centimeters by four centimeters (3.15 × 1.57 in.), except those for ballroom buffets, which should be half that size. The first edition of the *Larousse gastronomique*, published in 1938, lists more than fifty sandwich recipes in three long columns, relaying the regionalist vogue with specific names, from the Alsatian sandwich to the sandwich *antibois* (from Antibes).

Sandwiches also became a food adapted to new modes of transportation. As early as the 1790s, London grocers offered bread fillings. On roadsides a double loaf of bread topped with cold meat set the way for stops at post houses. The advent of railroads made sandwiches even more practical. In the 1860s station buffets offered them in various forms at prices ranging from ten to sixty cents. On top of these new offerings were all the domestic preparations that workers brought with them, making the sandwich a substitute for the mess tin or lunch box. Wrapped in newspaper or a brown paper bag, its portability and lack of eating protocol made it ideal for the miner's snap tin and for the metalworker's snack. In 1851 journalist Henry Mayhew counted street vendors in London delivering more than 436,000 sandwiches a year. By the 1930s travelers, cyclists, picnickers, and walkers were blending in with wage-earners, whether blue- or white-collar.

Supported by a broad customer base and a variety of uses across all levels of society, the sandwich market grew in every direction. As early as the 1930s, the practice of selling sliced bread gave American schoolchildren the chance to have their own sandwich. Since the second half of the twentieth century, cafés and bars advertising five or six kinds of "homemade" sandwiches have been joined by bakeries, which have broadened their customer base, in France as well as in Japan's *panyas*. Sandwich shops have specialized in fast food. And supermarkets have similarly moved in this direction, offering convenient foods on the go. Differences in types of sandwiches are reflected in their shapes, including a well-orchestrated symbolism: the thin club sandwich of posh circles around 1900, the thick verticality of American models in the 1930s, or the long half-baguette on Parisian café counters of the 1950s.

The universal nature of the sandwich has also given rise to local culinary specificities. The grilled *cubano* sandwich from Florida followed migrant Havana cigar factory workers. Banh mi, introduced in colonial Indochina on a French-style bread made from rice and wheat flour, did not disappear in Vietnam. In India, *vada pav*, distributed at the Dadar railway station in 1971, replaced British-influenced recipes. Finns immediately recognize a *porilainen* just as a Uruguayan may order a *chivito*. The Italian *panino* has followed in pizza's commercial footsteps. Scandinavian countries, where sandwiches did not exist, have now adopted it. Chains such as Subway, founded in Connecticut in 1965, could be seen as far away as Beijing thirty years later and contributed to producing new global standards, dominated by industrially prepared club sandwiches on white bread or Swedish bread varieties.

Behind this anecdotal history of the sandwich lurks a window into our societies, between modes of consumption and life experiences. Pop art has seized on the sandwich, with Claes Oldenburg sculpting the *Giant BLT* (bacon, lettuce, and tomato sandwich) in 1963 and Roy Lichtenstein dedicating one of his silkscreens to the "sandwich and soda" theme in 1964. A form of cultural heritage has taken shape through dedicated festivals, such as the Po' Boy Festival in New Orleans since 2007. Po'boys can be made with bread, mussels, fried shrimp or oysters, Cajun spices, and more. In some recipes seafood is replaced by roast beef. In Japan the identity of the *kissatens* is revealed by the offerings on the sandwich menu.

In economic terms, however, there is nothing anecdotal about the sandwich. In 1986 alone Americans consumed forty-five billion of them. Twenty years later, in France, more than two million ham-and-butter sandwiches were sold every day, and two-thirds of all sandwiches were still made with a baguette. Since 1990 the international *Sandwich & Food to Go News Magazine* has been tracking developments in a market that now has its own designers, prices, and business concerns. In 2013, following the posting online of a Subway sandwich that was one inch short of the twelve-inch regulation, a wave of class-action lawsuits against fast-food restaurants was unleashed across the United States. Indeed, the culinary criticism leveled at the "SNCF (French railway) sandwich," and its British Rail counterpart in 1947, which was reproached for its minimalist twenty-gram (.7 oz.) filling of sardines, now seems a distant memory. Warnings about the toxicity of unhygienic preparations and the standardization of sizes and production processes are proof that the sandwich is both a product for global consumers and a result of local innovations.

Jean-Pierre Williot

FURTHER READING

Julia Csergo. *Casse-croûte: Aliment portatif, repas indéfinissable.* Paris: Autrement, 2001.
Marc Jacobs and Peter Scholliers. *Eating out in Europe: Picnics, Gourmet Dining and Snacks Since the Late Eighteenth Century.* Oxford: Berg, 2003.
Bruce Kraig and Patty Carroll. *Hot Dog Culture in America: Man Bites Dog.* Lanham, MD: AltaMira Press, 2012.
Andrew F. Smith. "Sandwiches." In *The Oxford Encyclopedia of Food and Drink in America*, ed. Adam F. Smith, 2:191–95. Oxford: Oxford University Press, 2004.
Bee Wilson. *Sandwich: A Global History.* London: Reaktion Books, 2010.

FURTHER TRAVELING

Bagel, Baguette, Banh Mi, Hamburger, Pizza

Sardines (Canned)

In 1867, the rapporteur for the Universal Exhibition then being held in Paris described the situation in these terms: "Good canned fish is rare; they have however been successful in Nantes and on the Ocean coast, where powerful companies have been involved.... There is no point on the globe where these preparations cannot be found and have not become indispensable for consumption. Similar efforts have been tried elsewhere: in Brazil, in Spain, in Italy; but these more or less successful attempts are no match for our country's production." Like perfumes and the great wines of Champagne, Bordeaux, or Burgundy, sardines in oil had become a highly sought-after delicacy and were in great demand at the world's finest tables. Queen Victoria, Tsar Alexander II, King Albert I of Belgium, and many other crowned heads were fond of these little fried fish bathed in olive oil. In less than forty years the first industrial food product, made only in France, became a fundamental and irreplaceable part of a sophisticated meal. How did French canners achieve this hegemonic position in less than half a century?

Sardines are easy to catch on the Breton and Veneto coasts but are highly perishable. So, means were sought to preserve them early on. As early as the tenth century, sardines were salted in La Rochelle and pressed in Le Croisic, Groix, and Douarnenez. In the fifteenth century, they were "anchovied" (salted and placed in barrels) on Belle Île. The method used to preserve sardines in oil is quite different. It came from mixing the method invented by Nicolas Appert for preserving food by boiling and the tin canning method devised by the British. All that remained to be done was to coat the sardines with olive oil, as has been practiced since the eighteenth century on the shores of the Mediterranean.

As early as 1810, Grimod de la Reynière reported the existence in Nantes of sardines in oil, preserved in welded tin cans by Joseph Colin, a *"confiseur."* Perfectly mastered by 1820, the production process has hardly changed since. In the first phase the sardines are placed on inclined tables, sprinkled with salt, topped, and dipped in brine. After being washed they are placed on racks to dry. They are then cooked in boiling oil before being put into boxes. Tin cans full of sardines are filled with cold oil and sealed with a brazed lid, then sterilized in a large sheet-metal boiler.

Admittedly, manufacturing processes and packing materials have been improved, but the various stages involved in producing the finished product have remained unchanged for two centuries. Only the quality of the products used, chosen with some rigor, and the quality of the preparation, which is always done by hand, can differentiate excellent preserves from low-end products. The success of this preparation immediately met with great success beyond all expectations. This was not the case for all preserves at the time. Manufacturers of canned meat and canned ready-made meals found them difficult to sell, due to a strong taste that displeased customers. Canned meat is never as good as fresh meat, which is not the case with canned sardines. In fact, frying and preserving sardines in olive oil improves their taste considerably over time: sardines in oil may be considered to taste better than fresh sardines.

The spread of this innovation intensified after 1852 with the invention of the autoclave. At the same time, producers moved closer to the fishing grounds, between Camaret and the island of Noirmoutier, to sell their highly sought-after and expensive products all over the world. There they grew in increasing numbers: Rödel opened his workshop in Bordeaux in 1824, followed by Teyssonneau; Deffès moved to La Turballe in 1830. Bertrand and Feydeau were in Port-Louis in 1839; the Pelliers in La Turballe in 1841. Colin himself built "branches" in Le Croisic in 1842, then in Les Sables d'Olonne around 1844. The Lucas and Levraud factories were founded on Belle-Île around 1845. Finally, Amieux and Cassegrain set up shop on the Breton coast. French sardines in oil, like Bordeaux wine, became obvious signs of distinction. By serving them hosts could show their refined taste, experience (that is, culture), but also standard of living. Henceforth, good manners imposed the presence of this delicacy on tables of "superior taste" the world over. Exports grew steadily until 1885, when they accounted for three quarters of French production and the twelfth highest value in the country's foreign trade.

A refined product, sardines in oil were a luxury item destined for a small number of well-to-do households and public establishments, hotels, embassies, or consular offices—in short, the urban elite. It also aroused the appetites of industrialists the

SARDINES (CANNED) 281

world over, jealous of French success. Resounding court cases pitted French producers against foreign canners, who often made do with brisling (herring) rather than sardines, as in Norway or the United States, or used exotic oils, such as camellia oil in Japan. In 1892, the German firm of Bieler and Lippmann, based in Lisbon, was condemned for introducing boxes of sardines into France under the brand name "Le Jockey Club," near the Arsène Saupiquet company in Nantes. The tin was identical, only the Saupiquet name was replaced by Soupiquet.

At the same time, a new, national market emerged for factory workers: picnics and lunches on the grass. This new form of dining was imagined by the bourgeoisie so that social elites might escape the stiff constraints of formal dining and enjoy more leisurely pleasures. The picnic was the pretext for a convivial feast in which sardines in oil took center stage, invested with qualities that went far beyond mere nourishment. Canners quickly responded to this new market and offered a ready-made meal that could be stored indefinitely in any climate, and which also proved its worth on long-distance trips and excursions: so much so that Amieux wasted no time in meeting the needs of the ever-increasing numbers of travelers on France's roads and railways. The bourgeoisie flocked to Paris train stations to escape the noisy and dirty city. The company offered "picnic" boxes and "Illico" lunches, a package of three tins of fish, meat, and desserts for those in a hurry. One headed off to Nice, Deauville, Cabourg, Biarritz, or for other sites of ocean bathing for a few days during high season with plenty of time to enjoy the canned goods sold as *délicieuses* or *savoureuses* on the Orleans railway carriages.

Subsequently, canners continued to expand their production areas, setting up in Portugal in 1880, then in Spain and Morocco, but the quality remained low. In the 1980s sardines in oil became a common dish and lost their culinary distinction. To overcome foreign competition French canners produced low-cost, poor-quality sardines, often frozen and coated with common oils (peanut at best, but also sunflower or rapeseed). One could find sardines in school canteens. Nonetheless, a few surviving entrepreneurs have sought to present canned sardines as a luxury high-end food product. As a result, they are once again producing high-quality preserves, stamped as Label Rouge (Red Label) in efforts to revive the original values of this exceptional industry.

Jean-Christophe Fichou

FURTHER READING

Jean-Paul Barbier. *Nicolas Appert, inventeur et humaniste*. Paris: Royer, 1994.
Alberto Capatti. *Le goût du nouveau: Origines de la modernité alimentaire*. Paris: Albin Michel, 2004.

SARDINES (CANNED)

André Marie d'Avigneau. *L'industrie des conserves de poissons en France métropolitaine*. Rennes: Imprimerie Bretonne, 1958.

Jean-Charles Caillo Jeune. *Recherches sur la pêche à la sardine en Bretagne*. Nantes: Vincent Forest, 1855.

Félix Libaudière. *Des origines de l'industrie des conserves de sardines, 1824–1861*. Nantes: Mélinet, 1910.

Gourarier Zeev. "Manger hors du foyer." *Les français et la table*. Paris: Ministère de la Culture, 1985.

FURTHER TRAVELING

Ceviche, Fish and Chips, Olive Oil, Salt, Wine

Singapore Noodles

In 2020, Singapore's food culture found itself in the spotlight when its tradition of "hawkers" (communal dining) was officially added to UNESCO's list of Intangible Cultural Heritage of Humanity. As the island nation celebrated the event, its iconic noodle dishes were proudly featured in celebratory messages announcing the prestigious recognition. These noodles, loved and appreciated by generations of Singaporeans, included *char kway teow* (fried flat rice noodles), *hae mee* (shrimp and pork rib soup served with noodles), *wonton mee* (pork and shrimp ravioli served with thin noodles), and *bak chor mee* (noodles served with minced meat and mushrooms).

But there was one dish missing, the most internationally recognized of all: "Singapore noodles." And with good reason: while this recipe is ubiquitous in the United States and a number of other Western countries, it simply does not exist in Singapore itself. The dish that comes closest is stir-fried rice vermicelli (pronounced *"xingzhou mifen,"* 星洲米粉), more commonly known as "Star Island vermicelli" (one of Singapore's nicknames). How then can we explain the presence of such a dish under this name elsewhere than in Singapore?

One way to begin an investigation would be to describe the ingredients: rice vermicelli, curry powder, soy sauce, rice wine, red chili (better known as *chili padi* in Singapore), bean sprouts, shitake mushrooms, grilled pork (*char siu*) or shrimp, ginger, and a blend of spices. While not all chefs agree on the composition, they are virtually unanimous on the recipe's execution. The ingredients are simply stir-fried and are ready to serve in just a few minutes. Given the simplicity of this dish, it is hard to understand why and how it came to embody Singapore's diverse food culture in the Western imagination.

The next step in the investigation leads us to Hong Kong, the point of departure for a diaspora that popularized a local version of Singapore noodles in North America and Europe, distinct from a Malaysian recipe.

To reconstruct this history, one must start here. Malaysian Chinese restaurants, which from the 1920s–30s included many Cantonese chefs and owners, often featured *char siu* (grilled pork), one of their region's specialties, on the menu. This explains why the latter is part of the Malaysian version of Singapore noodles, while others ignored it. According to the origin myth, in the 1940s a Chinese restaurant in Kuala Lumpur received a customer just before its kitchen closed, forcing the chef to gather leftovers such as *char siu*, bean sprouts, eggs, and chilis. He then quickly stir-fried them with vermicelli to satisfy his customer. Enjoying his dish, the customer asked for the name of the dish, to which the chef, in a flash of inspiration, replied "Star Island vermicelli." Singapore (Star Island) was a more prosperous city than Kuala Lumpur, so the leftover dish benefited from the prestige of the wealthy city-state.

Fact or fiction, the economical nature of Malaysian noodles is reflected in another essential ingredient, ketchup. During the British colonial period, Lea & Perrins Worcestershire sauce was the main flavoring of the dish, but ketchup soon supplanted it since it was sweeter, cheaper, and readily available.

The cultural hybridity evidenced by this British influence is similarly characteristic of the Hong Kong version of "Singapore noodles," which includes curry powder. The yellow spice mix can be found in most Hong Kong restaurants (*cha chaan teng*), as well as in the restaurants of Hong Kong and Cantonese immigrants in North America and Europe. The addition of vegetables more commonly found in the West, such as broccoli or peppers (rather than *cai xin* or Chinese cabbage, for example), reflects an adaptation of the recipe to Western palates.

Curry powder is a condiment found in many local dishes, such as curried beef brisket and curried pork chop. As for the name "Singapore noodles" in Hong Kong, there are two possible explanations. It could come from the introduction of the dish by Cantonese chefs from Malaysia—which is what the first mentions in Hong Kong tend to prove, dating back to the 1950s, a decade after the alleged invention of "Singapore noodles" in Malaysia. But curry powder being an imported product, the name "Singapore" may simply have been chosen because the island was an important trading port, associated with imported products.

The use of curry powder as the main ingredient in "Singapore noodles" is equally remarkable as a revelation of the cultural influence of British colonialism in Hong Kong. The manufacture and marketing of curry powder is said to have resulted from imperial ambitions. Etymologically speaking, "curry" simply meant mixing spices (powders) with pieces of chicken or mutton to make them more digestible. At the height of British imperialism, the use of "curry powder" containing spices from Asia (particularly South Asia) became increasingly common throughout the Empire. The presence of curry powder in Hong Kong's "Singapore noodles" is therefore also a vestige of British colonial influence.

As a result of these influences, "Singapore noodles" spread through immigration to Western countries and were then presented as an emblematic dish of the city-state. Foreign to Singaporeans, they are in fact representative of the identity that Singapore seeks to project on the international stage. Born of multiple cultural exchanges as well as efficiency and ingenuity, "Singapore noodles" could well be, inadvertently, a dish embodying the diversity and richness of the island state from which it takes its name.

Jialin Christina Wu

FURTHER READING

Cecilia Leong-Salobir. *Food Culture in Colonial Asia: A Taste of Empire*. London: Routledge, 2011.

Casey M. K. Lum and Marc de Ferrière le Vayer, eds. *Urban Foodways and Communication: Ethnographic Studies in Intangible Cultural Food Heritages Around the World*. Lanham, MD: Rowman & Littlefield, 2016.

Chee Beng Tan, ed. *Chinese Food and Foodways in Southeast Asia and Beyond*. Singapore: National University of Singapore Press, 2012.

Rachel S. Y. Wong. "The Singapore in Singapore Noodles." In *Within & Without: Singapore in the World; the World in Singapore*, ed. Eng Fong Pang and Arnoud De Meyer, 66–73. Singapore: Research Collection Lee Kong Chian School of Business, 2015.

David Y. H. Wu and Chee Beng Tan, eds. *Changing Chinese Foodways in Asia*. Hong Kong: The Chinese University of Hong Kong Press, 2001.

FURTHER TRAVELING

Chili Pepper, Curry, Indomie, Ketchup, Noodles and Macaroni, Ramen, Soy Sauce

Soy Sauce

In November 1956 American voters were about to discover the face of their future president on their televisions. Then suddenly, a few minutes before the official announcement of the results, the Kikkoman logo appeared, followed by a short cartoon depicting a North American family, each joyfully holding up a small bottle of brownish liquid. While the jingle repeated the name of the Japanese brand, the main verse promoted the gustatory qualities of soy sauce as an ideal accompaniment to any barbecue.

Broadcast during this key moment in U.S. political life, the commercial represented a new departure for the Japanese brand of fermented soybean-based condiments. One year later Kikkoman set up its first sales office across the Pacific in San Francisco. It was not until 1972 that a soy sauce production plant opened its doors, this time in Wisconsin. The last decades of the twentieth century saw a proliferation of production sites abroad—in the Netherlands, the People's Republic of China, Singapore, and Taiwan—at the same time that the product range actually decreased.

But the Mogi family, originally from Noda north of present-day Tokyo and cofounders of Kikkoman, had not waited for the aftermath of the Second World War to enter the international market. The brand name was legally registered in California as early as 1879. Japanese emigration for the West Coast facilitated its establishment within the immigrant communities. Thirty years later, in 1910, Kikkoman accounted for more than half of all soy sauce exports from Japan, with nearly four million gallons a year (ca. 15 million liters) destined for places as varied as Honolulu, Portland, London, Berlin, and Shanghai.

Despite the importance of Kikkoman in the construction of a global market, the history of soy sauce is far from limited to one company. Just a glance at the shelves of supermarkets, both Asian and Western, where numerous brands and recipes rub shoulders, confirms this observation. Nor did it necessarily have its roots in the Japanese archipelago, despite the Soy Sauce Museum on the island of Shodoshima, where factories have been producing the famous sauce for four centuries.

It was on the Asian continent, between Korea and China, that the first amber-colored seasonings were concocted, foreshadowing today's *jiangyou* on the Chinese side and *kanjang* on the Korean side. Although some writings mention the arrival of soya in China from Korea, its production and consumption in the form of a fermented liquid then spread from the Middle Kingdom to the Asia-Pacific region. In Japan, it is attested by written sources from the eighth century onward. It was then found in Vietnam, nine centuries later. Recipes evolved as populations moved and were not always bound to commercial ventures. Japanese oral tradition has it that the current recipe for local soy sauce—called *shoyu*—originated in the thirteenth century with a Buddhist monk's journey to China.

Each territory has its own brown sauce, the diversity of which is only enhanced by its many names: *keçap* in Indonesia, *toyo* in the Philippines, but also *siaw* or *siave* on Réunion. There are some notable exceptions, however. In Cambodia the sauce has remained absent from everyday cooking, confined to urban catering, mainly in areas marked by the presence of Chinese diasporas.

Beyond Asia, colonization gave new impetus to the spread of soy sauce in the modern age. While Japan closed its doors to European explorers and traders, the exception granted to the Dutch on the island of Deshima, not far from Nagasaki, encouraged the spread of the Japanese version of the condiment. From 1737 onward the Dutch East India Company—Vereenigde Oostindische Compagnie, or VOC—traded it through colonial possessions in Southeast Asia. Between 1737 and 1762 no less than fifteen thousand liters (3,962 gal.) of soy sauce were shipped from Batavia, the VOC headquarters in present-day Indonesia, to the Netherlands. Once in Europe, the port of Amsterdam provided the link with the continent's consumer centers, while the British exported their own stocks from China. Soy consumption had a visible impact on culinary practices: from 1768 onward special bottles were manufactured in England to facilitate serving.

The boom also spread to territories across the Atlantic. While the holds of VOC ships were filled with barrels of soy sauce, retailers in the British colonies of North America were interested in this Asian product. As early as 1750 in New York they were offering half-liter bottles to customers, presumably for domestic use. It did not take long for Samuel Bowen, a British settler in Georgia, to decide to start growing soybeans, almost two centuries before the opening of the Kikkoman factories in the United States. He developed a recipe inspired by an

288   SOY SAUCE

alleged trip to China in the early 1760s, from which he was said to have brought back Chinese soy vetches. His slaves began planting the Asian bean around Savannah, and he sent his first sauce samples to learned societies before selling his stocks in major North American towns.

Favored by European imperialism on a global scale, the conquest of soy sometimes preceded territorial conquests: when the United States annexed Hawaii in 1898, soy sauce factories had already been set up there. The condiment was then the main ingredient of a local specialty, *pork shoyu*, bearing witness to the links between the Hawaiian and Japanese archipelagos. These contacts and the resulting hybridization only became more pronounced after World War II, with the creation of the Aloha Shoyu brand, the future leader in Hawaiian soy sauce, by five Japanese families installed in Kahili.

In the end, soy sauce flavors were constantly renewed through circulation. In England in the 1830s it was used as the secret ingredient in Worcestershire sauce, guaranteeing its success with raw meat lovers. In Europe, at the end of the twentieth century, it made its way into so-called Asian restaurants, in both savory and sweet forms, a far cry from the culinary traditions of China and Japan. Kikkoman was quick to catch on to this trend when in 2021 it launched a new version of its 1956 advertisement, featuring a new low-sodium product and the slogan "brewed in USA."

Sara Legrandjacques

FURTHER READING

Ang Chouléan. "Le tamarin dans la cuisine des villages d'Angkor: Des mémoires de Zhou Daguan à aujourd'hui." *Moussons* 30 (2017): 185–202.

W. Mark Fruin. *Kikkoman: Company, Clan, and Community*. Cambridge, MA: Harvard University Press, 1983.

H. T. Huang. *Science and Civilisation in China*, vol. 6, *Biology and Biological Technology, Part 5, Fermentations and Food Science*. Ed. Joseph Needham. Cambridge: Cambridge University Press, 2000.

William Shurtleff and Akiko Aoyagi, eds. *History of Soy Sauce (160 CE to 2012): Extensively Annotated Bibliography and Sourcebook*. Lafayette, CA: Soyinfo Center, 2012.

Ronald E. Yates. *The Kikkoman Chronicles: A Global Company with a Japanese Soul*. New York: McGraw-Hill Education, 1998.

FURTHER TRAVELING

Barbecue, Fish Sauce (Nuoc Mam), Maki, Sushi

Spam

In the heart of the Great Depression in 1937, American industrialist Jay Hormel launched a new canned pork meat product called "Spam." It was developed from preservation techniques perfected in 1810 by Nicolas Appert and Peter Durand. At Hormel's huge factories in Austin, Minnesota (a.k.a. "Spamtown"), Appert's process was applied not to beef (to produce the famous corned beef) but to pork shoulder, cooked for three hours in perfectly airtight rectangular metal cans. The result, described by Hormel as "miracle meat," was then sold as a pink, fatty, salty lump of meat surrounded by a layer of jelly.

Both scorned and adored, mocked and nostalgically treasured, few food products have divided consumers as much as Spam. Its unappetizing appearance partly explains the initial reluctance of American housewives who were suspicious of this "mystery meat" that requires no refrigeration, can be kept for several years, and was tainted by scandals. As early as 1906, novelist Upton Sinclair's *The Jungle* denounced the practices of the Chicago meat industry, which marketed products made from the carcasses of diseased animals and other waste products rendered unrecognizable by the addition of chemical substances. Spam, on the other hand, contains just five ingredients—pork (mainly shoulder), water, salt, sugar, and sodium nitrite—to which potato starch has been added since 2001 to reduce the jellylike coating that repels consumers. If Spam's poor reputation is partly undeserved, we now know that sodium nitrite, a preservative that provides its pinkish color and prevents the development of botulinum toxin, is a carcinogenic additive.

The history of Spam began in earnest in World War II and immediately took on a global character. Seduced by the advantages of this inexpensive, precooked, high-calorie meat, which was easy to store and transport thanks to its rectangular packaging, the U.S. Army Quartermaster's Office included Spam in soldiers' regular rations. GIs deployed in all theaters of war ate Jay Hormel's product (or an equivalent brand) daily. This everyday consumption contributed to Spam fatigue. Nicknamed "the ham that failed the medical exam" or "the meatloaf that didn't make the cut," Spam quickly became the butt of jokes, as Dwight Eisenhower confessed in a letter to Hormel's CEO in 1966. But nothing stood in the way of its dazzling success. In the United States, sales, stimulated by the rationing of fresh meat, doubled between 1939 and 1942. This success quickly spread to the rest of the world through food aid. Fifty thousand tons of Spam were used to feed America's allies in Europe and the Pacific. The British ate it in sandwiches, on toast, in fritters, or even, for special occasions, baked with cloves and a marinade of sugar, mustard, and vinegar. The little pink rectangle also fed Russian soldiers, threatened with starvation following the loss of direct access to fertile land in the Ukraine and the Caucasus. Nikita Khrushchev wrote in his memoirs: "Without Spam, we wouldn't have been able to feed our army," going so far as to admit that "it tasted good." In Italy and England Spam became a key black-market product, used to acquire services and information.

The tremendous success of Spam, born under the bad star of the economic crisis and associated with the dark days of World War II, could have ended there. However, the craze for the product spread throughout the twentieth century in the various theaters of operation of the American army. In the United States, Spam became synonymous with a degraded form of artificial nutrition, associated with mass industrialization. In several Asian and Pacific countries, notably the Philippines, Japan, South Korea, and the American islands of Guam and Hawaii, it acquired a prestigious status as an imported good. Here, the typically American food became synonymous with modernity and sophistication. In Korea, where the American army fought from 1950 to 1953, Spam was first incorporated into the local culinary repertoire by starving civilians who survived on products salvaged from American bases. Thus, *budae jjigae* (literally "army stew"), today a national dish, is prepared from local ingredients such as kimchi, tofu, and noodles, to which are added emblematic products of the American agri-food industry such as Spam, canned baked beans, and sandwich cheese. During the autumn festival of Chuseok, assorted tins of Spam are highly prized gifts, along with chocolates and fine spirits. In Hawaii, where Spam is so popular that the McDonald's fast-food chain added it to regional menus in 2002, locals have invented Spam Musubi: a sushi made with rice and a slice of grilled spam, all surrounded by a sheet of nori seaweed. Finally, in the Philippines,

Spam has given its name to one of the most popular variations of a breakfast dish: "spamsilog," a combination of *sinangag* (fried rice with garlic), *itlog* (fried egg), and a slice of fried Spam.

While it has become a key ingredient in the culinary repertoire of countries and territories formerly occupied by the U.S. armed forces, Spam has also found its way into the cupboards of many immigrant communities in the United States, where it is associated with nostalgic memories of childhood. More surprisingly, this is also the case for the descendants of Japanese Americans interned in detention camps set up in the western United States between 1941 and 1946. The food served in the communal dining halls included vegetables grown in the camps, as well as products supplied by the U.S. army that internees were not accustomed to eating, such as hot dogs, bread, ketchup, and . . . Spam. The cooks, recruited from among the prisoners, invented a hybrid cuisine, of which the "royal weenie," a mixture of rice, soy sauce, scrambled eggs, and chopped hot dogs, is one of the best examples.

Despite its success, Spam has remained an object of derision. In 1970 a famous Monty Python sketch featured two patrons of a restaurant that served nothing but Spam dishes, including a dish made of lobster thermidor with shrimp in mornay sauce served Provençal style with shallots and eggplant topped with truffle pâté, drizzled with brandy, and served with a fried egg and Spam, while a nearby table of Vikings sang the virtues of the product (the word was uttered 132 times in two minutes). Since then, the term "spam" has been used to describe the unsolicited e-mails that invade our inboxes. Initially annoyed by this negative publicity, Hormel eventually came to terms with it, going so far as to finance the musical *Spamalot* in 2005. It would be wrong not to: sarcasm has hardly stopped Americans from turning to Spam during difficult times, as was the case during the economic crisis of 2008, or more recently during the coronavirus epidemic of 2020, during which Spam sales increased by 70 percent.

Stéphanie Soubrier

FURTHER READING

Lizzie Collingham. *The Taste of War: World War II and the Battle for Food*. London: Penguin Books, 2012.

Robert Ji-Song Ku. *Dubious Gastronomy: The Cultural Politics of Eating Asian in the USA*. Honolulu: University of Hawai'i Press, 2014.

Rachel Laudan. *The Food of Paradise: Exploring Hawaii's Culinary Heritage*. Honolulu: University of Hawai'i Press, 1996.

Harvey A. Levenstein. *Paradox of Plenty: A Social History of Eating in Modern America*. Oxford: Oxford University Press, 1993.

Carolyn Wyman. "Spam." In *The Oxford Companion to American Food and Drink*, ed. Andrew F. Smith, 559–60. Oxford: Oxford University Press, 2007.

FURTHER TRAVELING

Hot Dog, Ketchup, Poke, Salt, Sandwich, Soy Sauce, Sushi, Tofu

Sparkling Water

In 1783 Johann Jacob Schweppe founded the first industrial company to manufacture artificial carbonated mineral water in Geneva. As such, he may be considered the founder of an industry whose initial product—sparkling water and its various avatars, including sodas—spread worldwide in the nineteenth and twentieth centuries. Almost ten years after setting up his company, the watchmaker and amateur chemist moved to London in 1792 to develop sales of his water, which was marketed under various names: soda waters, aerated waters, carbonated waters. In 1799 he finally sold his shares in the company and retired to Geneva.

Behind the transnational entrepreneur, a whole social, economic, and technical context emerges. Between the mid-1760s and the beginning of the nineteenth century, numerous innovations were introduced. In England, where naturally carbonated water was in short supply, the vicar Joseph Priestley mobilized knowledge accumulated throughout Europe to create a method for carbonating water, tested in 1767 and published in 1772. Priestley obtained "carbonated" water by lightly dissolving sodium bicarbonate in water laden with carbonic acid gas. The result was a soda water similar to Vichy water or many German springs.

From the first third of the nineteenth century onward, the number of companies producing artificially carbonated water multiplied in the United Kingdom and on the East Coast of the United States. Urbanization provided a major impetus, just as improved manufacturing techniques considerably reduced costs. Large companies established themselves alongside a number of small producers. In the United Kingdom, travelers were struck by the widespread distribution of these soft drinks, particularly in the "golden quadrilateral of consumer goods" between London, Cardiff, Edinburgh, and Glasgow. Soda waters were very popular, and the distinction between bourgeois, middle-class, and working-class consumers was reflected in the various brands. This early development paved the way for mass development after 1870. The consumption of bottled sparkling water at home was then complemented by the spread of soda siphons. The device, manufactured by the same companies that made the waters, became standard equipment in British middle-class dining rooms at the end of the nineteenth century and rapidly spread to European homes. These developments should not lead one to believe that there was a particular taste for temperance. Before World War I whiskey and soda was the most popular drink in Ireland and Great Britain.

The period after 1870 also witnessed the global spread of artificial and natural sparkling waters. Of course, the latter were particularly sought-after. They were mainly produced in continental Europe and marketed around a few major springs: Vichy, Badoit, and Perrier in France; San Pellegrino in Italy; Apollinaris, Gerolsteiner Brunnen, and Aachener Kaiserbrunnen in Germany. Other local producers sold waters in more limited markets. But the technical constraints of bottling, difficulties of transport, and the costs involved restricted sales to towns close to the source, or to the wealthiest customers. This is why manufacturers of carbonated water built factories close to the places where they were consumed. This was the case for Schweppes, which set up in Scotland (1865), Australia (1877), and New York (1884). The scale of international investment—mostly British—in bottled sparkling water is striking. One example is Apollinaris in Bad Neuenahr (Rhineland-Palatinate), controlled by London publisher George Smith, founder of the *Pall Mall Gazette*. The Harmsworth family, founders of the *Daily Mail* and owners of the *Times*, created the Perrier source in the south of France. The Aesculape and Hunyadi Janos springs in Hungary were also under British management. In March 1902 the House of Commons reported on a British company, Kobe Tansan Mineral Water Industry, which produced a sparkling mineral water in the Kobe district of Japan, employing several hundred people.

European imperialism also played an important role in the global circulation of sparkling water. From the 1880s onward the British and the French focused their exports on their empires. The name of the British trade journal, created in 1888, is revealing: *The British & Colonial Mineral Water Trade Journal*. European doctors and various guides recommended consuming carbonated water in countries with hot climates. Elites in these places also began adopting sparkling water along with other European customs. But these cases remained exceptional. In the Indian Raj and French North Africa, European drinking habits contributed to further segmentation of societies. This was not just the result of colonization. The great movements of population during the nineteenth and early twentieth centuries also favored the spread of sparkling water. Soda waters, for example, were widely consumed by Irish immigrants in New York's working-class neighborhoods, structuring notions of identity, health, Irish nationalism, and nostalgia. The consumption of sparkling water among non-Europeans should not be underestimated either. According to the *Qingbai Leichao*, a collection of stories and histories of the Qing dynasty published in Shanghai by Xu Qe in 1917, Helan Water was a Chinese domestic beverage, composed of carbonated water, some form of sweetener, and fruit juices, that was drunk seasonally, mainly in summer. The beverage's popularity is confirmed in the *Materia Medica & Natural History of China*, intended for medical missions in Central China and published by the American Presbyterian Mission Press in 1871.

The marketing and labeling of products played a fundamental role in the international development and specialization of mass-produced sparkling waters after World War II. Latin European and South American countries continued to regulate their water markets based on their therapeutic value. In the Germanic world, the proportion of minerals per liter strictly defined the natural mineral water's quality. These two areas remained the bastions of natural sparkling water. But in the United Kingdom, United States, and many other countries, the mineral water appellation was not bound to any specific regulations. Under these conditions, various additives were introduced such as sugars and colorants among others. This explains the turn of the *Mineral Water Trade* toward the soft drinks sector. British consumption of artificial sparkling water, which had been distinct from soft drinks since World War II, became almost nonexistent, even derided by some British MPs. In 1976, for example, Conservative Neil Marten argued that he agreed with his honorable colleague that people on the Continent drank a lot of bottled water, but it was not because their own tap water was impure, he argued. Instead, he insisted that bottled waters were laxatives, explaining a severe tendency toward constipation on the continent. "I'm not saying this in a hostile way," he clarified, "but it's the truth, I'm dead serious!"

Nicolas Marty

FURTHER READING

Sam Goodman. "Spaces of Intemperance & the British Raj 1860–1920." *Journal of Imperial and Commonwealth History* 48, no. 4 (2020): 591–618.

Meredith B. Linn. "Elixir of Emigration: Soda Water and the Making of Irish Americans in Nineteenth-Century New York City." *Historical Archaeology* 44, no. 4 (2010): 69–109.

Nicolas Marty. *L'invention de l'eau embouteillée: Qualités, normes et marchés de l'eau en bouteille en Europe, xixe–xxe siècles*. Brussels: Peter Lang, 2013.

Douglas A. Simmons. *Schweppes, the First 200 Years*. London: Springwood Books, 1983.

Nessim Znaien. "Cafés maures, débits européens et cadre colonial: Boire en Tunisie et en Algérie (fin xixe–milieu xxe siècles)." In *Boire et manger: Une histoire culturelle*, ed. Didier Nourrisson, 281–93. Lyon: La Diana, 2018.

FURTHER TRAVELING

Coffee, Food Coloring and Preservatives, Gin, Rocibos, Tea and Chai, Whiskey

Sushi

The first "sushi restaurant" (*sushi-ya*) outside Japan opened in 1965 in Los Angeles, California. Until then Kawafuku Sukiyaki ("The sukiyaki of the river of prosperity") offered mainly, as its name suggests, sukiyaki, a fondue mix of vegetables and meat in a Japanese-style broth. In an effort to diversify, the restaurateur took a culinary and commercial gamble on Japanese emigration.

From the 1930s onward Los Angeles was home to the largest community of Japanese migrants in the United States—thirty-seven thousand in 1940, representing over a third of the Japanese-American population (the Nikkei)—followed by San Francisco and San Jose. Its "Japantown," named Little Tokyo, located downtown, already included ten thousand Japanese before the 1907 law restricting Japanese immigration. Family reunification (prohibited in 1924) and the birth rate explain the increase in the number of Nikkei, which consisted of "first generation" (Issei, born before 1924) and a "second generation" (Nisei, born after 1924 in the United States and holding American nationality).

In 1964 Kanai Noritoshi moved to Los Angeles with his family. This Tokyo businessman had already enjoyed an adventurous lifestyle: *judoka* (judo practitioner), soldier, prisoner of war, and economics graduate, involved in various unsuccessful commercial ventures. Since 1952 he had been employed by the Tokyo branch of an import-export business, Kyodo Boeki, alias Mutual Trading Company (MTC), founded in Los Angeles in 1926. Kanai's mission was to develop Japanese food products on the American market. After an initial exploratory trip in 1956 he met Harry Goldberg, a Jewish American consultant, in Chicago in 1964 and hired him as an advisor. The two men traveled throughout

East Asia. In Tokyo, Noritoshi introduced Harry to sushi at a famous restaurant in the Kanda district.

For a century and a half this dish was a Tokyo specialty known as *Edomae-zushi*. Its now best-known variant, *nigiri-zushi*, consists of a cooked, vinegared rice dumpling topped with a garnish of fish, shellfish, or crustaceans. It was invented in 1824 in the Ryogoku district of the Lower Town (Shitamachi), by a clever restaurateur named Hanaya Yohei. His process made it possible to produce a large quantity of sushi rapidly and sell it as quickly as he made it. A kind of Japanese-style fast-food, it was initially aimed at the busy workers of Shitamachi, who ate standing up or on a stool in the open air in front of the "stall" (*yatai*). It later spread throughout Japan as a dish served at the counter.

Harry was captivated by this fresh, fast, apparently simple but potentially refined product. It was exotic but also reminiscent of Mediterranean (tapas) or Jewish (the bagel) gastronomy, or even of hot dogs or sandwiches. Back in Los Angeles, Kanai Noritoshi was convinced and urged Nakajima Tokijiro, owner of Kawafuku Sukiyaki since 1946, to take the plunge. The success was dazzling. The clientele, initially Japanese, soon expanded.

The times were right. The California counterculture was promoting vegetarian dietetics, macrobiotics, and products from Asia and the Far East. Eating raw was no longer scary. For the Nisei and the next generation of Sansei it was time to turn the disastrous page of the Pacific War, which scarred Japan and the United States. The preoccupation of Kanai Noritoshi and his friends was to spread the "taste of Japan" (*Nihon no aji*) as a form of rehabilitation. For the Americans it was a question of making amends for the unjust treatment meted out to the Japanese American community, which, despite overwhelmingly supporting the Allies, was herded by the thousands into concentration camps in California from the spring of 1942 onward. Kanai Noritoshi also counted on progress in transport and refrigeration, indispensable for fresh fish. And in 1962 a Japanese immigrant also succeeded in improving the rice grown in California to produce a variety that appealed to the particularly discerning Japanese palate, Kokuho Rose.

The conditions were ripe for the rise of the sushi bar (*sushi ba*). A wooden counter separated the cook from the customer, who busily made *nigiri* dumplings or *maki* rolls from the fish preserved in the cooling containers. Sitting on a stool, the customer observes the maneuver before tasting the preparations.

The success of Kawafuku led to the creation of other establishments. Roy Morishita, a Nisei, transformed his Eigiku café into a sushi bar in 1965. Imperial Garden opened in 1966. Tokyo Kaikan, a more upscale Japanese restaurant, followed suit in Los Angeles. Leaving California, the phenomenon spread to the prestigious Harvard Club in New York in 1972, then to major American cities and, gradually, to cities in Europe and elsewhere, in the wake of the fascination with Japanese culture and the J-Pop craze of the 1990s.

After visiting a beer bottling plant, Shiraishi Yoshiaki invented the "revolving sushi" (*kaiten-zushi*) counter in 1958. His restaurant was located in Higashi-Osaka, a working-class district of the Osaka megalopolis, and was initially aimed at a clientele of busy workers. With orders no longer compulsory, upstream preparation, the continuous presence of dishes on view, speed and convenience, the process appealed to both shopkeepers and customers. When *sushi-ya* was introduced to American and European cities in the 1990s, there was a departure from the sophisticated *sushi-ya* ritual, where the customer began with an appetizer (*kohada*) and was then guided by the chef's suggestions.

As sushi became more international, it also became less Japanese. In the 1970s restaurateurs on North America's West Coast competed to invent the aptly named "California roll." In a reversal of exoticism, the California roll made its way to Japan, much to the chagrin of purists. Depending on the availability, taste, and imagination of cooks, the range of sushi products expanded considerably around the world.

Paradoxically, the decline in Japanese fishing that began in the late 1980s, due in part to the creation of exclusive economic zones restricting access, accompanied the globalization of sushi. Japanese imports of fish products grew considerably. This was particularly true of bluefin tuna, which has traditionally been shunned by the upper classes as being too fatty and vulgar but is now becoming a favorite among the general public. Its demand has created something of a treasure-hunt effect in various seas (Gulf of Mexico and the Mediterranean in particular). Interest has dwindled in Japan with the economic crisis of the 1990s, but the powerful American tuna fishery has found a fallback market with the sushi bar craze in the West.

Within a generation, the exotic cuisine of sushi from an East Asian archipelago had become a worldwide craze, reconfiguring tastes and creating a new market. Of the 156,000 Japanese cuisine establishments in the world outside Japan in 2019, some of which offer sushi, three-quarters are Chinese-owned. The complex vagaries of the primary materials (depending on the season, location, quotas, and environmental restrictions) make the fishing economy fragile, as do the fortunes of the port communities that make a living from it locally, even though their ships often sail great distances. With sushi, the simultaneous presence of global trends and local processes, or glocalization, takes on its full meaning.

Philippe Pelletier

FURTHER READING

Michael Ashkenazi and Jeanne Jacob. *The Essence of Japanese Cuisine: An Essay on Food and Culture.* London: Curzon, 2000.

Jonas House. "Sushi in the United States, 1945–1970." *Food and Foodways* 26, no. 1 (2018): 40–62.

Sasha Issenberg. *The Sushi Economy: Globalization and the Modern Delicacy.* New York: Gotham Books, 2007.

Jordan Sand. "How Tôkyô Invented Sushi." In *Food and the City: Histories of Culture and Cultivation*, ed. Dorothée Imbert, 223–48. Cambridge, MA: Harvard University Press, 2015.

FURTHER TRAVELING

Bagel, Beer, Ceviche, Maki, Oyster, Sake, Sandwich

Tapioca

In 1837 starch manufacturer Groult opened a flour mill just outside of Paris in Vitry-sur-Seine. He was one of the first to recognize the industrial potential of tapioca, the tasteless, odorless, colorless substance derived from bitter cassava. Since the eighteenth century, agronomists, botanists, and pharmacists had been working on this multifaceted root. In 1764 the Dutch physician Fermin confirmed its dangerousness in the case of a poisoned slave in Surinam. Thirty-five drops of its juice were enough to kill him in five minutes, after horrible suffering. In 1835 a French pharmacist and chemist noted in a report entitled *Sur le principe vénéneux du manioc amer* (On the Poisonous Principle of Bitter Manioc) that slaves used the root to commit suicide. The process for extracting the hydrocyanic acid from the poisonous tuber was then invented: the root was grated and pressed to extract the starch, which was then steamed to destroy the cyanide and placed onto copper plates at 100°C (212°F) to make little pearls.

The metamorphosis also took place in the imagination. To make people forget the brown, poisonous tuber, manufacturers emphasized its "hygienic" character. In 1850 Maison Groult's "Tapioca from Brazil" claimed to be "recommended by doctors." It was advertised alongside cod-liver oil and date syrup. Supposedly analeptic, it was recommended for children, the elderly, and convalescents. Thanks to the success of his Parisian stores, Groult strengthened the association between children and tapioca by adding an orphanage to his factory, where boarders received a religious and domestic education. In return they had to "sort and package the cereals." As an added privilege, they could stay on as adults "at the factory to make tapioca." The public could admire the success of the work through displays of baby clothes, which implied that tapioca fed the orphans directly and indirectly. Tapioca did indeed enjoy a long-lasting success in Europe and North America as "baby porridge" that could be prepared in just a few minutes by sprinkling tapioca into water, soup, or milk.

Since the beginning of the nineteenth century, the foodstuffs industry had been searching for new starches to serve as the basis for recently identified carbohydrates, and the young science of nutrition was looking for a caloric material that could be preserved. Along with other exotic materials such as *sago* from India, arrowroot from Jamaica and *salep* from Persia, tapioca seemed ideal. *Le dictionnaire des substances alimentaires* (The Dictionary of Food Substances), published in 1874, noted that 500 grams (17.6 oz.) "of tapioca can nourish a man for up to twenty-four hours" because it "greatly increases in volume when cooked." The miracle powder could be used to make glue, for papermaking processes, and for linen starch. A tasteless, odorless material—whitish then translucent when baked—it could be transported in the form of flour, salted, or sweetened. As such, it was a dream for industrial transformation, just as rubber was in the same years. The beads could be colored and flavored: tapioca was like manna. Packaging was essential to give shape to a narrative and feed imaginations for a food that was decidedly abstract. Brand names, labels, and boxes for tapioca were registered on a massive scale from the 1850s onward, and to great success, since tapioca took root in Western kitchens. The brand name also had to give a certain authenticity to the product, especially in the face of the multiple counterfeits based on potato starch, rice, or horse chestnuts. At the end of the nineteenth century, this fat- and gluten-free starch was used to make light pastries, broths, and soups for weak stomachs and struggling livers. At the beginning of the twentieth century, its falling cost made it commonplace. From the 1950s onward it became a "texturizer" in the food industry, and a ready-to-use material to "help the housewife" consolidate and thicken puddings and gratins and make the creams and mousses of "modern cooking" impeccable.

As a result of this transfiguration, tapioca remains a product of uncertain origin in Europe and North America. Not only does manioc grow only in the tropics and the Southern Hemisphere, but the term *tapioca* also conceals its vegetable origin. A Portuguese word inspired by the Indian languages of Brazil, *tapiocha*, then *tapioka* and *tapioca*, spread from the seventeenth century onward. At the beginning of the nineteenth century the names "island tapioca" and "Brazilian tapioca" competed with each other; then at the end of the century, in keeping with the exoticism of the times, came "Japanese pearls." The industrial geography of tapioca added to the confusion: it was produced in the colonial cities of Marseille and Nantes (Robillard Petit Navire), but also in colonial port cities Vitry-sur-Seine and Nancy (Bloch). Indeed, supply channels changed regularly. As late as the 1800s tapioca arrived from South and Central America via Spain. When Groult opened his factory in 1837, tapioca was imported from Brazil and the West Indies via Le Havre. In 1876, 1,300 tons from Brazil passed through Le Havre, rising to 20,000 tons after World War I. It was also often imported raw from Madagascar and Réunion. In the United Kingdom it comes from the West Indies and British Malaya.

Manuel Charpy

FURTHER READING

William O. Jones. *Manioc in Africa*. Stanford, CA: Stanford University Press, 1959.
Dominique Juhé-Beaulaton. "De l'igname au manioc dans le golfe de Guinée: Traite des esclaves et alimentation au royaume du Danhomè (xviie–xixe siècle)." *Afriques* 5 (2014). https://journals .openedition.org/afriques/1669.
Mary Karasch. "Manioc." In *The Cambridge World History of Food*, ed. Kenneth F. Kiple and Kriemhild Coneae Ornelas, 181–87. Cambridge: Cambridge University Press, 2000.

FURTHER TRAVELING

Acheke, Feijoada, Tea and Chai

Tea and Chai

In 1842, the Treaty of Nanking was signed. It was, as Sun Yat-sen put it, the most famous of the "unequal treaties" imposed on China by the Western powers. The United Kingdom, at the end of the First Opium War in 1839, obtained freedom of trade with the Qing Empire and the opening of four new ports in addition to Canton and Amoy. Botanist Robert Fortune scoured China to collect plants. At the end of an expedition in 1848 for the British East India Company, he introduced twenty thousand tea plants to India. China no longer had a virtual monopoly on tea exports. Europeans, notably the British and their former colonies in America, had rapidly increased consumption since the end of the seventeenth century. They could now cultivate and distribute it, making it the most widely consumed beverage in the world after water.

This globalization was superimposed onto a more ancient form of distribution. Making beverages from *Camelia sinensis* leaves through infusion, decoction, and even maceration had been practiced in China since the first millennium BCE. Tea-related cultural practices were introduced to Korea and Japan in the second century CE. To the west, via the Eurasian Silk Roads, tea penetrated Central Asia in the first millennium CE before reaching Persia and then Russia. Mongol caravanners invented the samovar, which the Russians later made into a marker of their own identity. Further west, the spread of tea was held back by another, more recent hot beverage: coffee. This competitor became an important social practice in the Ottoman Empire, while copying its ritual objects from those of tea: the coffee pot derived from the teapot and the cup from the *gaiwan*, the Chinese tea bowl.

Tea was not introduced to Europeans via the Silk Road. Following in the footsteps of the Portuguese, the Dutch, then the English and French, brought tea back from China in the early seventeenth century. Initially the East India Companies traded with the Middle Kingdom from the south. So it was under the name of *te* in Malay, a word borrowed from Minnan, a language widely used in southern China, that Europeans discovered the infusion of *Camelia sinensis*. Hence the French term *thé*, the British *tea*, the Germans *tee*, the Spanish *té*, as opposed to the more easterly societies that came to the beverage through ancient Eurasian exchanges and draw the name from the term *chai*, derived from Mandarin and other northern Chinese languages. Russians and Arabs, but also Turks and Czechs, drink *chai*. The linguistic geography of tea opposes the East against the West, as a result of two successive historical phases of globalization. Portuguese *cha* is an amusing exception: the first Europeans to make direct contact with China in the sixteenth century were in fact subjects of the Portuguese king. They went as far as the court of Peking, where tea was known as *chai*.

In the seventeenth century the East India companies began importing tea to Europe, along with porcelain tableware for its consumption, but without any precise instructions for use. This led to the development of practices that reinforced the Chinese belief that they were dealing with savages: adding sugar and, even worse, milk to this delicate beverage. Of course, the tea imported to Europe was of the lowest quality: highly fermented black tea compressed into briquettes to withstand the long sea voyage from Canton to London. This casts doubt on the legend that attributes the addition of milk to the hostess of one of the most famous literary salons during the reign of Louis XIV, Madame de la Sablière, who was keen to preserve her precious Chinese cups. In the eighteenth century European consumption of tea went from anecdotal to massive. From the 1720s onward, with the introduction of regular fleet rotations by the East India companies, tea was drunk several times a day, initially by the wealthier classes but soon by the whole of British society. The practice of eating breakfast, which only spread to all social categories in the nineteenth century, emerged as well, along with 5:00 o'clock tea. New utensils, such as silver cutlery and porcelain dishes, were invented, helping to codify a typically British way of life. On the Continent, coffee clearly prevailed, from breakfast to the end of the last meal, reserving tea for the rather bourgeois and feminine practice of tearooms.

On the other hand, the English model spread widely throughout the British Empire. Tea consumption became significant enough in the thirteen American colonies that the massive increase in tea taxes imposed by George III, impecunious as a result of the Seven Years' War, provoked the first event of the American Revolution, the Boston Tea Party in 1773. The increase in Western demand for tea came up against a bottleneck: China did not purchase products supplied by the East India Company in exchange for tea exports. English merchants eventually identified a demand for opium that remained socially strong despite restrictions imposed by the Chinese state. So, to satisfy the West's growing appetite for tea, the British East India Company began drug trafficking. When in 1839 Lin Zexu, imperial commissioner of Guandong, had opium stocks destroyed in Canton and announced that all foreign ships would be searched, the British Parliament declared war on China, a conflict that ended three years later with the Treaty of Nanking.

Within a few decades British tea production exploded across the Indian Ocean. In 1903 the first tea bushes were planted in Kenya, followed by Uganda, Mozambique, Madagascar, and Mauritius. Highlands with cool nights were preferred for the tea plantations. As a result, they tended to be accompanied by colonial settlements in higher altitudes. One could discover the beautiful landscapes produced by regularly sheared *Camelia sinensis* bushes in Nuwara Eliya in central Sri Lanka or Darjeeling at the foot of Sikkim or Kericho near Lake Victoria. These were almost exclusively black teas produced for British consumers. The rapid spread of these plantations, set up by the great London trading houses (such as Twining, Earl Grey's company, founded in 1706), required an abundant and dependent workforce: coolies. Mainly from southern India, this forced emigration, which though not a slave trade resembled it in many ways, involved some eight million workers until 1938, when it was finally abolished. This dark side of tea history has a counterpart on the consumer side. Tea, an aristocratic practice in the early eighteenth century, became a popular drink in Victorian England. Sweetened with molasses, it provided 20 percent of workers' daily calorie intake, representing an essential fuel for industrialization.

Today, Kenya is only the third-largest tea-producing country, behind China and India, but the leading exporter. China consumes most of its production, while India is a more recent consumer. Although Hindu nationalists claim to have been drinking tea for a long time, going so far as to say that they introduced the beverage to the British, it was the arrival of Chinese tea plants during the Opium War that made tea the national drink. Indian tea is drunk with milk (directly from the teapot), but also spiced (hence the name *massala chai*). The British also played a key role in another practice that has become part of Morocco's local identity: mint tea. Having established themselves as importers in Russia, English tea companies were faced with unused stocks in 1855, due to the Crimean War, particularly in Gibraltar. Nearby Maghreb quickly became a market when tea was added to traditional sweet mint infusions.

The worldwide divergence of the words tea and chai is a reminder not only of two successive waves of diffusion but also of two quite different beverages. Today Chinese tea culture is also becoming globalized, as are the practices of countries that adopted it long ago: Japanese matcha or Taiwanese bubble tea. Tasting the cultural complexity of Chinese practices, playing on the variety and subtlety of plants and plantations, types of leaves and the diversity of fermentation techniques, is becoming a refined, global practice in the West. Tea is hardly at risk of losing its position as the world's leading beverage.

Christian Grataloup

FURTHER READING

Paul Butel. *Histoire du thé.* Paris: Desjonquères, 1997.
Victor H. Mair and Erling Hoh. *The True History of Tea.* New York: Thames and Hudson, 2009.
Sidney Mintz. *Sweetness and Power: The Place of Sugar in Modern History.* New York: Viking Press, 1985.
Helen Saberi. *Tea: A Global History.* London: Reaktion Books, 2000.
George van Driem. *The Tale of Tea: A Comprehensive History of Tea from Prehistoric Time to the Present Day.* Leiden: Brill, 2019.

FURTHER TRAVELING

Beet Sugar, Chicory, Coffee, Cornflakes, Roiboos, Yak Butter

Tikka

In 2001, Robin Cook, the British Foreign Secretary, declared that chicken tikka masala (CTM) was the country's true national dish, instead of the famous fish and chips, not only because this Indian dish, adapted to British tastes by the addition of a special sauce, was the most popular but also because it was a perfect example of how Britain adopts outside influences without weakening its own traditions or diluting its national identity. Tikka, a Punjabi word close to the Turkish term *tikk'*, meaning piece or morsel, refers to any piece of boneless meat or cheese that is marinated in a sauce made up of a mixture of spices dyed to a bright red color, and then grilled.

For the Labour minister, the status of chicken tikka was proof of British multiculturalism from the Celts, Romans, and Normans to recent immigrants from the former colonies. Tikka was thus placed at the heart of the immigration debate, not as specific to one ethnic group but as an icon of universality. Affirming one's taste for tikka would reflect openness to the world in a country no longer confined to bland or boiled dishes.

The food has been promoted since 1983 by major supermarket chains such as Sainsbury, Tesco, and Waitrose, for whom tikka is the spearhead of ready-made meals. A canned version, sold by Heinz, makes it part of the breakfast menu, alongside the brand's famous beans. Served in more than nine thousand restaurants in Great Britain, it quickly found its way into Indian, Pakistani, and Bangladeshi restaurants, as well as fast-food outlets such as Pizza Hut, Dominos, Subway, McDonald's, and Spudulike. British companies even export it to Pakistan, India, and Bangladesh.

This success prompted reactions from communities on the subcontinent, who laid claim to its heritage, insisting that the dish served in the United Kingdom not only had no connection to the authentic dish but was also as false as the country's proclaimed multiculturalism. The debate is part of the many international disputes surrounding the origins of culinary traditions, fostered by the European policy of Protected Designations of Origin or UNESCO's World Intangible Cultural Heritage label. Its close link with questions of nationalism demonstrates the powerful interweaving of food with issues of identity and cultural heritage.

As with many other culinary specialties, the origins of tikka lie in the world of legend and myth. Its discovery is attributed to King Babur (1483–1530), who conquered Punjab from Central Asia, ushering in four centuries of Mughal rule. Babur is said to have feared choking on meat bones and so ordered them to be removed before cooking in a specially designed earthen oven. Popularized in India as a piece of cheese served with a sauce or simply grilled, it was adapted to local practices, stuffed with crushed and grilled almonds in Kashmir, or in a Chinese style as *paneer tikka masala chow mein* in the northeastern provinces. Concerned with being once again dispossessed of their cultural heritage, many Indians today point to the contribution made by the Moti Mahal restaurant in Delhi in the 1940s. At the same time, the heritage of the dish in "Mughlai" cuisine is defended by chefs who claim to descend from the cooks of the last emperor, Bahadur Shah Zafar, deposed by the British in 1857. Others associate it with Punjab in the 1940s.

The British version, on the other hand, attributes its contemporary form to the Pakistani chef of an Indian restaurant in Glasgow in the 1950s. Faced with a complaint from a Scottish customer asking where the sauce was to accompany his chicken tikka, he heated up a can of tomato soup from the well-known Campbell's brand and added a few spices. Its entry onto restaurant menus inevitably brought about decisive changes, notably softening the strength of the spices by adding yogurt or cream, as well as versions with Nutella or potatoes. Along the way it has become an object of identity, community, and urban issues. In 2009, Mohammad Sarwar, Glasgow's Labour MP, proposed that his city be recognized as the place of origin of chicken tikka masala and that the dish be recognized as part of the European Union's Protected Designation of Origin. Although his proposal failed to be taken seriously, it reflected a desire to give the dish the same status as Cornish clotted cream or Welsh lamb.

Whether in India, Pakistan, Europe, the United States, or Mexico, immigration has played a central role in the spread of the dish. In London Pakistanis, Bangladeshis, and Indians opened restaurants from the 1950s onward, focusing on grilled meat. Each, depending on their origins, added their own touch through different combinations of spices. This gave rise to a wide variety of recipes with just one element in common: meat, either chicken or mutton. In this sense, Robin Cook's chicken tikka masala was a novelty. Its promotion by renowned chefs gave it the legitimacy of a dish that was both accessible and sophisticated, while at the same time claiming the heritage of the great cuisine of the Mughal emperors. As a result, it has been exported not only across the Atlantic but also to South Asia, Australia, and New Zealand. Its global trajectory is closely linked to the worldwide development of "Indian" restaurants.

Today, chicken tikka consumption is not confined to Great Britain, nor is it confined to the kitchen. It has also made its way into song, with titles such as "I sneak a chicken tikka masala at a gala event" (2008) by the Beastie Boys, "I got a tikka masala, that's the right idea . . ." by Scott Helman (2014) and the recent "Chicken Tikka" on TikTok (2021). In Australia, the #ChickenTikkaMasalaChallenge (2020) invited Australians to submit their version of the dish on TikTok or Instagram. The reward: win a year's supply of chicken tikka from the delivery company Deliveroo.

Carried by diasporas, commercial networks, or restaurateurs, acclaimed by more open-minded generations ready to experiment, chicken tikka masala has escaped a communitarian gastronomic tradition bound to insular nationalism that might exclude those who are not part of it. Tikka is an example of a modern, global cuisine, which can be found in restaurants and kitchens all over the world, whether Indian, Pakistani, Bangladeshi, British, American, Australian, African, or Latin American. While for some it may express nostalgia for a time of extreme refinement, when the Mughals dominated South Asia, its successful expansion beyond the culinary sphere into the worlds of tourism and the art scene has transformed it into a global icon, a status few culinary specialties have managed to achieve.

Arundhati Virmani

FURTHER READING

Amir Ali. "Chicken Tikka Multiculturalism." *Economic and Political Weekly* 36 (2001): 2821–22.

E. N. Anderson. *Everyone Eats: Understanding Food and Culture.* New York: New York University Press, 2005.

Arjun Appadurai. "How to Make a National Cuisine: Cookbooks in Contemporary India," *Comparative Studies in Society and History* 30, no. 1 (1988): 3–24.

Ashis Nandy. "Ethnic Cuisine: The Significant 'Other.'" *India International Centre Quarterly* 29, nos. 3–4 (2002–2003): 246–51.

"Robin Cook's Chicken Tikka Masala Speech." *The Guardian,* June 10, 2021.

FURTHER TRAVELING

Curry, Fish and Chips, Food Coloring and Preservatives, Naan, Yogurt

Tofu

When, on October 19, 1905, Li Yuying (Li Shizeng, 1881–1973), then a young attaché to the Chinese legation, presented a paper on "Vegetable Milk in China" at the Second International Dairy Congress in Paris, soy-based food products were virtually unknown to his French audience. While the brilliant student at the École Pratique d'Agriculture du Chesnoy in Montargis, France, was not trying to convince people of the qualities of vegetal milk or plant-based cheese (tofu), which he saw as comparable to those of the dairy specialties his listeners loved, he was trying to arouse scientific curiosity and introduce the Western world to an ancient food produced through Chinese inventiveness. The presence of tofu is attested in China as early as the tenth century and for several centuries in the parts of East and Southeast Asia under its influence.

The techniques used to make this vegetal cheese are similar to those used in cheese-making: the white liquid obtained from soybeans, ground after soaking and then filtered, resembles milk in both color and consistency. The curd obtained by adding coagulating agents (usually magnesium chloride or calcium sulfate) forms a mass similar in appearance to that of fresh cheese. This striking resemblance had already caught the attention of the first missionaries who discovered tofu in Japan and China as early as the seventeenth century, to the point of describing it, like Li Yuying, as "vegetal cheese."

A few years later, the anarchist and vegetarian Li Yuying had become a member of the Institut Pasteur in France. He attracted the attention of elite Parisian scientists in 1908–9 when he built the Caséo-Sojaïne factory at La Garenne Colombe (Les Vallées). With this ultramodern plant he inaugurated the production of tofu, which in his eyes were fresh, fermented, and smoked "soy cheeses" that he likened to Gruyere, Camembert, and Roquefort cheeses, depending on their taste. While this was indeed the first large-scale industrial venture of its kind in the West, Li Yuying was following a path already trodden in 1855 by the French Société d'Acclimatation, the first organization in the Western world to take an interest in the potential uses of "oleaginous peas."

It all began when a sample of the beans were sent to Buffon in 1740 by missionaries living in China. It is also said that a bag of seeds dated 1779 had been carefully preserved in the Cabinet du Roi. However, it was not until Auguste Pailleux's book on soya was published in 1881 that the history of this new legume in Europe became known thanks to scientists. Agronomists, arboriculturists, or horticulturists, and even the simply curious and literate, began experimenting with its cultivation on a private basis, using the few seeds distributed by the Société d'Acclimatation, which had received them from the French consul in Shanghai. Inspired by a precise description of the techniques for making "pea cheese" or tofu published in 1866, Pailleux, who had become an ardent defender of soya as a future food resource for the French population, succeeded after numerous attempts in achieving a satisfactory result. Despite these successful domestic trials, no large-scale enterprise was set up in France until the creation of Li Yuying's Caséo-Sojaïne, a pioneering factory, but without any followers. The fact that the young entrepreneur obtained the world's first patent on the tofu manufacturing process in London in 1910 hardly changed a thing.

To be fair, the "raw pea taste" attributed to soy cheese and soy milk was not very appealing and posed a real handicap to its distribution in France. Yet it was derived from a hygienically and digestibly impeccable "milk," which was not the case with cow's milk. Nonetheless, Caséo-Sojaïne rapidly went bankrupt.

Across the Atlantic, tofu was known long after its arrival in Europe and even then was rarely cultivated. It arrived thanks to the efforts of a handful of Asian grocery store owners at the end of the nineteenth century. Despite an official investigation into the composition of tofu in 1912 and a patent obtained in 1917 by a Japanese tofu manufacturer, the product was still unknown in America at the time of World War I. The efforts of a few scientists to make it known met with little success.

It was the Seventh Day Adventists who pioneered tofu production in the United States from 1929 onward at Madison College in Tennessee, where cafeteria menus included fresh tofu and soy milk. These Protestants had probably learned about tofu through their contacts with missionaries evangelizing in

China. Members of the congregation were committed vegetarians or vegans and had been involved in food reform movements since the early nineteenth century to improve the health of the American population. Physician John Harvey Kellogg, inventor of cornflakes and creator of the famous Battle Creek Adventist Hospital, was one of the first Americans to understand the nutritional potential of soy foods. But Kellogg was more interested in soy milk than tofu. For these reformers, tofu was ultimately a fresh, home-cooked food, whereas they were relentless in their efforts to transform soy into industrially produced, shelf-stable dietary by-products. Tofu was one of these. However, once canned, it failed to gain a reputation.

As a result, tofu disappeared from the dietary horizon of ordinary Americans and was forgotten until the 1940s. World War II and the government's rationing program gave tofu a new lease on life. The *Soy Cookbook* published in 1944 offered elaborate recipes for tofu, which the author described as appetizing and rich in protein, calcium, phosphorus, and minerals, useful in times of shortage. She treated tofu both as a food in its own right and as a substitute for cheese and meat.

After the bankruptcy of Li Yuying's company, tofu disappeared for over fifty years in Europe, since the marginal vegetarian movements did not use tofu in their diets, despite its well-known dietary value today (on average 40 percent proteins and around 20 percent lipids). Tofu then reappeared with the arrival of large contingents of Asians (Chinese, Cambodians, Vietnamese, and Laotians) in Europe and particularly in France during the period of decolonization of Indochina and the Vietnam War. These men and women from East Asia set up small tofu factories in the Netherlands, Belgium, England, West Germany, France, and Switzerland, since they could not do without a product that was essential to their daily diet. It was in the late 1970s that tofu became fashionable again among European youth, following the influence of the American counter-culture movement and new vegetarian currents inspired by "oriental" practices. Gary Landgrebe's culinary treatise *Tofu Goes West* (1978) provided the starting point for this trend, with its collection of recipes adapted to the style of American cuisine, and its title, which surprisingly suggested that tofu had never previously existed in the West. With the twenty-first century boom in veganism and vegetarianism, a lifestyle choice commonly adopted by younger generations, tofu has become popular worldwide. Perhaps it will escape being forgotten once again.

Françoise Sabban

314 TOFU

FURTHER READING

Guangzhu Hong. *Zhongguo doufu* (Chinese Tofu). Beijing: Zhongguo shangye chubanshe, 1987.

Camille Oger. *Tofu: L'anthologie.* Paris: La Plage, 2019.

William Shurtleff and Akiko Aoyagi. *The Book of Tofu: Protein Source of the Future—Now.* New York: Ballantine, 1975.

"Une usine chinoise fonctionne dans la banlieue parisienne." *Le Journal*, January 9, 1911.

Li-Yu Ying and L. Grandvoinnet. *Le soja, sa culture: Ses usages alimentaires, thérapeutiques, agricoles et industriels.* Paris: Éditeur Augustin Challamel, 1912.

FURTHER TRAVELING

Cornflakes, Parmesan Cheese, Roquefort, Soy Sauce

Turkish Delight

At the 1873 World's Fair in Vienna, an Ottoman confection in the shape of a sweet, gelatinous cube was awarded a silver medal. The product was referred to as *lokoum*, or Turkish delight in England and *loukoum* in France since the nineteenth century. Hadji Bekir, its maker, was the head confectioner of the Ottoman palace, owner of a sweets store in Istanbul dating back to 1777. He was awarded a second silver medal in 1888 at the Cologne exhibition in Germany, followed by two gold medals, one in Brussels in 1897 and the other in Nice in 1906. Hadji Bekir's establishment played an important role in the recognition of Turkish delight in Europe. In the nineteenth century, many foreigners wrote in their memoirs about this doughy dessert that melts in the mouth and leaves a delicious, fragrant aftertaste. In fact, Ottoman confectioners long kept the sweet a secret, ensuring its mysterious exotic flavor for Europeans.

Formerly known as *rahatü'l-hulkum* in Arabic, Turkish delight was among the most original flavors in Ottoman cuisine. The expression, meaning "that which passes easily through the throat," underwent modifications over time to become *lati lokum* ("comfortable Turkish delight"), later abbreviated to *lokoum*. It is not known exactly when the confection first appeared in history. References to *lok* could be found in writings on Arab culinary culture from the seventh century, when sugar obtained from sugarcane was first used. It was prepared with honey or sugar, fruit pulp, dried fruit, or mastic, which soothed the stomach and may have been the ancestor of *lokoum*. A second origin refers to an Ottoman dessert called *paluze* or *pelte*, prepared with honey or grape must, water, flour, or starch. Although *rahatü'l-hulkum* is first mentioned in Ottoman sources as a culinary term in the seventeenth century, the first similar recipe is for *paluze*, noted in an eighteenth-century manuscript. White sugar is boiled in water, and the syrup is mixed with a little wheat starch. The whole preparation is then stirred and cooked for three hours, after which rosewater is added. This *paluze* is turned over in a tray and moistened with almond oil. Once cooled, the sweet dough is cut into cubes with scissors and sprinkled with musk-scented white powdered sugar. This nineteenth-century preparation of Turkish delight fragrance became the most popular.

From the late 1880s onward, a more modern technique for making *lokoum* was developed. After transforming sugar and water into syrup, cream tartar was added with white starch diluted in water to prevent the sugar from crystallizing. At the same time, recipes multiplied: mastic, rose, almond, pistachio, and kaymak, a thick milk cream.

Originally Turkish delight was served primarily during religious feasts in wealthy homes of Istanbul. Along with marzipan and berlingots, it was presented on silver platters, accompanied by Turkish coffee in porcelain cups. Far from being consumed exclusively by the Ottoman elite, it was enjoyed by all. In the memoirs of Friedrich Unger, the head confectioner to King Otto I of Greece, which won its independence from the Ottoman Empire in 1832, Turkish delight is mentioned as one of the most sought-after tastes in the confectioneries of Athens and Istanbul. It then spread to Europe in the second half of the nineteenth century. During their trips to Istanbul, British travelers were very fond of the delicacy. They bought numerous tins and shipped them back to Great Britain. Turkish delight was offered as a luxury sweet at Christmas time. Because of its sugar content, it was an expensive commodity. From *Punch* magazine, which published an advertising cartoon in 1861, to Charles Dickens's *Mystery of Edwin Drood*, published in 1870, Turkish delight colonized British culture, partially because it had no competition from local production.

European confectioners had long tried to make this confection without success. For years, the famous English chocolate company Cadbury's sold a dark pink jelly made from fish gelatin and coated in chocolate like Turkish delight. But it could not compete. At the beginning of the twentieth century, the sweet was exported in large quantities to Marseille, where it became known as *ratacomb*, a deformation of the Turkish *rahatü'l-hulkum* according to the French painter Prétextat-Lecomte, one of the first foreign witnesses to describe its manufacture in detail.

From the late nineteenth century to the 1950s, Turkish delight began to spread throughout the world. From Napoleon Bonaparte to Queen Victoria and Queen Elizabeth, from Churchill to Picasso and Rita Hayworth, Turkish delight became a favorite of many statesmen and artists. During World War II, however, the constant risk of famine made its consumption difficult, especially given the high price of sweets and their scarcity.

In today's Turkey, *lokoum* continues to exist as a traditional sweet in competition with chocolate. Its production has an important place in the country's confectionery industry, and is exported to countries such as Germany, America, France, the Netherlands, England, and Belgium. An Ottoman culinary heritage, it also survives in the former territories of the Empire, from the Balkans to the Middle East, via the Maghreb countries. It is a tradition that Hadji Bekir, the oldest of the brands, continues to uphold.

Özge Samancı

FURTHER READING

Priscilla Mary Işin. *Bountiful Empire: A History of Ottoman Cuisine*. London: Reaktion Books, 2018.
——. *A King's Confectioner in the Orient Friedrich Unger, Court Confectioner to King Otto I of Greece*. London: Kegan Paul, 2003.
Timothy G. Roufs and Kathleen Smyth Roufs. *Sweet Treats Around the World: An Encyclopedia of Food and Culture*. Santa Barbara, CA: ABC-Clio, 2014.
Özge Samancı. *La cuisine d'Istanbul au xixe siècle*. Tours: Presses Universitaires de Rennes, 2015.
Özge Samancı and Sibel Özilgen. *Kadim Lezzetler—1*. Istanbul: Yeditepe University Press, 2015.

FURTHER TRAVELING

Christmas Pudding, Coffee, Sugar, Tea and Chai, Vanilla

Vanilla and Vanillin

In 1841 the secret of simple, large-scale artificial reproduction of vanilla was discovered. The breakthrough was made by a young enslaved man from the Bellier-Beaumont plantation in Sainte Suzanne on Bourbon Island, now Réunion. Edmond was a gardener with a mastery of plant science, including a rare knowledge of their Latin names. In 1841, building on the strength of his experiments with other varieties, the twelve-year-old succeeded in bringing together the male and female organs of a vanilla plant. This plant had arrived in Bourbon some twenty years earlier. The island had received several shipments from French Guiana in 1819, Java and the Philippines in 1820, then from Paris in 1822. However, like all specimens planted outside Mexico, the plants remained sterile, bearing flowers but no fruit. We now know that they lacked an essential element necessary for pollination, a species of bee (*Apis melipona*) native to Central America. With the help of a needle, Edmond invented the act of artificial pollination.

Not only was the young slave responsible for the globalization of vanilla, but he also helped spread his method. As Mézières Lepervenche, an amateur botanist and justice of the peace who witnessed the events of 1841, explained: "Word of this discovery soon spread throughout [the island]: all the vanilla owners wanted to see the truth for themselves and asked Mr Bellier to see his black boy, then aged 12, to come and teach them the mystery of vanilla fertilization he had invented. Edmond was sent to St. Benoît to Mr. Patu de Rosemond, to St. André to Mr. Floris, to Ste Suzanne to Mr. Joseph Desbassayns.... And at his young age, he was sent a carriage or a horse." Seven years before the abolition of slavery, Edmond shook the very foundations of black servitude. Planters and scientists were absorbed by his words and scrutinized his pioneering gesture. We can only

VANILLA AND VANILLIN

imagine the reaction of others as the young boy was listened to, praised, and solicited. How could slavery be justified when this slave was teaching science to masters?

Edmond's story remains complex. Remarkably, his invention was not stolen. Attempts were made, but all failed, not least thanks to the testimony of Mézières Lepervenche, who protected the discovery by publicly attributing it to him. However, despite this recognition, the story of the botanist slave did not have a happy ending. In 1848, following the abolition of slavery, Edmond was given the surname Albius. Was this an allusion to the "white" vanilla flower? Or was it a coincidence due to the urgent need to invent new surnames? Or was it a racist joke? Edmond's destiny was marked for a long time by his condition as a slave. Although as a free man he went on to achieve a certain notoriety—an engraving of his likeness adorns the local pantheon, *L'album de la Réunion*—he died in poverty in 1880 because his method of pollination was not patentable.

The Belgian Charles Morren was a few years ahead of Edmond. In 1836, in Liège, the scientist had succeeded in fertilizing a vanilla plant in the laboratory, producing several hundred pods over the following decade. But his slow and cumbersome greenhouse production technique, set up in a cold country, was never tested outside his laboratory greenhouses. Moreover, the sources show that the Morren method, however confusingly explained, only appeared in a few specialized journals not to be found in the libraries of Bourbon Island. Edmond could not have been inspired by it. Even today, vanilla professionals still use the Albius method.

Although it did not make his inventor a fortune, Edmond's discovery did ensure the prosperity of Réunion, since vanilla production soared; so much so that the name *Vanille Bourbon* was soon coined. In 1862 the island exported twenty-seven tons, rising to two hundred tons in 1898, while Mexico produced only forty-four tons of beans that year. Vanilla went from being a Mexican luxury item to a much more democratized product, mainly from the French colonies of Reunion, Comoros, Madagascar, and Tahiti, where the bean was introduced in 1846. Between the two world wars, they accounted for around 85 percent of the world's production.

In the second half of the nineteenth century, the United States and France in particular became great consumers of vanilla. It was no longer simply an adjunct to chocolate, as it had been in the previous century. Some ate it as an ice cream flavor, just as it added an exotic touch to pastries. A secret ingredient in Coca-Cola, it was also a component of other flavors. Demand was so great that a second race was launched to develop a chemical vanillin. This was discovered by French chemist Nicholas Goblet in 1858, and the first synthetic vanillin was produced in Germany in 1876. Ethyl-vanillin followed in the twentieth century. It was even cheaper to produce with a more intense aroma.

Vanillin is a molecule present in both real vanilla and synthetic vanilla-flavored products. Only a few machines can detect the difference between the two. The food market whetted the appetites of those who sought to replace agricultural materials with industrial substitutes for substantial profits. Thus, for a long time, the anal secretions of the beaver, or castorium, were used to achieve a vanilla scent, which was cheaper for producers. In the 1980s Canada took the lead with a vanillin produced from discarded paper pulp derivatives at a plant not far from Niagara Falls. More recently, Japanese chemist Mayu Yamamoto succeeded in developing a vanilla flavor from cow dung. And you must be well informed to know that behind the words "aroma" or "taste" of vanilla almost certainly lies the use of a synthetic vanillin. In this respect, the latter is an eloquent example of a contemporary substitution process, in which agricultural materials are replaced by industrial substitutes that are difficult for consumers to differentiate from the original.

Eric Jennings

FURTHER READING

Tim Ecott. *La vanille: À la recherche de l'orchidée au fruit noir*. Paris: Noir sur Blanc, 2014.

David Goodman, Bernardo Sorj, and John Wilkinson. *From Farming to Biotechnology*. New York: Basil Blackwell, 1987.

Eric Jennings. "Cartels et lobbies de la vraie vanille: Marketing, genre, nostalgie et réseaux postcoloniaux." *Revue d'histoire moderne et contemporaine* 66, no. 3 (2019): 128–55.

Emilio Kourí. *A Pueblo Divided: Business, Property and Community in Paplanta, Mexico*. Stanford, CA: Stanford University Press, 2004.

Raoul Lucas. *La Réunion: Île de la vanille*. Saint-André: Océan Éditions, 1990.

Serge Volper. *Du cacao à la vanille: Une histoire des plantes coloniales*. Paris: Quae, 2011.

FURTHER TRAVELING

Coca-Cola, Rum, Tea, Yogurt

Vodka

On January 15, 2008, the European Parliament issued a regulation on "the definition, description, presentation, labeling and protection of spirit drinks." According to this regulation, only spirits distilled from cereals (as in the case of Russian vodka) or potatoes (as in the case of its great rival, Polish vodka) would be entitled to the official designation of "vodka," unlike those spirits distilled, for example, from grapes or grape must. The aim of the regulation was to put an end to the vagueness surrounding the term "vodka," at least on the European market. More implicitly, given the financial stakes involved, the aim was also to better protect the appellation of the world's best-selling spirit. By 2020, vodka's annual worldwide consumption was estimated at 4.54 billion liters (1.2 billion gallons), representing almost 20 percent of all spirits consumed. More than four thousand brands share the market. At the same time, there is no reference to a specific region or terroir associated with this production; and while it is indeed dominated by Russia, countries such as Poland, the United States, Canada, Sweden, Finland, Switzerland, France, and New Zealand are also important producers.

These figures and the global spread of vodka may come as a surprise. The craze for this high-alcohol beverage can be explained neither by its sweet taste nor by its color (it is a white spirit) or by the bubbles that we tend to associate with festive occasions. Although vodka is now produced and widely available all over the world, for centuries it was intrinsically linked to the Slavic world. Russians and Poles alike dispute the paternity of the "little water," even as it remains impossible to establish its precise "date of birth." A Russian oral tradition claims that it was invented in 1430 by the monk Isidore at the Choudov monastery in Moscow's Kremlin, inspired by the work of a Persian physician and scholar named Ar-Razi. In the eleventh century, Ar-Razi is said to have been the first to extract ethanol from grapes by fermentation for medicinal use, since the consumption of alcohol was forbidden by the Quran. In Moscow, Isidore is said to have distilled fermented wheat and barley to produce an alcoholic beverage with a strength of around 20 percent. According to another version, the drink was introduced to Russia as early as 1386 by Genoese merchants who offered it to the grand prince of Moscow, Dimitri Donskoi. At the time, however, this grape brandy had not yet really seduced the Russians. It was not until the second half of the fifteenth century that vodka production, this time grain-based, began to develop in Russia, while in Poland "little water" was made from potatoes as early as the mid-seventeenth century.

Distilled from fermented cereals, primarily wheat and barley, vodka became a popular beverage with Russian sovereigns and their boyar companions in the early sixteenth century. Gradually, vodka began to be consumed by an ever-wider range of social classes, with peasants being tempted to distill the beverage themselves. As early as 1553 Ivan the Terrible realized the financial benefits of vodka and imposed a monopoly on its production and sale. From then on, vodka was drunk in state-controlled *kabaki* (taverns). In 1716, during the reign of Peter the Great, vodka production was no longer limited to imperial distilleries but opened to the landed nobility, who enjoyed substantial revenues. At that time, however, it had neither the translucent appearance nor the purity we know today. Not only did its color vary according to the impurities it contained or the aromatic herbs and fruits within it, but its alcohol content also ranged from 37 percent to over 80 percent! By this time, vodka's uses were already well established: it was reserved for toasts between men and was drunk neat.

In 1894, during the reign of Alexander III, vodka was fixed at 40 percent to facilitate the calculation and collection of taxes, since it was a major source of revenue for the state. Moreover, until the 1880s vodka was generally sold in dozen-liter (ca. 3.2 gal.) buckets, but the first bottles appeared, making it easier to transport, market, and consume. Colossal fortunes were made, including that of the Smirnovs, distillers and inventors of "vodka 21" (twenty preliminary tests were necessary to arrive at its definitive formulation), which was appreciated by the emperor and thus earned them the title of "official court supplier" in 1886. At the same time, alcoholism was becoming a veritable social scourge in the tsarist empire, justifying the first prohibition measures introduced during the war against Japan in 1904–5 and then during World War I.

Following the October Revolution, the Soviet authorities continued to ban vodka. Confiscating and nationalizing existing distilleries, they also forced the dispossessed Smirnovs to leave the country. In 1925, however, the ban was lifted, and the Kremlin revived national production from the former imperial state distilleries. For several decades the Cold War hampered the export of Soviet brandy, but de-Stalinization brought about a first boom. In 1953, Stolichnaya, produced at the Kristal distillery in Moscow, won a gold medal at the Berne International Fair. This marked the beginning of the internationalization of Soviet vodka and the growing popularity of Stolichnaya.

By the middle of the twentieth century Russia had once again become a producer and consumer of vodka, but it was not alone. White Russians uprooted and transplanted to the West played a key role in globalizing vodka. Settling in Paris, the Smirnoffs, who had Frenchified their family name, relaunched production before moving to the United States in 1933. The first years met with mixed success, but in the postwar years the infatuation of young Americans with cocktails—in particular the Bloody Mary—and the new cultural representations of vodka conveyed by the cinema (it was the preferred drink of James Bond, a lover of "vodka martinis," and it appealed to the great seductresses of Hollywood) quickly contributed to the worldwide success of this spirit, a success that has not declined since.

Marie-Pierre Rey

FURTHER READING

David Christian. *Living Water: Vodka and Russian Society on the Eve of Emancipation.* Oxford: Clarendon Press, 1990.
Patricia Herlihy. *Vodka, a Global History.* London: Reaktion Books, 2012.
Vilam Vasilevic Pokhlebkin. *Istoriia vodki* (History of Vodka). Moscow: Inter-Verso, 1991.

FURTHER TRAVELING

Beer, Gin, Port Wine, Raki, Rum, Sake, Vodka, Whiskey, Wine

Whiskey

The "trouble with the Engenglish is that their hiss hiss history happened overseas, so they dodo don't know what it means," mischievously declares the aptly named Whiskey Sisodia. Invented by Salman Rushdie, author of *The Satanic Verses* in 1988, the stammering Indian character was not wrong. Scotch, an Indian spirit accidentally invented by the British, is his favorite drink. Winston Churchill, a Johnnie Walker fanatic, discovered Plato, Darwin, and whiskey when he was in India in the late 1890s, claiming that the water was undrinkable and that to make it palatable he added whiskey until he developed a taste for it. Yet the British elite, in Highland mansions and London clubs alike, never saw it coming. Almost without warning, in the second half of the twentieth century, the former Indian colony became the world's leading consumer (nearly half the world's production) of this spirit and, in a great gesture of audacity, conquered the title of world's best whiskey at the 2019 Bartender Spirits Awards in San Francisco, consecrating the Amrut brand, launched barely fifteen years earlier. In barely a century, one of the symbols of Britishness had become the undisputed attribute of the new elites of America and Asia.

Nothing predisposed this golden potion, distilled from barley beer by Irish and Scottish monks in the Middle Ages, to such worldwide success. As its name suggests, *"uisge beatha,"* meaning "water of life" in Scots Gaelic, was first prized for its medicinal virtues, carefully detailed in the famous *Holinshed Chronicles* (1577):

> Being moderately taken, it slows the age, it cuts phlegm, it lightens the mind, it quickens the spirit, it cures the dropsy, it heals the strangulation, it pounces the

stone, it repels gravel, it pulls away ventositie, it keeps and preserves the head from whirling, the eyes from dazzling, the tongue from lisping, the mouth from snuffling, the teeth from chattering, the throat from rattling, the weasan from stiffing, the stomach from womblying, the heart from swelling, the belly from wincing, the guts from rumbling, the hands from shivering, the sinews from shrinking, the veins from crumpling, the bones from aching, the marrow from soaking, and truly it is a sovereign liquor if it be orderly taken.

Consumption of this elixir of monks and apothecaries, sometimes mixed with honey, spread more widely from 1536 onward when King Henry VIII dissolved the monasteries, dispersing the monks and their know-how to homes and farms across the country. Anyone could now ferment grains (barley, rye, wheat) with water and yeast, then distill the beer in a still. While the origins of whiskey remain obscure, its spread is well documented in the British Empire, with the massive emigration of the Irish and Scots to the four corners of the globe. But migration is hardly the whole story. Indeed, in the thirteen British colonies of North America, the colonists preferred gin, brandy (distilled wine liqueur), and above all rum. It was not until the American War of Independence that the consumption of rum, made from sugarcane and molasses produced in the British West Indies, came to an abrupt halt. The rebels replaced it with whiskey—with an "e" in the United States and Ireland—made from the distillation of North America's queen cereal, corn. In the aftermath of the conflict, the population became accustomed to it, while the "conquest of the West" increased corn production tenfold, with surplus corn being transformed into whiskey. Its new popularity helped structure the national economy and political life of the new federal republic.

In 1791, to pay off its war debts, the newly established U.S. Congress introduced a tax on alcohol, which provoked the "whiskey rebellion," where farmers violently attacked the collectors. In the eyes of Washington and Hamilton's Federalist Party, the repression of the distillers demonstrated the government's ability to impose its laws. The resistance to the tax was widespread, however, and was finally abolished in 1802 by the anti-Federalist President Jefferson, leader of the Republican Party. In a country where drinking water was often in short supply, whiskey was an everyday commodity. At only twenty-five cents a gallon (nearly four liters) in the 1820s, it was even less expensive than wine, beer, coffee, or even milk. At the time it was a currency of exchange in the West, where cents and dollars were still scarce.

This fervor had not yet spread to Europe, where, with the exception of Great Britain and Ireland, the bourgeoisie despised grain alcohol as too crude.

326   WHISKEY

However, production improved rapidly from the 1860s onward with the development of blends (a blend of malt and grain whiskeys) inspired by the techniques used by cognac makers. This improvement was not enough to conquer the continent. In the end, it was thanks to a microscopic aphid, *phylloxera*. Ravaging French vineyards between 1870 and 1880, it caused cognac to disappear from European drawing rooms for several years. Whiskey, now aged in brandy casks with milder blends adapted to continental palates, flooded Europe and France. Still arousing the ire of French spirits zealots a century later, comedian Pierre Desproges in his *Dictionnaire superflu à l'usage de l'élite et des biens nantis* (A Superfluous Dictionary for the Elite and the Well-Off, 1985) explained: "Whiskey is the cognac of the *con* [idiot]. Its bouquet evokes the Institut Mérieux's flu vaccine packaging room. Added to sparkling water, it insults the palate of the man of taste, which it splashes with the unseemly saltiness and ungodly bubbles that a Champenois would spit out of contempt for Albion. As it ages, whiskey gains in platitude what it loses in infamy."

Across the Atlantic, on the other hand, growth in production came up against the rise of the temperance movement and, above all, alcohol prohibition in 1920. The local whiskey industry collapsed, and the underworld organized itself methodically, bribing police officers, judges, and politicians and recruiting lawyers, accountants, and smugglers to import alcohol illegally. Irish whiskey distilleries, already weakened by the loss of colonial markets after independence in 1921, refused to negotiate with organized crime, unlike the Scots, who sold their production en masse to Canada, Cuba, and the Bahamas, from where it was then smuggled into the United States. Whiskey thus took advantage of Prohibition to strengthen its presence in a country plagued by counterfeit products made from ethanol and caramel.

At the same time, on the other side of the Pacific, Japan's Masataka Taketsuru began producing the spirit in the Japanese archipelago. After learning Scottish processes in Glasgow and Speyside in 1918, he founded the first whiskey distillery in Yamazaki in 1923 as part of the Suntory company. In 1936 he set up his own company, Nikka, in Yoichi, where the climate resembles that of the Highlands, with mineral-rich water. In 2014 the TV series *Massan*, which recounts his biography, sparked a consumption boom in Japan. Ten years earlier, Sofia Coppola's film *Lost in Translation*, featuring a former Hollywood star tasked with promoting the virtues of Suntory whiskey, had played a major role in popularizing Japanese production worldwide, whose excellence now rivals that of the finest Scotch. Following in Japan's footsteps, the Indians and Taiwanese, great fans of the spirit, are now promoting quality production of blends and single malts respectively, while the Singaporeans and Chinese are experimenting with distillation.

Today there is no doubt that the history of whiskey is being written in Asia.

Pierre Singaravélou

FURTHER READING

Grace Bellino. "Whiskey in Early America." *International Social Science Review* 94 (2018): 1–24.

Dave Broom. *The World Atlas of Whiskey*. London: Mitchell Beazley, 2014.

Vivien Deitz. "The Politics of Whiskey: Scottish Distillers, the Excise, and the Pittite State." *Journal of British Studies* 36 (1997): 35–69.

Martin Wagda. "Le whiskey, liqueur souveraine." *Hommes et migrations* 1226 (July–August 2000): 109–14.

Sandra White. "Smugglers and Excisemen: The History of Whiskey in Scotland, 1644 to 1823." PhD dissertation, University of Western Ontario, 2020.

FURTHER TRAVELING

Beer, Coffee, Gin, Port Wine, Rum, Sake, Sparkling Water, Wine

Wine

The year was 1735. King Louis XV received two sumptuous paintings for his *petits appartements*, commissioned from Jean-François de Troy and Nicolas Lancret. The first was *Le déjeuner d'huîtres* (the luncheon of oysters) and the second *Le déjeuner de jambon* (the luncheon of ham). Both glorified champagne, a new wine that was all the rage, and the joy it brought to any table. They marked the culmination of a revolution introduced by the invention of the thick glass bottle and the cork stopper. Wines could now be stored in small containers, aged, and transported over long distances without risk. It was also possible to serve different wines at different times of the day and to create subtle pairings with different dishes.

The history of fermented beverages goes back to the dawn of Neolithic times. Thanks to their euphoric powers and their ability to rouse the subconscious, fermented beverages have always played a role in sociability, artistic expression, the exercise of power, and initiatory, magical, or religious rituals. Every civilization has one or more fermented beverages and, since the invention of the distillation process, one or more spirits. Wine, however, enjoys a very special status. It first appeared around 5000 BCE in the mountains surrounding the Fertile Crescent, where the *Vitis vinifera* vine grew naturally and was domesticated by indigenous peoples who used the berry juice to make a delicious beverage (*wee-an* in Hittite, *vena* in Sanskrit). Its seductive power was far superior to that of beer, which was common in these parts, thanks to its colors ranging from straw to gold, ruby to garnet, as well as its fragrance, fruitiness, and refreshing acidity. As a result, it quickly supplanted beer in the aristocratic banquets and religious rituals of Mesopotamia and Egypt. At the same time, the Hebrews made it the drink of the Covenant between Yahweh and their people, as witnessed by the Bible, which repeatedly features it after attributing its invention to Noah. Around the fifth century BCE, the Greeks associated it with a new god from the east, Dionysus, son of Zeus and a mortal woman. Then Jesus gave it a status of exception, between his first miracle at the wedding feast in Canaan and the transubstantiation of the Last Supper, thus intimately blending Jewish and Greek traditions. Wine had already been popularized throughout the Roman Empire, and then Christianity reinforced its prestige. Thanks to the Church, wine survived the period of the Invasions and continued its conquest of Europe during the Middle Ages and then the world after 1492. In Islamic Africa and the Middle East, wine consumption was reduced to the bare minimum and tolerated among Jewish and Christian minorities.

By the end of the seventeenth century, Northern Europeans who suffered from the climatic cooling of the Little Ice Age imported wines from Champagne (which they sweetened in England with sugar from the islands to make it effervescent), Bordeaux (the new French claret), Porto (port wine), Jerez (sherry), Malaga, Marsala, and Madeira, and Constantia in South Africa. Most of these consumers were Protestant, so they did not believe in transubstantiation. They were, however, passionate about wine, which was considered a luxury and offered a moment of celebration. Their daily lives, on the other hand, were dominated by beer, whiskey, and gin. It was during this period that the secularization of wine began and continues to this day.

Although Thomas Jefferson was a great connoisseur of wine, as were his fellow WASP countrymen, few Americans drank it in the nineteenth century and the first half of the twentieth century. Hungarian Catholics such as Agoston Haraszthy, French Catholics such as Paul Masson and Georges de Latour, and later Italian Catholics such as Robert Mondavi expanded the vineyards of California, which had been planted initially by missionaries and early Spanish settlers. Georges de Latour's Beaulieu Vineyard even managed to obtain a waiver during Prohibition to continue production, officially intended for the celebration of Mass. Everything changed in the last decades of the twentieth century.

Americans' rising standard of living and passion for travel sparked a growing interest in wine. The preference was for stronger wines. Robert Parker, journalist and founder of *The Wine Advocate* in the late 1970s, heavily promoted this style. Such was his success that producers from all over the world sought to flatter his palate to obtain scores as close as possible to 100 in his ratings. The explanation for the American taste for full-bodied wines may be attributed to their being accustomed to Coca-Cola, hard liquor, hamburgers, ketchup, and barbecue sauces. It is no doubt for the same reason that wines from the Southern Hemisphere now resemble those from California, a factor compounded by hot summers. Fortunately, the trend has now turned toward a more balanced and delicate palate.

At the end of the twentieth century, other countries developed an interest in wine, especially in Northern Europe, Asia, and Russia. Countries that had traditionally been oriented toward beer also became wine lovers. In 1980, for example, the Japanese consumed ten centiliters (3.8 fl. oz.) of wine per person per year. The figure has now risen to 3.5 liters (118.4 fl. oz.), a thirty-five-fold increase.

This phenomenon is linked to globalization. A century ago, in the old wine-producing countries of Europe, wine was the most pleasant daily drink and, as Pasteur used to say, the healthiest and most hygienic, since water was often unsafe to drink. Around 1930 every French person of all ages consumed two hundred liters (53 gal.) of wine a year! There was no hesitation to mix it with water and serve it to children. Today the figure has dropped to less than forty liters (10.5 gal.), and many people never consume any at all. At the same time the quality of French wines has improved considerably, and the number of connoisseurs has grown, though not to the level of Swiss, Belgian, English, Japanese, Hong Kong, or Singaporean wine lovers. It would be fair to say that bad wines are no longer being produced in France or anywhere else in the world, with the exception of a few non-exporting regions in the Caucasus and some new vineyards in Asia whose methods are still approximate. Israel has become a producer of more than estimable wines. Even the most common wines produced in China today are of a certain quality, which was not the case in the last decades of the twentieth century. The global trend is toward the production of wines that are typical of each terroir and reflect the personality and talent of the winemakers who made them. In France, alongside very affordable high-quality wines, price speculation has been introduced on some of the most famous bottles, including rare Burgundies, Bordeaux crus classés, and prestigious cuvées of Champagne. To a lesser extent, the same applies to certain Rhine and Moselle wines, as well as some Barolo and Chianti, Rioja, and other appellations.

Drinking good wine, paying attention to its provenance, to the vintage, and, among the most enlightened consumers, to the winemaker who produced it, have become markers of refinement, openness to the world, and cultural exchange. This can be seen in the trendy bars of New York and in other major metropolises. The sight of Chinese President Xi Jinping or North Korean President Kim Jong-un toasting with a tasting glass full of red wine in hand shows that wine has lost its sacred, Western, or even capitalist connotations. It is now a sign of elegance, sharing, and conviviality, inviting smiles from even the most hardened dictators. May it spur them on to democracy and greater leniency

WINE   331

toward their peoples and others around the world. After all, did Goethe not declare that "art and wine bring people together?"

Jean-Robert Pitte

FURTHER READING

Hanna Agostini and Marie-Françoise Guichard. *Robert Parker, anatomie d'un mythe: Portrait non autorisé du plus grand dégustateur de tous les temps.* Paris: Scali, 2007.
Azélina Jaboulet-Vercherre. *Le vin, entre nature et culture.* Bordeaux: Féret, 2016.
Hugh Johnson. *Une histoire mondiale du vin, de l'antiquité à nos jours.* Trans. Claude Govaz. Paris: Hachette, 2002.
Jean-Robert Pitte. *Le désir du vin: À la conquête du monde.* Paris: Fayard, 2009.
Jean-Robert Pitte, ed. *Le bon vin entre terroir, savoir-faire et savoir-boire: Actualité de la pensée de Roger Dion.* Paris: CNRS Éditions, 2010.

FURTHER TRAVELING

Beer, Champagne, Coca-Cola, Gin, Hamburger, Ketchup, Oyster, Port Wine, Sake, Vodka, Whiskey

Yak Butter

In 1927, a former cabaret dancer versed in the arts and cultures of Asia, Alexandra David-Néel, published the *Journal d'une parisienne à Lhassa*, recounting her peregrinations on foot to the Tibetan capital, Lhasa. At that time, the capital was off-limits to foreigners, but she entered disguised as a Tibetan woman. This extraordinary moment was the culmination of a journey that she describes in detail. One prosaic detail has gone down in history: the recurrent use of yak butter as food, lighting fuel, and even cosmetics. Since then, one of these uses has become particularly well known outside Tibet as a famous beverage, (black) tea with (rancid) yak butter. Its consumption is served at stops for travelers in areas of Tibetan culture, not only in Tibet but also in Mongolia, Nepal, and above all India, where a large part of the diaspora settled following China's annexation of Tibet in 1959.

Henceforth, those who followed in the footsteps of Alexandra David-Néel (such as Éric Faye and Christian Garcin in their 2018 book) included this obligatory mention. From the point of view of trekkers and visitors to the high plateau, yak butter tea (*Po cha*) is the experience par excellence for Western taste buds that discover harsh Himalayan flavors. So much so, in fact, that mountaineer Wade Brackenbury, author of *Yak Butter & Black Tea: A Journey Into Tibet* (1997), has metonymized it to stand for Tibet.

A food as trivial as yak butter nonetheless helps grasp Tibet's complex position in globalization. The "roof of the world" (as it is called by its admirers) was indeed the starting point for the global circulation of religious ideas, beliefs, and practices, including Mahayana Buddhism (known as the "Great Vehicle"). Yet its material and food products (which make up the ordinary life of a traveler in Tibet) remain confined to the cultural space of the Himalayan foothills and circulate beyond them only as exotic vignettes feeding a fantastical imagination projected (for centuries) onto this isolated region. In the Tibetan temples that have sprung up by the thousands across the world, offerings are made to the great masters and deities of the Buddhist pantheon, and butter lamps are replaced by candles.

The same applies to the material and even most symbolic goods of Tibet. Tibetan Buddhism has been exported in an eminently ascetic form, stripped of some of its more elaborate cultural forms. The asceticism advocated by the lamas now irrigates the world on a vast scale, to the detriment of popular religiosity and magical-sorcery practices, too strongly rooted in local folklore to be transposable elsewhere. Of the cultures that have developed in this region, it is the most sophisticated that have traveled the world, mainly the arts, leaving behind the rough, rustic customs that continue to characterize the Tibetan terroir. Yak butter is one of these components. It is not a dish in itself but rather is used in temples as fuel for lamps or for tea and as an ingredient in a porridge composed mainly of roasted barley flour (*tsampa*) and served copiously during rituals. For those who have tasted it, yak butter, which is consumed rancid and transmits its exquisite flavor to the foods with which it is mixed, requires habituation for the palate. Contending with the strong, salty, and particularly viscous taste of the famous tea requires a real shift in perspective. Hence its consumption by the heroic trekkers who seek to surpass their athletic capacities or the pilgrims in search of heightened spirituality.

An exotic food par excellence, yak butter embodies that part of the Tibetophile imagination so strongly rooted in the habits, customs, and routines of these mountainous communities. For it remains a local product, dependent on an agropastoral production system of upland crops and a regional exchange economy. It is, moreover, subject to strict restrictions (like yak wool or farm animal hides) in interregional trade between India and China. Unlike Cantonese rice, sushi, curry, or, more recently, *bun bo xao*, the food itself has traveled little outside this zone and cannot be counted as a component of these now globalized Asian cuisines.

In consumers' imaginations and their consumption, yak butter seems to be diametrically opposed to ghee, the Indian clarified butter that has established itself on the world market of wellness products, distributed in the ever-increasing number of "organic" or similar shops. In India, ghee has deep cultural roots. Cited in mythology as a product of the gods, fuel for ritual lamps, and an ingredient in beverages, this butter is used in many Indian dishes. Outside Asia, it has a more ambivalent image, blending the idealization of a religious India with the current (and globalized) taste for a more "natural," even "spiritual" cuisine.

Clearly the conditions and logic of an "Indianization" of the world through the export of spiritual (Hindu meditation, yoga), prophylactic (via its now globalized Ayurveda medical system), and dietary (vegetarianism, curry spice or as a dish) techniques differ entirely from "Tibetization" across the world, which has been far less common. Despite an established presence in most of the world's major capitals, Tibetan restaurants are still few compared to their numerous Indian counterparts.

The paradox of globalization is that, according to the WHO, fatty products are on the rise in developing countries. In more developed countries, however, where ghee is exported widely but yak butter is more difficult to obtain, they are declining by virtue of changing dietary standards. In Tibet, this same globalization is responsible for the decline in consumption of the traditional beverage, which is losing ground to imported competitors. Yak butter, Tibetan tea, and *tsampa* are nonetheless timidly making their way into the kitchens of the world, particularly in the West, as part of a more "natural" diet with a spiritual and wellness dimension, following on the development of ghee. But like Buddhism, which has lost some of its cultural and cultic forms as it spreads around the world, yak butter tea has also lost its unique rustic taste. The recent appearance of "bulletproof coffee," made from coffee, cow's butter, and coconut oil, would seem to indicate a trend toward a new variant with dietetic virtues adapted to North American tastes. It may be some time before people start ordering *Po cha*.

Lionel Obadia

FURTHER READING

Sina Bianmu and Lindsay Neill. "Yak Butter Tea in Shangri-La: A Beverage Icon Under Threat." *Food Studies: An Interdisciplinary Journal* 10, no. 2 (2020): 1–18.

Alexandra David-Néel. *Voyage d'une parisienne à Lhassa à pied et en mendiant, de la Chine à l'Inde à travers le Tibet*. Paris: Presses Pocket, [1982] 1999.

Éric Faye and Christian Garcin. *Dans les pas d'Alexandra David-Néel: Du Tibet au Yunnan*. Paris: Stock, 2018.

Thierry Mathou. "L'Himalaya, 'nouvelle frontière' de la Chine." *Hérodote* 125, no. 2 (2007): 28–50.

World Health Organization. *Globalization, Diets and Noncommunicable Diseases*. Geneva: WHO, 2002. https://apps.who.int/iris/handle/10665/42609.

FURTHER TRAVELING

Curry, Sushi, Tea and Chai

Yogurt

In 1905, twenty-seven-year-old Stamen Grigorov discovered the bacillus that gives yogurt its acidity by transforming milk sugar lactose into lactic acid in yogurt samples from his native Bulgaria. Invited to the Institut Pasteur in Paris, Grigorov presented his work, which was well received. Professor Élie Metchnikov, assistant to the director of the institute, was curious about a possible link between yogurt consumption and longevity in Bulgaria's mountain communities. According to him, the pathogenic effects of certain bacteria were canceled out by the intake of lactic acid bacteria from sour milk. With Grigorov's discovery, he revealed the benefits of yogurt and highlighted the action of the ferment now known as *Lactobacillus bulgaricus* in the treatment of intestinal disorders in infants. In 1908 he was awarded the Nobel Prize in medicine for his work on immunity.

The invention of yogurt has been lost in the mists of time. Since humans first domesticated mammals in the Neolithic period (8500 BCE), nomadic tribes consumed fermented milk, which was easy to transport. The first herders in the Middle East realized that milk curdled spontaneously when preserved in wineskins made from cattle stomachs, the rennetting process. The traditional method of making fermented milk, the *rayeb* of the Near East, was always the same: fresh milk from the udder of a camel, donkey, or mare was left in an earthen vessel in the open air until it turned (curdled) spontaneously (within twenty-four to seventy-two hours, depending on local temperatures). It was then preserved in a goatskin casing and seasoned with sea salt. A piece of this spontaneous curd could then be used to seed the warmed milk. The "invention" soon spread along the caravan routes to the Balkans in the west and to India and China in the east. The oldest Chinese agricultural treatise, dating from 536 BCE, described how to ferment milk. Flavored with garlic, it was used as a sauce or in stuffing. It can still be found in the Indian state of Tamil Nadu under the name "milky mist curd" in English or *khayiv sadam* in Urdu, a sour rice pudding sometimes flavored with lemon. One of the earliest Western references to yogurt dates back to the first century, when Pliny the Elder noted that certain tribes knew how to "set milk to form a pleasantly acidic liquor," which he described as a "divine essence serving as a remedy for many ills."

The term yogurt is probably of Turkish origin. The verb *yogmak* means "to coagulate." In countries through which Turkish tribes passed, such as the Balkans, the word *yoghourt* was used in different forms: *yahourt, yogourt, yog-gourt*. The first mention of yogurt in Old French dates to the fifteenth century. In his book *Le voyage d'outre-mer* (1432–33), Chevalier Bertrandon de la Broquière explains how, on the way back, "the Turquemans gave us large (quantities) of curdled milk that they called yogurt."

If yogurt is consumed almost daily today—a French person consumes more than 21 kilos (46.3 lb.) a year, or 170 pots (second in Europe behind the Germans)—it is of course thanks to the industrial application of Grigorov and Metchnikov's discoveries. This was certainly not the first time that science has shaped the food industry. Émile Duclaux, Pasteur's successor at the head of the eponymous institute, developed dairy microbiology and promoted "pasteurization" even before the end of the century. Professor Mazé of the same institute selected lactic ferments for Brie cheese on behalf of industrialists in the Meuse region. It was not until after World War I that yogurt was industrially produced.

Two manufacturers turned yogurt into a mass-market product. The first, an Armenian from Constantinople named Deukmedjian Aram, left to study in Paris and in 1912 opened the Au Rendez-vous des Étudiants restaurant and the Cure de Yogourt store at 8 rue de la Sorbonne. For his specialty, "yogurt Aram," he obtained from the Pasteur Institute the label "sole supplier to Professor Metchnikoff" (the spelling of the time). The yogurt was sold with the following statement: "I have eaten and analyzed Aram yogurt. It is not harmful to one's health. On the contrary, it contains lactic ferments that are useful for our bodies." In 1921, Aram built a yogurt factory in the Parisian suburb of Montrouge.

The second industrialist was also a subject of the Ottoman Empire from the Balkans. In 1913, a Jew of Turkish origin named Isaac Carasso moved to Barcelona a few months after his hometown of Salonika had been captured by the Greeks and began producing yogurts in a modest workshop after the war. In 1923 his product was sold in pharmacies with a promising label: the College of

Physicians of Barcelona described it as "wholesome, natural and good for one's health." The company took the name Danone, the Catalan diminutive of Isaac's son Daniel's first name. The young Carasso, born in 1905, studied business in Marseille, then worked at the Pasteur Institute in Paris before founding the Parisian yogurt company Danone. Thanks to good advertising and marketing research, the product was sold in creameries. The product continued to employ the argument of good health: "delicious and healthy, Danone is the dessert for happy digestion," according to a 1937 advertisement.

When the Germans occupied France in 1941, anyone labeled "Jewish" had to flee, often to the United States. There, Daniel founded a new company, Dannon. On his return to France he took over the reins of the Franco-Spanish company and expanded in into an international group. From a simple health product, yogurt became a product of pleasure in the new consumer society. In addition to natural yogurt, the company offered fruit yogurt, flavored yogurt, and other light products. The "large supermarkets" that developed in the 1960s soon put Danone yogurts on their shelves. In 1967 the company merged with fresh cheese manufacturer Gervais and in 1973 with the BSN group. Daniel Carasso passed on the reins to Frank Riboud and then his son Antoine to lead the BSN-Gervais-Danone group. In 1994 the group changed its name to Produits Frais Danone. It comprised four divisions: dairy products, bottled waters (Evian, Volvic, Badoit), medical nutrition, and infant nutrition (Blédine, Gallia). The Danone Group is the world's fifth-largest food company. Today it is present in 120 countries, employs 100,000 people, sells 51 billion pots of yogurt a year, and is one of the world's top three food companies.

Not all yogurt manufacturers were so successful. In France alone, however, the industry has included such giants as Nestlé, Senoble, Lactalis (La Laitière brand), and the Yoplait cooperative (since 1965). In 1974, Yoplait launched the first drinkable yogurt under the name Yop.

By this time, modern manufacturing techniques were well established: milk heated to 50°C (122°F) to which milk powder is added. It is then homogenized at 70°C (158°F) and heated to 90°C (194°F) for fifteen seconds to destroy pathogenic bacteria and microorganisms in the milk; ferments are added at 45°C (113°F), and it is fermented for four hours; it is then cooled to 4°C (39.2°F), packaged in glass or cardboard jars, and stored in a cool place. Today, with the advent of yogurt makers and the newfound pleasure of "homemade" products, yogurt is also a popular household food in the West, as is Indian *dahi*, which is still consumed daily without being produced industrially.

Didier Nourrisson

FURTHER READING

Michèle Barrière. "Le yaourt." *Historia*, November 2017.

Mireille Gayet. *Petit traité de yaourt*. Gap: Éditions Le Sureau, 2013.

Didier Nourrisson. *Du lait et des hommes: Histoire d'un breuvage nourricier de la Renaissance à nos jours.* Paris: Vendémiaire, 2021.

A. Y. Tahine and R. K. Robinson. *Yoghurt: Science and Technology*. Boca Raton, FL: CRC Press, 1999.

Fatih Yildis. *Development and Manufacture of Yogurt and Other Functional Dairy Products*. Boca Raton, FL: CRC Press, 2010.

FURTHER TRAVELING

Beet Sugar, Salt

Index

acheke *(attiéké)*, 4, 6, 8–10
Acton, Eliza, 61
Acurio, Gastón, 43
Adant, Théophile, 30
African culinary arts, 8–10
African food: couscous, 3, 7, 89–91, 212; Indomie instant noodles, 4, 167–69; palm oil, 5, 117, 168, 217–19; rooibos, 7, 255–57; white pepper, 4
agribusiness, 31, 219
alcoholic beverages: beer, 25–28, 94, 134, 136–37, 146, 155–56, 247–49, 268–69, 324–25, 328–30; cocktails, 138, 165, 265; gin, 136–39, 325, 329; raki, 3, 247–49; rum, 7, 69, 263–65, 325; sake, 2, 47, 227, 267–69; vodka, 3, 38, 74, 248, 321–23; whiskey, 4–6, 163, 165, 246, 264, 269, 294, 324–27, 329. *See also* wine
Algerian food, 210–12
American food: California roll, 6–7, 182–83, 299; cornflakes, 2, 5, 85–88, 313; freeze-dried food, 4, 128–30, 251, 253; hamburgers, 1, 23, 95, 144–46, 237, 241; hot dogs, 155–57; ketchup, 31, 121, 129, 144, 157, 174–77, 284, 291, 329; pet food/treats, 228–30; Spam, 4, 7, 289–91; Tex-Mex food, 57–60, 184
Anderson, J. Walter, 145
Arabic food: couscous, 3, 7, 89–91, 212; dafina, 97–99; harissa, 98, 110, 148–50; hummus, 3, 159–61; Turkish delight, 2, 315–17
Archenhollz, Johann von, 245
Argentinian food, 189–91

Aristotle, 37
aromatics/spices: chili pepper, 3, 57–58, 61–63, 140, 148, 157, 226; curry powder, 61, 93–95, 283–85; pepper/peppercorn, 225–27; vanilla/vanillin, 318–20
Ashkenazi Jews, 11–12, 194–95
Asian food: banh mi, 16, 18–20, 277; *budae jjigae* (army stew), 7, 290; dim sum, 6, 101–3; fish sauce (nuoc man), 5, 120–23; Indomie instant noodles, 4, 167–69; lato, 178–80; maki *(makizushi)*, 4, 6, 182–84, 298; pho, 6, 232–34; poke, 43, 240–42; ramen, 3, 7, 167, 251–53; Singapore noodles, 95, 167, 283–85; soy sauce, 4, 19, 120, 214, 241, 251, 283, 286–88, 291; tea/chai, 6, 304–7; tikka, 2, 6–7, 118, 308–10; tofu, 5–7, 242, 290, 311–13. *See also* Chinese food; Japanese food
Aygün, Mehmet, 110

Bachelot, Roselyn, 14
bagels, 3, 11–13
baguette, 2, 14–19, 201, 277
Baker, Jack, 145
Bancroft, Hubert, 62
banh mi, 16, 18–20, 277
barbecue, 21–23, 151, 153, 261, 286, 329
Barthes, Roland, 7, 201
Basile, Giovanni, 236
Beckford, William, 62
beer, 25–28, 94, 134, 136–37, 146, 155–56, 247–49, 268–69, 324–25, 328–30

340 INDEX

beet sugar, 7, 29–31
Bekir, Hadji, 315
Benayoun, Claude, 59–60
Beton, Jean-Claude, 210, 211
Beton, Léon, 210–11
beverages, cold: Coca-Cola, 4, 5, 7, 73–76, 145, 156, 168, 175, 319, 329; Orangina, 210–12; Pepsi Cola, 5, 74; *sharbat* drink, 66, 210; sparkling water, 293–95, 326
beverages, hot: coffee, 6–7, 15–16, 28, 31, 54–55, 77–80, 94, 130, 141, 145, 191, 226, 304–5, 316, 325, 334; mate, 3, 189–91; rooibos, 7, 255–57; tea/chai, 6, 304–7
Big Food, 82–83
Boston Tea Party (1773), 3
Bowen, Samuel, 287–88
Brazilian food, 3, 6, 35, 112–14
bread foods: bagels, 3, 11–13; baguette, 2, 14–19, 201, 277; banh mi, 16, 18–20, 277; injera, 170–72; matzah, 3, 192–95; naan, 7, 200–202
British food, 2, 3, 7, 69–71, 94, 116–18, 308
Buarque, Chico, 112
budae jjigae (army stew), 7, 290
Bulgarian foods, 2

California roll, 6–7, 182–84, 299. *See also* maki
Camelia sinensis. See tea/chai
Cantonese food, 6, 101–3
capsaicin, 63
Carasso Daniel, 337
Carasso Isaac, 336–37
carcinogens, 5, 51, 126, 289
cassava, 8–10, 230, 301. *See also* acheke *(attiéké)*
cassoulet, 1, 6, 33–35
caviar, 37–39, 180
Cédard, Henri, 69, 71
ceviche, 2–3, 41–44, 242
chai. *See* tea/chai
champagne, 2, 4, 39, 45–48, 165–66, 260–61, 279, 328–30
charcuterie, 18, 20, 49–51, 127, 223
cheddar cheese, 19–20
cheese: cheddar, 19–20; feta, 2, 160; parmesan, 204, 221–24; Roquefort, 2, 132, 146, 259–61, 312
chicory, 7, 53–55
chili con carne, 4, 57–60
chili pepper, 3, 57–58, 61–63, 140, 148, 157, 226. *See also* harissa

Chinese food: dim sum, 6, 101–3; dogmeat, 105–7; tofu, 5–7, 242, 290, 311–13
chorba, 65–67
Choy, Sam, 241
Christmas pudding, 2, 69–71
Churchill, Winston, 138, 324
Civil War, 27, 50, 81
Coca-Cola, 4, 5, 7, 73–76, 145, 156, 168, 175, 319, 329
Coca-Cola Company, 4
cocktails, 138, 165, 265
coffee, 6–7, 15–16, 28, 31, 54–55, 77–80, 94, 130, 141, 145, 191, 226, 304–5, 316, 325, 334
Coffey, Aeneas, 137
Cold War, 23, 182–83, 234, 323
coloring/color additives. *See* food coloring/preservatives
Columbus, Christopher, 61, 264
Common Agricultural Policy (CAP), 208
condensed milk (sweetened), 5, 81–83, 86
condiments/sauces: caviar, 37–39, 180; fish sauce (nuoc man), 5, 120–23; guacamole, 140–43; ketchup, 31, 121, 129, 144, 157, 174–77, 284, 291, 329; lato, 178–80; mayonnaise, 3, 18–19, 41, 94, 183, 196–98, 261; soy sauce, 4, 19, 120, 214, 241, 251, 283, 286–88, 291
confectionaries: beet sugar, 7, 29–31; condensed milk (sweetened), 5, 81–83, 86; high glucose-fructose syrup (HFCS), 31; sugarcane, 29, 113, 165, 263–65, 315, 325; Turkish delight, 2, 315–17. *See also* desserts
Cook, James, 240
Cook, Robin, 7, 308
Corloux, Didier, 234
cornflakes, 2, 5, 85–88, 85–88, 313
Coste, Victor, 215
couscous, 3, 7, 89–91, 212
culinary arts, 1, 4, 9
cured meats, 5, 49, 51
curry dish, 6–7, 93–95, 333–34
curry powder, 61, 93–95, 283–85

dafina, 97–99
dairy foods: ice cream, 31, 164, 319; yak butter, 332–34; yogurt, 2, 111, 201, 249, 309, 335–37. *See also* cheese
Dakin, Thomas, 138
David-Néel, Alexandra, 332
Defour, Judith, 136

INDEX

Delicado, Francisco, 98
desserts, 2, 31, 69–71, 164, 319. *See also* confectionaries
Dickens, Charles, 70
dim sum, 6, 101–3
dogmeat, 105–7
döner kebab, 6, 109–11
d'Opobo, Jaya, 217
Duclaux, Émile, 336
Dumas, Alexandre, 236
Dumont, Émile, 276

East India Company, 79, 94, 137–38, 226, 287, 304–5
Edmond of Réunion, 318–19
El Maleh, Edmond Amran, 97
Empire Marketing Board (EMB), 71
Ermengem, Émile van, 49–50
Escoffier, Auguste, 35
Ethiopian food, 170–72
exotic foods, 1, 18, 41–43, 91, 121–22, 137, 180, 184, 242, 298–99, 302, 315, 333
Exquemelin, Alexandre-Olivier, 22

fast food, 3, 5, 20, 43, 110–11, 132, 134, 142–43, 145–46, 175, 237, 252, 261, 276–77, 290, 298, 308
fats/oils: hydrogenated oils, 186, 219; margarine, 185–87, 218–19; olive oil, 6, 36, 61, 149, 159, 187, 206–8, 279–80; palm oil, 5, 117, 168, 217–19
feijoada, 3, 6, 35, 112–14
Feltman, Charles, 156
feta cheese, 2, 160
Filipino food, 178–80
fish and chips, 3, 7, 94, 116–18, 308
fish/fish foods. *See* seafood
fish sauce (nuoc man), 5, 120–23
Food and Agriculture Organization of the United Nations (FAO), 126
food coloring/preservatives, 31, 103, 113, 124–27, 145, 185, 198, 204, 271, 273, 289
food identities, 2
Fortune, Robert, 304
Foucault, Michel, 88
François, Edmond, 8
freeze-dried food, 4, 128–30, 251, 253
French food: baguette, 2, 14–19, 201, 277; cassoulet, 1, 6, 33–35; champagne, 2, 4, 39, 45–48, 165–66, 260–61, 279, 328–30;

charcuterie, 18, 20, 49–51, 127, 223; mayonnaise, 3, 18–19, 41, 94, 183, 196–98, 261; Orangina, 211–12; Roquefort cheese, 2, 132, 146, 259–61, 312
french fries, 3, 7, 110, 117, 132–34
French Revolution, 15–16, 54, 77–78, 196, 203

Garba, Dicoh, 10
General Company, 244
Georghehner, Johann, 155
German food, 95
Gibbon, Edward, 275
gin, 136–39, 325, 329
Ginsbert, Benjamin, 256
Ginsbert, Charles, 256–57
Giraud, Charles, 54
Glass, Anna, 144
Glasse, Hannah, 93, 116
globalization of food: acheke and, 8, 10; baguette and, 17; beer and, 25; beet sugar and, 31; cassoulet and, 35; Coca-Cola, 74; fish and chips, 117; fish sauce and, 120–21; hamburger and, 146; harissa and, 149–50; hummus and, 161; Indomie and, 167–68; lato and, 180; maki and, 184; noodles and macaroni, 205; olive oil and, 208; pet food and treats, 229–30; phases of, 6; pho and, 234; pizza and, 236; Roquefort and, 261; sake and, 267–69; sushi and, 299; tea and chai, 304–5; vanilla and vanillin, 318; Westernization of culinary habits, 7; wine and, 330; yak butter and, 332–34
Goblet, Nicholas, 319–20
Goldberg, Harry, 297–98
Gorrie, John, 165
Greek food, 2, 6, 36, 61, 149, 159, 160, 187, 206–8, 279–80
Grigorov, Stamen, 335
Groult, Maison, 301, 303
guacamole, 140–43

hamburgers, 1, 23, 95, 144–46, 237, 241
Hamoud, Youcef, 211–12
harissa, 98, 110, 148–50
Hawaiian food, 240–42
hedgehog stew, 3, 151–53
Heinz Company, 4, 129, 174–77, 198, 308
high glucose-fructose syrup (HFCS), 31
Hormel, Jay, 289
Hosokawa Tadatoshi, 268

342 INDEX

hot dogs, 155–57
hummus, 3, 159–61
hydrogenated oils, 186, 219

ice cream, 31, 164, 319
ice cubes, 163–66
Indian food: curry dish, 6–7, 93–95, 333–34; naan, 7, 200–202; pepper/peppercorn, 225–27; tikka, 2, 6–7, 118, 308–10
Indomie instant noodles, 4, 167–69
industrialization, 2, 4–5, 10, 26–27, 30, 51, 58, 81, 87, 134, 142, 145, 164, 176, 194–95, 212, 222, 228, 230, 237, 252, 265, 274, 290, 306
infant formula, 82–83
Ingram, Edgar Waldo, 145
injera, 170–72
instant noodles, 4, 167–69, 219
Israeli food, 159–61
Italian food: macaroni, 4, 203–5, 221, 236; parmesan cheese, 204, 221–24; pizza, 2, 3, 6, 17, 187, 201, 236–38

janissary corps, 66–67
Japanese food: curry, 95; ice desserts, 164–65; maki (makizushi), 4, 6, 182–84, 298; ramen, 3, 7, 167, 251–53; sake, 2, 47, 227, 267–69; sushi, 6, 17, 182–84, 242, 290, 297–99
Jefferson, Thomas, 203, 329
Jewish food, 3, 97–99, 192–95
Joint Expert Committee on Food Additives (JECFA), 126–27
jouissance, 1
junk food, 133, 161, 219, 261

Kahe Nakagawa, 164
Kanai Noritoshi, 297–98
kebab. See döner kebab
Kellogg, John Harvey, 13, 31, 85–87, 313
Kerner, Justinus, 49
ketchup, 31, 121, 129, 144, 157, 174–77, 284, 291, 329
Khusro, Amir, 200
Kim Jong-un, 330
Korean War, 7, 128
Krakow Jews, 11–12
Krieger, Frédéric, 133–34
Kroc, Ray, 145
Kuykendall, Ralph Simpson, 240

Landgrebe, Gary, 313
lato, 178–80
Lebanese food, 159–61
Lender, Murray, 11
Lepervenche, Mézieres, 318
Le Play, Frédéric, 15
Lescallier, Daniel, 22
Leslie, Eliza, 275
Lespes, Léo, 186
Lévi-Strauss, Claude, 265
Lichtenstein, Roy, 155–56
Liebig, J. von, 125
Linschoten, Jan Huyghen van, 93
Li Yuying, 311–13
Lorius, Claude, 163

macaroni, 4, 203–5, 221, 236
maki (makizushi), 4, 6, 182–84, 298
malnutrition, 7, 82
Malouin, Paul-Jacques, 204
margarine, 185–87, 218–19
Margherita pizza, 2, 237
Mason, Charlotte, 275
mate, 3, 189–91
matzah, 3, 192–95
Mayhew, Henry, 276
mayonnaise, 3, 18–19, 41, 94, 183, 196–98, 261
McDonald's, 145–46
medicinal food, 5, 273, 335
Mediterranean food: hummus, 3, 159–61; olive oil, 6, 36, 61, 149, 159, 187, 206–8, 279–80; Orangina, 210–12
Mege-Mouries, Hippolyte, 185–86
Menon, Joseph, 204
Metchnikov, Élie, 335
Methuen Treaty (1703), 243, 245
Mexican food, 57–60, 140–43, 184
Mexican Revolution, 59
Mezquita, Agustín Trigo, 211
Michelet, Jules, 77–78
Mikhailovich, Alexis, 38
Moench, Émile, 124
Montagu, John, 275
Morren, Charles, 319
Mukhopadhyay, Bipradas, 94

naan, 7, 200–202
Napoleon I, 16, 53–55

INDEX

Napoleon III, 185, 215

Nazi Germany, 7, 74, 194, 265

Nestlé Company, 81–83, 337

Nguyen Kim Bach, 234

nitrite salts, 5, 51, 127, 289

Nofras Nortier, Pieter, 256

non-alcoholic beverages. *See* beverages

noodles/pasta: couscous, 3, 7, 89–91, 212; Indomie instant noodles, 4, 167–69; macaroni, 4, 203–5, 221, 236; ramen, 3, 7, 167, 251–53; Singapore noodles, 95, 167, 283–85

Normann, Wilhelm, 186–87

nourishment, 1, 53–54, 58, 77, 82–83, 102, 187, 232–33, 242, 251, 281, 302

Obama, Barack, 1, 33, 140

Obata Rumiko, 269

obesity, 5, 88, 117, 133, 146

October Revolution, 38–39, 322–23

oils. *See* fats/oils

Oldenburg, Claes, 277

olive oil, 6, 36, 61, 149, 159, 187, 206–8, 279–80

Orangina, 210–12

origin myths, 3, 284

Ottoman Empire, 66, 109–10, 159, 230, 247–49, 304, 315–17, 336

oysters, 2, 213–16, 241, 277

palm oil, 5, 117, 168, 217–19

Parker, Robert, 329

parmesan cheese, 204, 221–24

Parr, Martin, 132

pasta. *See* noodles/pasta

Pemberton, John, 73–74

pepper/peppercorn, 225–27

Pepsi Cola, 5, 74

Pepys, Samuel, 137

Perkin, W. H., 125

Persian Empire, 37–39

Peruvian food, 2, 41–44

pet food/treats, 228–30

pho, 6, 232–34

Pinto, Fernao Mendes, 105

pizza, 2, 3, 6, 17, 187, 201, 236–38

Pizza Hut, 236–37, 308

poke, 43, 240–42

port wine, 5, 243–46, 329

preservatives. *See* food coloring/preservatives; nitrite salts

Priestley, Joseph, 293

protected designation of origin (PDO), 5

raki, 3, 247–49

ramen, 3, 7, 167, 251–53

raw fish, 3, 182–83, 240–42, 268

Redding, Cyrus, 243

red wine, 14, 45, 330

rooibos, 7, 255–57

Roosevelt, Franklin Delano, 155

Roosevelt, Theodore, 74–75

Roquefort cheese, 2, 132, 146, 259–61, 312

rum, 7, 69, 263–65, 325

Rushdie, Salman, 324

Russian food, 3, 37–39, 74, 248, 321–23

Saint-Hilaire, Auguste de, 189–90

sake, 2, 47, 227, 267–69

Salmon, D. E., 196

Salmonella bacteria, 196

salt: in baguettes, 16; in curry, 94; on fish, 280; in harissa, 149; Hawaiian salt, 241; in marinades, 111; in matzah, 193; nitrite salts, 5, 51, 127, 289; overview, 271–74; as preservative, 22, 37, 49, 51, 124, 144; sea salt, 335; in Spam, 289

Salt March (1930), 3

Sánchez, Mari, 98

sandwich foods, 13, 18–20, 31, 110, 156–57, 197–98, 275–78

sardines (canned), 4, 19, 35, 277, 279–81

saturated fatty acids, 5, 219

Schweppe, Johann Jacob, 293

seafood: caviar, 37–39, 180; ceviche, 2–3, 41–44, 242; fish and chips, 3, 7, 94, 116–18, 308; oysters, 2, 213–16, 241, 277; poke, 43, 240–42; raw fish, 3, 182–83, 240–42, 268; sardines (canned), 4, 19, 35, 277, 279–81

seaweed foods, 178–80

Seven Years' War, 133, 305

sharbat drink, 66, 210

shawarma, 7, 109–10. *See also* döner kebab

Shiraishi Yoshiaki, 299

Short, William, 203

Sinclair, Upton, 289

Singapore noodles, 95, 167, 283–85

Singer, Isaac, 193

INDEX

Sinophobia, 105
Société Ivoirienne de Technologie Tropicale, 10
sodium nitrate. *See* nitrite salts
soup/stews: *budae jjigae,* 7, 290; cassoulet, 1, 6,
    33–35; chorba, 65–67; dafina, 97–99; feijoada,
    3, 6, 35, 112–14; hedgehog stew, 3, 151–53; pho,
    6, 232–34
South African food, 7, 255–57
soy sauce, 4, 19, 120, 214, 241, 251, 283, 286–88, 291
Spam, 4, 7, 289–91
sparkling water, 293–95, 326
sparkling wine, 45, 47, 223
spices. *See* aromatics/spices
Spratt, James, 228
sugarcane, 29, 113, 165, 263–65, 315, 325
Sun Yat-sen, 304
supermarket sector, 13, 16, 120, 122, 140, 161,
    186, 195, 201, 223, 276–77, 287, 308, 337
sushi, 6, 17, 182–84, 242, 290, 297–99

tapioca, 5, 9, 301–3
Tcheng Ki Tong (Chen Jitong), 106
tea/chai, 6, 304–7
Terry, Edward, 93
Tex-Mex food, 57–60, 184
Thai food, 95. *See also* Asian food
Theron, Annetjie, 257
Tibetan food, 332–34
tikka, 2, 6–7, 118, 308–10
tofu, 5–7, 242, 290, 311–13
Trinaranjus syrup, 211
Turkish delight, 2, 315–17
Turkish food, 3, 6, 109–11, 247–49

UNESCO, 89
United Nations Industrial Development
    Organization (UNIDO), 149

Uring, Nathaniel, 21

vanilla/vanillin, 318–20
vegetarian food, 3, 5–6, 65, 85, 107, 161, 298,
    311–13, 334
Vernon, Edward, 264–65
Vietnamese food, 5, 6, 120–23, 232–34. *See also*
    Asian food
vodka, 3, 38, 74, 248, 321–23

Warhol, Andy, 144
whiskey, 4–6, 163, 165, 246, 264, 269, 294,
    324–27, 329
white wine, 45, 223
wine: champagne, 2, 4, 39, 45–48, 165–66,
    260–61, 279, 328–30; overview, 328–31;
    port wine, 5, 243–46, 329; red, 14, 45, 330;
    sparkling wine, 45, 47, 223; white,
    45, 223
Wöhler, F., 125
Wolf, Frederick William, Jr., 165
Woodforde, James, 245
Woodruff, Robert, 74
World Health Organization, 5, 51, 83, 126, 196
World Trade Organization, 122
World War I, 15, 27–28, 34–35, 47, 55, 70, 74, 121,
    187, 249, 260, 312, 322
World War II, 7, 63, 74, 82, 90–91, 128, 145, 151,
    155, 165, 182, 187, 206, 229, 245, 256, 289–90,
    313, 316–17

Xavier, Francis, 267–68
Xi Jinping, 330

yak butter, 332–34
yerba mate, 189–91. *See also* mate
yogurt, 2, 111, 201, 249, 309, 335–37

GPSR Authorized Representative: Easy Access System Europe, Mustamäe tee 50, 10621 Tallinn, Estonia, gpsr.requests@easproject.com

www.ingramcontent.com/pod-product-compliance
Lightning Source LLC
Jackson TN
JSHW020251140825
89344JS00006B/145